QUEERING THE ENLIGHTENMENT
KINSHIP AND GENDER IN EIGHTEENTH-CENTURY FRENCH LITERATURE

QUEERING THE ENLIGHTENMENT
KINSHIP AND GENDER IN EIGHTEENTH-CENTURY FRENCH LITERATURE

TRACY L. RUTLER

Published by Liverpool University Press on behalf of
© 2021 Voltaire Foundation, University of Oxford
ISBN 978-1-80085-980-7
Oxford University Studies in the Enlightenment 2021:11
ISSN 2634-8047 (Print)
ISSN 2634-8055 (Online)

Voltaire Foundation
99 Banbury Road
Oxford OX2 6JX, UK
www.voltaire.ox.ac.uk

A catalogue record for this book is available from the British Library

The correct style for citing this book is
Tracy L. Rutler, *Queering the Enlightenment: kinship and gender in eighteenth-century French literature*
Oxford University Studies in the Enlightenment
(Liverpool, Liverpool University Press, 2021)

Cover illustration: Achille Devéria et Louis Philippe Alphonse Bichebois
(dit Bichebois Aîné). *Le Roman du Jour* (IFF 250). Lithographie, 1832.
CC0 Paris Musées / Musée Carnavalet – Histoire de Paris.

Printed and bound by TJ International Ltd, Padstow, Cornwall,
PL28 8R

QUEERING THE ENLIGHTENMENT
KINSHIP AND GENDER IN EIGHTEENTH-CENTURY FRENCH LITERATURE

Liminal periods in politics often serve as points in time when traditional methods and principles organizing society are disrupted. These periods of interregnum may not always result in complete social upheaval, but they do open the space to imagine social and political change in diverse forms. In *Queering the Enlightenment: kinship and gender in eighteenth-century French literature,* Tracy L. Rutler uncovers how numerous canonical authors of the 1730s and 1740s were imagining radically different ways of organizing the masses during the early years of Louis XV's reign. Through studies of the literature of Antoine-François Prévost, Claude Crébillon, Pierre de Marivaux, and Françoise de Graffigny among others, Rutler demonstrates how the heteronormative bourgeois family's rise to dominance in late-eighteenth-century France had long been contested within the fictional worlds of many French authors. The utopian impulses guiding the fiction studied in this book distinguish these authors as some of the most brilliant political theorists of the day. Enlightenment, for these authors, means reorienting one's relation to power by reorganizing their most intimate relations. Using a practice of reading queerly, Rutler shows how these works illuminate the unparalleled potential of queer forms of kinship to dismantle the patriarchy and help us imagine what might eventually take its place

Contents

List of illustrations

This book is dedicated to Beatrice and River.
You remind me what true love is every single day.

Preface: "le patriarcat est fini"

On January 22, 2020, the French Senate voted to open medically assisted fertility treatment (*procréation médicalement assistée*, or PMA) to all women. Previously, legal fertility treatments were limited to heterosexual couples experiencing infertility issues, or in which one of the partners had a disease which could be transmitted to the child. While this law finally opened up the possibility of medical assistance to single women and lesbian couples, by offering financial assistance only to women experiencing infertility issues, it effectively continues to deny this pricey service to women unable to afford the treatments. Moreover, the procedure remains unavailable to trans and nonbinary individuals who are forced to travel to other countries in order to conceive. In short, while some have seen this law as a victory for women, others recognize the extreme limitations of the decision.

So why, in the twenty-first century, should it be so difficult to pass legislation opening up fertility treatments to all? In an address to the National Assembly in favor of passing the PMA legislation in September of 2019, Jean-Luc Mélanchon, leader of the recently formed political party La France insoumise, stated plainly the reason why so many were opposed to the bill: Opening up this type of fertility treatment to lesbians and single women means that men are no longer required in the reproductive process. In sum, this was a "revolution of the principle of filiation, proclaiming that *patriarchy is finished* [*le patriarcat est fini*]." After highlighting the fact that this would finally allow women to have children without the permission of a man, he asks, "from what do you hope to protect the child? From the absence of a father? This is a preconceived notion, the idea of filiation has never been anything but a social and cultural construction."[1]

1. Jean-Luc Mélanchon, "Addresse à l'Assemblée nationale: compte rendu intégral

While the hyperbole of Mélanchon's statement serves as an important political tool, it also remains wildly optimistic. To imagine the end of patriarchy, the end of millennia of patriarchal rule, will take a lot more than granting women permission to have children as they please. It will entail, as Mélanchon points out, a reform of systems of affiliation, but it will also require a gutting of so many of the structures that organize our daily lives. Not only does marriage remain a necessity for many because of the rights accorded only to married couples (such as adoption, tax, and end-of-life policies), but women, ethnic minorities, and members of the LGBTQ+ community continue to be hired at lower rates than cisgender men and are consistently paid less than their male counterparts. In other words, we remain politically and economically dependent upon the structures of patriarchy.

Still, while Mélanchon's statement speaks to the persistence of patriarchy, it also demonstrates a hope that has long been seized by queer activists. The year 2019 marked the fiftieth anniversary of the Stonewall riots. Those spontaneous uprisings constituted one of the most important steps in openly fighting for rights of LGBTQ+ people. Within the last fifty years, there have been marches and protests in countries around the globe, anti-discrimination laws have been passed, in 2013 France legalized same-sex marriage, and in 2015 the United States Supreme Court struck down all state bans on same-sex marriage. The success of these laws demonstrates that the utopian energy of queer activist movements can translate into systemic change. I began writing this book in part as a way to demonstrate the long history of such queer, utopian experiments. By showing how authors in the eighteenth century were also examining what might be added to a discussion of family if we were to include within that definition diverse and nonheteronormative structures, I thought I could demonstrate how the eighteenth century was more present than ever. I still feel that way today, but perhaps for different reasons.

Like many people from all parts of the political spectrum, I now read the daily news in a combination of awe and horror as I see the rights for which we have worked so hard over the course of so many years and decades being stripped away one by one. The word "family" has become a terrifyingly pertinent one as families escaping horrible

---

de l'Assemblée nationale XVᵉ *législature,* seconde session extraordinaire de 2018–2019, première séance du mercredi 25 septembre 2019" (emphasis added), http://www.assemblee-nationale.fr/15/cri/2018-2019-extra2/20192011.asp (last accessed February 22, 2021).

situations in their own countries seek asylum in First World countries, only to be turned away or ripped apart upon their arrival. The same people in these developed countries who would turn a blind eye to the separations of children and parents occurring at the borders are often the first to label themselves "pro-family." These examples remind us of the inextricability of family and politics. In fact, if there is one very important lesson we can learn from queer theory, it is that politics has *always* been about families, and, in particular, children.

The work of queer scholars such as Leo Bersani and Lee Edelman in the 1990s and early 2000s provoked discussions in queer theory that forced us to reckon with the role of heterosexual reproduction and the figure of "the child" in politics, as well as to think about how a non-child-centered politics might make room for queer rights. Anti-relational theory argues that supporting heteronormative systems of relationality will never work for queer individuals, and that those individuals should, therefore, resist relational forms stemming from the child and its heteronormative family. Given that many of the atrocities we are witnessing today are, in large part, a product of those very (heteronormative) forms of relationality, Edelman's oft-cited call to shout, "fuck Laws both with capital ls and with small; fuck the whole network of Symbolic relations and the future that serves as its prop," seems more pressing than ever.[2]

While I deeply admire Edelman's critique of politics, as well as his reading of the death drive, and greatly sympathize with this impulse, I would like to take a more optimistic turn in ending this preface toward the work of the late José Esteban Muñoz. Muñoz found Edelman's anti-relational theory both overly pessimistic and unrealistic for queer women and persons of color who, he argued, could not afford the type of systemic refusal proposed by Edelman. While Muñoz agreed that there is no place for the Queer (as a mode of being and doing) in a politics based on heteronormative modes of sociality, he nevertheless saw the hope in other modes of relationality already existing in queer communities. Rather than describing himself on the side of relationality, he states his position as one of "anti-anti-relationality"; instead of focusing on the here and now, as does Edelman, Muñoz longs for the not-yet-here of the future.[3] Both authors base their positions on a psychoanalytic understanding of desire as a lack that

2.   Lee Edelman, *No future: queer theory and the death drive* (Durham, NC, 2004), p.29.
3.   See José Esteban Muñoz, *Cruising utopia: the then and there of queer futurity* (New York, 2009).

can never be filled, but Muñoz encourages us to at least keep desiring, arguing that it is the hope of what may come of that desire that keeps us going through the bad times.

As we face our own tough times, I choose to draw hope from thinking about queer ways of relating to one another in times when relationality has become harder than ever. In the past ten years in the US and in Europe, politics has become ever more divisive as the gulf between the left and the right grows deeper. This divide has undoubtedly caused problems within families. In the absence of what had been believed to be reliable networks of support, many individuals have increasingly found themselves wondering what to do, how to handle the breakdown of their own families. Without the support from blood relatives, many have begun to seek out their own queer forms of relationality, taking a cue from the queer folks who have been relying upon chosen families for hundreds of years. These forms include communities of friends and strangers getting together to share a meal and offer support to one another (even if they are now masked and socially distanced), as well as communities emerging from virtual spaces such as the #blacklivesmatter and #timesup movements, or in France #balancetonporc and #ellessimposent, that not only lead to changes in policy and socially acceptable behavior, but also give voice to traditionally underrepresented groups – amplifying the voices of the perennially unheard through the sympathy and support of others from across the globe. Moreover, the current global pandemic which has effectively shut down domestic and international travel and forced people to remain distant from one another has inalterably changed the ways we connect with others. Moments such as these make us rethink relationality, rethink family, and rethink intimate communities. If this preface presents a moment of supreme despair, it also presents one of renewed hope. For now, all I can do is remain optimistic against all odds and hope that, by the time this book is published in the not-yet-here that Muñoz describes, we will have seen a new moment of change. There will likely still be battles to fight, but hopefully we can get through them with the support of our own queer communities.

Acknowledgments

Writing about queer kinship has invited me to reflect more thoughtfully than ever on those friends, family members, mentors, and colleagues who constitute my world and make day-to-day life enjoyable (or at least bearable), even in these difficult times. Like many first books, the kernel for this project began as a dissertation while I was at the University of Minnesota, and I would like to thank Daniel Brewer for being the most thoughtful and dedicated adviser I could have asked for. Juliette Cherbuliez, Mária Minich Brewer, Mary Franklin-Brown, and Nancy Luxon also shaped this project in so many helpful ways. My time in Minnesota was made so much better by friends in the Department of French and Italian – especially Anna Rosensweig, Sarah Jones-Boardman, Sara Wellman, Greta Bliss, Melanie Bowman, Robert St. Clair, Lia Mitchell, Becky Halat, Deborah Lee-Ferrand, and François Vozel. Outside of the department, Roberto Rebolledo, Tom Cannavino, Aly Penucci, Benedict Stork, Colleen Quesnell, and Andre Quesnell became the best family I could have asked for.

At Penn State, I have the great fortune of having exceptionally brilliant colleagues who have informed this book in so many ways. Though there are undoubtedly too many to name here, I will name just a few who have supported my academic and intellectual endeavors over the years. Thanks to my colleagues in the departments of French and Francophone studies and Women's, Gender, and Sexuality studies, with a special thanks to Christine Clark-Evans, whose probing questions enriched several chapters of the book, Willa Silverman, who has provided invaluable support, and Bénédicte Monicat, an incredible mentor who never ceases to inspire me. I have also received financial and intellectual support from the Fulbright Commission and the Humanities Institute at Penn State, as well as a welcoming community in Penn State's Center for Early Modern Studies. I am also particularly grateful to those graduate students who took my "Kinship and Enlightenment" seminar a few years ago, and who helped me to work through many of the ideas that appear in this book.

As I have moved through my career, I have been lucky enough to have created my own forms of queer community in various spaces. During my time at Dartmouth, I worked with some amazing people who have become dear friends, including Aimee Bahng, Bill Boyer, Tish Lopez, Jason MacLeod, Alysia Garrison, Mary Coffey, and Amy Allen (now also my colleague at Penn State). And now in State College I have found support among an equally wonderful group of folks including Sophia McClennen, Alicia Decker, Sarah Townsend, Julie Kleinman, Hil Malatino, C. Libby, Sam Tenorio, AnneMarie Mingo, Sara Grossman, Grant Wythoff, Chris Castiglia, Janet Lyon, Erin Heidt-Forsythe, John Christman, Kathlene Baldanza, Christopher Moore, Laura Kooistra, Sc'Eric Horner, and Susan Squire. Although I do not recommend having a baby while trying to finish a book manuscript, having a supportive group of parent friends definitely makes the process better, and for that I thank Ariane Cruz, Alyx Lee, Betsy VanNoy, Alicia Palmer, Jess Garrity, as well as Pamela VanHaitsma, whose advice was also crucial in defining some of the key concepts of this book. Additionally, Jessamyn Abel, Jonathan Abel, Maryam Frederick, Samuel Frederick, Ben Schreier, Sarah Koenig, and Jens-Uwe Guettel make up the intimate community that I am so thankful for in this town. Finally, although group texts have recently replaced hangouts, Heather McCoy and Abigail Celis keep me laughing when Canvas makes me want to cry, and conversations with Jennifer Boittin over drinks at Local Whiskey (in pre-COVID times) nourish my body and soul, and I doubt this book would have gotten finished without her love, suggestions, and support.

I have presented much of this work at conferences and am grateful to have found a group of scholars and academics whose feedback, mentorship, and friendship have been crucial to the success of this project, including Suzanne Pucci, Mary McAlpin, Logan Connors, Katharine Jensen, Andrew H. Clark, Annelle Curulla, Laurence Mall, Yann Robert, Scott Sanders, Masano Yamashita, Karen Santos Da Silva, Rudy Le Menthéour, Jennifer Tamas-Le Menthéour, Jennifer Row, Fayçal Falaky, Christopher Breu, Sean Grattan, Pierre Saint-Amand, Ourida Mostefai, and especially Valentina Denzel, my partner in the "Legacies of the Enlightenment" project and overall magnificent friend. I would also like to extend my thanks to Gregory Brown, who has supported this project from the beginning, Leah

Morin for her expert editorial work, Emma Burridge, Ally Lee, and the team at Liverpool University Press for making this book see the light of day, and the anonymous reader of the manuscript whose feedback made this book stronger.

Finally, the biggest thanks go to my family. I'm pretty sure my mother was disappointed when the daughter she had long wished for wanted to play school instead of dolls, but, in spite of our disagreements over the years, her encouragement led me to become a first-generation college student, and, without her help in those early years with my first daughter, I'm not sure I ever would have finished college or graduate school. Thanks also to my brother, Fred, who has long been a source of support. I met my partner, Christian, right before I started writing the dissertation that would eventually become this book. He has probably read about a thousand different versions of this project over the years, and somehow has never complained. I am in awe of his constant dedication to those around him, and I owe him more than I can ever repay. Thank you for being my best friend, an incomparable father, and for supporting and growing with me. Finally, to the last two members of our wonderful little family, my daughters Beatrice and River, to whom this book is dedicated. Beatrice, you and I have been through so much together, and loving you has kept me going even when I wanted to quit everything. River, you arrived only recently but your smile makes everything so much brighter, even in the darkest of times. Although my relationship to kinship has often been rocky, being a mother to the two of you has made me realize just how nurturing family can be.

Author's note

On pronouns

Many of the characters in this book present across a broad spectrum of gender. Most often, these characters adhere to binary notions of gender, changing from male to female at different points in the story; however, there are also characters for whom gender falls outside of the binary, or who present as their nonassigned gender throughout. Because understanding the characters' gender presentation at a given point is crucial to my analyses of the novels and plays, I have chosen to use the pronoun associated with each character's gender in any given scene. This means that some characters will be referred to with both male and female pronouns, with the choice remaining faithful to the context of the scene. In all cases in which the gender has no bearing on the interpretation, gender-neutral pronouns (they/them) are used.

On spelling and translations

In keeping with the bilingual spirit of the series, I have provided English translations for all primary French texts, with the original text in footnotes or directly following the translation for block quotes. Unless otherwise noted, translations are my own. For all pre-1800 French texts, I have kept the spelling of the editions cited, keeping all variant spellings and using modern or eighteenth-century spellings as necessary.

I

Family remains

Introduction: the specter of patriarchy

A father! What a subject in a century such as ours when it seems we haven't the foggiest idea of what a father is!

Un père de famille! Quel sujet dans un siècle tel que le nôtre, où il ne paraît pas qu'on ait la moindre idée de ce que c'est qu'un père de famille!

Denis Diderot, *Entretiens sur le fils naturel*

If you take a stroll through the Sully wing on the third floor of the Louvre, you will likely encounter two magnificent paintings by Jean-Baptiste Greuze: *Le Fils ingrat* (*The Ungrateful son*) and *Le Fils puni* (*The Punished son*). The two tableaux, known collectively as *La Malédiction paternelle* (*The Father's curse*), were completed around 1777–1778 and were famously described by Denis Diderot in his literary salons.[1] In *Le Fils ingrat* (see Figure 1), we see a scene of familial chaos. The eldest son has just enrolled in the army and is about to leave his paternal home. In the corner, an older officer stands waiting in the doorway to take him to a future far away from his family. The father and son occupy opposite sides of the painting, a symbol of the gulf separating the two even prior to the son's departure. The son tries desperately to leave, but the mother blocks his path, begging him to stay, as the eldest

---

1. Diderot admires the work of Greuze in his 1765 salon. He is, in fact, commenting on early ink sketches of the two paintings that Greuze completed in 1765. Although there are several changes between the sketches and the final tableaux, the theme of the paintings remains the same. See Denis Diderot, *Œuvres complètes*, vol.14: *Salon de 1765: essais sur la peinture*, ed. Else Marie Bukdahl, Annette Lorenceau, and Gita May (Paris, 1975).

1

Figure 1: Jean-Baptiste Greuze (1725–1805). *Le Fils ingrat, la malédiction paternelle* (*The Ungrateful son, the paternal curse*), 1777. Oil on canvas, 130 × 162 cm.

Figure 2: Jean-Baptiste Greuze (1725–1805). *Le Fils puni, la malédiction paternelle* (*The Son punished, the paternal curse*), 1778. Oil on canvas, 130 × 163 cm.

daughter prays that he not leave. The father rises from his chair to
lunge at the ungrateful son, but he too is held back by one of his
dutiful daughters. In the small, disheveled room, this family drama of
paternal-filial separation plays out in the most extraordinary of colors,
movements, and emotions.

We understand the consequences of the son's flight only in the
second piece of the diptych, *Le Fils puni* (see Figure 2). In it the
ungrateful son arrives home from the army, devastated to learn of
his father's death. The injured son enters, bent over and disheveled
with his crutch lying on the floor in front of him. With his head in his
hand, he realizes the grave situation caused by his actions. The family
gathers around the bed of the father, dressed in mourning clothes,
each wearing various expressions of shock and sadness. The father
and son once again occupy opposite sides of the frame, with the father
on the deathbed and the son in the doorway. This time, however, the
son moves toward rather than away from the father as the hands of the
mother, sisters, and brothers all point toward the patriarch who has
just died. The only figure in the painting not gesturing to the father
is a dog that had been absent from the last painting. The presence of
the dog serves as a reminder that the canine was a friend more loyal
to the father than the son had been. The son's punishment for having
left the family is the death of his father.

Both of these paintings, displayed for the first time in the latter half
of the eighteenth century, translate the raw emotions of family life in
France. Even in its earliest sketches, this diptych had such a strong
effect on Diderot that he wrote of it, "I can't say what effect this short,
simple description of a sketch for a painting will have on others; for
myself, I confess that I've not written it without emotion."[2] Diderot
found in these tableaux images to adequately express the passions
he had already been creating on the stage for his spectators, the
emotional language of familial intimacy. At the center of this intimate
scene, both in life and in death, we find the father. The father of these
paintings, much like the fathers in Diderot's *drames bourgeois*, depends
on the love and, more importantly, the devotion of his children—
without it, he withers away. As we see in the second painting, however,
his corporeal presence is felt deeply, even after his death. Whereas the

2.   Diderot, *Diderot on art: the salon of 1765 and notes on painting*, translated by John
     Goodman (New Haven, CT, 1995), p.108; *Salon de 1765*, p.199. "Je ne sais quel
     effet cette courte et simple description d'une esquisse de tableau fera sur les
     autres; pour moi, j'avoue que je ne l'ai point faite sans émotion."

focus was split between father and son in the first painting, after his death, almost all eyes are on the father, whether it be on his corpse or toward the sky in search of his departed spirit.

Given Greuze's interest in historical painting, one cannot help but imagine that the presentation of this diptych in its final form in 1778 encouraged viewers to reflect upon the loss of another patriarch, Louis XV, who had died just a few years prior in 1774. Beyond the portraiture for which Greuze is often remembered, what the painter demonstrated with *La Malédiction paternelle* (as well as other tableaux depicting scenes of familial intimacy such as *The Paralytic* and *The Village bride*) was a fascination with the delicate relations of the patriarchal family. Viewed globally, his *œuvre* explores not the death of one father in particular, but the ailing state of patriarchy in general. One reason for such an intense meditation on fatherhood might be found in the transitional period during which many of Greuze's most provocative paintings were produced. Although Louis XV did not die until 1774, an attempt on his life in 1757 as well as parliamentary revolts in the 1760s had already begun to demonstrate the precarity of the king's position. These were also the years in which Greuze finished such masterpieces as *Epiphany*, *Septimius Severus and Caracalla*, and *The Village bride*—each of which depicts a father interacting with his children. In other words, during the final years of Louis XV's reign, as well as during the transitional years between one king and the next, Greuze's paintings tend to examine the possibilities for how a man might govern his family. As Abby Zanger points out, liminal periods (such as the years following the death of a king) serve as points in time when the traditional methods and principles organizing society are disrupted and called into question.[3] These periods do not always result in reversals of society or radical changes, but they do at least open the space to imagine social and political upheavals in many diverse forms. In this book I also analyze obliquely the ailing state of patriarchy, largely through the alternative systems that authors propose to take its place, but I do so by turning the years and decades during and following the regency of Philippe II, duke of Orléans.

Prior to his death, Louis XIV had transformed himself from the leader of France into the very symbol of virility and unfettered power. Following England's Glorious Revolution of 1688, which resulted in a more powerful Parliament and clear limits on the British king's power,

3. See Abby E. Zanger, *Scenes from the marriage of Louis XIV: nuptial fictions and the making of absolutist power* (Stanford, CA, 1997).

the Sun King worked hard to avoid a similar uprising in France.[4] In moves to centralize and grow his power, the French king, who had recently relocated the court to Versailles in order to more closely monitor his subjects' behavior, signed the Edict of Fontainebleau, stripping Protestants' rights. By revoking the Edict of Nantes, Louis XIV hoped to avoid any religious uprisings that might threaten his position. Between decrees, wars, and a daily, ritualistic scrutiny of aristocrats and civil servants at Versailles, the French king showed no outward signs of weakness. On the contrary, his position seemed stronger than ever. However, as we will see in France in 1789, and again in 1830 and 1848 (and arguably even today), during times when power becomes consolidated in the hands of one or a few individuals, there will almost inevitably be growing voices of dissent amongst the people.[5] These voices may be loud and direct in the form of protests or strikes, or they may be much more subtle and subversive. It is to those subversive voices of dissent that I turn in this book—those who were imagining new futures through fiction for, as Voltaire writes in a poem to Mme Elie de Beaumont, "history tells what one has done; a good novel, what *must be done*."[6]

Queering the Enlightenment argues that, following the death of the Sun King, many authors took up the pen to propose exactly what the French subjects *must do*. These authors did not just record history or tell interesting stories; they distinguished themselves as some of the most brilliant political theorists of the day within the pages of their novels and plays. Enlightenment, for these authors, meant reorienting one's relation to power by reorganizing their most intimate relations. Only by imagining family as a grouping of individuals of diverse genders, social strata, and races who come together for the sake of love and pleasure (rather than duty and obligation) could these

4. For a detailed analysis of the post-Glorious Revolution period in France, see *A Court in exile: the Stuarts in France, 1689–1718*, ed. Edward Corp (Cambridge, MA, 2009). This collection charts the relationship between the recently deposed James II and his cousin Louis XIV in the years following the Glorious Revolution.

5. Recent politically motivated gatherings of people such as those occurring during the Nuit debout, the Gilets jaunes, or the Black Lives Matter protests attest to the continued importance of vocal dissent to France's political identity.

6. Voltaire to Anne Louise Dumesnil-Morin Elie de Beaumont, 29 June 1764 (D11956). *Correspondence and related documents*, ed. Th. Besterman, in *Œuvres complètes de Voltaire*, vol.85–135 (Oxford, 1968–1977), vol.111, p.453 (emphasis added). "L'histoire dit ce qu'on a fait; Un bon roman, ce qu'il *faut faire*."

authors bypass the rigid rules of a patriarchal system (and, with it, its powerful regime) that regulates governance through specific practices of reproduction and inheritance. In their fiction, we see not a blueprint for the Revolution or the democracy that formed after 1789, but rather the forms of democracy that might have been. In particular, I focus on novels and plays written and performed during the 1730s and 1740s because this period in French literature provides particularly fertile ground for assessing the precarity of the patriarchal family structure. From 1715 to 1723, following the death of Louis XIV, France was ruled by the late king's nephew, Philippe II. During this period of regency many hardline rules of absolutism were relaxed, opening up the space for a collective family romance in which the French became symbolically orphaned and some began to more openly conceive of ideal models of leadership.[7] I examine several canonical authors from the first half of the eighteenth century, such as Pierre de Marivaux and Françoise de Graffigny, who came of age during this brief interlude between regimes of patriarchal power. The misfits and outsiders who populate the pages of their works enact a loosening of systems of alliance and morals, inviting readers to follow a utopian impulse to *recreate*—rather than procreate—a society of equals. Recreation, for these authors, implies both attending to the many pleasures offered by social life and *re*-creation, or proposing new forms of intimate community by rearranging the various components of family life. These authors imagine a utopian expansion of the possibilities for intimate communities. They grapple with the potential loss of the patriarch and the resulting vacuum of power by proposing new types of kinship that might rise to take its place.

   Scholars such as Nancy Armstrong, Carol L. Sherman, and Lynn Festa have established that domestic and sentimental fiction and national politics share mutual concerns.[8] Both sentimental fiction and national politics are interested in how individuals engage with one another, and both take on the task of organizing and managing

---

7. For an analysis of what a French family romance looks like, see Lynn Hunt's *The Family romance of the French Revolution* (Oakland, CA, 1992). Although Hunt focuses on the precarious time period following 1789, when the newly fatherless society scrambled to decide how, exactly, democracy would take the place of the monarchy, we see similar questions arising following the death of Louis XIV.

8. See Nancy Armstrong, *Desire and domestic fiction: a political history of the novel* (Oxford, 1990); Carol L. Sherman, *The Family crucible in eighteenth-century literature* (Burlington, VT, 2005); and Lynn Festa, *Sentimental figures in eighteenth-century Britain and France* (Baltimore, MD, 2006).

communities of people. By contrast, scholars such as Michel Delon and Srinivas Aravamudan have assessed the political import of salacious stories in the less prestigious genres of the libertine or oriental tale.[9] This book aims to bridge the gap between these two positions by considering the places where the domestic and the illicit or exotic overlap. What can be gained, I ask, by examining the moments in which figures of normativity such as the good son or the well-mannered daughter stray into unfamiliar territory? And conversely, what happens when exotic figures are brought into typically heteronormative spaces such as the patriarchal household? In these instances of estrangement, normal psychic processes falter and subjects begin to question the social situations in which they find themselves. The rules of family politics that had previously shaped these protagonists' existence are replaced with new ways of life that test their beliefs. These scenes of disjunction, confusion, even discomfort open the space for authors to seize upon a utopian impulse to challenge the status quo of patriarchal politics by proposing radical forms of kinship. Uncovering these alternative intimate communities will require us to be open to the breaks between the content of literature and its form. This is a process I call "reading queerly" and it allows us to find the radical potential in works that may seem otherwise tame. We will return to this notion in more depth later in this introduction, but first, we need to understand the theoretical apparatuses that compel such a reading, and that make it possible.

The regime of the father

Because of its focus on the relation of individuals, kinship, and power, this book draws primarily on theoretical concepts from three distinct disciplines: psychoanalysis, structuralism, and political theory. Theorists such as Jacques Lacan, Michel Foucault, and Jacques Rancière have relied heavily on epistemological concepts that emerged from eighteenth-century philosophers as a way of understanding the internal and external structures that guide and inform our everyday lives. The eighteenth century in France was a time of movement and change; from the fall of the monarchy to the reconfiguration of the public sphere, this moment is often regarded as the country's entry into modernity. Along with these political and social transformations,

9. See Michel Delon, *Le Savoir-vivre libertin* (Paris, 2004); and Srinivas Aravamudan, *Enlightenment orientalism: resisting the rise of the novel* (Chicago, IL, 2011).

literature was changing as well. As we have learned from the vast
number of studies on what has come to be known as the "rise of
the novel," scientific and technological advances, combined with the
separation of critical inquiry from the Church, led to a heightened
desire for new forms of literature that would explore these transitions
in an enjoyable form.[10] As Marthe Robert points out, the novel
emerges as a "bastard" of literature, departing from the romances
that preceded it. Generic and stylistic changes in literature reflect, if
not historical events, then at least a general mood in Europe—a mood
desirous of something new.

Central to each of the discussions in this book are the ways in which
power circulates according to two primary constructs: Foucault's
assessment of the apparatuses of alliance and sexuality that overlap
and compete with one another; and the transfer of paternal power via
the Oedipus complex, especially as it is articulated by Lacan. Each
of these thinkers grapples with how power emerges and circulates in
modern societies, although through very different means. In order to
better guide the readings that occur in the chapters that follow, we will
examine these two concepts here.

Foucault argues that the family unit serves as a generative site
of power in early modern European societies. In the first volume
of *History of sexuality*, he renders explicit the connection between the
family and sexuality. For Foucault, sexuality replaces blood as the
primary mode of social reproduction and becomes "an especially
dense transfer point for relations of power."[11] He writes that, in the
eighteenth century, specific mechanisms of knowledge and power were
being formed that were centered on sex. These mechanisms included
new theories on female physiology and childhood sexuality, and
invited more surveillance from within the home. Husbands watched
their wives and parents observed their children, looking for any signs
of aberrant behavior. Furthermore, the family home was opened up
to the outside world in previously unknown ways. Family members
increasingly relied on the outside influence of doctors and specialists
to govern one another, disrupting the autonomous reproduction of

10. Some of the most well-known studies on the rise of the novel include: Marthe
     Robert, *Origins of the novel*, translated by Sacha Rabinovitch (Brighton, 1980);
     Ian Watt, *The Rise of the novel* (Oakland, CA, 1974); and Aravamudan, *Enlight-
     enment orientalism*.
11. Michel Foucault, *The History of sexuality: an introduction*, vol.1, translated by Robert
     Hurley (New York, 1991), p.103.

paternal power within the family. Until the early modern period sexual relations had determined practices of marriage and the formation of kinship structures in a way that ensured the transmission of names and possessions from one generation to the next. This system, the apparatus of alliance, relied on and maintained the social body; laws governing alliances between families were firmly fixed, with severe repercussions for breaking the laws. Beginning in the eighteenth century, Foucault argues, a new system emerges that governs and is governed by sexual relations. This system, the apparatus of sexuality, is superimposed upon and coexistent with the apparatus of alliance, and shifts the importance away from the link *between* bodies, that is, the transmission of power from one generation to the next, to the sensations *of* the body. Against alliance, which is motivated by a constant compulsion to reproduce, sexuality finds its motivating force not in reproduction but in penetrating individual bodies "in an increasingly detailed way, and in controlling populations in an increasingly comprehensive way."[12] Sexuality continues to develop, according to Foucault, as the family coheres into its modern bourgeois form in the eighteenth century.

Given his scrutiny of sexuality and power, it is unsurprising that Foucault's work has served as a touchstone for scholars of gender and sexuality. Critics such as Nancy Fraser, Judith Butler, and Elizabeth Grosz have demonstrated how Foucault's unique positioning of sexuality as an apparatus of power and control has allowed us to rethink such categories as gender, corporeality, and sexed material.[13] However, by and large these works take for granted the apparatus of alliance as a bygone institution. Even Nancy Hartsock's important critique of the universalizing characteristics of power in Foucault implicitly suggests that domination begins (or at least becomes overbearing and stifles the possibility for resistance) only with the introduction of an apparatus of sexuality.[14] Although alliance disappears from many contemporary arguments, for Foucault, the division between the two apparatuses is not so cut and dry. Alliance and sexuality

12. Foucault, *History of sexuality*, p.107.
13. See Nancy Fraser, *Unruly practices: power, discourse, and gender in contemporary social theory* (Minneapolis, MN, 1989); Judith Butler, *Gender trouble: feminism and the subversion of identity* (New York, 1990); and Elizabeth Grosz, *Volatile bodies: toward a corporeal feminism* (Bloomington, IN, 1994).
14. See Nancy Hartsock, "Foucault on power: a theory for women?," in *Feminism/postmodernism*, ed. Linda Nicholson (New York, 1990), p.157–75.

exist simultaneously, overlapping and intertwining as they alter the laws governing individual bodies and the social body. According to Foucault, familial relationships (particularly those between husbands and wives, and parents and children) serve as ideal nodes in which to locate the mechanisms of power operating in both alliance and sexuality. Those protagonists of eighteenth-century fiction who are still bound by the strict rules of lineage and inheritance typical of alliance, and yet who are opening outward toward a society in which the family (as a patriarchal institution) is in peril and sexuality as an apparatus of power is beginning to emerge, therefore, are precisely the kinds of heroes who can show us just what happens to power in transitional moments. These are the kinds of heroes that allow us to imagine radical forms of kinship.

The forms of kinship on display in the works examined in this book inhabit the nexus of these two apparatuses, demonstrating how these diverging models of power networks at times overlap with one another, and at others seem far apart. We find in the pages of these works intense studies of individual human sexuality often embedded within a strict sense of familial duty. It is from the gap between these two apparatuses that we find depictions of the family that are revolutionary in their divergence from the norm. Nevertheless, in order to arrive at these revolutionary models of kinship, we must also understand the transformation of the individual subject taking place. Long soliloquies, letters in which one's soul is laid bare, and memoirs that record the most intimate details of one's life—these forms of literature allow us to assess the human psyche in ways that will become more evident in the nineteenth century with the introduction of the free-indirect style. Central to the styles we see in these novels and plays are the ways in which the form of the works may diverge from their content. For example, in Crébillon fils's libertine novel *Le Sofa* (*The Sofa*) the frame contains dialogue between a narrator and extradiegetic interlocutors that calls into question the veracity of the story itself. Wrapped up in plots of familial intrigue, the form of these works allows us to glimpse quite intimately the subjective formation of the protagonists. In many cases, the form of these novels and plays stages a literary family romance.[15]

15. According to Freud, the family romance occurs when a child begins to realize the deficiencies in their own parents and imagines the parents' deaths and subsequent replacement with better parents. See Freud, *Collected papers*, vol.5, ed. and translated by James Strachey (New York, 1959), p.74–78.

One of the primary functions of family, according to psychoanalysis, is the introduction, circulation, and transfer of desire and, with it, power. Since Sigmund Freud, psychoanalytic theory has located the primal scene of familial desire in the story of Oedipus Rex. In *The Interpretation of dreams*, Freud introduced a foundational concept that he named the Oedipus complex.[16] Not only did Freud find in Sophocles's ancient Greek tragedy *Oedipus Rex* a compelling story for explaining human emotions, but he also noted that the structure of the play resembles the work of psychoanalysis itself. All of the actions are completed prior to the first act, and the entirety of the tragedy consists in a slow revelation of the myriad of tragedies that befall the unlucky Oedipus and Jocasta. Because the plot centers on the king of Thebes uncovering long-lost memories, there could be, in Freud's opinion, no better representation for the process of psychoanalysis. It is no wonder, then, that the story of Oedipus has now become inseparable from the story of human psycho-subjective development.

According to Freud, the scene of oedipal crisis unfolds when the son, unconsciously desiring the mother, enters into competition with the father.[17] He sees the father as his sexual rival, competing with him for the attention of the mother. Once the son discovers the sexual differences between males and females, he begins to experience castration anxiety, fearing that the father will castrate him, thus leaving him both literally and figuratively emasculated. The successful resolution to the crisis, according to Freud, occurs only once the son identifies with the father and realizes the father's authority over himself and his mother. Only once he identifies with the father and understands paternal authority can he begin to form his own superego that will let him distinguish between right and wrong. In this chain of desiring, all happens at the level of the unconscious, and the child becomes a normative sexual subject only through a successful resolution of the crisis. Two of the most consistent feminist and queer critiques of the Oedipus complex as elaborated by Freud have been first, its reliance upon biological notions of gender, and second, the

16. Sigmund Freud, *The Interpretation of dreams*, translated by James Strachey (1899; New York, 1955).
17. Although the Freudian interpretation of the crisis is often elaborated in terms of same-sex and opposite-sex parent, when referring to a normal psychic progression Freud himself repeatedly describes the complex in terms of fathers and sons. Discussions of daughters continue to focus on the vital role of the father.

primary position accorded to the male in the formation of young boys and girls.[18] The result of the Freudian oedipal complex is a circulation of desire that always favors male over female, understanding the lack of a penis to be the most profound privation one can endure.

By theorizing the oedipal complex as a linguistic, rather than biological, process, Lacan diverges from the gender essentialism apparent in Freud. The locus of power is no longer the penis but the phallus—a signifier of sexual difference rather than a male genital organ. For Lacan, as for Freud, the complex constitutes an essential formation of the normative subject, but, unlike Freud, desire circulates through a chain of signifiers. The Lacanian process divides the psyche into three major structures: the Real, the Imaginary, and the Symbolic. Although Lacan's position on the primacy of one structure over the others will shift throughout his career, the oedipal crisis can be divided into three main points, which follow the three structures. The psychic experience of these structures is messy, and they may intersect with one another and repeat themselves in a disorderly fashion, but for the sake of clarity I will outline them here in a relatively chrono-logical manner. First, the infant exists only in the Real, as language has not yet come to alter or obfuscate desire.[19] The drives of the infant are intimately tied to need. For example, the infant desires the mother because it is hungry and in need of nourishment. The child enters the Imaginary during a period Lacan calls the Mirror Stage, when the child understands its body and desires as separate from the mother. While we will discuss the function of anxiety during this stage in chapter 3, for now it is important to note that at this stage in the child's psychosexual development meaning is whole—signs do not diverge from signifiers and signifieds. The child understands that its father is a figure of authority but does not yet realize that this father

18. For some of the most famous of these critiques, see Simone de Beauvoir's *The Second sex*, translated by Constance Borde and Sheila Malovany-Chevallier (New York, 2011), particularly ch.2; Luce Irigaray's *Speculum of the other woman*, translated by Gillian Gill (Ithaca, NY, 1985); Monique Wittig's *The Straight mind and other essays* (Boston, MA, 1992); and Juliet Mitchell's *Psychoanalysis and feminism: a radical reassessment of Freudian psychoanalysis* (New York, 2000).

19. The Real is a structure that will change throughout Lacan's career. Unless otherwise stated, I will be working from articulations of the Real from his later works (especially the twentieth seminar), as it is in these works that he seems to elaborate upon the structure most clearly. See *The Seminar of Jacques Lacan XX: on feminine sexuality, the limits of love and knowledge 1972–73*, ed. Jacques-Alain Miller, translated by Bruce Fink (New York, 1998).

is but one among many fathers. Castration anxiety, for Lacan, occurs only in the third and final stage of the oedipal complex. It is at this point that the child realizes the power of the father as belonging to a larger system of signs and signifiers, thus fracturing meaning. Finally, the child enters into the Symbolic Order, receiving from the father a *non/nom-du-père*. For Lacan, the father's name is not a name at all, but rather a symbol of the power he holds as a master of language.

Lacan finds in *Oedipus Rex* another way in which this tragedy teaches us about human desire—through death. The analyst's earlier examinations of the complex are very much focused on the psychosexual development of the child that we have just discussed. In subsequent writings, however, he elaborates more fully on the complex's relation to desire and death (and the death drive). Most notably, he reminds us that the process is neither linear nor unique, and that one can move through the oedipal complex as if on a continuum throughout one's lifetime. To think through the relation of desire and the death drive, Lacan returns to a reading of Sophocles's tragedy in his seminars on the ethics of psychoanalysis. He argues that, although the king does not die after the revelations of his crimes, he does suffer what Lacan calls a "true death in which he erases his own being."[20] In other words, Oedipus's symbolic death (in which he loses his eyes, the kingdom, and his wife and children) allows him to prepare for the death to come (that of the body), and Oedipus thus "shows us where the inner limit zone in the relationship to desire ends."[21] The act of self-erasure demonstrates that point between the death drive and the pleasure principle in which an individual comes closest to pure *jouissance*. *Jouissance* is not exactly joy and nor can it be rendered simply by its English equivalent (orgasm); it is an unconscious drive that is tied up in, yet distinct from, one's conscious desires. To live beyond life is to know the value of living—and, more specifically, of living in the here and now. I will discuss the ethical implications of *jouissance* in chapter 3, but I point it out here because its emphasis on the freedom of the psyche in the moment—a freedom from the structures and strictures of oedipal society—explains why psychoanalysis, and Lacanian psychoanalytic theory more specifically, has played a crucial role in much of the feminist and queer theory to be discussed in this book.

20. Jacques Lacan, *The Seminar of Jacques Lacan VII: the ethics of psychoanalysis 1959–60*, ed. Jacques-Alain Miller, translated by Dennis Porter (New York, 1992), p.306.
21. Lacan, *The Ethics of psychoanalysis*, p.306.

In many ways, psychoanalysis and Foucault's structural articulation of power could not be farther from one another. Psychoanalysis is, in fact, one of the very institutions Foucault critiques in part due to its taxonomic divisions of sex and behavior that govern societies in the most pernicious of ways. It is likely for this reason that critics rarely bring these two discourses together.[22] However, restoring a place of importance to Foucault's apparatus of alliance with its focus on the transmission of power through laws based on reproduction and inheritance, and analyzing how it becomes entangled with the apparatus of sexuality, will help us to see how the structures of the psyche replicate and are replicated by the structures governing society in the early eighteenth century in France. At the base of each of these structures is, in one way or another, a patriarch.

The specter of patriarchy

"Le roi est mort, vive le roi!" ("The king is dead, long live the king!") This proclamation, first uttered after the death of Charles VI, serves as the thread that stitches one monarch's rule to the next. When one king dies, another rises to take his place. For centuries in France, this was the traditional succession of power. Sometimes the transfer of power was relatively seamless, but other times, particularly when the new king had not yet reached the age of majority, his power was given over temporarily to a regent (or board of regents). Between each king, certainly, but particularly in extended periods between the death of one king and the next king's assumption of the throne, subjects experienced a life that was, essentially, between two kings. As Ernst Kantorowicz famously described back in 1957, the decree, "the king is dead, long live the king," made visible the duality of the king's body.[23] On the one hand, the king was, like any individual, a corporeal being of flesh and bone, whose body grew and changed as he lived and breathed. This body remained at risk of disease and death. This was the king's body natural. On the other hand, the king was a being of almost mythical proportions. This body was symbolic—immune to the disasters of everyday life and capable of immortality. This

22. A few notable exceptions are Nancy Luxon, *Crisis of authority: politics, trust, and truth-telling in Freud and Foucault* (Cambridge, 2013); and Jill Gentile, *Feminine law: Freud, free speech, and the voice of desire* (New York, 2016).
23. Ernst Kantorowicz, *The King's two bodies: a study in medieval political theology* (Princeton, NJ, 2016).

was the king's body politic. From at least the medieval period until the early eighteenth century, this was a phenomenon that was easily understood.[24]

At some point in the late seventeenth and early eighteenth centuries, however, something began to change. As Jay Caplan points out, a semiotic crisis occurred in the years following Louis XIV's death that made clear the crumbling of absolutism that had been taking place for at least several years before his death.[25] In the wake of the king's (real) death, Caplan argues, the names for things no longer necessarily matched the things themselves, and new systems of language had not yet successfully taken the place of the old. This was because the king's real death was accompanied by a symbolic death—the slow death of absolutism. This moment between the two deaths, the time separating the comma of the first clause in the proclamation from the first word in the second clause ("The king is dead, ... long live the king!"), is a time of confusion, a time when the natural order of things is thrown into disarray. In Lacanian terms, the body that exists between two deaths is one that embodies the death drive but becomes evacuated of desire. This is the body on an unstoppable mission, but one that ultimately has only one possible outcome—death. Staring down its own death, that body can do nothing more than fight to preserve its life for as long as possible. At that point, it is up to the subjects—the philosophers and the writers—to assess and diagnose the ailing state of patriarchy, and to try to think of what to do, as Caplan says, in its wake.

Following Lacan, scholars often invoke *Antigone* and *Hamlet* when referring to figures that demonstrate the persistence of the body beyond death.[26] The presence of both bodies (the corporeal and the

24. Eric Santner argues that this division does not disappear after the French Revolution and other uprisings in Europe that result in the end of monarchies, but rather that it is displaced onto the people. This ill-fitting symbolic power, which he describes as an excess of "flesh," is sublimated into many of our everyday practices that replicate the theological powers of the king. See Santner, *The Royal remains: the people's two bodies and the endgames of sovereignty* (Chicago, IL, 2012).

25. Jay Caplan, *In the king's wake: post-absolutist culture in France* (Chicago, IL, 1999).

26. See, for example, Judith Butler, *Antigone's claim: kinship between life and death* (New York, 2000); Joseph Margon, "The death of Antigone," *California studies in classical Antiquity* 3 (1997), p.177–83; and for a legal take on the subject see Maria Aristodemou, "To be or not to be a (dead) father," *Journal of international dispute settlement* 9:1 (2018), p.103–22.

spectral) resonates in the world of the living as an apparition or a ghost. For Antigone, this death is a symbolic one from the start since she marks herself as dead before the action of the play even begins. Her corporeal presence, then, is ghostlike, it reminds spectators of the death to come. In *Hamlet*, the ghost is much more literal with the spirit of Hamlet's dead father haunting his son as well as his soldiers. In each of these plays, the ghosts are feared because of the radical power communicated by their bodies. The female body of Antigone, beholden to justice, poses a serious threat to the royal power of the king. The ghost in *Hamlet* serves as a reminder of the power of the state, wreaking vengeance on those who would question such power. In each of these cases, the persistence of these specters serves as a reminder of justice.

Although the monarchy in France will not be dismantled until the end of the eighteenth century, it weakens, beginning to assume a ghost-like quality, after the death of Louis XIV. Much like the ghost of Hamlet's father, the ghost of patriarchy in eighteenth-century France also serves as a reminder, but, in this case, it is a reminder of a dying system. As we will see in chapter 1, the specter of patriarchy had already begun to haunt political theory even before a postmortem was declared on the monarchy. The gap between the king's symbolic and real deaths is filled with an anxious energy among the people, whose futures remain uncertain. Rather than being declared dead from the very beginning, he is born into eternal life. As king he is guaranteed a body that will not die. His is an apparition manipulated through a series of elaborate rituals and practices.

As children, we learn to fear ghosts. Ghosts are what hides under our beds or lurks in our closets. Scary stories warn us that ghosts are almost always out to destroy us. These apparitions threaten not just our happy way of life: They threaten our lives altogether. However, as Carla Freccero points out, haunting can be a useful tool of analysis.[27] Building on Jacques Derrida's notion of hauntology, Frecerro proposes the practice as a means of describing when something seems temporally "out of joint." For Derrida, as for Freccero, this does not necessarily mean an unearthing of the past—it can also be a presence from the future; in short, hauntology is a means of sensing something that seems of the wrong time.[28] Whereas Derrida

---

27. Carla Freccero, *Queer/early/modern* (Durham, NC, 2006).
28. For a recent example of how this kind of reading can unearth new possibilities for eighteenth-century literature, see William F. Edmiston's exceptional monograph

assesses a sensitivity to a certain sublime ontology, Freccero offers spectrality as a way of doing queer historiography. She proposes that, as a method of historical research, spectrality might "describe a more ethical relation to the past and the future than our current models permit."[29] To "do history" through the method of spectrality allows one to let the ghosts speak without making them speak in service of the literary critic, historian, or anyone else. The danger of making specters talk is that it presumes an understanding of the subjectivity of one rendered an object. To speak for someone from beyond the grave is to eliminate the intricacies of the subject, rendering them flat in an attempt to stabilize meaning. What Freccero proposes instead is to take the queer approach of letting the past live in the present; "This is what [...] doing a queer history means, since it involves an openness to the possibility of being haunted, even inhabited, by ghosts."[30] Spectrality is a way of making the past present and of unburdening the past of its duty to be an origin. It lets the past exist as if on a continuum of time that allows us to engage with history and the literature of the past without a sense of mastery or progressed state over the material.

Queering the Enlightenment means letting go of certain long-held principles of Enlightenment thought such as a belief in linear progress or a teleological string of events. In order to understand literature through this lens, we need to learn to read it a little queerly. The practice of reading queerly that I propose emerges primarily from two sources: Eve Kosofsky Sedgwick's notion of "reparative reading" as articulated in *Touching feeling* and Lee Edelman's concept of "homographesis" as explained in his essay collection of the same name.[31] Both of these texts have given us powerful tools for learning how to be open to the queerness of literature by reorienting our awareness of temporality as circuitous (rather than linear and progressive), by rendering us more sensitive to literary modes that express queer subjectivities and experiences, and by demonstrating how queer reading seizes upon the contingencies and unexpected surprises of literature.

Sade: queer theorist, SVEC 2013:03. To date, this remains one of the few critical books to bring together eighteenth-century French studies and queer theory.

29. Freccero, *Queer/early/modern*, p.70.
30. Freccero, *Queer/early/modern*, p.80.
31. Eve Kosofsky Sedgwick, "Paranoid reading and reparative reading, or, you're so paranoid, you probably think this essay is about you," in *Touching feeling: affect, pedagogy, performativity* (Durham, NC, 2003), p.123–51; Lee Edelman, *Homographesis: essays in gay literary and cultural theory* (New York, 1994).

For Sedgwick, reparative reading allows us to diverge from paranoid methods of reading that seek to anticipate and eliminate any element of surprise. The paranoid hermeneutic appears to emerge from the point at which literary criticism and psychoanalysis meet. This hermeneutic, according to Sedgwick, is necessarily homophobic because of its Freudian origins.[32] Although Sedgwick does not name specific "paranoid" reading practices, she does state that they are strong theories of negative affects that are reflexive, mimetic, anticipatory, and seek to expose something.[33] Given her explanations of these categories, we can assume that paranoid reading is synonymous with much of poststructuralist theory more generally, which aims to discover the truths of objects by interrogating them. This paranoid practice mimics psychoanalysis, the goal of which has been to uncover truths about the human psyche by finding hidden meanings in the stories we tell about ourselves. Freud's (and later Lacan's) presumption that the psyche is structured oedipally assumes an obligatory heterosexuality centered on the primary position of the patriarch. Put differently, the analytic process—which is replicated in paranoid reading practices—assumes heterosexuality and is, therefore, homophobic. Sedgwick's reparative reading ventures away from such homophobic origins by turning to psychologists and analysts such as Melanie Klein and Silvan Tomkins who focus less on drives than on affect, and who are, therefore, less concerned with Oedipus.

Although Sedgwick's reparative reading practices have recently sparked a "postcritical" turn among certain academics, her work is not necessarily opposed to theory (even as she criticizes her earlier, paranoid pieces of scholarship—most notably *Epistemology of the closet*).[34] For one thing, as Heather Love points out, Sedgwick's essay on reparative reading participates in the very paranoid reading practices it calls out. Love argues that reparative reading should exist alongside paranoid reading practices, gesturing to the moments in Sedgwick's

---

32. In his famous Schreber case (1896), Freud proclaims that his patient's paranoid delusions are the result of a repressed homosexual conflict within the subject. The work of the analyst is to bring these homosexual feelings to the surface in order to work through them so that the patient can attach his sexual feelings to more appropriate (female) objects.
33. Sedgwick, "Paranoid reading," p.130.
34. One of the most outspoken proponents of the postcritical turn has been Rita Felski, who proposes that postcritical practices should augment critique. See Felski, *The Limits of critique* (Chicago, IL, 2015).

article that demonstrate the benefits of paranoia.[35] Still, Sedgwick's article insists that paranoid reading practices are inextricable from homophobia, because they are based on Oedipal drives. Sedgwick's anti-homophobic reparative reading, therefore, embraces hope rather than focusing on paranoia. While I do not wish to return to paranoid practices of reading that seek to squash out the unexpected in the search for an ultimate truth, I do wish to take the utopian hopefulness of Sedgwick's reparative reading, a hopefulness that I believe also lives in the pages of the novels and plays studied in this book, while still attending to those oedipal drives that Sedgwick leaves behind. If, as Sedgwick argues in *Touching feeling*, Oedipus has been less definitional to queer thought than earlier writings on the subject had assumed, then, one might ask, why return to those oedipal drives at all? As I hope will become clear throughout this book, I believe that shedding Oedipus might not be as easy or as productive as Sedgwick (along with many feminist and queer theorists since) has claimed.

Sedgwick argues that we do not need Oedipus for queer readings because queer relationality doesn't function oedipally. She writes:

> The dogged, defensive narrative stiffness of a paranoid temporality, after all, in which yesterday can't be allowed to have differed from today and tomorrow must be even more so, takes its shape from a generational narrative that's characterized by a distinctly Oedipal regularity and repetitiveness [...] But isn't it a feature of queer possibility—only a contingent feature, but a real one, and one that in turn strengthens the force of contingency itself—that our generational relations don't always proceed in this lockstep?[36]

In other words, queer relationality allows for differences and unexpected occurrences in ways not available to the linear logic of Oedipus. However, it is quite a leap to assume that, at least in many Western societies, our psychic lives and lived experiences are not still largely structured by an oedipal relation to society, as much as we may wish that not to be the case. The continued debates about what does and does not count as a family, or who does and does not count as human, such as those surrounding access to PMA in France, or immigration in the US and Europe discussed in the preface, attest to

---

35. Heather Love, "Truth and consequences: on paranoid reading and reparative reading," *Criticism* 52:2 (spring 2010), p.235–41. Love has also been a leading voice in the postcritical turn.
36. Sedgwick, "Paranoid reading," p.147.

a lingering power of Oedipus. These debates assume two things: first, that we must define *what* a family is (whether or not that includes a patriarch); and second, that there is an "us" and a "them" and that we are constituted differently (whether or not that means we should be open to "them"). These are two of the hallmark outcomes of Oedipus. Therefore, while I agree with Sedgwick that one of the beautifully hopeful aspects of queer relationality is the openness to surprise and the understanding that "our [queer] generational relations don't always proceed in this lockstep," I also believe that oedipal drives still have their role to play in our assessment of queer possibility. This is even more the case in the eighteenth century, when the conditions that will allow Freud to make his assertion about Oedipus in the nineteenth century begin to take shape.

Edelman's queer readings remain indebted to psychoanalysis (and particularly an account of the drives). He proposes the term "homographesis" as a way of describing both how homosexuality is put into writing, and how the use of metaphor, allegory, and other literary modes invokes a process of *différance*, thus avoiding a normalization of queer writing.[37] Much like homographs, which are words with a double and disparate meaning, homographesis also names a double operation: It simultaneously codifies identities, all while resisting that categorization.[38] Homographesis, he writes, is "intent on *de*-scribing the identities that order has so oppressively *in*scribed."[39] While this process of *différance* involves a retroactive meaning-making (ascribing new meanings to previous encounters once the legibility of the queer body becomes visible), it is also made possible only by an initial misrecognition of desire precisely because desire is structured oedipally within the Symbolic Order. Homographesis thus attends to the metonymic slippage within texts to elucidate how homosexual difference is both produced and undermined. In other words, Edelman takes the old adage "seeing is believing" and flips it on its head, demonstrating how only by believing that something exists can we (retroactively and henceforth) see not just that it exists, but that it has existed all along.

37. Edelman, *Homographesis*, p.9–10.
38. To give an example of a homograph, the word "shed" can mean a small structure used for storage, or to remove, lose, or discard an item (such as clothing), among other meanings. Although the words sound and are spelled alike, they each have very different etymologies.
39. Edelman, *Homographesis*, p.10.

While reading queerly certainly attends to the circulation of desire and sexuality in the novels and plays at hand, it also means paying attention to the gaps between form and content that allow us to assess the disjunctions between the Symbolic and the Real. Although the notoriously elusive Real will continuously change and take different shapes for Lacan, by the end of his career he will argue that the Real is always unattainable. It is the utopian dream of wholeness—a dream of an existence unmediated by language—that is simply impossible for us who are, for better or worse, fractured subjects constituted by language. My desire makes sense only within a vast network of meaning in which desire in all its variations has always already existed. Moreover, the potential meanings of my desire have been framed by the rules of the society in which I exist. In this system, drives are always only partial, never expressing the entirety of sexuality. It is precisely the disjunction between one's desire for wholeness and the fractured system that structures the relation to society that renders all expressions of sexuality unsatisfactory (in the sense that they are partial). Reading queerly then means seizing these disjunctions between the part (the subject) and the whole (the Order) by paying particular attention to the fruitful fractures between and within narration and language. Analyzing these moments when the content of literature becomes unhinged from its form will allow us to uncover queer, utopian impulses even in works of seemingly heteronormative literature.

To provide one brief example of how such a reading works, let us turn to an early-eighteenth-century play that questions notions of sex and gender: Pierre de Marivaux's *La Fausse Suivante* (*The False servant*). This 1724 comedy opens with a young Parisian woman who has been promised to a man named Lélio. Uncomfortable with marrying a man they have never met, this woman decides to disguise themself as a knight and befriend Lélio to get to know his character better. Through conversations, they learn that the male suitor is actually already promised to another young woman, and that he is interested only in marrying the one who will bring him the most money. Realizing that Lélio is ill-suited to their tastes and also hoping to save their fellow woman from a terrible marriage, the Knight decides to trick the Countess into falling in love with them instead. Moreover, they convince Lélio that this will be in his best interest, since it will allow him to exit the arrangement without repercussions, thus freeing him to marry the wealthier woman. The Knight succeeds and their true identity is revealed only at the very end of the play much to the dismay of Lélio (who is now left with no wife) and the Countess (who had wanted to marry the Knight).

A traditional reading of the play is to see in the messy love triangle nothing more than a hashing out of heterosexual desire in the most normative of ways. Indeed, this is what Henri Coulet and Michel Gilot argue in their important edition of Marivaux's theater.[40] Such a reading is relatively easy; throughout the early modern period, actors often played roles across genders, and characters in many of Marivaux's own plays utilize drag as a means of escaping familial restrictions without necessarily invoking queer desires or sexualities. In the end of this play, the Knight returns to *his* "true" gender and *she* marries neither the loser nor the coquette. We see no true fulfillment of queer desire.

However, as Elena Russo has pointed out, there is something a little queer about a character who becomes "all things to everybody; she is everyone's focus of desire, and she is also the one who coaxes them into believing that she will fulfill their secret aspirations."[41] This character embraces the male gender so fully in the play that they are provided no other name than "Chevalier" ("Knight"). It is certainly true that there is much precedent for depictions of queer romance in French fiction. In the seventeenth century Isaac de Benserade's *Iphis et Iante* (*Iphis and Ianthe*) deals very explicitly with lesbianism, and the fairy tale coauthored by François-Timéon de Choisy, Marie-Jeanne L'Héritier de Villandon, and Charles Perrault, *Histoire de la marquise-marquis de Banneville* (*The Story of the marquise-marquis de Banneville*), tells the love story of a man-raised-woman who meets and falls in love with a woman who lives life as a man. Even though the tale ends in a scene of reproductive bliss, the fact that the characters choose not to assume a gender that would match their biological sex suggests the possibility for queer forms of kinship. *La Fausse Suivante*, compared to these earlier works, might, in fact, seem conservative in its portrayal of queer desire. This is the point at which the practice of reading queerly becomes important. Rather than looking for overt representations of queer individuals or desires, to read queerly means to look for those

40. Coulet and Gilot write: "Marivaux follows convention in that he doesn't use disguise as a means to probe doubts about one's sexuality," arguing that no one actually believes the Knight to be a man. See Pierre de Marivaux, *Théâtre complet*, vol.1, ed. Henri Coulet and Michel Gilot (Paris, 1994), p.941–42.
41. Elena Russo, "Libidinal economy and gender trouble in Marivaux's *La Fausse suivante*," *MLN* 115:4 (2000), p.690–713 (712).

cracks in all literature (queer or not) through which the possibility for queer intimacy peeks out—spectrally—letting us sense its presence even if we cannot fully grasp it.

Aside from the fact that the main character never receives a "female" name, even after they reveal their gender at the end, the last scene of the play can show us one of these moments when the spirit of queer desire inhabits the scene of heterosexual romance. One might assume that this play would end with the concretization of heteronormativity in a scene of marriage, and it almost does. Just after Lélio tells the Countess that his feelings for her have changed, she asks what they should do about the disavowal:

Lélio
We'll manage, Madame, I would be honored to marry you.

The Countess
What's that! You will marry me even though you no longer love me?

Lélio
That doesn't mean anything, Madame, it shouldn't stop you.

Lélio
Nous le tiendrons, Madame, j'aurai l'honneur de vous épouser.

La Comtesse
Quoi donc! vous m'épouserez, et vous ne m'aimez plus?

Lélio
Cela n'y fait de rien, Madame, cela ne doit pas vous arrêter.[42]

As Lélio points out, love should have nothing to do with marriage. As he sees it, marriage is a contract between two parties (one that guarantees him money) and little more. This is, in fact, how marriage should function following the rules of the apparatus of alliance. The subtraction of love from the heteronormative institution of marriage reminds the spectator that desire, intimacy, and marriage are not commensurate things. If desire is disconnected from marriage, then we might understand the *potential* of queer desire. Even if marriage in Marivaux's fiction follows rules of heteronormativity (after true

---

42. Pierre de Marivaux, *La Fausse suivante, L'Ecole des mères, La Mère confidente*, ed. Jean Goldzink (Paris, 1992), p.126.

identities are revealed, men marry only women), nonheteronormative desire can still circulate outside of contractual marriage. Such desire is amplified by the Knight's dialogue with the Countess once they reveal to the latter their true, female, identity. She first announces her female identity to Lélio by stating, "You were told that she [the Parisian lady] was beautiful, you were tricked because here it is, my face is *the original of hers*."[43] The Knight's face is thus doubled as male and female identities overlap with one another. Now presenting as female, she proceeds to speak to the Countess in a way that implies she is not wholly averse to a relationship with another woman:

The Knight
My metamorphosis is not to the taste of your tender feelings, my dear Countess. *I would have taken you so far if I could have kept you company*: well, I guess that's love lost, but, on the other hand, it has saved you a good sum of money; I'll tell you about the nice little trick one was about to play on you.

Le Chevalier
Ma métamorphose n'est pas du goût de vos tendres sentiments, ma chère Comtesse. *Je vous aurais menée assez loin, si j'avais pu vous tenir compagnie*: voilà bien de l'amour de perdu, mais en revanche, voilà une bonne somme de sauvée; je vous conterai le joli petit tour qu'on voulait vous jouer.[44]

Although the Knight expresses no words of regret that the Countess no longer desires her company, she continues to speak of a future in which the pair would have been together. The Knight thus proposes a queer future for the two women, even if only in the past conditional. In the absence of romantic desire between women, she offers a substitution—sisterly affection. Even if the two will not be together (in a future perfect) the Knight will at least save her fellow woman from marrying a monster, demonstrating a preference for the happiness of another woman over that of a man. In this case, intimacy between women will win one way or another.

Although desire does not circulate in this play in an oedipal fashion—that is, the shared object of desire is the Countess who is caught in a queer triangle with no clear order to desire—the story

43. Marivaux, *La Fausse suivante*, p.127. "On vous écrit qu'elle [la demoiselle parisienne] était belle; on vous a trompé, car la voilà, mon visage est *l'original du sien*."
44. Marivaux, *La Fausse suivante*, p.127 (emphasis added).

does end with an admission to a symbolic order. By demonstrating the possibility that one can simultaneously embody two genders, the Knight teaches readers and spectators about the confusion of language. Bringing to the surface that which remains buried in language is also the goal of this book as I expand my energy outward from that ultimate signifier (the father) to encompass all of the confusion brought by other familial signifiers as well. This is the goal of reading queerly—not to clear up misunderstandings brought about by the poetic language of literature, but to ground ourselves within that confusion and to see what it has to teach us about the relation of gender, sexuality, and power in eighteenth-century France.

Intimate networks of knowledge

Reading queerly not only allows us to uncover the queer, utopian impulses of domestic fiction, but it also provides us with a new understanding of what it means to be (or to become) "enlightened," in eighteenth-century France. As Kant famously described in his response to the question "What is Enlightenment?," achieving enlightenment means shedding one's self-imposed immaturity and "daring to know!" "This enlightenment requires nothing but freedom," he writes, but he addresses this message to those who have the legal capacity to *become* free.[45] Women, slaves, and children, those who have few rights as autonomous individuals, are excluded from such enlightenment. As Foucault pointed out two centuries later, Kant's seemingly simple text in fact poses much larger problems in that it proposes a change that is universal without considering the material conditions of life outside of a very specific subset of individuals.[46] However, Foucault also proposes that the Enlightenment is an event (*événement*), an attitude, and a philosophy of which he is an inheritor. While his reader is able to trace a certain ontology of enlightenment, these discrepancies in the term's meaning (an event is rigid, for instance, while an attitude is more fluid and apt to change) leave us wondering just how to define it. So, what is/was/will be the Enlightenment? And what does family have to do with it? The possible answers for the first question have always varied,

45. Immanuel Kant, *Political writings*, ed. H. S. Reiss, translated by H. B. Nisbet, 2nd ed. (Cambridge, 1970), p.54–60.
46. See Michel Foucault, "Qu'est-ce que les Lumières?," in *Dits et écrits*, vol.4 (Paris, 1984), p.562–78.

but there has been a common movement over the years, and it is one I intend to trace briefly here.

Modern academic study of the European Enlightenment begins on the eve of World War II with Ernst Cassirer's *The Philosophy of the Enlightenment*. In this foundational work, Cassirer draws together the threads of various Enlightenment thinkers, proposing a relatively cohesive philosophy of the period. One of the most important contributions of the Enlightenment, he argues, is that it brought philosophy down from the realm of pure ideas, and into the material world as a creative force of change. Using a metaphor of construction, he creates a very positive image of the Enlightenment, seeing in its philosophy a radical force of change (perhaps one that might offer hope in a prewar Germany where anti-Semitic sentiment was already gaining momentum). He writes:

> It [the philosophy of the Enlightenment] opposes the power of convention, tradition, and authority in all the fields of knowledge. But it does not consider this opposition as merely a work of negation and destruction; it considers rather that it is removing the rubble of the ages in order to make visible the solid foundations of the structure of knowledge. These foundations are looked upon as immutable and unshakable; they are as old as mankind itself. The philosophy of the Enlightenment, accordingly, does not understand its task as an act of destruction but as an act of reconstruction.[47]

Here the philosophy of the Enlightenment takes on corporeal form, desiring and opposing, as do human beings. It has a goal, and that goal is to shake things up. To present the Enlightenment as a philosophic system whose goal is to rebuild better systems in the place of its older, stodgier, and detrimental counterparts, as utopian as it may seem, is still to present the Enlightenment as a monolithic system with common desires and goals.

On the other side of World War II, we find Max Horkheimer and Theodor Adorno's *Dialectic of Enlightenment*. In this critical work, all of the utopian energy and hope of Cassirer's text falls away and is replaced by a deep pessimism and sadness for what they understand as the failures of the Enlightenment. For them, the Enlightenment was not looking to "remov[e] the rubble of the ages," to replace it with something new; according to Horkheimer and

---

47. Ernst Cassirer, *The Philosophy of the Enlightenment*, translated by Fritz C. A. Koelln and James P. Pettegrove (1932; Princeton, NJ, 2009), p.234.

Adorno, "Enlightenment's program was the disenchantment of the world."[48] It was a mass deception because it could not live up to its promises; in spite of all the advancements in knowledge, humans failed to make things better for humankind. The dogmatism and discourse of freedom and equality for all contrasted with material conditions that left many behind. Eventually, they argue, the intellectual curiosity opened up by the Enlightenment led to an alienation of humankind, paving the way for fascist leaders to gain power without much of a fight. If Cassirer's Enlightenment is a system of creative forces, the Enlightenment of Horkheimer and Adorno is a persistent destructive force that continues to threaten humanity.

In the late 1960s Peter Gay devoted much of his career to restoring a good name for the Enlightenment. In several works, but particularly in his two-volume series entitled simply *The Enlightenment*, he describes the Enlightenment neither as a system nor as a force, but instead he speaks of a movement populated with thinkers who, while being pioneers, were also troubled. By demonstrating the dynamic nature of the Enlightenment's key thinkers, he did much to vivify this intellectual (pagan) movement and bring it back into critical academic discourse.[49] Scholars have meticulously scrutinized the Enlightenment's origins, effects, and afterlives, and they have continued to ask themselves what, exactly, the Enlightenment was. Was it an event? Was it a movement? Was it a philosophy? Whatever *it* was, most were in agreement that it was a dividing point in history and thought—one that separated the premodern from the modern. In the 1970s and 1980s, scholars continued to interrogate the social, political, and ethical meanings of the works of Enlightenment philosophers, authors, scientists, and artists. In the 1990s and 2000s we have begun to study the Enlightenment from different angles, considering the point of view of those who had previously been excluded from discussions of the Enlightenment. Jonathan Israel examined the role that Spinoza's materialist philosophy played in what he calls the "Radical Enlightenment"; feminist scholars such as Dena Goodman, Joan DeJean, and Joan Landes began to tell us what women contributed to the Enlightenment; and Srinivas Aravamudan, Doris Garraway, and Nick Nesbitt, among many others, have begun to interrogate the role

48. Max Horkheimer and Theodor Adorno, *Dialectic of Enlightenment*, ed. Gunzelin Schmid Noerr, translated by Edmund Jephcott (Stanford, CA, 2002), p.2.
49. See Peter Gay, *The Enlightenment*, vol.1: *The Rise of modern paganism* (New York, 1966), and its second volume, *The Science of freedom* (New York, 1969).

of race and colonialism in the production of knowledge and power.[50] Furthermore, Aravamudan, Garraway, and Nesbitt, among others, have opened up the discussion of an Enlightenment beyond European borders—considering an enlightenment that happens along with, but remains distinct from, that of the most famous European names.

Within the past few years, two new works have emerged that interrogate the crucial role of the family and intimate communities in the production and maintenance of knowledge and power in the Francophone world: Meghan K. Roberts's *Sentimental savants* and Jennifer Palmer's *Intimate bonds*.[51] Roberts dispels the myth of the solitary genius, revealing that scientific and philosophic production was, in many instances, a collective effort within families. Palmer, by contrast, argues that, as the French colonial empire expanded, the meanings of families and households changed. The intimate relations she examines had lasting effects not only for individual families, but also for our very understanding of race and gender. Both of these studies demonstrate the role that families (or other intimate communities) play in the circulation of knowledge, as well as in the distribution and leveling out of power hierarchies. Both Roberts and Palmer offer historical accounts that revise narratives of externally imposed laws and solitary genius, contextualizing such narratives within the nucleus of the family.

Bringing together critical studies of kinship and the Enlightenment with Cassirer's groundbreaking text seems fitting for the current study. By reading queerly, I hope to recapture some of the optimism expressed by Cassirer, while allowing for the diversity that is necessarily inherent to the Enlightenment. The Enlightenment here is something that is persistent and flexible. It has been a movement, a discourse, a practice, and it now functions like a drive, influencing social, scientific, and

---

50. See Jonathan Israel, *Radical Enlightenment* (Oxford, 2001); Dena Goodman, *The Republic of Letters: a cultural history of the French Enlightenment* (Ithaca, NY, 1994); Joan DeJean, *Tender geographies: women and the origins of the novel in France* (New York, 1991); Joan B. Landes, *Visualizing the nation: gender, representation and revolution in eighteenth-century France* (Ithaca, NY, 2001); Srinivas Aravamudan, *Tropicopolitans: colonialism and agency, 1688–1804* (Durham, NC, 1999); Doris Garraway, *The Libertine colony: creolization in the early French Caribbean* (Durham, NC, 2005); and Nick Nesbitt, *Universal emancipation: the Haitian Revolution and the radical Enlightenment* (Richmond, VA, 2008).

51. Meghan K. Roberts, *Sentimental savants: philosophical families in Enlightenment France* (Chicago, IL, 2016); Jennifer Palmer, *Intimate bonds: family and slavery in the French Atlantic* (Philadelphia, PA, 2016).

political practices to this very day. It is this drive that challenges us to seek out and constantly revise knowledge. This was perhaps the drive that brought together the authors discussed in chapters 2 through 5 of this book. Through their attendance at some of the same salons, their letters back and forth to one another, and their engagement with one another in fictional writings, Prévost, Crébillon, Marivaux, and Graffigny formed an imaginary coterie which sought to interrogate the very nature of politics and power through a subversive discourse of the family. By engaging in this imaginary coterie—the eighteenth-century social network—these authors participate in a common project of breaking apart and rebuilding the family in various forms. In doing so, they demonstrate with great hope and optimism the potential for a new, father*less* (if not father-free) society. In other words, before Simone de Beauvoir, before bell hooks, before Ruth Bader Ginsburg, these were among the first thinkers teaching us how we might smash the patriarchy and try again with something new.

As we shall see, these authors take something that is inherently familiar—the family—and render it unfamiliar. They do not just break the family down; they take its pieces and see how they might fit together differently. When the roles of husband and wife, or mother and daughter, are called into question, so too is the unilateral and hierarchal passage of knowledge. In response, these authors demonstrate various means of enlightenment and growth; some paths are atomized—scattered throughout a network of unrelated individuals—some are predicated upon a willful ignorance, and some challenge notions of what, precisely, constitutes acceptable knowledge. Throughout their novels and plays, the use of familial signifiers serves to queer the meaning of family and furthermore of knowledge. Put differently, these authors, whom we have long accepted as canonical, use the tools afforded to them by fiction, that is, the invocation of emotions and the imagination of utopian worlds, to queer the Enlightenment.

Queering the canon

As I have shown, the presence of queer sexualities in French fiction was nothing new in the eighteenth century. Already in the *fabliaux* of the Middle Ages, queer sexualities were prominently displayed, and it seems that little stigma was attached to them. However, in the early decades of the eighteenth century, much of the overtly queer sexualities is evacuated from literature in favor of heteronormative romance and platonic friendship. In this book, I argue that those queer tendencies did not disappear or even go underground (although there were certainly queer pornographies that circulated underground).[52] Instead, queer sexualities are sublimated into kinship structures that appear, more often than not, relatively tame. But, while uncovering the queer aspects in these texts is an important first step, the second step I take is to show what these queer kinship constructions can reveal about the utopian forms of language and politics contained therein. From atomistic and orgiastic scenes of anarchic governance to matriarchies, to feminocentric utopias, these plays and novels (some of which have constituted the canon for years, others that have rarely before been critically examined) propose non-normative intimate formations that capture the desire for something new in the wake of Absolutism. Aside from Voltaire and Montesquieu, most of the authors I examine have never really been considered serious political theorists. Although scholars have often unearthed the political importance of works by Marivaux and Graffigny, among others, they have most often considered them authors of fiction first who happen to have something political to say. I take a different approach. I consider each of the authors studied in this book—Prévost, Crébillon fils, Marivaux, and Graffigny, as well as Montesquieu and Voltaire—to be important political theorists who choose to communicate their philosophy through literature. Additionally, thanks to letters and other personal writings (especially Graffigny's letters, which were meticulously written and thoughtfully preserved), we can grasp the extent to which these authors' lives were intertwined with one another. In addition to the many hours spent attending the same salons, such as Jeanne Quinault's Société du bout du banc, these authors talked together, dined with one another, and wrote letters back and forth in which they discussed life, writing, and politics. As such, they not only wrote about queer forms of kinship, but they formed a sort of queer intimate community of their own.

The authors studied in *Queering the Enlightenment*, although canonical, are also revolutionary in three major ways: Their works depict intimate communities of otherwise unrelated individuals; they offer paradigms of subjectivity that will not come into focus until the end of the nineteenth century with the arrival of Freud and psychoanalysis;

---

52. For more information on the underground trade in pornographic fiction see Robert Darnton, *The Forbidden best-sellers of pre-revolutionary France* (New York, 1996).

and their works often remain unfinished, refusing to provide answers and instead demonstrating the potential of utopian ways of life. These authors situate their utopian forms of society and subjectivity within the very real and present framework of the family. By seizing upon the fluid nature of kinship (marriages, births, and deaths change its structure all the time), these authors take the most basic form of social organization—the family—and rearrange its components, stretching it to its limits and showing readers not what has been, or even what will be, but merely what might be possible for a nation in the midst of a changing political climate. In 2021, during a time when the global political landscape is changing at a much faster pace than we could have imagined, a book that unearths various possibilities of social and political organization—even those of a period long past—is timelier than ever.

According to Susan Lanser, any work that engages in queer studies must also include serious discussions of gender, and I would add that it must also consider the fluidity of gendered embodiment.[53] To propose a single coming-to-queerness would be to elide the very real distinct histories of lesbians, gay men, trans folks, and so many other queer individuals. While discussions of male- and female-centered communities overlap in this book (often calling into question the very stability of the terms "male" and "female"), they will be featured separately to attend to the unique questions raised by each. The book is therefore divided into three parts. Part I, "Family remains," tells a story of patriarchy in decline, and then looks to the authors of the early decades of the eighteenth century, analyzing how they were imagining the ways it might be repaired in a more functional way. Part II, "Prodigal sons," examines the productivity of wastefulness in sons who do not marry and have children. It uncovers the potential of changing relations between men in public and intimate spheres. Finally, Part III, "Narrative spinsters," analyzes the crucial role of unmarried (and often unaffiliated) women in the construction of the modern family. It explores the various ways in which women form intimate communities that do not necessarily rely upon men.

In this introduction, I have laid out the story of patriarchy in decline. In chapter 1, by contrast, I begin to examine how it starts to be redefined in the works of two of the most important French political philosophers of the eighteenth century, Montesquieu and

---

53. Susan Lanser, *The Sexuality of history: modernity and the sapphic, 1565–1830* (Chicago, IL, 2014).

Voltaire. Unlike the other authors studied in this book, these two were well known for their overtly political writings. This chapter, however, is concerned with their earliest works of fiction. Voltaire's restaging of the Oedipus story (*Œdipe*), along with his failed follow-up play *Artémire*, and Montesquieu's orientalist novel about two Asian men's views of French culture (*Lettres persanes*) give us a very important insight into the earliest political philosophies of both authors. These works uphold patriarchal values, but certain details and formal devices in each reveal the fragility of patriarchy and propose, even at this early stage, a reformation of the father's role within the family. These two authors' adherence to patriarchal rule, even if in a different form, separates them from the other authors studied in this book. They may not fully belong to the imaginary familial coterie, but they open up the space that makes such a coterie possible.

Chapter 2 examines several works of Antoine Prévost, looking at how the ghosts of women, dead from the beginning of the story, disrupt masculine desire and yet restore relations between men. The circulation of desire in these novels undermines oedipal progression in a way that flattens out hierarchies, creating a more egalitarian mode of masculine relations. In chapter 3, I examine Crébillon's *Egarements du cœur et de l'esprit* (*Wayward head and heart*) and *Le Sopha* (*The Sofa*), arguing that the utopian impulse in his work lies in envisioning a form of social organization in which encounters with others produce pleasure rather than offspring. While critics tend to focus on the overtly sexual and political in these novels, or on the productive form of Crébillon's orientalism, this chapter moves beyond a politics of the overtly sexual and exotic to focus on what I call a politics of the encounter. I propose that these novels are organized by an ethos of cruising, whereby desire is displaced outside of the oedipal structure, circulating from one encounter to the next. Turning to the ways in which female subjectivity is formed differently from that of men, chapter 4 explores how Marivaux imagines a maternal symbolic from which women's subjectivity may emerge. Because each of the works examined in this chapter features families of women with no fathers, oedipal desire falters. In this world of no fathers, enlightenment becomes something shared among mothers and daughters. In the final chapter, I demonstrate not only how Graffigny carefully constructs a world for women, but also how she continues to revise that world throughout her life, creating an adaptive language of sisterhood as an alternative to the regime of the brother. Taken individually, the authors and playwrights studied in this book construct a canon of literature that we have long taken for granted as rather heterogeneous in voice although relatively heteronormative in their message. Read together, however, we will see how these canonical authors perform the radical task of queering the Enlightenment.

1. Toward a queer politics of kinship

> "Politics" should never have become a noun.
> It should have remained an adjective. An
> attribute and not a substance.
>
> "Politique" n'aurait jamais dû devenir
> un nom. Ç'aurait dû rester un adjectif.
> Un attribut, et non une substance.
>
> Comité invisible, Maintenant

In one of the most famous last lines of Western literature, Voltaire's eponymous hero Candide tells his optimistic teacher Pangloss (who has just chained together all of the events of the hero's life in a series of cause and effect, reiterating that he inhabits the best of all possible worlds), "that is very well put, but let us cultivate our garden."[1] This line, with its simple and honest language, has been interpreted repeatedly since its publication by authors, literary critics, historians, and philosophers who have argued that this garden represents: a parable of morality (Goldzink); a space where diverse individuals can share and cultivate both the earth and relations between human beings (Hirvonen); an articulation of materialist skepticism that paves the way for modern ecocriticism (Feder); a supreme parody of the kind of novel represented by Prévost's *Cleveland* (Stewart); a contingent and temporary utopian community of nonrelated individuals of divergent social stations that rivals Rousseau's Clarens (Howells); a pre-Marxist critique of labor (Pomeau); and a practical application of metaphysical philosophy (Henry).[2] Such varied critiques demonstrate

---

1. Voltaire, *Candide, ou l'Optimisme*, ed. Michelle Béguin and Jean Goldzink (Paris, 1998), p.189. "Cela est bien dit, mais il faut cultiver notre jardin."
2. See Jean Goldzink, "La métaphysique du mal," *Revue Europe* 72 (1994), p.63–78;

the impossibility of assigning any one meaning to the novel. It is a novel that has succeeded in delighting readers for centuries, all while failing to communicate a unified message. Its failure to signify concretely is, in fact, one of the things that makes it such a compelling story. However, as the novel's subtitle, *or Optimism*, makes clear, this novel will at least provide an intense reflection on this newly coined term.[3] Voltaire felt that Leibnizian optimism needed to be seriously reconsidered in the aftermath of such devastating catastrophes as the Lisbon earthquake of 1755. If this was the best of all possible worlds, as Leibniz argued, how could such terrible things happen to so many people? And if this is the best of all possible worlds, is that sufficient to explain human actions (or inactions)?

In the pages of *Candide*, we see that Voltaire's critique of optimism is a critique of metaphysics more generally. Abstract theories, he felt, provided a bleak outlook for humanity. If the events of the world are predetermined and decided upon by a deity with no regard for humanity, then what would be the point of human existence at all? As Patrick Henry points out, Candide's final rejection of Pangloss's optimism is not a rejection of philosophy and enlightenment *tout court*; it is instead an acceptance of the kind of reason that comes with being in the world. Not only is this kind of reason grounded in reality, but it is also capable of "unit[ing] together over and above the speculative differences that tend to separate us and to contribute ultimately to our suffering."[4] Put differently, Candide's idea of enlightenment is not just being in the world, but it is being there with other people.

One of the distinctive features of Voltaire's enlightened utopia is its reliance upon bringing together a diverse group of individuals.

Ari Hirvonen, "Voltaire's garden," *Pólemos* 8:2 (2014), p.223–34; Helena Feder, *Ecocriticism and the idea of culture: biology and the bildungsroman* (Burlington, VT, 2014); Philip Stewart, "Holding the mirror up to fiction: generic parody in *Candide*," *French studies* 4 (1979), p.411–19; Robin Howells, "*Candide* and *La Nouvelle Héloïse*," *Journal for eighteenth-century studies* 29:1 (2006), p.33–46; René Pomeau, "Candide entre Marx et Freud," *SVEC* 89 (1972), p.1305–23; and Patrick Henry, "Raisonner in *Candide*," *Romanic review* 80:3 (1989), p.363–70. There are obviously more interpretations of this famous scene than I can realistically offer here; I offer this list as a demonstration of the vast variety of interpretations of this sentence.

3. Although the word *optimum* (the best) existed in ancient Greek, the word "optimism" was coined only in 1737 by the French Jesuits in reference to Gottfried Wilhelm Leibniz's *Theodicy*.

4. Henry, "Raisonner in *Candide*," p.370.

As Robin Howells points out, unlike Rousseau's Clarens, Voltaire's *métairie* contains a "motley crew": "There is no family unit, and the group has been assembled mainly by chance."[5] These individuals, whose various failures have all led them to one another, work together to make life more bearable in the moment. In other words, this novel ends with the construction of a queer community of characters who have all been altered by their encounters with the world. Although the story does end with a long-awaited marriage (that of Candide and Cunégonde), that marriage is, by and large, a disappointment. In fact, the last chapter of the novel begins, "Candide, deep in his heart, had no desire to marry Cunégonde."[6] This is not the romantic fairy tale ending ("ils vécurent heureux et eurent beaucoup d'enfants").[7] Although the pair will live (relatively) happily ever after, they will do so only as one part of a larger group of people, and they will not fulfill the second proposition of having many children. In fact, rather than focusing on the heterosexual couple and their reproductive habits, the end of *Candide* opens out onto the entire community. Cunégonde becomes an excellent baker, Paquette (the prostitute) does the embroidering, and even Giroflée (the monk), who had been useless all along, becomes a great carpenter. Unlike Clarens, there are no children, no servants, and no hierarchies in this household; all work together to maintain the group in the present.

One way to understand *Candide*'s ending is to see in it a complete rejection of metaphysical philosophy in favor of manual labor and collective action. However, the hero's dedication not only to work at cultivating the garden but to do so with his "motley crew" demonstrates a different kind of optimism. These individuals have been burned, beaten, raped, hanged, and disemboweled, and yet they all end up together—still alive and thriving through the collective cultivation of their land. The future is not prescribed, but they do continue to work for a future that is, at the present time at least, completely new and unknown. This is not a complete rejection of optimism; this is

5. Howells, "*Candide* and *La Nouvelle Héloïse*," p.43.
6. Voltaire, *Candide*, p.184. "Candide, dans le fond de son cœur, n'avait aucune envie d'épouser Cunégonde."
7. I use the French in this instance, rather than the traditional English fairy tale ending ("they lived happily ever after") because the English version lacks the imperative to "have a lot of children" found in the French version. While it may be possible to argue that Candide and Cunégonde do live a happy life (if not as romantic partners then at least as a part of the group), there is no indication that they will or even could reproduce.

optimism bolstered by collective pragmatism. While the Candide of the beginning of the novel is optimistic to the point of being naive, by the end of his journey, the protagonist has learned his lesson. Breaking the last sentence into two clauses demonstrates his turn away from the metaphysical ("that is very well put") toward the pragmatic ("but let us cultivate our garden")—Candide effectively shifts the conversation from words to actions. However, the second clause does not negate the first. The hero does acknowledge the importance of words (and an ethos) that chain the sequence of events together leading each of the characters to that little garden outside of Constantinople. In praising the words while calling to action, Candide moves from an optimistic ethos to a politics of optimism and failure that allows for a future built by and for the people.

Finding optimism in failure has been an important project for certain queer theorists. Jack Halberstam's *Queer art of failure* and José Esteban Muñoz's *Cruising utopia: the then and there of queer futurity* both attest to the political power of failure for queer communities. Halberstam describes failure as, among other things, "a story of art without markets, drama without script, narrative without progress. It quietly loses, and in losing it imagines other goals for life, for love, for art, and for being."[8] This is a failure of a specific kind—one that refuses the dictum to repeat the past and reproduce a politics organized around heterosexual reproduction. In the end, this refusal constitutes a political action that is absolutely future oriented, and yet it is one that is completely unconcerned with grand narratives of success that depend upon jobs, promotions, heterosexual marriages, and reproduction. For Muñoz, queer failure is also a rejection of "normative protocols of canonization and value," and is a necessary component of all performances of utopia.[9] If success depends upon

---

8.   Jack Halberstam, *The Queer art of failure* (Durham, NC, 2011), p.88; Muñoz, *Cruising utopia*. On queer optimism, see also Michael D. Snediker, *Queer optimism: lyric personhood and other felicitous persuasions* (Minneapolis, MN, 2008). Snediker was among the first queer theorists to propose queer optimism as a positive counterpoint to queer theory focused on negative affects and the death drive. While not explicitly equating optimism with happiness, Snediker examines how queer optimism offers a way to think about good feelings. Although it is a very important work for theorizing queer optimism, given its focus on presentism (rather than future-oriented politics), along with its overall focus on positive affects (to the exclusion of the uneasiness that may accompany failure), it is not included in the present discussion of optimism.

9.   Muñoz, *Cruising utopia*, p.153.

following a pattern set by practices of the past, then the imagination of something new requires failure. Thus, unlike the antisocial queer critics (most notably Edelman and Bersani) for whom failure is an ethical position that dismisses any future based on heterosexual reproduction and revels in the *jouissance* of not imagining any future at all, Halberstam and Muñoz argue that only a politics of failure can create a world in which there will be a future for queers.[10]

Failure doesn't have to be an end; it can also be the articulation of a new beginning—one that will be different from what precedes it. From the earliest pages of *Candide*, Pangloss teaches his young student that all the chains of events that have happened and that will happen are necessarily strung together in the best order possible. "It is demonstrable," Pangloss declares, "that things cannot be otherwise; for all things having been created for a purpose, everything is necessarily made for the best end."[11] The optimism of this statement lies in the belief that all will work out for the best in the end, but undeniably ignores the real and present pain and suffering of individuals. This form of optimism forecloses the possibility of altering the future. However, Candide learns from the many failures of the novel. As early as the fourth chapter, he begins to question the philosophy of his master. Upon learning of Cunégonde's death, he cries out, "Oh! Best of worlds, where are you?"[12] His skepticism grows as he continues his journey, leading to that famous last line. He refuses to accept the inevitability of time, and instead bands together with those he meets along the way to work toward a different future. This ending demonstrates what Lauren Berlant might call a kind of cruel optimism. Cruel optimism is an attachment to an object (or set of objects) that might feel anything but optimistic at times, but that nonetheless allows us to structure meaning in our lives. In fact, one of the definitions Berlant provides for optimism describes quite nicely the final scene in Voltaire's *métairie*: optimism is "a scene of negotiated sustenance that makes life bearable as it presents itself

---

10. See Edelman, *No future*, and Leo Bersani, *Homos* (Cambridge, MA, 1996). The antisocial school of queer theory along with *jouissance* will be discussed more thoroughly in chapter 3. For an excellent explanation of the social and antisocial divide in queer theory, see Mari Ruti's *The Ethics of opting out: queer theory's defiant subjects* (New York, 2017).

11. Voltaire, *Candide*, p.34. "Il est démontré que les choses ne peuvent être autrement: car, tout étant fait pour une fin, tout est nécessairement pour la meilleure fin."

12. Voltaire, *Candide*, p.48. "Ah! Meilleur des mondes, où êtes-vous?"

ambivalently, unevenly, incoherently."[13] The beauty of *Candide* lies in the way in which this thrown-together community of aging, ugly misfits demonstrates a kind of optimism for a future that lies outside of the familiar and familial system of reproductive kinship politics, and is built instead upon a politics of collective action.

Although the queerness of *Candide* certainly merits further inquiry, such an extended reading lies outside the scope of this book.[14] Rather than examining the more mature works of the author, I would like to turn back to where he began. Within even his earliest writings, François-Marie Arouet (Voltaire) marked himself as a rebellious trailblazer. As a young man, he was exiled and then imprisoned in the Bastille for his verses that criticized the monarchy and mocked Philippe II, alluding to the regent's incestuous affair with his daughter. However, in addition to his blatant challenges to king, regent, and court, the philosopher also demonstrated more passive forms of political resistance in his early plays. *Œdipe* (first performed in 1718) and *Artémire* (first performed two years later in 1720) staged regal drama as a way to interrogate the role and actions of kings. Around this same time, Charles de Secondat (Montesquieu) was beginning to write a collection of letters, assembling them into what would become the *Lettres persanes* (*Persian letters*), which would offer poignant observations on the morals and customs of France under both Louis XIV and the Regency. These pieces would seem to have little in common, but the fact that both Voltaire and Montesquieu, authors who would become known as some of the greatest political philosophers of their time, were writing about tragically flawed families falling apart in the most horrendous of ways merits a closer look than it has been given up until now. I begin with a study of the earliest works of two of the most recognizable names in eighteenth-century political philosophy not because they necessarily provide examples of the kinds of queer communities we will see in the other works examined in this book, but because they *fail to do so*. There is optimism in this failure found in a simultaneous failure to reproduce and reinforce patriarchal and

---

13. Lauren Berlant, *Cruel optimism* (Durham, NC, 2011), p.14.
14. I am unaware of any queer interpretations of Voltaire's *Candide*; however, scholars have begun to investigate the queerness of Leonard Bernstein's operatic adaptation of the novella. See, for example, Matthew J. Jones, "'Enough of being basely tearful': 'glitter and be gay' and the camp politics of queer resistance," *Journal of the Society for American music* 10:4 (2016), p.422–45.

heteronormative kinship structures.[15] Their early works appear for the first time at an important, transitional moment (during the Orléans Regency) and interrogate the weakening state of patriarchy in ways that open up the discursive space necessary for the formation of our familial literary coterie.

Voltaire's earliest works are his tragedies, which are by nature framed by stories of familial intrigue. Montesquieu, by contrast, framed his own works of fiction by the family largely in its absence, distance, or disarray. These authors, who have become household names both in France and abroad due to a political savvy that remains as relevant today as it was 300 years ago, first entered into political discussions not necessarily in the form of pamphlets or treatises, but by means of fictional literature. We may look to Voltaire's letters, dictionary, and treatises to answer some of our most pressing philosophical questions, and Montesquieu's *Esprit des lois* (*Spirit of the laws*) may still inform our discussions about the division of political branches and the distribution of governmental power, and yet we can also gain a tremendous amount of insight into their visions for social organization by turning to their fiction. It is in some of the most ubiquitous of their novels and plays that we can identify certain utopian experiments that open the space to question the very nature of the family and, by extension, systems of governance modeled on family politics. The patriarchs of *Œdipe*, *Artémire*, and the *Lettres persanes* fail over and over again, but a queer reading of these works will reveal a certain optimism for the future emerging from that failure. This particular future does not eliminate paternal power as an organizing force for kinship and government, but it does allow us to begin to imagine something outside of heteronormative frameworks of community. In this chapter, I thus place these two authors into dialogue as contemporary political philosophers, staging the dialogue largely through a reading of their earliest artistic productions. As we shall see in the pages that follow, by demonstrating the fragile position of seemingly powerful men, these authors open up the space for thinking about alternative intimate communities and move us one step closer to a queer politics of kinship.

---

15. For various perspectives on heteronormativity in the eighteenth century, see *Heteronormativity in eighteenth-century literature and culture*, ed. Ana de Freitas Boe and Abby Coykendall (New York, 2014).

On the shores of patriarchy

While the turn to optimism in queer theory has largely been framed by affect theory, at least one group of queer theorists have turned to another, rather unlikely, source—French political philosopher Jacques Rancière. In a 2009 issue of the e-journal *Borderlands*, several critics examine what we can learn by pairing queer theory and activism with Rancière's articulations of politics.[16] Why the pairing with a philosopher who, by his own admission, is relatively unconcerned with queer studies? The editors, Samuel A. Chambers and Michael O'Rourke, explain that, among other reasons, "even a superficial reading of Rancière's conception of politics and police orders, of his understanding of subjectivization (*assujetissement*), of his theory of the subject as 'in-between' reveals powerful affinities with queer theory's thinking of norms, subversion, and subjectivity as positionality, as relationality."[17] In the issue, scholars propose such varied uses of the pairing as: the development a Rancièrian influenced queer theory; the drawing out of points of contestation (or irritation) between the philosopher and queer theory by focusing on the "disagreement" so central to Rancière's work; and the exposure of methodological resemblances between the two different fields such as an insistence on the connection between aesthetics, performativity, and politics. Each of the articles in this issue, whether through a discussion of politics or aesthetics in the philosopher's *œuvre*, provides compelling arguments if not for a full inclusion of Rancière within the field of queer studies, then at least for being open to the interesting swerves that may result from the marriage between his work and that of certain queer theorists.

In one of the issue's articles, Nina Power places Rancière into dialogue with Edelman, arguing that the "no future" of the French philosopher's politics, based as it is on the local and occasional quality of the event of politics, provides us with a more optimistic (yet still pragmatic) way to engage meaningfully in the present than does Edelman's *sinthomosexual*.[18] While the *sinthomosexual* is deeply narcis-

16. *Borderlands* 8:2 (2009), special issue: *Jacques Rancière on the shores of queer theory*, ed. Samuel A. Chambers and Michael O'Rourke.
17. Chambers and O'Rourke, *Jacques Rancière on the shores of queer theory*, unpaginated. On Rancière's criticism of queer theory, see his short journalistic piece, "L'héritage difficile de Michel Foucault," in *Chroniques des temps consensuels* (Paris, 2005), p.183–89.
18. See Nina Power, "Non-reproductive futurism: Rancière's rational equality

sistic, refusing to signify in a world not made for it in the first place, Rancière's wronged subject, who also fails to signify in a *demos* from which it is excluded, instead seeks justice (and therefore signification) within that realm. Put succinctly, while Edelman's subject takes immense pleasure in its outsider status, Rancière's subject seeks only recognition based on the basic equality that is the law of the *demos*.[19] It is the voice of that one subject, what Rancière calls the "one-too-many" (*l'un-en-plus*), that sets into motion the process of politics, whose object, as noted above, is the righting of wrongs. We will see many of these voices in the literature studied in this book, especially within epistolary novels. Whereas epistolary novels in France prior to the *Lettres persanes* focused on letters sent from one individual to another, Montesquieu's unique treatment of the back-and-forth of letter-writing and -receiving creates a cacophony of voices from which we might just be able to hear that one-too-many (or even many-too-many) that stands out from the rest.

In addition to the reasons cited above, in this chapter, I turn to Rancière's work for two principal reasons: First, although he rarely cites Montesquieu, his debt to the eighteenth-century philosopher is undeniable; and second, while democracy is often understood as a process of building consensus, Rancière's insistence on politics as a process of dissensus (with its focus on the voice of the one-too-many) can help us understand how the form of a text such as Montesquieu's *Lettres persanes*, with its proliferation of voices, can be a subversive tool against the absolutism of the early-eighteenth-century French monarchy. The novel's two main protagonists, Usbek and Rica, do not just write letters: They also receive them in return. Although plurivocal texts exist prior to the *Letters* (Marguerite de Navarre's

---

against Edelman's body apolitic," in *Jacques Rancière on the shores of queer theory*, ed. S. A. Chambers and M. O'Rourke, unpaginated. Edelman proposes the neologism "sinthomosexuality" in ch.2 of *No future*, combining Lacan's "sinthome" (an archaic spelling of *symptome*, which Lacan argues is the trace of *jouissance*) and "homosexuality." Edelman argues that the sinthomosexual proposes itself as against the future by failing to signify and insisting instead upon *jouissance*.

19. For Rancière, the *demos* is a collectivity of individuals that never fully succeeds in having a political voice because of its occasional and diverse nature. That each person is an individual subject with individual desires, and that each individual is equal to each other individual, means that consensus within any given demos is impossible. For a more detailed explanation of this, and other key terms in Rancière's *œuvre*, see *Jacques Rancière: key concepts*, ed. Jean-Philippe Deranty (New York, 2010), as well as Oliver Davis's *Jacques Rancière* (Malden, MA, 2010).

Heptameron, for instance, demonstrates brilliantly the utility of dialogue in the novel), Montesquieu's is the first epistolary novel to truly exploit the possibilities opened up by the vast geographic and temporal space separating letter-writers. These letters blend the personal with the general, the moral with the political, the religious with the secular. By multiplying voices in the novel, the author incorporates various perspectives, allowing the reader to become involved in the scrutiny of both Western and Eastern culture and politics. The form of the novel in which women write to men, slaves write to masters, and men question their faith in letters to religious leaders democratizes the circulation of knowledge by granting power to the otherwise powerless in the form of letters. In other words, the form introduces a politic of the many.

In *Aux bords du politique (On the shores of politics)*, Rancière gives a name to a concept he had been working through since much earlier in his career: *le politique*.[20] By substituting the masculine article *le* for the feminine *la*, Rancière distinguishes between what he calls "la cuisine gouvernementale," or governmental machinations (*la* politique), which is also a process of emancipation, and *le politique*, or the stage upon which justice occurs. *Le politique*, according to the philosopher, is the meeting place between two separate but integral processes: The first is the government, or the rules that manage societies (*la police*); and the second is equality, or the presupposition that in a given society each individual is equal to each other (*émancipation*). Rancière refers to the latter process as a "realist utopia" given its impractical (in the sense of unable to achieve in practice) nature. Emancipation involves a constant fluctuation (since populations are always changing), and therefore can be thought of only relationally. The dream of such unilateral and universal equality is utopian because true equality between all members of the *demos* never occurs and therefore *le politique* becomes the meeting place between utopian ideals of equality and the

20. Jacques Rancière, *Aux bords du politique* (Paris, 1998). Rancière also elaborates on many of the important political concepts (such as emancipation, radical equality, and the division between doing politics and being a subject thereof) in his earlier works including *Proletarian nights*, translated by John Drury (London, 2012); *The Philosopher and his poor*, translated by John Drury, Corinne Oster, and Andrew Parker (Durham, NC, 2004); and *The Ignorant schoolmaster*, translated by Kristin Ross (Stanford, CA, 1991). He continues to work through these concepts until at least his more recent turn to aesthetics. Because of the importance of gendered nouns and pronouns to his work (which do not exist in English), I will use French in the text.

process that occurs between the government and the governed aimed at achieving, or at least constantly working toward, that equality. Because the process is in a state of constant anarchic motion, and because universal equality is always just out of reach, for Rancière democracy is not a process of consensus, but rather one of *dissensus*. There must be a dissenting voice, one who has been wronged, that demands the righting of that wrong. The righting of wrongs is precisely the responsibility of *le politique*.

The distinction between *le politique* and *la police* relies upon a basic separation of laws (that govern) and the essence (or spirit) of these laws that is dictated by the needs of a given society; this is precisely the distinction that Montesquieu proposes in *Spirit of the laws*, a foundational text for many modern democracies.[21] Montesquieu's call for a system of checks and balances to ensure the execution of justice was crucial to the formation of the French parliament, and his division of the three branches of government defined the very notion of democracy in the United States. In short, Montesquieu is one of the most essential theorizers of Western democratic principles. This may be one of the reasons why Rancière, who is concerned less with the mechanisms of governmental systems than with the instances within societies where the struggle for emancipation occurs, is so dismissive of Montesquieu.[22] Furthermore, Montesquieu himself might be surprised to learn of his influence on modern democracies. He did indeed help to revolutionize governmental structures, but what he proposes throughout his lifetime is *not* revolution—it is reform. A pure democracy, according to Montesquieu, would be chaotic and ultimately untenable and, for this reason, he favored a limited monarchy similar to that of England after the Glorious Revolution. As we will also see in Voltaire, Montesquieu calls absolutism into question by proposing an alternate form of monarchy—one in which the king's power is limited. The form of his politics thus draws on familiar structures, but the content and the relation between constituents (in this case the king and his subjects) change. This is why turning to the *Lettres persanes* becomes such a fruitful endeavor; analysis of the eighteenth-century philosopher's

---

21. Charles de Secondat, baron de Montesquieu, *The Spirit of the laws*, ed. Anne M. Cohler, Basia C. Miller, and Harold S. Stone (1748; New York, 2002).
22. In fact, in *Disagreement*, he writes, "if Montesquieu did stumble on such a spirit, in his own way, this is because it was already harnessed to the law in the original philosophical determination of political law." J. Rancière, *Disagreement*, translated by Julie Rose (Minneapolis, MN, 1999), p.67–68.

fiction will allow us to witness those moments of irritation and disagreement between letter-writers when politics, in the Rancièrian sense, occurs. These instances of politics have little to do with the foundation of democracy, and show us instead how the struggle for recognition can take many forms. We will now turn to the first several letters of the novel to demonstrate how a multiplicity of voices can undermine the seemingly strong position of the patriarch.

Within the first four letters, one can already see the ways in which a multiplication of voices provides both richer stories and more dynamic characters. The novel opens with a letter from Usbek to his friend, Rustan, back home in Ispahan. In this letter we can sense both nostalgia and hope in Usbek, who has now been away from his home and harem for twenty-five days. The letter is filled with sentences beginning with the first-person plural pronoun *nous* (we), in a way that communicates to Rustan what he and Rica have been doing since their departure, and that also invites the friend, the male recipient of the letter, into the conversation. At one point Usbek boasts, "Rica and I are perhaps the first Persians to have left our country for the love of knowledge, to have abandoned the attractions of a quiet life in order to pursue the laborious search for wisdom."[23] This statement appears to set Usbek and Rica apart from their Persian comrades, presenting them as fearless explorers and seekers of knowledge. Yet, in the very next paragraph, Usbek implores his friend to send him news about what people are saying about them back home. So far away from his home and people, he wants to remain a part of the community he left behind, even if only as a legend. The letter ends on a loving note of friendship: "be assured that wherever I may be on earth, you have a faithful friend."[24] From the first letter we might expect to read a tale of homosocial bonding through letters—one in which we witness the formulation of a friendship Montaigne would admire.

The next letter, however, alters our expectations. The tone of the letter shifts from friendship to duty and authority as Usbek writes to the head black eunuch of his harem.[25] The *nous* disappears completely,

23. Montesquieu, *Persian letters*, translated by C. J. Betts (New York, 2004), p.41; *Lettres persanes*, ed. Jean Starobinski (1721; Paris, 2003), p.51. "Rica et moi sommes peut-être les premiers, parmi les Persans, que l'envie de savoir ait fait sortir de leur pays, et qui aient renoncé aux douceurs d'une vie tranquille, pour aller chercher laborieusement la sagesse."
24. Montesquieu, *Persian letters*, p.41; *Lettres persanes*, p.52. "Sois assuré qu'en quelque lieu du monde où je sois, tu as un ami fidèle."
25. There is a strict hierarchy even among the slaves of the harem, dependent

along with the descriptions of the trip, and is replaced with a much more pointed and isolating *tu*.[26] The trajectory of the letter moves from a gentle tone of a benevolent master to a firmer one, reminding the slave of his duty, and finally to a more threatening tone. The last paragraph of the letter begins, "Remember the nothingness from which I took you [*tu*]," reminding the slave of his debt to the grand patriarch.[27] Whereas the Usbek of the first letter was soft and kind, we see a different side of Usbek in the second letter, one that uses language to demonstrate power and his superior condition. The strength of his words, he hopes, will serve as a reminder of his great power even though he is far away. In this letter, we thus begin to see the despotic leader that Montesquieu will critique so sharply in the years to come.

These first two letters draw on one of the most important aspects of the epistolary novel: the ability to communicate the capricious nature of individuals by providing readers with letters written to different recipients at different times and for different purposes. This form allows us to glimpse the letter-writer's psyche in ways that predate the free-indirect style of nineteenth-century Romantic literature. In the letters we see a man who is a kind friend and a severe master. However, these letters, which both emanate from Usbek, would also seem to establish the inequality characteristic of the patriarchal politics of the harem; Usbek speaks (or writes) and others must listen and obey. In fact, the first black eunuch (who is addressed in the second letter) will not write back to his master until much later when, in letter 41, he defends his decision to replace a deceased eunuch by castrating another one of the slaves. This arrangement in which the servant and the master write to one another without engaging in conversation reinforces the master–slave dynamic in which one man commands and another prostrates himself.

Although Usbek reads only groveling letters from his head eunuch that reinforce the former's powerful position, we, the readers, discover other letters from the eunuch addressed not to his master, but to other slaves. For instance, in letter 9 he writes to Ibbi, a servant who accompanies Usbek on his journey, and describes the seraglio as a

---

largely upon race. For a more complete discussion of the hierarchies, see Michel Delon, "Un monde d'eunuques," *Europe* 574 (1977), p.79–88.

26. Translated into English as "you," the informal *tu*, as opposed to the formal *vous*, highlights the letter-receiver's lowly position within the power dynamic.

27. Montesquieu, *Persian letters*, p.42; *Lettres persanes*, p.52. "Souviens-toi du néant d'où je t'ai fait sortir."

"dreadful prison." In his youth, the eunuch had been tormented by the beautiful women rendered unavailable to him by his position and castrated state. Now, as an old man, he continues to be tormented both by the women's humiliating requests, and by the knowledge that the women may turn on him at any time, leaving him hated by everyone. The only pleasure he finds in life is exerting what little power he does have over the wives. The man who is doomed to penetrate each recess of the harem with no hope of sexual satisfaction thus satisfies his desires with an imaginary form of patriarchy.

The *demos* of Montesquieu's novel up until this point has relied upon the suppression of female voices, but letters 3 and 4 introduce two new female characters and letter-writers, Zachi and Zéphis respectively. These two wives of Usbek write to him from the harem, and their letters shift the content and tone of the novel significantly. Zachi's letter recounts a highly erotic scene from a previous time in the harem when the wives were competing to be the favorite of their master. Usbek examined his wives "in the simplicity of nature" one by one until finally declaring Zachi his favorite and delivering to her orgasms she believes would have devastated the other wives if they could have heard them. In this letter, sexuality is presented as a public display and a game for power among the women of the harem.[28] This letter, with its overtly sexual language, invites the reader to imagine the harem as what Christophe Martin calls "a sort of laboratory in which the softening of bodies and consciousnesses is experimented upon."[29] In this laboratory, the morals of polite society fade away, and its results are uncovered throughout the novel. While the desire evoked in this letter remains structured by heteronormative desire (that between a husband and wife), this letter nonetheless presages the experimentation to come. The memory Zachi evokes is framed in the letter by a double absence: first, Usbek's absence from the seraglio, and second, the displacement of the wives from the harem to the

28. Janet Gurkin Altmon discusses this game as being one that involves collective action and intellectual development in "Strategic timing: women's questions, domestic servitude, and the dating game in Montesquieu," *Eighteenth-century fiction* 13:2–3 (2001), p.325–48. Suzanne Pucci, by contrast, finds in this same game a process of individualization in which letter-writers become alienated from one another. See Suzanne Rodin Pucci, "Letters from the harem: veiled figures of writing in Montesquieu's *Lettres persanes*," in *Writing the female voice: essays on epistolary literature*, ed. Elizabeth Goldsmith (Boston, MA, 1989), p.114–34.

29. See Christophe Martin, "L'institution du sérail: quelques réflexions sur le livre XVI de *L'Esprit des lois*," *Revue Montesquieu* 5 (2001), p.41–57 (47).

countryside. She begins, "we ordered the Chief Eunuch to take us out in the country," and the letter ends with a reproach to her husband who has performed a violence against the wives by leaving. Her final cry, "Ah! my dear Usbek, you should learn how to be happy," signals a crumbling of his power that begins precisely with this move out of his realm. Her voice thus reminds us that the pleasure brought by sanctioned desire is already a thing of the past.[30]

Already in the next letter, another wife, Zéphis, alludes to orgasms of a much different nature. After being accused by the head eunuch of a lesbian romance with her servant, she writes to Usbek to deny the allegations and complain of having lost her handmaid. Her desires become clearer as the language she uses to defend herself and her slave, Zélide, reinforces the erotic nature of the relationship between the two women. When she states, "Zelide who serves me so faithfully, whose *deft hands* create beauty and grace wherever they go," she returns the reader's attention to the previous letter in which such "ornaments" had served as distractions from true desirability.[31] Placing this letter immediately after a letter describing the pleasures of heterosexual (if polygamous) sex may seem to suggest that the patriarch's absence throws the rules of heteronormativity into chaos, allowing for the free circulation of queer desire. After all, Zélide will later be accused of having seduced at least one other wife (and it is insinuated that she has pleasured many more) with her "deft hands," and we will also learn of illicit affairs between wives and eunuchs, the latter of whom are entrusted with the wives precisely because of their emasculated state. Yet to read in this letter a complete loss of patriarchal power would be misleading. For one thing, while the language of Zachi's letter openly discusses sexuality and orgasms, desire and sexuality in Zéphis's letter exist only as subtext, and for another, the letter is written first and foremost as a denial of sapphic desire. In other words, while queer desire exists on the shores of Usbek's harem (literally—the wives are carried across a body of water on their journey to the country), within these early letters of the novel such desire is expressed largely as a means to shore up patriarchal power.

30. Montesquieu, *Persian letters*, p.43–44; *Lettres persanes*, p.53–54. "Nous avons ordonné au chef des eunuques de nous mener à la campagne," "Ah! mon cher Usbek, si tu savais être heureux!"
31. Montesquieu, *Persian letters*, p.44; *Lettres persanes*, p.55 (emphasis added). "Zélide qui me sert avec tant d'affection, et dont les *adroites mains* portent partout les ornements et les grâces."

My goal here is not to go through and inspect each of the letters one by one (as does Usbek with his wives) in order to demonstrate Usbek's many faces and the various forms of desire. I examine these first four letters in succession to demonstrate the very careful arrangement of the letters. The first two introduce a strong and severe patriarch, while the second pair give voice to those who, in the politics of the harem, would not otherwise have one—the women. The careful curation of these letters thus provides a stage upon which we, the readers, might hear the voices of the oppressed. In other words, the form of the novel demonstrates a politics that runs parallel to that of the content. Even before we see Usbek's harem fall into chaos, those letters, with their multiplicity of writers who express individual thoughts and desires, provoke an instance of politics. The arrangement of the letters is brought to the reader's attention all the more because of the chronological *dis*order of the letters. In fact, were we to put the letters in chronological order, letter 3—Zachi's letter of sensual and aesthetic pleasure—would have been the opening letter.[32] Perhaps Montesquieu felt that to open with such a sexually charged scene would send the wrong message about the book's content, but then why go to the trouble of creating a system that, once uncovered, places this letter first?

While many authors of the time, especially authors of tragedies such as Voltaire (as we shall see in the next section of this chapter), use a number of dramatic effects, character additions, and aesthetic devices to foreshadow the tragic outcomes of their protagonists, these methods remain inaccessible to the writer of (especially epistolary) novels. Because of the nature of the epistolary novel, such overt devices become difficult. Anyone alive in the early eighteenth century would

---

32. The letters are listed out of chronological order and instead ordered to tell a particular story. Montesquieu himself alludes to a secret chain (*chaine secrète*) that unifies the letters, and readers and scholars have been trying to unlock it since the book's publication. For a few examples from the past several decades, see R. L. Frautschi, "The would-be invisible chain in *Les Lettres persanes*," *The French review* 40:5 (1967), p.604–12; Elizabeth Cook, *Epistolary bodies: gender and genre in the eighteenth-century Republic of Letters* (Stanford, CA, 1996); Randolph Runyon, *The Art of the Persian letters: unlocking Montesquieu's "secret chain"* (Newark, DE, 2005); and Theodore E. D. Braun, "Montesquieu, *Lettres persanes*, and chaos," in *Disrupted patterns: on chaos and order in the Enlightenment*, ed. Theodore E. D. Braun and John Aloysius McCarthy (Amsterdam, 2000), p.79–90, among others. For an explanation of dates and chronology in the *Lettres*, see Robert Shackleton, "The Moslem chronology of the *Lettres persanes*," *French studies* 1 (1954), p.17–27.

be familiar with the time it takes for a letter to reach its destination. An epistolary novel that told a linear story in a chronological fashion, all while dealing with multiple letter-writers, would, therefore, be unrealistic. Since, as the preface to the novel indicates, realism is key to the novel's reception, the author must necessarily intertwine the various matrices of writers composing and sending letters from one country (and continent) to another.[33] To foreshadow tragic events in any obvious way would also break the facade of realism so carefully crafted by the author. The reader is not meant to read the letters in chronological order just as the recipients of the letters might not receive them in chronological order, a fact that is alluded to in letters such as letter 21 from Usbek to his chief white eunuch, in which he chastises the servant for not opening sooner a letter the master had sent him. To order the letters as Montesquieu does, therefore, allows him to maintain a sense of realism of the novel, and create a system of narrative suspense through its structure.

The suspense builds to a climax in the final, fateful letter from Roxane to Usbek. Hers is the final voice we hear and the one that will provoke an unresolvable dissensus as her actions betray the devastating failure of the patriarch. Many feminist critics have argued that Roxane's suicide in the final letter dramatizes a moment of supreme female agency.[34] The woman whose rape is misinterpreted as foreplay by her master/husband in letter 26 ends the novel on a vengeful note:

You were surprised not to find me carried away by the ecstasy of love; if you had known me properly you would have found in me all the violence of hate.

But you had for a long time the benefit of thinking that a heart like mine was subject to you. We were both happy: you thought that I had been deceived while I was deceiving you.

33. Realism is here a relative term related solely to the experience of letter-writing and -receiving. Montesquieu makes clear in the preface to the novel that he does not believe readers will be fooled by the aesthetic and narrative devices he employs.
34. See, for example, Katherine M. Rogers, "Subversion of the patriarchy in *Les Lettres persanes,*" *Philological quarterly* 65:1 (1986), p.61–78; Pauline Kra, "Montesquieu and women," in *French women and the Enlightenment*, ed. Samia Spencer (Bloomington, IN, 1984), p.272–84; and Mary McAlpin, "Utopia in the seraglio: feminist hermeneutics and Montesquieu's *Lettres persanes,*" in *Gender and utopia in the eighteenth century: essays in English and French utopian writing*, ed. Nicole Pohl and Brenda Tooley (New York, 2007), p.87–106.

Such language is new to you, no doubt. Is it possible that after having overwhelmed you with grief I could force you to admire my courage? But it is all over, the poison is destroying me. I am losing my strength, the pen is falling from my hands, I can feel even my hatred growing weaker; I am dying.

Tu étais étonné de ne point trouver en moi les transports de l'amour: si tu m'avais bien connue, tu y aurais trouvé toute la violence de la haine.

Mais tu as eu longtemps l'avantage de croire qu'un cœur comme le mien t'était soumis: nous étions tous deux heureux; tu me croyais trompée, et je te trompais.

Ce langage, sans doute, te paraît nouveau. Serait-il possible qu'après t'avoir accablé de douleurs, je te forçasse encore d'admirer mon courage? Mais, c'en est fait, le poison me consume, ma force m'abandonne; la plume me tombe des mains; je sens affaiblir jusqu'à ma haine: je me meurs.[35]

With her final breaths, Roxane turns Usbek's own words against him. Letter 26, the first letter from Usbek to Roxane, describes the first sexual encounter between the two from Usbek's point of view. "Do you remember," he writes nostalgically, "how, when everything else had failed [...] you took a dagger and threatened to destroy the husband who loved you if he continued to demand something that meant more to you than he did."[36] Mary McAlpin, who has written extensively on both of these letters, emphasizes that what we read in the first of the letters to Roxane is, first and foremost, a rape scene.[37] Usbek's letter to Roxane begins, "Roxana, how fortunate you are to be in the sweet land of Persia, and not in these polluted climates, where modesty and virtue are unknown."[38] He claims to be protecting his wife from France with its "poisonous climates." In other words, he claims to be doing her a

35. Montesquieu, *Persian letters*, p.281; *Lettres persanes*, p.341.
36. Montesquieu, *Persian letters*, p.76; *Lettres persanes*, p.94. "Vous souvient-il lorsque toutes les ressources vous manquèrent [...] Vous prîtes un poignard, et menaçâtes d'immoler un époux qui vous aimait, s'il continuait à exiger de vous ce que vous chérissiez plus que votre époux même."
37. See M. McAlpin, "The rape of Roxane and the end of the world in Montesquieu's *Lettres persanes*," *Romanic review* 107:1–4 (2016), p.55–74.
38. Montesquieu, *Persian letters*, p.75; *Lettres persanes*, p.93. Although the translation indicates that the climates are "polluted," the French word *empoisonné* is better translated as "poisonous," thus highlighting the irony in Roxane's choice to use poison to take her life. "Que vous êtes heureuse, Roxane, d'être dans le doux

favor by keeping her locked up as a prisoner.[39] A comparison of the two letters between Usbek and Roxane demonstrates the same kind of foreshadowing that we see in the tragedies of the greatest playwrights. Roxane's suicide is also foreshadowed in another earlier letter (141). In it, Rica tells the story of a utopian female harem in which the master's words are also used against him. Roxane may have been spared the poisonous climates of France, but her last words to him are written as a literal poison courses through her veins in the climate that should have been, according to Usbek's account, her salvation. Like the powerful Phèdre before her, Roxane, mistreated by a husband, takes revenge on him by taking her own life.

The end of the novel is also the end of life. There is no future for Roxane, and we are left to believe that there is no future for Usbek, or at least none that he would recognize. On the one hand, we might see in Roxane a perfect example of Edelman's *sinthomosexual*. By using Usbek's words, she appears to take pleasure in depriving him of a future with her. We are taken along with her to the edge of death as she subtracts herself from a society that had no place for her voice. Yet, if she did want to live only in the present with no regard for any future, why write to Usbek at all? By using the last moments of her life to write to the man who had enslaved and raped her, she demands to be heard. She is the voice that calls attention to the vast chasm between the spirit of the laws, which claim to protect women from Persian society, and the laws themselves, which create a space of exploitation. The politics that she sets into motion by demanding to be heard is not neat or pretty; in a society based on inequality, her voice is but one of many subjects of Usbek's power. However, the description of her death leaves the reader with a demand for a future justice. It will not be justice for Roxane, but hers is the voice that sets into motion a serious questioning of the reigning system of governance that she has known. This is the future opened up through dissensus.

---

pays de Perse, et non pas dans ces climats empoisonnés, où l'on ne connaît ni la pudeur, ni la vertu!"

39. Montesquieu will echo this sentiment in the *Spirit of the laws* when he writes that women in the East are locked up for their own protection. For a discussion of Montesquieu's rationale, as well his contradictory statements about the harem in *Spirit of the laws*, see Martin's "L'institution du sérail."

An Oedipus for a new age

In Voltaire's earliest tragedy, *Œdipe* (1718), instances of politics occur not necessarily through a proliferation of voices, but rather by redistributing the weight given to each of the play's characters. He does make some changes to the lineup (such as adding Philoctetes as a romantic rival to Oedipus and eliminating the blind prophet Tiresias), but, as we shall see, his most important innovations involve structural change resulting from a heightened focus on Philoctetes and Jocasta, as well as a change to the overall mood of the play. The playwright alters the tone by writing characters who dare to question the gods rather than simply accept their fate. His reimagining of Sophocles's ancient tragedy infuses Oedipus and Jocasta with a fury against the gods for the cruel trick played upon them. While melodrama is crucial to each retelling of this ancient story, a fury aimed specifically at the gods is absent or muted in the earlier versions by Sophocles and Corneille. Voltaire turned away from what he believed too traditional an interpretation offered by Corneille, in which both the king and the queen of Thebes are implicated in their crimes—guilty of offenses against nature (both incest and regicide/parricide). By endowing humans with the power to question the gods, Voltaire alters the mythology of Oedipus, making it less about mysticism and a veneration of the gods and more about reckoning with the effect of familial relations upon humankind. Moreover, by decentering the patriarch, the young playwright invites the voices of the oppressed to question the legitimacy of absolute power.

During the years of the Orléans Regency, Voltaire wrote his two first tragedies: One was the hugely successful *Œdipe*; the other was the colossal flop *Artémire*.[40] The latter play was performed first in February of 1720 and received a devastatingly negative reception. After revising the play, Voltaire allowed it to be performed eight more times before finally pulling it out of the theater for good. Although his play was slightly better received after the revisions, the playwright was so disappointed with it that he never allowed the manuscript to be published, and what we can access today is merely a lacunae-ridden reconstruction based on fragments provided by several editors. Like *Œdipe*, *Artémire* tells a story of love, betrayal, and death, but unlike *Œdipe* it provides a new story that is relatively unpredictable (rather

---

40. Although we have only fragments of *Artémire*, we can assume much of its general content and form by the pieces that remain.

than a retelling of an ancient tragedy). The author takes familiar names and renders them strange; Cassandre, for example, one of the main love interests of the play, is not the beautiful Greek prophetess of the epic tragedies as one might expect. Instead, he is a mighty and vengeful king who has killed the father of his wife, Artémire.[41] So why is it that one became an overnight sensation while the other fell quickly into oblivion? And how does each offer new and different views on familial relationality? To answer these questions requires close consideration of the content, form, and family politics of both plays. We will first turn to *Œdipe*.

As I have established, Oedipus, that tragic hero of ancient times, has become, in modernity, a name that helps us to understand the psychological structures of human desire, even if, as many feminist scholars and analysts have pointed out, the focus on Oedipus's role in this psychic drama, to the exclusion of that of Jocasta, can explain, to a certain extent, the persistence of gender discrimination and sexism in psychoanalytic theory and practice.[42] This is a deeply personal story and one that has been rewritten again and again from Antiquity up to the present day. The choice to restage a production of an ancient tragedy at a given point in time is rarely without political motivation, and the retelling of *Œdipe* in particular, which recounts the story of a king's fall from grace, is among the most seditious.[43] Voltaire's choice to adapt the tragedy, by comparison, seems obvious and timely. The Sun King's passing provided the perfect opportunity to reflect on what a king does and should do for his people.

Voltaire's new take on this ancient tragedy was a huge success, quickly replacing the long run of Corneille's *Œdipe* at the Comédie-Française. The new version played to sold-out crowds for over a year.

41. The choice of the name Cassandre appears to come instead from the Italian *commedia dell'arte*, which influenced many French playwrights in the seventeenth and eighteenth centuries.

42. Some of the earliest feminist critics of psychoanalysis were Freud's own contemporaries Karen Horney and Helen Deutsch. More recently, scholars such as Juliet Mitchell and Luce Irigaray have examined both the sexism inherent in (especially Freudian) psychoanalysis, and how the field might still be essential for feminist scholarship. For a thorough discussion of the engagement of feminism with psychoanalysis, see Mitchell's *Psychoanalysis and feminism*.

43. For instance, as Hélène Bilis points out, Corneille's production of *Œdipe* (first presented in 1659) was highly motivated by a desire to highlight the distinction between the king's mortal and royal body and to reinforce the supremacy of Louis XIV's divine reign. See Bilis, "Corneille's *Œdipe* and the politics of seventeenth-century royal succession," *MLN* 125:4 (2010), p.873–94.

The public, it seemed, was ready for a break from tradition, and Voltaire was happy to bring that change. Whereas Corneille's retelling of the ancient Greek tragedy altered the story to focus on Oedipus's legitimacy as king (contrasting it with Laius's known daughter and heir, Dircé), Voltaire's eliminates the character of Dircé altogether, along with her competing claims to the throne.[44] Like Corneille, Voltaire also alters the characters from Sophocles's version; Tiresias, for example, that blind prophet of old, is completely absent from this eighteenth-century retelling, replaced instead by a high priest. And, although Dircé is no longer competing with Oedipus for the throne, Philoctetes (the prince of Euboea) arrives as a competitor for Jocasta's affection. These two changes, among others, alert us to a shift in focus of the play. The absence of Tiresias, whose presence produces a hyper-awareness of blindness on the stage thus doubling the prophecy of Oedipus's terrible fate in the final act of Sophocles's play (when Oedipus gouges out his own eyes to avoid seeing the devastation wrought by his actions), both shifts our focus away from ancient mysticism and suggests that the final unveiling of the unlawful acts is less important than the process leading to discovery. Rather than blindness being foreshadowed by the presence of a blind seer, it is implied through Oedipus's own gaps in memory. Philoctetes's appearance as a romantic rival to the king also opens up the intrigue of sexual politics. The king's legitimacy is called into question by a sexual rival to his wife rather than a blood rival to the throne. The introduction of sexual rivalry into the transmission of power from one king to the next illustrates in a dramatic fashion how an apparatus of sexuality becomes entangled with one of alliance, as the rules governing succession through blood and tradition compete with new rules more concerned with the sexual being of bodies.

Had the play been written at a different time, Philoctetes's rivalry with Oedipus might have occupied a large portion of the play. In the *drame bourgeois* that will appear just a few decades after Voltaire's play, romantic rivalry and deception often serve as the main points of the

---

44. For a detailed analysis of the variations between Corneille's and Voltaire's versions of this tragedy, see Hélène Bilis, "Poétique tragique et pensée politique: la mise en scène de la souveraineté dans l'*Œdipe* de Voltaire," *Symposium* 64:4 (2010), p.258–74. Hélène Mordrelle also outlines some of the most important differences between the versions of Sophocles and Voltaire in "De l'*Œdipe Roi* de Sophocle à l'*Œdipe* de Voltaire: l'histoire et les enjeux d'une réécriture," *Bulletin de l'Association Guillaume Budé* 1 (2010), p.210–32.

plot. In this early period in the century, however, the romantic rivalry serves merely as a pretext to examine loyalty to the patriarch. As it is written, the rivalry is quelled relatively early based on what Philoctetes perceives as a higher law. Oedipus has defeated the Sphinx and saved the Thebans, and he therefore deserves Jocasta's hand in marriage. Already by the end of the first scene of the play, Philoctetes cedes Jocasta to his rival:

DIMAS

What do you hope to gain from a love fatal at best?
Did you come from the Estate to set ablaze all that rests?
Will you steal Jocasta away from her new spouse?

PHILOCTETES

Her spouse, good heavens! What are these words you pronounce?
Jocasta!... A second marriage, what could this mean...

DIMAS

Oedipus has joined his fate to this queen...
For his hard work it was the greatest reward.

PHILOCTETES

O dangerous charms that I so adored!
O how fortunate is Oedipus!

DIMAS

Quel fruit espérez-vous d'un amour si funeste?
Venez-vous de l'Etat embraser ce qui reste?
Ravirez-vous Jocaste à son nouvel époux?

PHILOCTÈTE

Son époux, juste ciel! ah que me dites-vous?
Jocaste!... il se pourrait qu'un second hyménée...

DIMAS

Œdipe à cette reine a joint sa destinée...
De ses heureux travaux c'était le plus doux prix.

PHILOCTÈTE

O dangereux appas que j'avais trop chéri!
O trop heureux Œdipe![45]

45. Voltaire, *Œdipe*, ed. David Jory and John Renwick, in *Œuvres complètes de Voltaire* (hereafter *OCV*), vol.1A (Oxford, 2001), p.15–284 (177). Philoctetes's acceptance

Although Jocasta and Philoctetes will both later admit to their mutual love for one another, they also agree that duty to the higher law is more important that human passion. The addition of Philoctetes in this version does not entirely undermine the foundations of patriarchy, and would seem on the contrary, at least in this early scene of the play, to bolster them.

Still, the entry of Philoctetes into the court of Oedipus does offset the balance of power in a different way. In fact, Voltaire's version opens not with a powerful Oedipus addressing his people, but with a private scene between Philoctetes and his friend Dimas. Act 1, scene 1 opens with Dimas pronouncing the doomed name of his friend:

> Philoctetes, is it you? What frightful blow of fate
> has made you seek death in this infested place?
>
> Philoctète, est-ce vous? quel coup affreux du sort
> Dans ces lieux empestés vous fait chercher la mort?[46]

Ironically, it is Philoctetes whom we learn is in danger of dying at this point, not Oedipus. The prince of Euboea has arrived back in Thebes during a terrible plague that has tormented the people since the assassination of their king, Laius. In addition to the plague, the prince's life is also in danger as it is he whom Oedipus suspects of having killed Laius. As the people have learned from the prophetic priest, the righting of a wrong through finding and punishing the king's assassin can rid the kingdom of the plague. By beginning the play with a private scene between two friends, the playwright emphasizes the importance of emotion, confidence, and intimacy to the story.

Oedipus's reaction upon learning of Philoctetes's arrival in Thebes demonstrates the patriarch's confusion regarding his own role, as well as the roles of those around him; Oedipus is now the king of Thebes, but he owes a great debt to the older Philoctetes who, along with Hercules, introduced him to the valiant life he now leads. The prince invokes these names as a warning to Oedipus:

---

of fate is, in fact, even clearer in the first edition of the play in which he says, "Oedipus is so fortunate! I am not surprised; / and he who saves his people is deserving of such a prize: / The heavens are just" ("Œdipe est trop heureux! je n'en suis point surpris; / Et qui sauva son peuple est digne d'un tel prix: / Le ciel est juste").

46. Voltaire, *Œdipe*, p.169.

I know what crimes they use to place a stain on my life;
My Lord, do not expect me my good name to justify;
I revere you too much, and do not take the position
That you could lower yourself to such base suspicion.
On the same path our steps coincide,
To your glory, my own is closely tied.
Theseus, Hercules, and I, we opened your eyes
To the glorious path upon which you now rise;
Do not dishonor with such aspersions abound
The splendor of these names to which yours is bound,
And finally deserve by a generous enterprise
The honor I give you in placing you by their side.

Je sais de quels forfaits on veut noircir ma vie;
Seigneur, n'attendez pas que je m'en justifie;
J'ai pour vous trop d'estime, et je ne pense pas
Que vous puissiez descendre à des soupçons si bas.
Si sur les mêmes pas nous marchons l'un et l'autre,
Ma gloire d'assez près est unie à la vôtre.
Thésée, Hercule, et moi, nous vous avons montré
Le chemin de la gloire où vous êtes entré;
Ne déshonorez point par une calomnie
La splendeur de ces noms où votre nom s'allie,
Et méritez enfin par un trait généreux
L'honneur que je vous fais de vous mettre auprès d'eux.[47]

These verses remind us that Oedipus is much younger than his rival, the latter having already traveled the world at the side of Hercules. By placing his name next to that of Hercules, a god known primarily for his incredible strength, the prince further emphasizes his own power. He has fought beside Hercules, and he is alive whereas the strong hero has died. Thus, this scene sets up a secondary rivalry: Having renounced his claim to Jocasta, Philoctetes instead demonstrates his heroic superiority. He simultaneously praises and provokes the king, discussing his esteem for Oedipus and in the same breath insulting his baseness (by citing his rival's ill-informed suspicions). The rocky relationship between the two men will continue throughout the play as Philoctetes chides and supports the king in turn.

The king's response to Philoctetes's rebuke betrays his own insecurities. He declares that if given the choice he would have been the victim of the assassination. He further claims that dying for

47. Voltaire, *Œdipe*, p.197.

one's people is the most heroic action a king can take. However, in doing so he has used his first words against the accused to create an image of himself as victim; as such, he contrasts himself to the virile Philoctetes, whom he hopes to convince of his power. He has rhymed *moi* (me) with *roi* (king), but he has also paired *crime* with *victime*, foreshadowing through rhymed couplets his guilt as assassin of the former King Laius. While the end of this proclamation intends to establish greatness through clemency typical of a Corneille-esque king, it might also be understood to demonstrate a weakness. Oedipus begs his rival to declare himself innocent, suggesting first that he does not wish to exact revenge on the great Philoctetes, and second that he is incapable of imposing his own will. After discussing a king's duty to die for his people, he says of heroic death:

> It is an honor too grand to give it away.
> I would have sacrificed mine, and defended your days;
> I would have saved my people a second time.
> But, Lord, the liberty of choice is not mine;
> It's a criminal blood that we must take:
> You stand accused, your defense you should make;
> Appear innocent, it will be so pleasant for me
> To honor in my court a hero such as thee,
> And I would be so happy to treat you as I please,
> Not as an accused man, but as Philoctetes.

> C'est un honneur trop grand pour le céder à d'autres.
> J'aurais donné mes jours, et défendu les vôtres;
> J'aurais sauvé mon peuple une seconde fois.
> Mais, seigneur, je n'ai point la liberté du choix;
> C'est un sang criminel que nous devons répandre:
> Vous êtes accusé, songez à vous défendre;
> Paraissez innocent, il me sera bien doux
> D'honorer dans ma cour un héros tel que vous,
> Et je me tiens heureux, s'il faut que je vous traite,
> Non comme un accusé, mais comme Philoctète.[48]

He has called forth imagery of himself as victim and one who should be dead, while giving his rival a heroic description. He implores Philoctetes to declare his own innocence, even though we will later learn that Philoctetes's innocence comes at the price of Oedipus's guilt. Furthermore, the king's declarations of a love for one's country

48. Voltaire, *Œdipe*, p.198.

that is best performed through one's death are betrayed by the ending in which the guilty Oedipus does not kill himself, but merely mutilates his face by gouging out his eyes. In his attempt to project a strong and powerful image of himself, he has instead affirmed his place as an unworthy heir to the throne.

Eighteenth-century viewers of the play could not have helped but see traces of their own king in the role of Oedipus. The youth of the king who is at least young enough to be Jocasta's son, along with the frequent allusions to his inexperience, might well have conjured up visions of Louis XV: The new king who was only eight years old at the time of *Œdipe*'s first performance.[49] Perhaps this play could be seen as an indictment of the French monarchy so embedded in outdated traditions as to fill the highest post of the land with a child, but more likely it served as a gentle warning. With youth comes a lack of knowledge. Even though Oedipus was clever enough to beat the Sphinx, the gaps in his memory reflect the limits to both his knowledge and his power. The scene in which Oedipus discovers himself to be guilty of regicide unfolds between the knowing priest, a relatively calm Philoctetes, and an increasingly belligerent Oedipus:

THE HIGH PRIEST
Once you discover the fate with which he is overcome,
You will shudder with horror at the very name of the guilty one.
The god who uses my voice to speak to you at present,
Commands that exile be his only punishment:
But soon, feeling a gruesome desperation,
His hands will add to the celestial tribulation.
Your eyes by his dreadful torment will be surprised,
And you will believe your days well paid for at this price.

OEDIPUS
Obey.

PHILOCTETES
Speak.

---

49. Furthermore, in letters written to the editor about the play, Voltaire explicitly states that his Jocasta is at most thirty-five years old, judging by the fact that she would have married Laius at a very young age. Strangely, this does not stop him from declaring that the Jocasta of Corneille's and Sophocles's tragedies is more likely sixty. See "Lettres écrites par l'auteur qui contiennent la critique de l'Œdipe de Sophocle, de celui de Corneille, et du sien," ed. David Jory and John Renwick, in *OCV*, vol.1A, p.323–81.

OEDIPUS
This is too much defiance.

THE HIGH PRIEST, to Oedipus.
It is you who force me to break the silence.

OEDIPUS
Oh how these delays anger me through and through!

THE HIGH PRIEST
As you wish... well!... it's...

OEDIPUS
Get to the point; who?

THE HIGH PRIEST, to Oedipus.
You.

LE GRAND-PRÊTRE
Quand vous serez instruits du destin qui l'accable,
Vous frémirez d'horreur au seul nom du coupable.
Le dieu qui par ma voix vous parle en ce moment,
Commande que l'exil soit son seul châtiment:
Mais bientôt éprouvant un désespoir funeste,
Ses mains ajouteront à la rigueur céleste.
De son supplice affreux vos yeux seront surpris,
Et vous croirez vos jours trop payés à ce prix.

ŒDIPE
Obéissez.

PHILOCTÈTE
Parlez.

ŒDIPE
C'est trop de résistance.

LE GRAND-PRÊTRE, à Œdipe.
C'est vous qui me forcez à rompre le silence.

ŒDIPE
Que ces retardements allument mon courroux!

LE GRAND-PRÊTRE
Vous le voulez... eh bien!... c'est...

ŒDIPE

Achève; qui?

LE GRAND-PRÊTRE, à Œdipe.

Vous.[50]

By trying to demonstrate his power, Oedipus is forced to reckon with the truth. In this scene the first of his crimes, that of regicide, is revealed to him. Surprisingly, the reaction is one of disbelief even by Philoctetes, who had been accused of the murder himself. Rather than taking contentment in the fall of his adversary, he demonstrates solidarity with the king, blaming instead the gods for their false words. It will take until the next act of the tragedy for these gaps in memory to begin to be filled in. As Oedipus talks privately with Jocasta, he realizes the moment when he accidentally killed Laius, mistaking the latter for a scoundrel attacking the king's party in the woods.

For Oedipus, the first scene of the final act serves to fill in the gaps in his own memory; for the spectator, a new crime is unfolding—that of incest. As Jocasta recounts her own mistrust of the priests, the spectator realizes through her story the incestuous truth of her relationship to Oedipus. The spectator, in other words, becomes more knowledgeable than the king, realizing that Oedipus is the long-lost son of Jocasta and Laius. This not only adds to the suspense of the tragic action, it also serves to democratize the circulation of knowledge. Oedipus will not learn the truth until act 5, scene 3, but, while Sophocles's Oedipus becomes so enraged that he runs through the house hoping to tear out the womb from Jocasta's body in a supreme act that would separate the two functions she performs in his life (wife and mother), Voltaire's Oedipus becomes introverted and sullen—angry at the gods who have dealt him this horrible fate. As he stands alone in the next scene he cries:

> The dreadful oracle has been realized
> My fear only hastened the inevitable demise!
> And I now find myself, by a turn of events so tumultuous
> Incestuous and parricidal, *and yet still virtuous.*

> Le voilà donc rempli cet oracle exécrable
> Dont ma crainte a pressé l'effet inévitable!
> Et je me vois enfin, par un mélange affreux
> Inceste et parricide, *et pourtant vertueux.*[51]

50. Voltaire, *Œdipe*, p.212-13.
51. Voltaire, *Œdipe*, p.249 (emphasis added).

The details of his crime come rushing back in the same breath with which he declares himself virtuous. This Oedipus does not seek revenge on the body of his wife; instead he tries to figure out how he can serve his people, even when the gods have forsaken him. Once he has been enlightened to the truth, Voltaire's king becomes the benevolent king that he feels the French people need. In this way, the play serves not only as a warning, but also as a plea. In the aftermath of the Sun King's absolute monarchy, the playwright urges the new young king to listen to his people and act in their best interests instead of his own.

And what of Jocasta? If my analysis of the play up until this point has remained largely silent about her role, this is not because of a lack of importance invested in her by Voltaire. In fact, while the Jocasta of the ancient Greek tragedy hangs herself long before the end of the play, Voltaire grants his Jocasta the final word. One of his biggest critiques of both Sophocles's and Corneille's versions of the tragedy is the misuse of this particular character. He writes of these versions: "As for Jocasta, of which the role should have been interesting since she shares all of the hardships with Oedipus, she is not even the witness [to them]; she does not appear at all in the fifth act when Oedipus learns that he is her son, in a word, she is a useless character."[52] By expanding Jocasta's role, Voltaire demonstrates the necessity of a cast of loyal subjects surrounding the king. Rather than Oedipus gouging his eyes out *after* finding his dead mother/wife, by the time Jocasta takes her own life, her son/husband is already blind. More importantly, however, Voltaire builds a sense of solidarity between Oedipus, Jocasta, and even Philoctetes. As I have already mentioned, Philoctetes gives up his hopes of a union with Jocasta in favor of a duty to Oedipus early in the play, but what is more radical is Voltaire's inclusion of Jocasta—a woman—in this otherwise masculine network of individuals. In this dramatization of Oedipus, Jocasta becomes a heroine just as important for understanding political power as Antigone. While Antigone's virtue lies in her belief in a power higher than that of the king, Jocasta's virtue lies in her refusal to accept mystic power.

---

52. Voltaire, "Lettres," p.357. "Pour Jocaste, dont le rôle devrait être intéressant, puisqu'elle partage tous les malheurs d'Œdipe, elle n'en est pas même le témoin; elle ne paraît point au cinquième acte, lorsqu'Œdipe apprend qu'il est son fils: en un mot, c'est un personnage inutile."

Initially, Jocasta had felt that being a good queen meant protecting the life of her husband at all costs. This is why, upon hearing about her tragic fate from the priest, she sends away the son borne of her union with Laius in order to have the child killed. Unlike another tragic Greek heroine, Medea, Jocasta endeavors to kill her offspring out of love rather than spite. In the final scenes, however, she learns the impossibility of escaping that which fate has destined for her. Her actions lead to the fulfillment of the prophecy, and for that reason she decides to end the tragedy of the prophecy by ending her own life. In *Tragic ways of killing a woman*, Nicole Loraux makes the provocative argument that a woman's death in ancient tragedies serves as a moment of relative gender equality.[53] Although men die in battle and women take their own lives or are sacrificed as virgins, it is only in the moments beyond their deaths that women are finally permitted to speak. While they have been forced to remain silent during their lifetimes, their bodies attest to the heroism of their lives in their absence. These moments of life beyond death are particularly crucial for women, whose death often carries with it the message of the play. Female bodies, hanging or slain, remain visible to the citizens to whom they had previously been invisible. In this way, the tragic death of the Greek heroines accompanies a symbolic death of a specific type of positionality of the woman. For Jocasta, this means that her voice, as she curses the gods for what they have done to her family, is the last we will hear. In life, her role was to support her husband; in death she decides to educate the people on the dangers of blind faith.

So many centuries after Sophocles and Euripides were writing these silent heroines, Voltaire had a different take on the importance of a woman's voice. Distinct from many other tragic heroines, Jocasta does not waste her final words to weep about her bad fate or misfortune; instead she uses her last breaths to blame the gods for what they have done.

JOCASTA

And me, I punish myself.
(She stabs herself.)
By a frightful power reserved for the incestuous soul,
Death is the only good, the only god to which I hold.
Laius, receive my blood, I follow you to the resting place of the dead;
I lived virtuously, and I die with no remorse in my head.

---

53. Nicole Loraux, *Tragic ways of killing a woman*, translated by Anthony Forster (Cambridge, MA, 1987).

CHOIR
O unfortunate queen! O fate that I despise!

JOCASTA
Pity only my son since he is still alive,
Priests, and you Thebans, who my subjects you have been,
Honor my funeral pyre, and believe until the end,
That amidst the horrors with which fate oppressed me
I made blush the gods who forced this crime upon me.

JOCASTE
Et moi, je me punis.
(Elle se frappe.)
Par un pouvoir affreux réservée à l'inceste,
La mort est le seul bien, le seul dieu qui me reste.
Laïus, reçois mon sang, je te suis chez les morts;
J'ai vécu vertueuse, et je meurs sans remords.

LE CHŒUR
Ô malheureuse reine! Ô destin que j'abhorre!

JOCASTE
Ne plaignez que mon fils, puisqu'il respire encore,
Prêtres, et vous Thébains, qui fûtes mes sujets,
Honorez mon bûcher, et songez à jamais,
Qu'au milieu des horreurs du destin qui m'opprime,
J'ai fait rougir les dieux qui m'ont forcée au crime.[54]

In this final scene, not only does Jocasta assert her virtuousness, but she also reclaims her political power. This is the inverse of the opening scene of the tragedy in which two friends, two men, have an intimate conversation with one another. The last scene is very public. The spectator no longer feels like a voyeur peeking into a closed-off scene: They feel like a true part of the crowd. Jocasta uses her death to criticize the gods, and she does so in front of her subjects. She reminds the people of Thebes, as well as those in the audience, that she is in charge of her own death, and that this death should bring people into a sense of community with one another—and against the gods.

Much like Roxane's suicide at the end of the *Lettres persanes*, Jocasta's suicide calls for the righting of a wrong. At this point, the stage upon which emancipation occurs is transposed onto the spectators. Once

54. Voltaire, *Œdipe*, p.254.

again, this suicide signals the failure of a kind of patriarchy that relies on outmoded traditions. The erasure of these women's desires throughout both Montesquieu's novel and Voltaire's tragedy causes a rupture between the imaginary world of the patriarchs and the lived world of the heroines—a rupture that eventually forces the reader/spectator to reckon with the supreme inequalities and violences of the patriarchal system. These women's refusal to be contained and controlled (by patriarchs or gods) demonstrates the failure of the laws (both those of the land and the Law of the Symbolic Order) to account for a changing world. In both pieces, we witness a *demos* in flux; the structure of the novel and the play invites us to sense a certain equality between characters that does not exist in content, and the content demonstrates the individual desires of each. The deaths of these women at the end may signal, as Loraux claims, a point of relative gender equality. What is more radical, however, is that they first demand it in life.

Voltaire's *Œdipe* undoubtedly tells a different story from Sophocles's *Oedipus Rex* or Corneille's *Œdipe*, because what the people needed was an old story made new. Following the loss of the Sun King, Voltaire chose to return to the story of the *Son* King, demonstrating how power and laws might look different if we alter the relationality between members of his intimate network of family and friends. By augmenting the characters of Philoctetes and Jocasta, the playwright moves themes of kinship and intimacy from the motivating forces to the main plot. Power still resides in the king who ultimately outlives his mother/wife, but he nevertheless requires the support of others. Much as Voltaire will do years later in *The Age of Louis XIV*, he transforms this ancient tale about a devastated and lonely king into a story about the people of Thebes. In his next play, the playwright will take an even bigger risk—killing off the belligerent king altogether. This unexpected death, however, does not alter intimate relations in ways that we might expect. Let us now turn to *Artémire* to examine what happens when the king is displaced completely, and the queen's voice dictates the actions of the play.

On the heels of *Œdipe*'s success, Voltaire wrote another tragedy featuring an unhappy king and queen, *Artémire*. In the play, the eponymous heroine is unhappily married to Cassandre, the king of Macedonia. As in *Œdipe*, a lover long believed to be dead is revived, so to speak, as Philotas returns to Larissa to find the woman to whom he has remained faithful during his absence (Artémire). Given the unusual choices of names and the invented nature of the story, this seems to be one of Voltaire's earliest risky literary experiments, but, because of its incomplete and fragmented nature, and because of its complete lack of success, critics have largely neglected the playwright's second attempt at tragedy. When mentioned in scholarly studies on the author, it is often evoked either to highlight its failure, or to discuss the playwright's affair with Adrienne Lecouvreur who played the title role.[55] It is, indeed, difficult to judge the play's artistic value given that the existing fragments are passed on only secondhand (through editors' notes); however, fitting the pieces together and imagining what might have filled those missing gaps will help us to understand the important questions the playwright raises about the legitimacy of dynastic rule.

Like *Œdipe*, the first act of *Artémire* also opens onto a scene of intimate conversation between two friends, except this time the two friends are women. Artémire is alone with her friend, Céphise, discussing her fear at the return of her husband, Cassandre. Although she is the queen, she explains to Céphise that, at the hands of her husband, she is a slave:

> A slave in my own palace, I wait here for my master;
> Excuse me, I could not call him my husband.

> Esclave en mon palais, j'attends ici mon maître;
> Pardonne, je n'ai pu le nommer mon époux.[56]

The conversation continues as Artémire provides a long list of atrocities committed by Cassandre—among the most egregious are the murders first of her father (after he had arranged the marriage of his daughter to his assassin) and then of her lover, Philotas. The first act, therefore, introduces a love triangle similar to the one we saw in Voltaire's first tragedy. There is a king, a lover, and a queen, and in both cases the lover is believed to be dead only to return unexpectedly.

The structural similarities between the two plays mask vast

---

55. Aside from a few scant references, the play has rarely been studied. Some studies that mention the play (and its failure) are Isabelle Degauque's *Les Tragédies de Voltaire au miroir de leurs parodies dramatiques: d'Œdipe (1718) à Tancrède (1760)* (Paris, 2007), and Thomas Wynn's "Collaboration and authorship in eighteenth-century French theater," *Romanic review* 103:3–4 (2012), p.465–81. For more information on the affair between the playwright and the actress see, Ian Davidson, *Voltaire, a life* (New York, 2010), especially ch.4.

56. Voltaire, *Artémire*, ed. D. Jory and J. Renwick, in *OCV*, vol.1A, p.409–61 (412).

differences in content. Unlike Philoctetes, Philotas does not renounce his love for the queen out of duty to the king. Cassandre appears as a truly despised king, so much so that even his most trusted confidant, Pallante, plots against him, trying to convince Artémire to conspire with him against the king. Unlike Oedipus, Cassandre is truly alone. It is not incestuous relations that render nominal signifiers confusing in this play, but rather the king's detachment from others and, by extension, from humanity itself. Artémire often talks of forgetting to call her husband by the proper title. She calls him "master," "unworthy," and "barbarian," among other names, but she consistently refuses to call him her husband. The detachment of the familial signifier (husband) from the character demonstrates from the beginning a symbolic order in disarray, and thus a fragility of patriarchal law.

The symbolic laws may be in trouble, but the heroine is still beholden to the tragic form. In true tragic style, she refuses to break her vows. She may be married to a monster, but the bonds of marriage are the law she is bound to follow. Like Philoctetes, Artémire respects the word of the law, even if it will bring about her death; in fact, in this play she talks about little more than her untimely end to come. After learning that Cassandre has ordered Pallante to kill her, she embraces the idea. One can even sense the disappointment in her words when she learns that her husband has revoked her death sentence. In an address to Cassandre following the reversal of his decision, she states:

> Death has already presented itself to me;
> Without regret I would have accepted it calmly;
> So impatient to spare me, must it be that your hate
> Wanted to reserve for me an even worse fate [than death]?
> Is it not enough that I join my father?
> Does your anger stretch beyond the slaughter?

> La mort à mes regards s'est déjà présentée;
> Tranquille et sans regret je l'aurais acceptée;
> Faut-il que votre haine, ardente à me sauver,
> Pour un sort plus affreux m'ait voulu réserver?
> N'était-ce pas assez de me joindre à mon père?
> Au-delà de la mort étend-on sa colère?[57]

57. Voltaire, *Artémire*, p.445.

Much like the heroines described by Loraux, Artémire understands
the power of her own death. The law of death is the only one that
can supersede the king's law. And yet, Artémire is different from
the heroines of ancient Greece; the protagonist of Voltaire's modern
tragedy does have a voice, and she uses it throughout the play to
promote virtue.

As innovative as this play may have been, it was a failure. Voltaire
succeeded in writing a modern tragedy, but the people were not
impressed by it. This is likely in part due to a combination of high
expectations after *Œdipe* and a lackluster plot that involved few
of the dramatic elements that characterized the ancient tragedies.
As Voltaire had hoped, the play focused less on the mythical and
more on the mundane. The heroes faced worldly problems such as
treachery, mistrust, and jealousy, breaking away from the gods and
their interference in human affairs. Public desire to bring stories down
to earth, so to speak, might have been a miscalculation on Voltaire's
part. But what if the playwright was not writing the wrong play, but
just writing the right play at the wrong time? Both plays offer new
takes on what we now call the Oedipus complex.[58] They each examine
the circulation of desire and the difficulties it encounters along the
way, and both locate the circulation of desire within the familial
drama. Freud's initial formulation taught us about desire and the role
of paternal prohibition, and Lacan's reformulation taught us about the
language and circulation of desire; but what might we learn about the
Oedipus complex from these two plays?

First, each of Voltaire's plays alters the role of the women in the
oedipal transfer of power. In a traditional construction, the woman
serves merely as a conduit for paternal power. She is the locus
of desire, and becomes the object that enables the transfer of the
name and power from one male to another. In Sophocles's *Oedipus*,
the diminished role of Jocasta and her early death reinforce her
powerless position. Further, the king's desire to tear out her womb,
the site of sexual reproduction as well as the site of the transfer of
paternal power, signifies the woman's role as mere vessel and object
of desire. In Voltaire's plays, however, the woman takes an active
role in the circulation of power. In *Œdipe* the mother/wife offers the

---

58. It is important to note, as Lacan reminds us, that Oedipus never completes
an oedipal crisis, and neither does Cassandre or any of the characters of these
plays. Their stories provide the bases upon which inquiry into the human psyche
is founded but they are not instructional manuals to be followed.

last word, invoking her own power against that of the gods, and, in *Artémire*, the protagonist is rewarded for her virtue with her life and the understanding of a husband just before she is freed of him. The woman, in this construction, plays a vital and active role. She is the object of desire, but the desire is decidedly *not* the transfer of paternal power through reproduction—instead it is the desire for enlightenment itself. By seizing language in the final moments of the play, the women alter the tragic stories spectators had come to know. The woman's role is not reduced only to a vessel for death or biological reproduction—these women are the bearers of knowledge. Jocasta's children (of Oedipus's issue) remain unnamed, and Artémire has no children with Cassandre. These plays do not propose a future for the children; they embrace the political importance of sharing knowledge and power in the here and now.

In the end, it is Cassandre, that ill-suited leader, who dies and not the virtuous Artémire. Here virtue is rewarded both with life and with compassion from a husband who finally learns the importance of tempering his bellicose nature on his deathbed. Whereas Oedipus declared that a true leader should die for his people, Cassandre actually does it. His death symbolizes the death of a certain symbolic, and yet the hanging ending means that there is nothing yet to fill it. Much like those brothers of the revolution that Lynn Hunt describes, who have killed off the patriarch but have no clear idea of how to fill the vacuum of power left in his absence, this play alerts the spectator that something is wrong in a system that favors the views of one man over an entire nation, but we, as readers of a future time, do not know how or if he proposed to fix it.[59] Even if we cannot know how to fill the king's absence, the mere death of the king allows us to think about how to do so. That is the revolutionary quality of this play—it is about opening up the space for thinking about a change to the symbolic order as we know it. Morality is not something dictated and decreed by one man: It is something that is discussed, evaluated, and frequently reassessed.

Loosening the reign of patriarchy

In letter 112, Rhédi asks several questions of Usbek that will lead to a long discussion about world populations. He writes, "Perhaps you have not noticed something which continually surprises me. Why is

59. See Hunt, *The Family romance*.

it that the world is so thinly populated in comparison with former times? How is it that nature has managed to lose the prodigious fertility that she had originally? Could she be already in old age, and failing from lack of strength?"[60] Usbek's response will fill the next ten letters and will include thoughts on disease, climate, and, most of all, sex. In Muslim countries that allow men to have multiple wives, men are having too much sex; in Christian countries that prohibit divorce, people are not having enough; and religious practices in both cultures render a large portion of the population useless for the reproduction of the species anyway. Put differently, while the novel is famous for its sensual depictions of life in the harem, the author never talks about sex more than when theorizing about demography. In the relationship between the book and its reading public, sex serves as a method of drawing the reader in, inviting them to peek voyeuristically into a scene of sensual pleasure. Within the philosophical logic of the story, however, sex serves a much more practical purpose—as a way to think about reproduction, populations, and, therefore, as a way to think about social politics and the laws that govern populations.

In Voltaire's plays, sex is never discussed by the main characters and is only alluded to by the great priest who prophesizes the incestuous relationship between Oedipus and Jocasta. Sex plays almost no role at all in *Artémire*, and in *Œdipe* it plays a role only in its reproductive qualities. In each of the works explored in this chapter, therefore, sex is rarely mentioned but undeniably important to the process of reproduction. And yet, for all the talk of reproduction and repopulating the earth (especially in Montesquieu), the products of those acts—children—are rarely discussed in relation to parents and family. Oedipus's kinship is invoked as a transgression against nature, the children produced from his union with Jocasta are mentioned but never named, and, although we know that Usbek has one child (a girl), she is only briefly mentioned in one letter from Zélis to Usbek.[61] In short, in spite of Montesquieu's concern with repopulating the earth, the products of repopulation are nowhere to be seen. The future for

---

60. Montesquieu, *Persian letters*, p.202; *Lettres persanes*, p.246. "Tu n'as peut-être pas fait attention à une chose qui cause tous les jours ma surprise. Comment le monde est-il si peu peuplé, en comparaison de ce qu'il était autrefois? Comment la nature a-t-elle pu perdre cette prodigieuse fécondité des premiers temps? Serait-elle déjà dans sa vieillesse? et tomberait-elle de langueur?"

61. In letter 62, Zélis proposes to Usbek that they bring the daughter into the seraglio at age seven rather than waiting for the child's tenth birthday.

these authors is made possible by reproduction, but the child as a living subject is ultimately unimportant.

The exclusion of children makes sense following what we know of childhood from scholars such as sociologist Philippe Ariès. In *Centuries of childhood*, Ariès explains the evolution of the concept of the child as it moves from being paternal property to a distinct and cherished living being.[62] Due to a number of factors including high infant mortality rates (coupled with a bad understanding of bacteria and germs), expectations of laboring families, social expectations of aristocratic women, and educational expectations, among many others, children in earlier times did not perform the affective labor they now do of inviting us to imagine the future. If the child is not meant to be our ultimate focus in these tales that appear to be intimately wrapped up in social reproduction, then this allows us to look more closely at that which is being produced in these novels and plays—the stories themselves. By reading these works queerly, we can see in their pages a gestation period for a reproduction of another sort. Theories of social reproduction do emerge from them, although that reproduction is not dependent upon heterosexual, childbearing relations.

Up until this point, our readings of Voltaire and Montesquieu have focused largely on the ways in which the patriarch finds himself in crisis when his family falls apart. To read the works from beginning to end is to witness, in one sense, the crumbling infrastructure of patriarchy. However, instead of focusing on the fall of the great patriarch, I would like to examine what we are left with in the end by performing a reading in reverse; that is, by starting at the culminating events of these plays and novels (the death of the wife or the blinding of the king) and working our way backward, we can better understand the structures that existed, and maybe we will find that they were never so stable to begin with.

Artémire is the sole work we have discussed thus far that does not end with the death of a wife. Instead, the virtuous heroine lives to see the death of the cruel and belligerent husband who has caused her so much pain. But, of course, there is a twist; at the time of his death, Cassandre realizes the error of his ways and repents for the atrocities he has committed. In true tragic fashion, this brief apology on the deathbed is enough to satisfy Artémire. As Cassandre laments that

---

62. See Philippe Ariès, *Centuries of childhood: a social history of family life*, translated by Robert Baldick (New York, 1960).

he has to leave his wife on the very day he has realized her worth, Artémire responds,

> O! My Lord, since you finally value virtue,
> Live, deign to enjoy the days that enlighten you.
> I still belong to you in spite of your cruelty;
> Your virtuous remorse brought my husband back to me.
> Live in order to erase Pallante's crimes;
> Live to protect an innocent wife;
> Don't lose any time, accept that a prompt recovery...

> Ah! seigneur, puisqu'enfin la vertu vous est chère,
> Vivez, daignez jouir du jour qui vous éclaire.
> Malgré vos cruautés je suis encore à vous;
> Vos remords vertueux m'ont rendu mon époux.
> Vivez pour effacer les crimes de Pallante;
> Vivez pour protéger une épouse innocente;
> Ne perdez point de temps, souffrez qu'un prompt secours...[63]

As the hanging rhyme suggests, we do not—and will never—hear the last lines of the play. The last bit of the fragment we read is simply a sentence indicating the action taking place on the stage; Cassandre dies after pardoning Philotas and bringing justice (*rendre justice*) to the queen. This is exactly the ending that we, as modern readers, may have expected—the evil king dies leaving the protagonist to marry her true love. This is not, it seems, what contemporary audiences had in mind. According to the rules of courtly society, the evil had been rectified; the king apologized, and the queen remained true to the promise she had made him, in spite of years of a terrible marriage. The real tragedy in this play, then, is the fact that the king dies just when all should have been right.

The disappointment with this play among Voltaire's contemporaries can be explained both by theatergoers' ever-changing expectations and by the playwright's subversion of the tragic genre. The rise of reason in the eighteenth century encountered a fascination with sentimentality. Both of these elements are exhibited plainly in this piece, but they compete with one another for domination and, as any theatergoer knows (and as Voltaire admits himself in letters), spectators care little for reason in the face of raw emotions.[64] Having spent five

---

63. Voltaire, *Artémire*, p.461.
64. Voltaire writes, "It seems to me that, if you find you have not quite mastered

acts witnessing Cassandre's evil deeds and learning of Artémire's love for Philotas, to have that all reversed in the last soliloquy of the tragedy subverts emotional expectations. Yet in another way it completely fulfills the expectations of the tragicomedy. Much like Auguste in Corneille's *Cinna*, Cassandre ends the play on a benevolent note. He declares his love and admiration for his wife, and pardons his enemy and sexual competitor. By confounding the tragedy and the tragicomedy at the last minute, Voltaire performs a bait and switch, leaving spectators in the awkward position of not quite knowing what they should be feeling.

To read the play in reverse would be to alter the moral of the story dramatically. We would see a benevolent king betrayed by the woman he loves as he falls deeper and deeper into a tyrannical state. In fact, to read the *Lettres persanes* or *Œdipe* in this same fashion would tell us a very similar tale; men betrayed by the women they love (or claim to love) deal with the betrayal by meticulously managing the affairs of their households (or kingdoms). To read these texts queerly allows the reader to retroactively attach signifieds to signifiers, adding new meaning to what we thought we understood. The suspension of disbelief in the reader/spectator is made possible by joining the fictional patriarchs in their complete obliviousness to what is happening around them. Incapable of understanding the language that takes place throughout the novels and plays—language that foreshadows the downfall of their houses—these protagonists exist only in the present, thinking of how society might be shaped to better support the structures of family and government in existence.

One of the few instances in which the illusion of presentism is broken in *Lettres persanes* occurs in the last letter (in order of publication) written by Usbek, letter 155. As he writes to his friend Nessir in Ispahan, he laments the exile which has kept him away from his home (*patrie*) for so long. He wishes to be back in the land of his enemies if only to see his friends and wives. The discussion of his harem, though, centers not on a love for the wives, but rather on an

---

the art, you should always strive to be interesting rather than exact, for the spectator forgives everything, except boredom, and once he finds himself moved [by the play], he rarely stops to examine if he should have been" ("Il me semble que, lorsqu'on se trouve si peu maître du terrain, il faut toujours songer à être intéressant plutôt qu'exact: car le spectateur pardonne tout, hors la langueur; et lorsqu'il est une fois ému, il examine rarement s'il a raison de l'être"). Voltaire, "Lettres," p.367.

anxiety he feels that all might be going terribly wrong in his absence. This letter is littered with questions about what would happen should he return: "if I find any of them [the wives] guilty, what will become of me? If the mere idea of it appalls me when I am so far away, what will it be like when I am present and it is more vivid?"[65] He continues to question his potential future responses to events that, we will soon learn, are actually happening in his harem as he writes. This letter serves as a wink to the reader, who is already aware of some of what is taking place in the seraglio in his absence, but it also serves a much more important purpose: In placing the patriarch's worries about the disorder of his house alongside what we know to be a disorder in the letters, it also binds together different temporal registers, rendering Paris and Ispahan closer than ever. His worries about what might be happening in his own household are imposed upon precisely what is happening in the household that is France at that very moment. Thus, it is not only the allusions to French aristocratic society that make this novel so important politically; to understand its full political import, it is also crucial to pay attention to the form.

The gap between the novel's content and its form in a letter that Rica writes to Usbek (in which he recounts the story of a Persian tale he has invented for a French woman) presents a particularly telling conundrum. As McAlpin points out, letter 141 serves as a microcosm of the novel itself with its plurivocality, embedded tales, and disparate opinions.[66] In this letter, Rica recounts to Usbek a story that he sent to a French aristocratic woman, passing it off as a Persian tale. The woman, whom he had met at a party and who had bombarded him with "thousands of questions about the ways of Persian men and the life of Persian women," asked Rica to tell her tales from his home country. She was particularly interested in learning more about the harems, which she found distasteful; "She was unable to contemplate the happiness of the one without envy and the state of the others without pity."[67] And so he embellishes an old Persian tale in a manner he hopes will be to her liking. In it, he tells of Anaïs, who is killed by

---

65. Montesquieu, *Persian letters*, p.276; *Lettres persanes*, p.335. "Si j'y trouve des coupables, que deviendrai-je? Et si la seule idée m'accable de si loin, que sera-ce, lorsque ma présence la rendra plus vive?"

66. See Mary McAlpin, "Between men for all eternity: feminocentrism in Montesquieu's *Lettres persanes*," *Eighteenth-century life* 24:1 (2000), p.45–61 (45).

67. Montesquieu, *Persian letters*, p.247; *Lettres persanes*, p.302. "[M]ille questions sur les mœurs des Persans, et sur la manière de vivre des Persanes," "Elle ne put voir, sans envie, le bonheur de l'un; et sans pitié, la condition des autres."

her husband, Ibrahim, for speaking out against him. In death, she is carried away to her own harem, where men who have been created for her desire please her over and over again. Because she has promised to save the wives she left behind at the harem from the cruelty of their master, she sends one of her sex slaves back to the real world disguised as Ibrahim himself. Once he arrives, the double sends the real Ibrahim to a place far away. After the real harem has been transformed into a place of female delight by empowering the women with unheard of freedom and by ensuring their continual sexual satisfaction, the real Ibrahim returns home to find that his happy wives have produced thirty-six children with the imposter.

The story itself seems a very liberating one—women who have freedom and satisfaction in marriage will not only be happy, they will also fulfill more readily their wifely duties of reproduction. However, this letter serves as a microcosm for the book also in the departure of content from form for, as McAlpin points out, the story that we read here is reproduced in a letter from one man to another. The construction of the letter, therefore, reminds us of the structure of the Freudian joke; the fun can be had only at the expense of the one (woman) who is excluded.[68] The receiver of the original story had asked for a true Persian tale and believes she has received one. Instead, however, she hears a tale altered by Rica—its true form known only to Rica and Usbek. Even the reader remains oblivious to the tale's original source.[69] The letter we read, which seems like a feminine utopia in content, serves instead to shore up masculine homosociality. In this instance, the disjunction between content and form forces us to reckon with some of the most difficult problems in imagining space for female sovereignty within patriarchal regimes. The series of dead wives that includes Anaïs and Roxane appears to disrupt masculine narratives of power by inserting their agency into the story. While their ultimate erasure allows for the continued rule of men, the ambiguous message communicated by their lives and deaths is one of the features that makes the novel so worthy of inclusion in the current discussion. Given the novel's abrupt ending, we can only imagine what

68. In Freud's theory of humor, a joke is passed between two men and requires the exclusion of a third party (most often a woman), at whose expense the joke is being made. Joking is then one of the foundational pieces of male homosociality.
69. McAlpin points out that, while there are hints alerting the reader to the fraudulent nature of the story, the source material of the letter is never revealed. See McAlpin, "Between men for all eternity."

will happen next for Usbek and Rica, but the disjointed nature of the novel, which offers letters like pieces of an epistemological puzzle meant to be put back together, allows us to imagine an ending that reproduces society in extrapatriarchal formations. The patriarch of this novel is not dead, but we can at least imagine a world in which patriarchy just might be.

If, as Cassirer argues, Enlightenment philosophers saw their job as one of archaeology, removing the rubble of time and history to find the solid foundations of modern society, in these works, we can almost see its inverse. As the houses crumble, the wreckage piles around the defunct patriarchs, falling into place and forming a thick layer of sediment through which future authors will wade to find what had been beneath all along. The sediment that forms confuses concepts often believed to be nearly as old as language itself such as father, wife, and child. As Jay Caplan argues, meanings of such terms begin to shift before subjects and philosophers can even begin to contemplate the meanings that might take their place.[70] What rises from these ruins is not anything solid but rather more questions, or, as Usbek puts it, "what will it be like, finally, if I have to pronounce verdicts which will be a permanent record of my shame and despair?"[71] The world may, in Montesquieu's opinion, need desperately to be repopulated, but the work of organizing and governing those ever-increasing populations will be the work of philosophers for years to come.

Toward a queer politics of kinship

In each of the works analyzed in this chapter, patriarchy is presented as an extremely ambivalent category. Usbek is the supreme ruler of his household, but he remains impotent as his harem crumbles around him; Cassandre shows himself to be a dynamic character, capable of reason and change; and Oedipus must continue to rule even after having lost everything that is most important to him. The ambivalence might help us to bring together the anti-relational queer theories discussed in the introduction to this chapter with its more futural (anti-anti-relational) interlocutors to which I will turn more intently in the next chapter. There is a certain foreclosure of the future in works

---

70. Caplan, *In the king's wake*.
71. Montesquieu, *Persian letters*, p.276; *Lettres persanes*, p.335. "Que sera-ce enfin, s'il faut que des châtiments, que je prononcerai moi-même, soient des marques éternelles de ma confusion et de mon désespoir?"

that end in death and the destruction of heterosexual ideals of family. In content, these works gesture to nothing outside of the here and now of kinship relations. In form, however, we can sense the utopia of what Muñoz describes as a more akin to a not-yet-here for, as he states, "queer aesthetics map future social relations."[72] The aesthetics of these plays and novels extends beyond their content, and even beyond the political imagination of Voltaire and Montesquieu. The two authors who argued in their nonfictional political writings that the best replacement for a bad king was a better, more enlightened one opened up the space in their fictional productions for future writers to imagine what might happen if there was no king at all.

Since Clovis I united the Frankish tribes, the people of what would later become known as the kingdom, and then the republic, of France had been ruled by a king. The crown, which was passed down through many men from many dynasties, represented familial rule in France. The family might change and with it the country's political ambitions, but the patriarch, as the corporeal representative of the Divine, had long been the ultimate symbol of France. To imagine anything outside of this would be not only treasonous, but also incredibly difficult. Such a task was made more difficult after Louis XIV's consolidation of power at Versailles. It is unsurprising, therefore, that early Enlightenment thinkers would imagine futures in which the king was not replaced but the position was reformed. The politics of kinship, for these *philosophes*, would naturally be framed around a politics of patriarchy. However, sometimes subversive elements, those that will slowly and subtly lead to the downfall of seemingly invincible institutions, emerge in spite of the authors' intentions. A queer politics of kinship is an optimistic one and one that is fleeting and ultimately based upon failure. The failure of the patriarchs in the stories of Montesquieu and Voltaire, the failure to articulate a queer form of political engagement, the failure to depict queer communities, signals at least an opening up of the possibilities for something new. This allows for an optimism of the unknown, the same kind of practical, yet hopeful, optimism that Candide will adopt by the end of his quixotic journey. When there is no possibility to reproduce sameness, something new must emerge, even if these authors remain limited in imagining what that difference might resemble. Imagining the futures that might rise up from these ruins will be the intellectual project of future authors, including those studied in the rest of the chapters of this book.

72. Muñoz, *Cruising utopia*, p.1.

II

Prodigal Sons

2. Oedipus interrupted: Prévost's regime of the brother

> The Oedipal complex being a universal human occurrence, there is no fiction, no representation, no artistic image that is not in some manner a veiled illustration of it.
>
> Le complexe d'Œdipe étant un fait humain universel, il n'y a pas de fiction, pas de représentation, pas d'art de l'image qui n'en soit en quelque manière l'illustration voilée.
>
> Marthe Robert, *Roman des origines et origines du roman*

The endings of Antoine-François Prévost's *Histoire du chevalier Des Grieux et de Manon Lescaut* (*Story of the chevalier Des Grieux and of Manon Lescaut*) (1731) and Honoré de Balzac's *Père Goriot* (1835) bear some striking resemblances. In the last paragraphs of each, a young, solitary man mourns the death of a father, reflects upon the journey that led him to this point, and decides the next steps he will take that will shape the rest of his life. Although the details of the paternal loss and the paths that lead each hero to this endpoint differ vastly, they each offer readers a story of transformation and education in the young, male protagonists. It is no wonder, then, that scholars have long regarded Eugène de Rastignac as an iconic hero of the bildungsroman genre, and also not all that surprising that some have even found in the chevalier Des Grieux an excellent early example of just such a hero.[1]

---

1. Some early and important discussions of the genre expound upon the importance of Balzac's contributions to the formation of the French bildungsroman, particularly through the works that form *La Comédie humaine* (including *Le Père Goriot*). See, for example, Georg Lukács's *Theory of the novel: a historico-philosophical*

Both heroes begin their stories as naive and inexperienced young men, and end them with a much deeper understanding of the world.

However, while most examples of the French bildungsroman emerge from the Romantic tradition of nineteenth-century literature, Prévost's earlier example is decisively different. As Franco Moretti points out, the French bildungsroman is marked by the hero's transformation.[2] According to Moretti, rather than moving toward a fixed outcome as do German and British protagonists, the French hero wanders aimlessly into modernity; it is precisely his *journey*, rather than any ending, that is most valued. He is not meant to mature; instead, he is meant to keep wandering until the very end. Such is not altogether the case for Des Grieux. His wanderings were always meant to come to an end—and a very specific one. As the second son of an aristocratic family in the early eighteenth century, he was destined from the beginning to return to the paternal household (or at least to paternal authority) until the father should die leaving the eldest son to take his place. Unlike Rastignac who plunges headfirst into the abyss of modernity, Des Grieux stands only at modernity's precipice, finding himself momentarily out of time but ultimately pulled back into the traditions of premodernity, however distorted the structure of those traditions may have become since the beginning of his journey.

Much like Des Grieux's account in *Manon*, Rastignac's story also depends greatly upon a patriarch, but the father in Balzac's novel experiences a very different fate from the father of *Manon*. *Père Goriot* demonstrates the slow and painful death of the father. While Goriot's physical death may come swiftly and only at the close of the novel, his story unfolds as the gradual dismantling of patriarchy while his daughters and sons-in-law take both his earthly possessions and his dignity bit by precious bit. Although Goriot is not a biological father to Rastignac, his death leaves a void in the protagonist's life, and the novel's abrupt ending leaves the reader perpetually wondering what

---

essay on the forms of great epic literature (Cambridge, MA, 1971), or Franco Moretti's *The Way of the world: the bildungsroman in European culture* (New York, 2000). Other scholars claim that Enlightenment traditions that valued the search for knowledge were particularly important steps leading to the formation of the bildungsroman, and that Des Grieux's journey in *Manon Lescaut* models an important precursor to the genre. For two notable examples, see Giovanna Summerfield and Lisa Downward, *New perspectives on the European bildungsroman* (London, 2010), and Alison Finch, "The French bildungsroman," in *A History of the bildungsroman*, ed. Sarah Graham (Cambridge, 2019), p.33–56.

2.   Moretti, *Way of the world*, p.7.

will come to fill that void. In short, modern youth is left alone to forge a new path once Oedipus has failed. This sentiment is most powerfully expressed in the last lines of the novel:

> Rastignac, now all alone, walked a few paces to the higher part of the cemetery, and saw Paris spread out along the winding banks of the Seine, where the lights were beginning to shine [...] He gave this murmuring hive a look which seemed already to savour the sweetness to be sucked from it, and pronounced the epic challenge: "It's between the two of us now!"

> Rastignac, resté seul, fit quelques pas vers le haut du cimetière et vit Paris tortueusement couché le long des deux rives de la Seine où commençaient à briller les lumières. [...] Il lança sur cette ruche bourdonnant un regard qui semblait par avance en pomper le miel, et dit ces mots grandioses: "A nous deux maintenant!"[3]

With those words, the protagonist and all of the disaffected youth in the burgeoning capitalist city of Paris are left to reimagine a France without a father figure.

Des Grieux, by contrast, is not alone. He returns to France with his childhood friend, and, once he hears the news of his father's recent death, he decides to return home into the welcoming arms of his older brother. The brother, who has now inherited the father's estate, becomes a figurehead for a new kind of tradition—one that embraces the form of patriarchy, all while rearranging its contents. In other words, rather than a complete toppling of the oedipal triangle such as we see in *Père Goriot*, this novel simply tips it on its side, leaving the triangular structure in place, but flattening out its hierarchal tendencies. What we see in Des Grieux's story, therefore, is the gradual replacement of Oedipus with a system that requires a triangulation of a different sort. This is the system of male homosociality that will begin to restructure social and political relations, eventually replacing patriarchy with brotherhood in late-eighteenth-century France.

The concept of homosociality, as famously introduced by Eve Kosofsky Sedgwick in *Between men*, is structured, much like the oedipal crisis, along the form of a triangle.[4] Sedgwick's triangle, like

---

3. Honoré de Balzac, *Père Goriot*, translated by A. J. Krailsheimer (Oxford, 1991), p.263; *Le Père Goriot* (Paris, 1971), p.367.
4. Eve Kosofsky Sedgwick, *Between men: English literature and male homosocial desire* (New York, 2016).

Freud's, requires two men and one woman, although her focus is less on the subjective formation of one man than on the solidification of masculine bonds through the exchange of, or shared focus on, the woman.[5] Power in this triangle does not necessarily rely on a hierarchy between men (father and son) as it did for Freud and, to a lesser extent, Lacan. Instead, the woman, as symbol of the heterosexual love object, serves to sublimate the more powerful attraction of one man to another. Rather than attaining or maintaining the woman, the objective of this triangle is, therefore, to bring men closer together.

Although nearly all of Prévost's stories deal with plots of heterosexual love, passion, longing, and heartbreak, a thorough reading of them reveals almost unfailingly that male bonding takes precedence over any heterosexual romances. Prévost d'Exiles, as he called himself after leaving France, loved to blend history and thrilling travel narratives. His protagonists traversed the globe, exploring so many corners of the world. In their journeys, the author often translated his own experience of never feeling truly at home.[6] There is one space, however, into which he rarely ventured—that of the female psyche. Of his many novels, only two titles bear the name (or at least the indication of a name to come) of a woman: *Histoire du chevalier Des Grieux et de Manon Lescaut* (1731) and *Histoire d'une Grecque moderne* (*The Greek girl's story*) (1740).[7] That the first of these novels has been more commonly referred to as simply *Manon Lescaut* almost since its publication would seem to reinforce the centrality of a woman to the story being told. And yet, although the stories do follow the adventures of Manon and Zara (who will rename herself Téophé, or "she who loves the gods"), we actually learn very little about the women themselves. What we

5. Sedgwick's work is thus heavily informed by Gayle Rubin's "The traffic in women: notes on the 'political economy' of sex," in *Toward an anthropology of women*, ed. Rayna Reiter (New York, 1975), p.157–210. Rubin's article brings psychoanalysis into conversation with the structural anthropology of Claude Lévi-Strauss to critique the exchange of women that Lévi-Strauss argues is foundational to the formation of Western societies.

6. In *Prévost romancier*, Jean Sgard explains the connection the author feels with his protagonists as an outsider: "Prévost d'Exiles has always been a foreigner, and the heroes in which he sees himself are always more or less exiled. Their work begins once they become aware of their difference; at that point they feel excluded from their family, as orphans or outcasts." See Sgard, *Prévost romancier*, 2nd ed. (Paris, 1989), p.409.

7. I exclude *Histoire de Marguerite d'Anjou* (*The Story of Marguerite d'Anjou*) (1740) from this list because, while it is highly fictionalized, it is presented by the author as a historical account rather than a novel.

learn of Manon's story, as well as that of Téophé, is relegated to their time spent with the male protagonists. All that we learn of them remains suspect, filtered as it is through various male voices. Of the qualities of these two women we know only that they are beautiful and that men easily fall in love with them. In the end, one gets the impression that Manon and Téophé could have been any woman, provided that she was young, beautiful, and had an inescapable allure.

Furthermore, if we take a closer look at the legacy of Prévost's novels, we will find an intriguing paradox: In various retellings and representations of his work, stories of heterosexual romantic intrigue eclipse almost all other aspects of the plots. In fact, one of the reasons that *Manon* offers such a compelling example of familial transformation over time is that its legacy in various artistic endeavors is often contradictory to the author's initial story. In the nineteenth century, for example, three separate composers produced operas based on the novel, and all three were quite popular in their initial runs. French composer Daniel Auber's *Manon Lescaut* was first performed in 1856; almost thirty years later Jules Massenet's *Manon* appeared on the stage (1884); and in 1893 Giacomo Puccini's *Manon Lescaut* (which is still frequently staged in opera houses today) was performed for the first time in Turin. Although the plot of each of these operas borrows from the novel to varying degrees, they each end with the same famous scene—the moment of Manon's death in Louisiana when a weeping Des Grieux laments the loss of his true love. In each opera Manon is played by a soprano who performs a series of emotionally charged arias. The story that emerges from these operas is one of true and passionate love between a young man and woman against all odds. In Prévost's novel, however, Manon remains little more than a faint presence. Her inescapable allure and her love affairs structure the novel, and yet she hardly speaks throughout. In other words, the operas demonstrate a desire for heteronormative love above all other forms of intimacy that, as we shall see later in this chapter, could only have emerged after the February Revolution of 1848, which solidified in many respects the transformation of male homosociality from a social to a political practice in France. The Manon of the nineteenth-century stage is a willing participant in this love affair. Conversely, as Naomi Segal points out, the eighteenth-century novel's story requires that men talk about the heroine in her absence.[8] Segal writes of the

8. Segal points out that this follows the structure of the Freudian joke. See Naomi Segal, *The Unintended reader: feminism and Manon Lescaut* (New York, 1986).

novel that it is "a text full of men and a communication between men."[9] In the novel, Manon's voice is remarked only in its absence.

Although *Histoire d'une Grecque moderne* offers more dialogue between Téophé and her male interlocutors than *Manon*, she too is remarked largely in her absence. In fact, the novel's very first lines inform us that we cannot trust what the narrator says about the Greek girl:

> Will I not arouse suspicion by the very confession that serves as my introduction? I was in love with the beautiful Greek girl whose story I begin here. Who will believe the sincerity of this account of my pleasures or of my suffering? Who will not be skeptical about my descriptions and my praise? Will my violent passion not distort everything that passes through my eyes or hands? In short, how much objectivity can one expect from a pen guided by love?

> Ne me rendrai-je point suspect par l'aveu qui va faire mon exorde? Je suis l'amant de la belle Grecque dont j'entreprends l'histoire. Qui me croira sincère dans le récit de mes plaisirs ou de mes peines? Qui ne se défiera point de mes descriptions et de mes éloges? Une passion violente ne fera-t-elle point changer de nature à tout ce qui va passer par mes yeux ou par mes mains? En un mot, quelle fidélité attendra-t-on d'une plume conduite par l'amour?[10]

As we will discover in the last lines of the novel, Téophé, like Manon before her, is already dead before the narrator begins writing the story. What we read, then, is a memory of the Greek girl in her ultimate absence. If all that we know of Téophé and of what she says and does comes from the Ambassador who narrates the story, and if this narrator is not to be trusted because of his violent passion for her, then how are we to believe that she speaks at all? Are her words not also those of a man who speaks, by and large, to other men? In both novels the women's voices serve merely as conduits for altering relations between men and are, therefore, crucial to reorganizing both forms of power and the very structure of male subjectivity and homosociality.

In Prévost's literature, fiction mingles with history, resulting in novels that become entangled in contemporary political debates.

---

9.   Segal, *The Unintended reader*, p.126.
10. Antoine Prévost, *The Greek girl's story*, translated by Alan J. Singerman (University Park, PA, 2014), p.29; *Histoire d'une Grecque moderne*, in *Œuvres de Prévost*, vol.4, ed. Allan Holland (Grenoble, 1978), p.11–121 (11).

Readers recognized in *Grecque moderne* the story of Charles de Ferriol, a French diplomat who served in Turkey and returned to France with a very young girl, Charlotte Aïssé, with whom he was rumored to be in love.[11] And while *Manon* is not a *roman à clef*, it is the only one of Prévost's novels in which the narrative ventures beyond Louis XIV's reign and into the time of the Regency.[12] Historical events thus provide the backdrop for his stories; however, his focus on historical events through the lens of erotic encounters allows for a reading of the function of desire in the creation of the political subject. For both Des Grieux and the Ambassador the introduction of the desired and desirable woman threatens to fracture the subjective identity each had constructed prior to the first encounter, thereby causing a prolonged state of anxiety. Their stories cannot exclude women because they are perpetually haunted by the ghosts of the women who have shaped their desire. In this chapter we will take a close look at the ghosts of Prévost's dead women and see what stories they tell us from beyond the grave. How do their presences, as well as their absences, interrupt the transfer of masculine power? And furthermore, how do they alter or disrupt networks of male desire in ways that confuse both gender and sexuality, and allow for the exploration of new models of both patriarchy and brotherhood?

What is crucial to understanding masculine subjectivity and relations between men in Prévost's *Manon Lescaut* and *Histoire d'une Grecque moderne* (and remains completely lacking in the operas briefly mentioned above) is the attention given to depictions both of the oedipal crisis and of an affirmation of homosocial bonds between men, including most importantly the gradual replacement of the former by the latter. For this, and other reasons to be elaborated over the course of this chapter, I argue that *Manon Lescaut* and *Grecque moderne* tell essentially the same story written from two different perspectives. Both tell the stories of men who fall desperately in love with women whom they will follow until those women are dead. In both novels,

11. Françoise de Graffigny reveals the similarities between the two stories in a letter to her friend François-Antoine Devaux, writing that she has just read the novel and stating, "it's believed to be the story of Father Pontevel [Ferriol], who was ambassador to the Porte" ("On prétend que c'est l'histoire du père de Pontevel [Ferriol], qui a été ambassadeur à la Porte"). See Graffigny to Devaux, 19 September 1740 (letter 307), in *Correspondance de Mme de Graffigny*, ed. J. A. Dainard *et al.* (Oxford, 1985–2018), vol.2, p.448.

12. Louis XIV's death occurs when Des Grieux and Manon are in America. The protagonist returns, therefore, to a France under Philippe II's regency.

the women try to escape through various means (for Manon this takes the form of other affairs, for Téophé this means several requests to go to a convent), only to have their desire to leave ignored by the men who claim to love them. Finally, while both women are traded from one man to the next during their lives, the exchange of these women becomes even more valuable after their deaths when their stories are exchanged in the same ways their bodies had been previously. Stripped of their subjectivity, these women become little more than objects of desire in a world made for men. These are both novels that announce by their titles the story of a woman but that ultimately reaffirm relations between men. Prévost thus plays a crucial role in defining what will later be known as sociable brotherhood.

Liberty, equality... fragility?

The February Revolution of 1848 led to the fall of the Orléans monarchy and resulted in the creation of the Second Republic. Having overthrown King Louis Philippe, the majority of French Republicans once and for all embraced the term that would become the third part of France's tripartite motto, *fraternité* (fraternity), as a concept capable of uniting all citizens.[13] The term was officially added to the constitution and fraternity was even celebrated with its own festival, "La fête de la fraternité," which took place on April 20, 1848. As Jean-Claude Caron points out, fraternity became a unifying term because it overrode other divisive categories such as class, race, and gender.[14] Although the term was not officially added to the French constitution until 1848, fraternity had served as an organizing

13. The term *fraternité* had, and continues to have, a difficult history in France. It first emerged after the 1789 Revolution, but during the Terror became quickly associated with Robespierre's call for "fraternity or death" (*la fraternité ou la mort*). Its association with exclusionary (and deadly) practices rendered it a poor fit for the motto of a French democratic republic based on liberty and equality. Battles over the term continued to surface until its adoption in 1848. For more information on the history of this term see Mona Ozouf, "Fraternité," in *Dictionnaire critique de la Révolution française*, ed. Mona Ozouf and François Furet (Paris, 1988); Florence Gauthier, *Triomphe et mort du droit en Révolution 1789–1795–1802* (Paris, 1992); and Marcel David, *Fraternité et Révolution française* (Paris, 1987).

14. Jean-Claude Caron, "La fraternité face à la question sociale dans la France des années 1830," in *Fraternité: regards croisés*, ed. Frédéric Brahami and Odile Roynette (Besançon, 2009), p.135–57.

principle of the French Republican citizenry since at least 1792.[15] In the years following the Revolution of 1789 questions began to arise in the newly elected National Convention on what actions, precisely, should be taken against the defunct king, Louis XVI. Many wondered who could try the king and how it could be done; the most pressing question, however, was whether or not he should be executed. Some argued against such action, fearing this would only replicate the kinds of violence they hoped the regime change would eliminate. But these Republican brothers, like the brothers of *Totem and taboo*, eventually tried and executed the king in 1792. Patriarchy, it must have seemed to the executioners back then, was dead.[16]

Of course, the return of various forms of monarchy over the course of the next hundred years attested to the lingering power of patriarchy, even from beyond the grave. Such relapses can be explained, at least in part, by the anxiety that began to reign in the absence of the king. As Lynn Hunt demonstrates, much of the political and artistic production of the years following the king's execution betrayed the lingering anxiety over what could replace the monarchy. Fathers and mothers began to disappear from stories, she claims, replaced by tales and images of brothers and sisters. *Fraternité* became the term that many hoped would explain the governmental shift in familiar (and familial) terms that could be easily understood by the public. Fathers admonished and punished their children; brothers, they believed, were equals within the family who got along with and helped one another—each encouraging the liberty of the other. Once anxiety creeps in, however, it is difficult to maintain a sense of utopian egalitarianism. Hunt explains:

> Republicans tried hard to imagine a world for themselves in which brothers got along peacefully with each other; they even tried to ensure it in legal terms by equalizing inheritance and providing for a system of universal education. Nevertheless, competition, conflict, and violence between brothers was an undeniable fact of life during the Revolution. To explain the continuing threat of failure to achieve liberty, equality, and fraternity, republicans looked for and found enemies everywhere. The Terror was invented as a system for forcing them into submission.[17]

---

15. See Mona Ozouf, "Liberté, égalité, fraternité," in *Les Lieux de mémoire*, vol.3, ed. Pierre Nora (Paris, 1992), p.583–629.
16. For a thorough study of the debates that occurred surrounding the decision to execute Louis XVI, see Hunt's *Family romance*.
17. Hunt, *The Family romance*, p.88.

Simply put, the anxiety produced in the father's absence led to precisely the types of violence the brothers had hoped to avoid—and this on a massive scale. In the span of just one year, over 16,000 French citizens were sentenced to death during the Reign of Terror.

While anxiety spread among brothers regarding who should rule and how, it also spread to those populations excluded from Republican notions of brotherhood such as women and slaves. In the past several decades, scholars have critiqued the supposed universality of brotherhood, reminding us of all those not protected by such a political system.[18] Fraternity assumes that it is up to the sons, and not the daughters, to take up the mantle of the deceased father; brotherhood, by nature, excludes the sister. As Juliet Flower MacCannell argues, "negating the relation to the past is not the only feature of the Regime of the Brother. It must also deny the sister."[19] Her analysis begins with those famous brothers of *Totem and taboo* whose oedipal desire leads them to kill the father.[20] In the father's absence, desire transforms into guilt, which leads to a prohibition among the brothers of any and all incestuous relations. MacCannell argues that the true danger (for women at least) of this regime lies in the brother's lack of symbolic power. Having killed off the superego he becomes the ego ideal. This brother who lacks power must still act *as if* he has power, making his power untenable and unstable. In order to create an aura of symbolic power, he must work harder than the father to retain it; it is for this reason that the regime of the brother turns out to be worse for women than patriarchy. The brother possesses a supremely narcissistic ego that answers to no one.

The regime of the brother is so pernicious, MacCannell argues, that it is to be blamed for the failure of modern democratic societies to live up to Enlightenment promises of universal liberty and equality. Indeed, brotherhood works as a unifying concept for nation-states precisely because it defines the boundaries of a nation by the land and peoples excluded from it. These are the same exclusionary practices

---

18. See for instance Joan B. Landes, *Women and the public sphere in the age of the French Revolution* (Ithaca, NY, 1988); Annie Smart, *Citoyennes: women and the ideal of citizenship in eighteenth-century France* (Newark, NJ, 2011); Nick Nesbitt, *Universal emancipation*; and Garraway, *The Libertine colony*.

19. Juliet Flower MacCannell, *The Regime of the brother: after the patriarchy* (New York, 1991), p.24.

20. Freud first introduces the story of Oedipus in *Totem and taboo: resemblances between the psychic lives of savages and neurotics*, translated by James Strachey (1913; London, 1950).

being used today by leaders of wealthy First World countries to deny rights and reparations to indigenous populations, and to turn away and intern migrants at their borders. The rhetoric often repeated by governments when turning away asylum-seekers and refugees is based on a protection of an "us" through an exclusion of a "them." In order to create a cohesive social and political ego, a brotherly regime requires us to accept fraternity (now more frequently called patriotism) or face the consequences of (social) death by political exclusion, or, as Robespierre put it, "la fraternité ou la mort."

MacCannell offers Jean-Jacques Rousseau as the prime theorizer of the regime of the brother, citing the ways in which his analysis of the ego's relation to the sociopolitical anticipates Freud and Lacan. The superego proposed by Rousseau is narcissistic, and his society therefore also becomes a narcissistic one founded upon a model of fraternal homosociality. However, if we look back a few decades before the publication of *Julie* and the *Social contract* (two of the works cited most often by MacCannell), we will find a slightly different version of brotherhood. These are not the narcissistic brothers who sense the father's impending demise and plot to take his place; instead, these brothers, unaware of the insecure position of the patriarch, are rebellious but not quite ready to let go of the father completely. These brothers are not (forcibly) narcissistic. They are anxious.[21] Much like the brothers in the wake of the Revolution, these brothers sense a change but are as yet unable to comprehend its full meaning as it pertains to them.

In the introduction I discussed the ways in which desire circulates in the oedipal formation from one man to another (father to son) via the womb of the woman. The power (of language) is transferred to the son at the expense of a mother. In spite of her inability to enter the scene of desire as a subject rather than an object, the mother plays a pivotal role in the transfer of power from one man to the next. The oedipal crisis is resolved successfully with the transfer of a *nom-du-père*. The son inherits the father's name, and with it the power, and this transfer can happen only once the father has demonstrated his possession of the mother, thus prohibiting the son's incestuous desire. In Prévost's tales of masculine subjectivity, however, mothers are absent. The household that Des Grieux knows is a completely masculine space

---

21. We can assess a narcissism in both of Prévost's male protagonists discussed in this chapter, but here narcissism is more a symptom of anxiety than an organizing principle.

consisting of a father and a brother. The missing mother causes a disruption to the oedipal transfer of power, resulting in a confusion of familial relations. In *Histoire d'une Grecque moderne*, the oedipal crisis is completely displaced as the familial players are replaced with foreign dignitaries. It is not with a father but with an influential pasha that the Ambassador must compete for the desire of a woman. Throughout the novel, the protagonist will repeatedly attempt to demonstrate his power through mastery over the young Greek slave, as well as over other men. With the mothers gone and the fathers thus incapable of maintaining the circulation of oedipal desire in their absence, what we are left with is a network of men trying to figure out alternative methods of dealing with desire. In these two novels, protagonists set up impossible triangulations of desire that replace mothers with lovers. The problem with replacing a mother with a lover is that the father's lack of desire renders the transfer of power via oedipal means impossible. What unfolds in its place is a scene in which men are united not by heterosexual desire, but by anxiety.

Anxiety takes several forms in these novels—fathers are anxious about losing their sons, men are anxious about losing the women they love, and all are anxious about the unknown. As Lacan notes in his tenth seminar, anxiety functions very similarly to desire. Motivated by a drive and thus remaining at the level of the unconscious, anxiety manifests itself rather as a symptom that attempts to attach itself to an object. The current discussion of anxiety draws very specifically on a Lacanian understanding of affect and desire. Like Freud, Lacan associates anxiety with castration but, whereas Freud understands anxiety as stemming from the fear of losing an organ (and the resulting lack), anxiety for Lacan is, at the risk of oversimplifying, the lack of the lack. To put it differently, when confronted with the object of desire, the subject must account for the other's desire and, consequently, it tries to find its own role within the other's frame of desire. This affective exchange cannot be represented symbolically because it involves a proliferation and confusion of multiple matrices of desire, and thus calls into question the legitimacy of the symbolic order for the anxious subject.

The introduction of anxiety into the narrative of the protagonists' lives presages the falling apart of the self that will occur over the course of their stories. In the pages following Des Grieux's and the Ambassador's introductions, meaning becomes unhinged for both narrator and reader. Signs become evacuated of meaning in a world that is both dominated by, and incomprehensible to, our male protagonists. Lionel Gossman ties this masculine loss of meaning to the indecipherability of the female objects of desire, writing, "if woman, as the emblem of the fallen world—the sign of the sign—is always represented as ambiguous, uncertain, undecipherable, the elusive object of man's quest for mastery and control, man himself turns out to be something less than the straightforward, entire, self-sufficient being he claims to be."[22] Gossman uncovers a central tension in these two novels and one that has made them so captivating to readers for generations: Each of the characters in these novels is so deeply fragmented, even when—and maybe especially when— they appear to us as whole, that the reader is able to configure and reconfigure the stories into a number of different readings.[23] Once the supremacy of the sign fails, language itself falls into chaos as signifiers for such categories as gender, sex, and kinship, categories that are foundational to our comprehension of the world around us, become muddled and lead to confusing and quasi-incestuous relations. In this world signifiers designating brothers, fathers, lovers, and sisters blend into one another and the organization of the family structure is open to change.

The very frame of *Manon* invites such confusion. The story is recounted to a father-like figure, Renoncour, who then shares the story with his readers. Because *Manon* is the seventh and final volume of Prévost's *Mémoires et aventures d'un homme de qualité* (*Memoirs and adventures of a man of quality*), readers would have already come to know Renoncour as a stand-in father to another young aristocratic man, thus reinforcing his paternal qualities.[24] Upon meeting Renoncour for the first time, Des Grieux begins to tell him a story:

> I was seventeen years old and was finishing my philosophy studies at Amiens, where my parents, who belonged to one of the finest families in P..., had sent me. I led a life so good and well-mannered that my

22. Lionel Gossman, "Male and female in two short novels by Prévost," *The Modern language review* 77:1 (1982), p.29–37 (33).

23. Gossman also warns that such interpretations repeat the possessiveness of Des Grieux and the Ambassador. "Male and female," p.36.

24. *Mémoires et aventures d'un homme de qualité* follows the adventures throughout Europe of Renoncour and his charge, Rosemont. In many ways, Des Grieux serves as a less virtuous counterpart to Rosemont. See Antoine Prévost, *Mémoires et aventures d'un homme de qualité qui s'est retiré du monde: histoire du chevalier Des Grieux et de Manon Lescaut*, in *Œuvres de Prévost*, vol.1, ed. Pierre Berthiaume and Jean Sgard (Grenoble, 1978).

professors held me up as an example at school. Not that I made any extraordinary efforts to earn this praise; but I am soft-spoken and tranquil by nature: I devoted myself to my studies by inclination, and people counted as virtues in me some natural aversions I had to vice. My birth, my success in school, and some exterior advantages meant that I was well known and held in high regard by all the good inhabitants of the town.

J'avais dix-sept ans, et j'achevais mes études de philosophie à Amiens, où mes parents, qui sont d'une des meilleurs maisons de P..., m'avaient envoyé. Je menais une vie si sage et réglée, que mes maîtres me proposaient pour l'exemple du collège. Non que je fisse des efforts extraordinaires pour mériter cet éloge; mais j'ai l'humeur naturellement douce et tranquille: je m'appliquais à l'étude par inclination, et l'on me comptait pour des vertus quelques marques d'aversion naturelle pour le vice. Ma naissance, le succès de mes études et quelques agréments extérieurs m'avaient fait connaître et estimer de tous les honnêtes gens de la ville.[25]

This introduction would appear to announce a solid young man from a noble family. At this point in his story (a point long past by the time he relates it to the *homme de qualité*), the family remains intact. His parents have provided him with a proper education in which he has excelled, and have raised him to be a young man who loves virtue. Nothing is missing from this romanticized scene of a man's passage into adulthood except a wife with whom he will start a family and carry on familial traditions.

And yet, the story of the paternal denial of filial desire as told in *Manon* diverges from the traditional oedipal dilemma of the competing desire of father and son for the wife/mother in two ways. First, the desired woman of this story, Manon, is neither mother nor wife, and therefore the oedipal triangle of masculine desire for the woman appears impossible. Because of the initial feminine lack (of the dead mother), Des Grieux must learn to navigate feminine space outside of the family. In so doing he becomes feminized as he struggles to comprehend underdefined gender roles in his relationship with Manon. Rather than standing beside the father, as a wife would, Manon stands in direct opposition to him. I will return to the ways in which Manon disrupts the hero's subjective formation in the next section of this chapter. For now, I would like to focus on a second divergence, which

25. Prévost, *Manon Lescaut*, p.367.

is found *within* the hero's family. As the younger son, Des Grieux can inherit neither familial wealth nor the patriarchal role. Throughout the story we do see the process of transference of the *nom-du-père* (and with it the father's function) from father to son, but this process takes place with the older brother rather than the hero. In the masculine space of the protagonist's family, Des Grieux's maturity is consistently called into question. In this space he is perpetually infantilized, unable to exit the stage of adolescence, which thus reinforces the impossibility of the hero's oedipal formation.[26]

Although much has been written on the character of Manon—about her absence, her masculinity, her femininity, her terrible fate, the list goes on and on—relatively little scholarly attention has been devoted to the character of the older brother in this story. This neglect seems logical, given that the older brother is perhaps the one character in the novel who speaks *less* than Manon. Yet his presence, like that of the women of Prévost's novels, haunts the entire story. With his mother deceased, Des Grieux grows up in a household in which the familial structure is completely masculinized. Rather than identifying himself only through his father, Des Grieux must also attempt to identify himself both with and against his older brother. Knowing that it is the older brother, and not himself, who will inherit the father's name and power, the protagonist enters into a crisis of subjectivity. If he cannot inherit the father's name, what will his own name be? Moreover, freed from the obligations of maintaining property and traditions that the older brother will face, Des Grieux is able to speculate about what kind of person he will be in ways inaccessible to the older brother.[27] The older brother occasionally acquires the fatherly role by seconding his father and scolding the hero, thus prohibiting the latter's desire, yet in several scenes, he is also presented as compassionate and almost

26. Segal aptly notes that the hero's role as younger son makes him "everyone's baby." Segal, *The Unintended reader*, p.149.
27. In addition to Des Grieux's position as younger son, Maurice Daumas argues that a changing in the role of fathers also contributes to the hero's subjective crisis. This phenomenon, which he calls the "Des Grieux syndrome," is a crisis in which an old order (strict father/obeying son) fades away without a fully formed new order to take its place. As Daumas points out, the absence of a mother in *Manon* allows Prévost to fully explore the evolving roles of fathers and sons. Fathers, sons, and brothers abound in this story, beginning with Renoncour, the *homme de qualité* who collects Des Grieux's story, and ending in America with Synnelet. See Daumas, *Le Syndrome Des Grieux: la relation père/fils au XVIIIᵉ siècle* (Paris, 1990).

motherly. Existing alongside the father in paternal and maternal capacities, the older brother joins the father in blocking Des Grieux's sexual desires, leaving the protagonist in a perpetually infantilized state.

Des Grieux's role as the youngest son produces two distinct results. First, as the non-inheritor of the paternal lineage, he must construct his identity by other means. The symbolic erasure of the paternal name once the hero is christened the chevalier Des Grieux allows him a certain freedom in his behavior that the eldest son cannot possess. Put differently, whereas the eldest son is bound by a sense of duty to the name and estate he will inherit, the younger son, because he is destined for the Order of Malta, is separated from both the land and the name. In this way his movement and actions are freer than those of his older brother. Second, although the hero is bound to the father by blood, because of the nominal link between the father and the eldest son that he lacks, he feels a sense of alienation within the family. For Des Grieux the paternal household represents a "world of fathers" in which each male inhabitant exercises power over him.[28] Only by being removed from the paternal household and its masculine relations can the hero grow beyond his perpetual adolescence.

Alienated from this world of fathers *intra muros*, Des Grieux seeks out new types of masculine relationships outside of the home. Each man with whom he forms relations (Tiberge, Lescaut, M. de T...) is roughly close to him in age, although their social status varies, and with each he will form distinct relations that call social and gender norms into question. Manon's brother, Lescaut, for instance, enters the story as the very symbol of masculinity. Bursting into Manon and Des Grieux's home uninvited, cursing and insulting his sister, he immediately asserts his dominance in the house that should be ruled by the chevalier. Lescaut takes over everything in the home, even assuming control of their carriage: "It was a complete takeover since he soon got so used to seeing us, and with such pleasure, that he made himself at home in our house and somehow made himself

---

28. Segal uses this phrase "the world of fathers" to indicate a broader society in which both Des Grieux's own father and other father figures like the old G. M. hold power over him even outside of the paternal household. I use the phrase here to indicate that the world of the fathers can, in fact, permeate the paternal household as the eldest son also serves as would-be father to Des Grieux. Segal, *The Unintended reader*, p.66.

the master of everything we owned."[29] Although Lescaut immediately refers to the hero as his brother, he very quickly pushes Des Grieux aside, taking his place beside the sister as the dominant male in the family. The hero reinforces Lescaut's powerful position when he begins referring to the brother as "Mr. Lescaut." The brother-in-law then begins dictating the hero's life, first by choosing a career for him (gambling), then once again by infantilizing the hero in the scheme to steal from the elder G... M..., introducing Des Grieux as Manon's "sad little orphan brother."[30] In this scene, Des Grieux is assigned an invented familial relationship with Manon for the second time (the first occurring during their first encounter when she pretends to be his cousin). Although playing the young brother does allow him to remain close to his desired object (as did the previous role), it once again strips him of power, renders him a child, and disrupts his process of formation. It also clearly demonstrates the blurring of boundaries between oedipal and homosocial desire. Although Des Grieux and Lescaut share a brotherly bond, Lescaut's actions place him in a position of power over the protagonist. The attempt to form a new identity as Manon's lover and Lescaut's brother ultimately renders him once again the younger brother within his love nest and reproduces the hierarchal form of power found within the paternal home.

Tiberge, by contrast, serves as a different kind of brother figure in *Manon*. There are many similarities between Des Grieux's relationship with Tiberge and that with his biological brother. He has been raised with both (first at home with his brother, then at school with Tiberge), Tiberge and the brother are both slightly older than the hero, and both believe that Des Grieux's happiness can be achieved only by leaving Manon—urging that he opt for a happiness based on reason and reflection rather than volatile passion. The most obvious distinction between the two relationships lies in the origins and motivations for each. Des Grieux's attachment to his brother stems from filial bonds of kinship, whereas his attachment to Tiberge develops as a result of mutual affection. Rather than simply replicating the brotherly role, which would reinforce an unequal distribution of power, Tiberge

---

29. Prévost, *Manon Lescaut*, p.380–81. "Ce fut une prise de possession, car il s'accoutuma bientôt à nous voir avec tant de plaisir, qu'il fit sa maison de la nôtre et qu'il se rendit le maître, en quelque sorte, de tout ce qui nous appartenait."

30. Prévost, *Manon Lescaut*, p.390. "Pauvre petit frère orphelin." In fact, René Démoris posits Lescaut as the inverse of Des Grieux. See René Démoris, *Le Silence de Manon* (Paris, 1995), p.59.

offers an idealized form of brotherhood in which power between men is equally distributed.

Given that the older brother serves a fatherly role with respect to Des Grieux, and that so many similarities exist between the two brother figures (the older brother and Tiberge), it is easy to understand why some scholars have attributed a fatherly role to Tiberge as well.[31] Like the older brother, he desires the hero's happiness and, like the traditional father, he supports Des Grieux financially. However, Tiberge cannot fulfill this function in the way that the natural brother can because he remains firmly outside of the family and furthermore outside of paternal rule. Although the two are best friends from childhood, we never hear of Tiberge entering Des Grieux's paternal home; conversely, the older brother leaves the paternal household only to bring the hero back.[32] In fact, while the older brother stands in for the natural father, Tiberge stands in direct opposition to him. After having lost all of his money in a fire, Des Grieux momentarily considers writing to his father for help; however, he promptly remembers that his father's help will come at the cost of losing Manon. Rather than turning to his brother for help, which he understands will lead to the same fate, the chevalier turns to his friend. In Tiberge, the hero finds a friend who can only chastise; unlike the father (and by extension the older brother), this friend has no power to keep him from Manon.

While the older brother will take up the fatherly role after the natural father's death, his main role for as long as the father is alive is as an intermediary to paternal power. During the father's life, the brother's power, like that of the brothers described by MacCannell, is largely imaginary rather than symbolic—the older brother can act only *as if* he were the hero's father. He is simultaneously in a position of power over his brother and equal to him; the older brother of this novel thus bridges the gap between the world of fathers and the regime of the brother. He prohibits desire like a father, soothes pain like a mother, and chides like an older sibling. The older brother is uniquely capable of understanding the youthful bodily sensations of

---

31. See for example Segal, *The Unintended reader*, p.148, as well as Michèle Respaut, "Des Grieux's duplicity: *Manon Lescaut* and the tragedy of repetition," *Symposium* 88:1 (1984), p.70–80.

32. Catherine Cusset argues that all of what she defines as "lieux du père" are enclosed spaces, which prohibit the son's escape. The enclosed nature of such spaces also renders them exclusionary, prohibiting those outside of the immediate family. See Catherine Cusset, "Loi du père et symbolique de l'espace dans *Manon Lescaut*," *Eighteenth-century fiction* 5:2 (1993), p.93–103.

the younger brother while at the same time maintaining his duty to the paternal name.

The difference in the relational dynamic between Des Grieux and the father on the one hand, and Des Grieux and the brother on the other, becomes particularly evident in the scene in which the brother brings the protagonist home from his love nest with Manon. Although the father demands the hero's return home, it is the older brother who carries out the request. The brother extracts the hero from the feminized space of his Parisian home, but immediately infantilizes Des Grieux when he hugs him in the carriage and offers to talk to their father first in order to soften the patriarch's anger. In this scene the brother demonstrates an almost maternal form of love as he hugs Des Grieux tightly, cries tears of joy, and watches him sleep on the way home. In this space of transition in the carriage, the older brother gently bridges the gap between the feminine space of a house run by Manon, and the masculine space of the paternal household. The fraternal relationship resumes a more masculine register upon the return to the paternal household when the brother joins the father in chastising Des Grieux. In addition to mediating the father's desire, the older brother must also learn to play diverse kinship roles simultaneously.

While the transfer of Des Grieux from the paternal home in the beginning of the novel to the fraternal home in the end (after the father's death) may seem like a lateral move for the hero who simply shifts from one form of hierarchal authority to the next, in fact, the paternal home based on brotherhood propels the traditional family toward modernity. Because the story that the hero chooses to tell focuses on the in-between time, the time of youthful rebellion when Des Grieux is physically removed from paternal authority, his return to the familial home now governed by the eldest son/older brother reflects the tension inherent to a transition from tradition to modernity.[33] The hero's defiant journey first in France and then in America is more than simple youthful rebellion. In addition to a personal journey of formation, this adventure signals a time of familial transformation and a move to a new order of governance, one that still resides in the home but where the power dynamic has been altered. Although it would be

---

33. The words "tradition" and "modernity" are borrowed from Daumas, who describes the traditional father as adhering strictly to the rules of alliance, and the modern father as being more sensitive to the desires of his children. See Daumas, *Le Syndrome Des Grieux*.

inaccurate to read Des Grieux's return to the brother as a complete acceptance of the modern, democratic principles of *liberty, equality*, and *fraternity*, the hero's ultimate acceptance of the older brother's authority does signal a relaxing of the strict system of alliance. Such a loosening eases the entry of a system of governance based on brotherhood.

In *Histoire d'une Grecque moderne*, fraternity develops in less obvious ways. In fact, we do not even learn of the Ambassador's family until the final pages of the novel. We learn that Théophé has a brother, but his appearance in the home of the Ambassador provokes at first jealousy (when the Ambassador perceives him as a rival), and eventually paternal (rather than fraternal) tenderness. Brotherhood in this novel, rather than emerging from shifting familial relations, follows a more sociable model. We read about how the Ambassador bonds with (unrelated) men through the exchange and shared desire of women. In this novel fraternity arises as a concept in which men are united to one another by uniquely homosocial means through the desired (female) object.

Even though it is largely Téophé's story that is recounted on the pages, she remains first and foremost an object that solidifies fraternal relations between men. In the novel, an Ambassador living in Turkey falls in love with a Greek slave girl he meets in Chériber's harem. Much of the novel centers on the Ambassador's deteriorating mental state following his first encounter with Téophé; however, I would like to begin this analysis of him, as I did with Des Grieux, by taking a look at how he describes himself prior to that fateful encounter.

> I was the king's emissary in a court whose customs and intrigues held no mystery for me. My advantage in speaking perfectly the Turkish language upon arrival in Constantinople helped me gain almost immediately a measure of acceptance and confidence that most officials achieve only after a long period of probation; and the very rarity of a French man who appeared just as Turkish, if I may use the expression, as the native inhabitants of the country, brought me from the outset of my stay an unending stream of compliments and honors.

> J'étais employé aux affaires du roi dans une cour dont personne n'a connu mieux que moi les usages et les intrigues. L'avantage que j'avais eu en arrivant à Constantinople de savoir parfaitement la langue turque, m'avait fait parvenir presque tout d'un coup au point de familiarité et de confiance où la plupart des ministres n'arrivent qu'après de longues épreuves; et la seule singularité de voir

un François aussi turc, si l'on me permet cette expression, que les
habitants naturels du pays, m'attira dès les premiers jours des caresses
et des distinctions dont on ne s'est jamais relâché.[34]

Like the young Des Grieux, the Ambassador begins his story by
giving a flattering description of his character. Rather than focusing
on the family he came from, the Ambassador notes his nobility by
emphasizing his presence in, and knowledge of, the Turkish court. In
addition to endearing him to the members of the Turkish courts, his
knowledge of foreign customs plays a secondary role—it highlights
his nobility in the French court of Louis XIV. Only his privileged
position could have allowed him such thoughtful preparation for his
time in Constantinople as the Turkish ambassador. He serves not only
as a representative of France in Turkey, but also as an extension of the
French king himself. Without mentioning any fathers, he demonstrates
that his is *the* French patriarch.

As the diplomat notes, his adeptness with Turkish customs wins
him the favor of several influential men. We learn throughout the
story that Turkish women must wear a veil and keep away from
strange men. We must assume, then, that in the time leading up to the
beginning of the novel the narrator had encountered very few women,
although he admits a certain curiosity by pointing out his frequent
glances toward the harem of Bacha Chériber. Although his knowledge
of customs and his status as gentleman prohibits the Ambassador from
asking about the harem directly, Chériber takes note of his interest
and, after several visits with the diplomat, invites the Ambassador
in to see the women. The scene we encounter next is quite different
from the harem we saw in the *Lettres persanes*. In this scene, orientalism
and male fantasy are matched only by the peaceful order that
reigns among the women.[35] The scene is fairly long, but I will cite
it in its entirety here for two reasons: first, because this is our first
introduction to women in the novel, and it has much to teach us on
the narrator's feelings about women; and second, because it introduces
the important themes of masculine desire and anxiety, foreshadowing
the story to come and laying the groundwork for Prévost's experiment
in masculine precarity:

34. Prévost, *Greek girl's story*, p.29–30; *Grecque moderne*, p.11.
35. As Julia Douthwaite points out, the scene balances Western expectations of
    Eastern practices with the repetition of the same prejudices in the West as those
    we read about in the East. J. Douthwaite, "Embattled eros: the cultural politics
    of Prévost's *Grecque moderne*," *L'Esprit créateur* 32:3 (1992), p.87–97.

The pasha's women, twenty-two in number, were gathered in the apartment reserved for their activities. Each of them was free to pursue her own interests, some painting flowers, others sewing or embroidering, according to their talents or inclinations. The fabric of their dresses appeared to be the same; the color was uniform, in any case. But their coiffure was varied, and I realized that it was arranged in harmony with each woman's face. A large number of servants of both sexes, the males being eunuchs,[36] stood ready in the corners of the apartment to carry out their slightest wishes. The crowd of slaves withdrew as soon as we entered, and the twenty-two ladies, rising without leaving their places, appeared to be awaiting the orders of their lord and master, or the explanation of a visit that they appearently found quite surprising. I examined each one in her turn, noting the differences in age; but while none seemed to be over thirty, I didn't see any as young as I had imagined, the youngest being at least sixteen or seventeen.

Les femmes du bacha, qui étaient au nombre de vingt-deux, se trouvaient toutes ensemble dans un salon destiné à leurs exercices. Elles étaient occupées séparément, les unes à peindre des fleurs, d'autres à coudre ou à broder, suivant leurs talents ou leurs inclinations, qu'elles avoient la liberté de suivre. L'étoffe de leurs robes me parut la même; la couleur du moins en était uniforme. Mais leur coiffure était variée, et je conçus qu'elle était ajustée à l'air de leur visage. Un grand nombre de domestiques de l'un et de l'autre sexe, dont je remarquai néanmoins que ceux qui paraissaient du mien étaient des eunuques, se tenaient aux coins du salon pour exécuter leurs moindres ordres. Mais cette foule d'esclaves se retira aussitôt que nous fumes entrés, et les vingt-deux dames se levant sans s'écarter de leurs places, parurent attendre les ordres de leur seigneur, ou l'explication d'une visite qui leur causait apparemment beaucoup de surprise. Je les considérai successivement, leur âge me parut inégal; mais si je n'en remarquai aucune qui me parût au-dessus de trente ans, je n'en vis pas non plus d'aussi jeunes que je me l'étais figuré, et celles qui l'étaient le plus n'avoient pas moins de seize ou dix-sept ans.[37]

Although the women of the harem are introduced as having the "liberty" to follow their inclinations, their reaction to the entry of

---

36. Although the English translation posits the eunuchs as specifically male, the French is less certain, stating that the eunuchs *seemed to be* (*paraissaient*) of the same sex as the narrator.
37. Prévost, *Greek girl's story*, p.31–32; *Grecque moderne*, p.12.

the two men into this female space demonstrates the limits of their liberty. Their primary function is to be observed and judged by men; when the two men enter, therefore, it is not only surprise that interrupts their activities as the narrator points out, but also a sense of obligation. Although Chériber tells the Ambassador that at his age he has no sexual desire for these women, the narrator quickly delimits the women as appropriate objects of sexual desire by discussing their dress, hair, and ages. They are roughly between the ages of sixteen and thirty; in other words, they are all in their prime sexual and childbearing years. In this scene the veil is lifted, and the diplomat sees the potential of his sexual desire, and all thanks to the man who allowed his entry into this forbidden space.

In the very same moment that he describes the exotic scene of desire, the narrator expresses, even if inadvertently, another primal feeling: fear, or anxiety, to be more precise. His eyes observe not only the women, but also the men (at least those that *seemed* to be men). Thus, as soon as our attention is drawn to the beautiful female objects of desire, it is also drawn to the potential for castration. It is just after this moment that he speaks to Zara for the first time. As he begins to congratulate her on her ability to adapt so quickly to life in the harem, the discussion turns almost instantly to treachery. Commenting on the docility of the subservient women (slaves) in the seraglio, the Ambassador laments that such qualities are missing in the women of France. In France, he says, men treat women like queens, "asking in return only sweetness, love, and virtue," but notes that men "almost always discover that they have made a bad choice of spouse."[38] In other words, the protagonist demonstrates within his first words to the heroine his admiration for men who possess and control women.

The Ambassador will try to ignore his desire, but he is drawn back to the harem as if by the force of Zara's charm. He stays away as long as he can in order to assuage any fears the pasha (Chériber) may have, but he cannot help returning. After several visits and a request from the young Greek slave, he decides to try for the first time to possess this fine object. However, rather than buying her directly, he involves several men in the transaction. The Ambassador must first engage his language instructor to translate since he does not speak adequate Greek, and he then proposes to buy Zara from the pasha in

---

38. Prévost, *Greek girl's story*, p.34; *Grecque moderne*, p.13. "Ne leur demandant pour unique retour que de la douceur, de la tendresse et de la vertu, ils se trouvent presque toujours trompés dans le choix qu'ils font d'une épouse."

the name of a third man, the *sélictar*. In so doing, the narrator avoids the risk of offending or hurting the pasha. Since this kind of exchange of women as material goods is common in the East, he reasons, a transaction involving another Turkish man will not seem out of the ordinary. Scholars have written extensively on the meaning of this trade, arguing that this allows the Ambassador to keep a veneer of disdain for Eastern customs that treat women as objects; that because the story is a *roman à clef* the author is merely recounting the story as he has heard it; or that the trade between multiple men serves as a breaking apart of Zara that allows the reader to reconstruct her in multiple ways, just as they would have constructed Manon.[39] At this point in the Ambassador's story, he describes his motives for buying Zara as nothing more than gentlemanly duty, claiming that he would do it for any of the slaves should they ask. He is increasingly concerned, however, with the feelings and emotions of Chériber and the *sélictar*. As she is passed between the men, Zara becomes the object that reinforces homosocial bonds.

Although the Ambassador is not feminized in his relationships in the same manner as Des Grieux, his masculinity is scrutinized through a discourse on cultural difference. His descriptions of individuals are not relegated to the women and eunuchs in the seraglio, but apply also to the men he befriends. In fact, the first Turkish man we encounter in his story, Chériber, would appear to be the very symbol of virility. He is, after all, the master of twenty-two women. And yet, as I mentioned above, one of the first things he tells the narrator upon entering the feminine space of the seraglio is that he is too old for sexual desire. Chériber's impotence is quickly countered with the hero's virility when the Ambassador describes his many affairs with women in France and instantly strikes up an intimate relation with the first slave to whom he speaks. However, sexually impotent as the pasha may be, we see in the Ambassador's dealings with him that, unlike Usbek, this master still remains powerful within his harem. He may not sleep with these women, but he owns them, and they obey him. In his harem, women do not only serve as sexual objects; they also provide him with cultural capital that facilitates his relations with other men.

39. See for example Douthwaite, "Embattled eros"; James Gilroy, "Prévost's Théophé: a liberated heroine in search of herself," *The French review* 60:3 (1987), p.311–18; and Allan J. Singerman, "The abbé Prévost's 'Grecque moderne': a witness for the defense," *The French review* 46:5 (1973), p.938–45.

Can we assume, then, that the Ambassador's desire to liberate/purchase Zara might also be tied to a desire to reassert his masculinity by controlling a woman of his own? The Ambassador does indeed talk about his own desire, but he is careful to note that his is *not* a sexual attraction to the slave he is going to buy. He uses a rhetoric of granting Zara's wishes by removing her from the cloistered space of the harem, but, by repeating the nonsexual nature of his desire, he symbolically castrates himself. His attention to the eunuchs during his first visit to the harem might be seen, therefore, less as a fear than as an affective bond. He does not necessarily identify with them because he does not understand them (saying they *seem* like his sex), but he cannot help but be drawn to their state as well. Their lack of a clearly defined sex allows them free movement between masculine and feminine realms. In symbolically castrating himself in his relationship with Zara he aligns himself with the sexless eunuchs and, like them, he too has the freedom of movement between masculine and feminine realms. However, like the eunuchs as well, his passage between these two worlds remains dictated by other men. He can only penetrate the feminine space with the pasha's permission. In buying Zara for himself, he hopes to be the master of his own realm, allowing himself free passage between masculine and feminine as master rather than slave.

And yet, once he successfully gets Zara (who quickly changes her name to Téophé) into his home, his situation changes very little. His desire to blend Eastern and Western customs leads him to grant freedom to his new ward, but that freedom also renders him as impotent as Chériber. He has assumed the role of master, but he has also enticed Téophé with the promise of a house governed by French customs in which women, as the Ambassador told her the first day they met, are treated like queens. The night of her arrival in his house in Oru demonstrates the stark contrast between male and female desire in this situation. When Téophé rejects the *sélictar*'s advances, the Ambassador mistakes this refusal as a sign of her desire for himself. Once they arrive at the house, however, Téophé's intentions become clear even though she has not yet said a word. When she expresses her desire to go to her room and sleep, the Ambassador once again misreads this cue as an invitation.[40] The Ambassador leads Téophé to the bedroom, which he has had prepared for the both of them, but,

---

40. We will recall the scene in *Lettres persanes* in which Usbek also willfully misunderstands Roxane's protest as a sign of desire on the first night of their marriage. In

as his servant begins to undress him, Téophé stands frozen. Until this moment, his intentions remained unstated. He has misunderstood his own desire as the desire of the other.

Having mistaken her hesitation for impatience, he tries to lighten the mood:

> I became concerned and made some playful comments about my fear of becoming bored if I had to wait too long for her. This manner of speaking, whose meaning was apparently all too clear from the situation, threw her into a state of utter dejection. She moved away from the mirror where she was still standing, and dropping listlessly down to the couch, she remained there, her head in her hands, as if she were trying to hide her face from me [...] Growing more and more concerned, I grabbed one of her hands, the very one her head was resting on, and tried to draw it toward me. She put up some resistance. Finally, using the same hand to wipe away some tears that I could still see on her face, she asked me if I would be so kind as to send away the two servants so that we could speak for a minute in private.

> Je hasardai avec inquiétude, quelques expressions badines sur la crainte que j'avais de m'ennuyer beaucoup à l'attendre. Ce langage, plus clair apparemment par les circonstances, acheva tout à fait de la déconcerter. Elle quitta le miroir devant lequel elle était encore, et se jetant languissamment sur un sofa, elle s'y tint penchée, le front appuyé sur la main, comme si elle eût cherché à me dérober la vue de son visage [...] Mon inquiétude augmentant, je saisis une de ses mains, celle même sur laquelle sa tête était appuyée, et je fis quelque effort pour l'attirer à moi. Elle résista quelques moments. Enfin, la passant sur ses yeux pour essuyer quelques larmes dont j'aperçus les traces, elle me demanda en grâce de faire sortir les deux domestiques, et de lui accorder un moment d'entretien.[41]

Standing in front of the mirror, Téophé is forced to reckon with her dual identity. She has renamed herself in the image of the gods, but the Ambassador continues to see her as Zara, the sex slave. The breaking apart of the woman in this scene allows the reader to distinguish her desires from those of the Ambassador and yet, at this moment, the Ambassador remains unaware. It is finally Téophé's

---

both instances, masculine anxiety translates into a usurpation of the woman's subjectivity.

41. Prévost, *Greek girl's story*, p.87; *Grecque moderne*, p.48.

tears that communicate to him that she is a subject separate from him with her own desires. This realization, that he has mistaken his desire for hers, provokes the primal scene of anxiety in the male protagonist who must now also choose between the doubles of his self. He must now choose between being the tyrant who forces the object to bend to his will, and the respectable master he has presented to his new ward, who allows her the freedom she had been denied in the harem. This scene demonstrates the extent to which signifiers have been dislodged from their signs; each of the protagonists has miscommunicated their desire to one another, leading to an agreement that has been reached on false premises. The moment when actions and words fuse into one meaning will break the spell. Once the Ambassador speaks aloud his intentions, symbols retroactively take on a different sense.

While words, actions, and meaning become fused for Téophé once she realizes the Ambassador's true intentions, for him they are ripped apart. His retrospective meaning-making inspires not realization, but rather anger. For the first time (but certainly not the last), we will see his jealousy translate into a hyperbolized version of masculinity. Rather than matching the reasoning that he inspired within Téophé—to become a virtuous and respectable woman—he reminds her of her baseness and recalls other men she has slept with. He insists that she is not his slave, but strongly encourages her to desire him of her own accord. In other words, he reinforces his desire to control, rather than merely to sleep with, Téophé. Alone in his room later, he curses her name and metonymically transforms her back into Zara—the slave—by continually looping her name in with thoughts about seraglios and other prostitutes. In this instance, his heightened sense of masculinity has the side effect of erasing the subjectivity he purports to grant Téophé.

As we will see through the Ambassador's repeated failures in his sexual advances with Téophé, it will take the recognition of other men to truly fulfill his desire. Based on a true story of Ferriol's time in Turkey, Prévost describes a party planned by the Ambassador to celebrate Louis XIV. After a regime change in Turkey, the Ambassador fails to receive permission from the new vizir to throw his magnificent party. In anger he lashes out like a child, threatening to set fire to all of the explosives in his house, blowing to bits himself and everyone around him. It is in this state of fury that he sees Téophé's brother, Synèse, whom the Ambassador had taken in as a son, with a

group of men in the process of kidnapping Téophé.[42] He sets his men
upon the band of kidnappers, killing two of the men, and frightening
Synèse and his friend into giving up their swords. The act of two men
handing their swords to a third man with a more powerful sword
needs little psychoanalytic explanation. The striking part is what
comes next. At the same instant the fight ends, the narrator learns that
the new vizir, being so frightened by the earlier threats, has agreed
to let him have the party as planned. At this moment, the narrator
finds an unusual sense of calm. The ambassador having now been
reaffirmed by three men, his anger disappears. Rather than punish
Synèse, he lets him go—anger has been replaced by pity for the other
man. He finally realizes the power he has so desperately desired and
thus has nothing more to prove. Téophé's fear at being kidnapped
never even enters his mind. The pleasure he feels from this extreme
act of masculinity, and its affirmation in the eyes of other men, has
erased her subjectivity completely.

Although there are more fits of jealous behavior in the book before
the Ambassador renounces his desire for Téophé altogether, having
felt the pleasure of homosocial affirmation, he now feels more at ease
taking on the fatherly role that Téophé has desired from him all along.
He returns to Téophé's birth father, père Condoidi (whom he had
previously sought out to render her birth legitimate), to make a final
plea that the father recognize his daughter, only this time it is in the
hope that Téophé's having a proper name will make it easier for him
to marry her to someone else rather than himself. He accepts his role
as stand-in father just pages before we learn that Téophé has died. In
fact, her death is the cause of the story:

> I did not even learn of her death until several months after the tragic
> event, owing to the care that my family and all the friends who
> came to see me in my solitude took to conceal it from me. It was
> immediately after receiving this news that I began to plan to record
> in writing the whole story of my relations with this lovely foreigner,
> and to put the public in a position to judge if my esteem and love were
> misplaced.

42. Synèse appears in the story as Téophé's brother, although their actual relationship
     remains ambiguous due to her uncertain origins. It is clear that Synèse desires
     Téophé as a lover rather than a sister, and it is for that reason that he attempts
     to kidnap her. I will return to a discussion of the heroine's birth family later in
     the chapter.

Je n'ai même appris sa mort que plusieurs mois après ce funeste accident, par le soin que ma famille et tous les amis qui me voient dans ma solitude ont eu de me la déguiser. C'est immédiatement après la première nouvelle qu'on m'en a donnée que j'ai formé le dessein de recueillir par écrit tout ce que j'ai eu de commun avec cette aimable étrangère, et de mettre le public en état de juger si j'avais mal placé mon estime et ma tendresse.[43]

He had tried to control her, prohibiting her from leaving to go to the convent, and so she exits the only other way she can, through death. His anxiety has thus always already been one that centers on the desire of the other, only we realize at this point that his has always been about the desires of other men. As he addresses the reader, he asks them to judge Téophé. He does not want to read Téophé, he wants her to be read and shared, much like Des Grieux wanted to share his precious object (Manon) with other men. In each case, the woman's ghost haunts the tale, reminding the reader that this is not a story about her, it is a story about reaffirming relations between men. In sharing these narratives about women, the narrators essentially tell a story about brotherhood.

Specters of desire, or the impossible woman

After their arrival in France, the Ambassador's jealousy reaches a strange apex. Believing Téophé to be cheating on him with the comte de M. Q., whom they met on the boat from Constantinople to Marseille, he sneaks into her room after she leaves for a morning walk around the garden. Looking for signs of her treachery he finds a small door with a staircase that leads to an alley. Although he finds the door securely locked, he becomes convinced that this has been the entry point for the count. At this moment his mind (and body) wanders to the most logical source he can think of for an answer— Téophé's bed. Desiring that this object tell him the truth about her, he begins to investigate the contours of her bed. Were this a story by Crébillon, we might expect the bed to actually tell us what it had seen, but we will have to wait until the next chapter for such a story. For the Ambassador, he will have to use his detective skills, examining the shape of the sheets and the state of her mattress. His jealousy drives him to extremes as he measures the space he believes her body should

---

43. Prévost, *Greek girl's story*, p.201; *Grecque moderne*, p.121.

occupy, making sure that the disorder does not exceed the imagined limits of her body.

In a supreme manifestation of masculine anxiety, the Ambassador becomes so overwhelmed with the absence that represents a past presence of Téophé that he claims to feel the residual heat of her body as well as the sweat she had excreted during the hot summer night. The scene continues:

> the sight of the place where my dear Téophé had just rested, the outline of her body that I could still see in the sheets, a trace of warmth that still lingered there, the dampness left by her gentle perspiration, moved me so profoundly that I pressed my lips a thousand times to the places she had touched. Tired as I was from staying awake all night, I lost myself so entirely in this pleasant activity that my senses succumbed to sleep, and I remained in a deep slumber in the very place that she had occupied.

> la vue du lieu où ma chère Téophé venait de reposer, sa forme que j'y voyais imprimée, un reste de chaleur que j'y trouvais encore, les esprits qui s'étaient exhalés d'elle par une douce transpiration, m'attendrirent jusqu'à me faire baiser mille fois tous les endroits qu'elle avait touchés. Fatigué comme j'étais d'avoir veillé toute la nuit, je m'oubliai si entièrement dans cette agréable occupation, que le sommeil s'étant emparé de mes sens, je demeurai profondément endormi dans la place même qu'elle avait occupée.[44]

Thus, the anxious male literally sleeps with the lack representing the woman who refuses to grant him access to her body. Attempting to fulfill the desire of an impossible woman, the protagonist participates in a moment of unbridled *jouissance* that signals both a going beyond, and a return to, the threshold of reality. Making love to the ghost of a woman substitutes for the sexual relation between two bodies. Although he had experienced a reprieve from his jealous obsession after the masculine affirmation discussed in the previous section, this becomes the moment at which the Ambassador will, once and for all, renounce his desire for Téophé. This scene demonstrates the extent to which women's bodies are insignificant in the construction of the masculine subject in Prévost's fiction. Reproduction in his novels emerges from a completely masculine construction.

In order to see how this masculine reproduction works, let us take

44. Prévost, *Greek girl's story*, p.174; *Grecque moderne*, p.104.

a moment to analyze Téophé's "birth," that is, her transition from the slave Zara to the virtuous Téophé. As previously noted, Zara's escape from Chériber's harem is filtered through a series of men. Wanting to spare Chériber's feelings, the Ambassador colludes with the *sélictar* and his language instructor to deliver Zara into his world. This provides an innovative portrayal of the exchange of women that is necessary to the reproduction of power in masculine societies. In Prévost's formulation, the woman is not a gift, as in Gayle Rubin's or Claude Lévi-Strauss's articulation of the circulation of women in patriarchal societies; the woman of this novel is a commodity to be bought and sold by and for men.[45] This means that the woman in this transaction is not traded to become a spouse and therefore to enter into a marital and reproductive arrangement, but instead her role is ambiguous. On the one hand, she is the object of desire, but the conditions of her purchase by the Ambassador lead her to think of him as a father, and this is the title she gives him upon her arrival in his house. A sustained confusion of names and titles is key to understanding the politics of love and kinship in *Histoire d'une Grecque moderne*.

Desperately seeking a way out of his paternal duties (so that he might fill those of lover instead), the protagonist decides to solve the mystery of Téophé's birth. Knowing that she had been sold into slavery as Zara, and believing the man who sold her to have stolen her from another family, the Ambassador seeks out the man he believes to be her true father—a noble Greek man named Paniota Condoidi. Condoidi is thus the name the Ambassador hopes to bestow upon his ward so that he might clarify his own relation to her. If she has the name of another man, then his own name can be offered under the guise of a lover instead of a father. However, when Condoidi refuses to recognize her, Téophé is slightly upset but nevertheless relieved. Knowing that the crook who had given her a slave name (Zara) is not the man to whom she owed her true name is enough for her. Rather than clarifying the Ambassador's relation to her, this serves as further proof that he is the only father she needs. As the Ambassador tells the reader, "she owed her birth to me."[46]

45. See Rubin's "The traffic in women" and Claude Lévi-Strauss, *The Elementary structures of kinship*, translated by James H. Bell, John R. von Sturmer, and Rodney Needham (Boston, MA, 1969).
46. Prévost, *Greek girl's story*, p.68; *Grecque moderne*, p.36. "C'était à moi qu'elle croyait devoir la naissance."

The Ambassador tries several times to convince Condoidi to recognize his daughter but to no avail. The father, having already designated his inheritance to his three sons, has neither the desire nor the need for a daughter. There is, however, one member of the Condoidi family eager to accept Téophé—the youngest brother, Synèse. He is so eager to get to know his sister that he runs away from the paternal home, and it is he who convinces the devout Téophé to run away to Europe. When they are caught by the Ambassador in the act of attempting to flee, Synèse pleads with him to be allowed to join the family as well. At this point, the discovery of the former slave's family has provided more confusion than clarity as Synèse joins Téophé as a brother (experiencing incestuous desire for his sister) but under the rule of a surrogate father.

Much like in *Manon*, what we end up with once again is an oedipal configuration with a missing mother, which leads to tremendous confusion regarding the circulation of desire. This triangle also contains a father, a son, and a lover, only in this example the father is the one with no relation to either party. Both the Ambassador and Synèse (the father and brother) desire her, but it is the woman— who simultaneously has no name (no father) and two names (Zara/ Téophé)—who interrupts the cycle of desire. This kind of semblance of power in the heroine might be one reason why James Gilroy has argued that Prévost (if not his male characters) respects the heroine's freedom as a liberated subject.[47] However, her power is by no means absolute. She may politely request that these men stop desiring her by reminding them of her rebirth as a virtuous woman and of their paternal and fraternal duties, but the men may, and in fact do, refuse to listen. In scenes that make modern readers cringe, these men continually ignore her interdiction, stalking her, sneaking into her room, trying to kidnap her, and even dueling over her. She would be long dead before sexual harassment would become a familiar term, but it is something she experiences intimately and often.

In this confusing and highly incestuous triad, symbolic logic falls apart. Father, sister, lover, and brother—these words fail to signify in a web of desire that contains an orphaned slave girl, an adoptive father, and a would-be brother. The lack of a signifying chain of desire reveals the constant threat of everything falling apart. The Ambassador's actions toward Téophé bounce back and forth between overwhelming desire and jealous disdain; Téophé is torn between a devotion to the

47. See Gilroy, "Prévost's Théophé."

man who saved her and a desire to escape his ever-tightening grasp; and Synèse, like Des Grieux, uses the veneer of kinship to remain closer to the object of his desire. The result is a perversion (*père-version*) of the nuclear family in which subjects and objects, along with the relations between them, bear improper names.[48] The man who gave birth (*a donné naissance*) to a woman in the absence of a mother has disrupted the channels of desire, resulting in an anxiety that will haunt him throughout the story.

Let us now see how masculine reproduction occurs in *Manon*. In an intriguing reading of desiring relations in *Manon*, Segal offers an alternative oedipal structure. She suggests that Manon takes up the role of mother by financially (and to an extent emotionally) supporting Des Grieux. Discussing Manon's duplicitous language and her power to make decisions for the hero, Segal writes, "we have the image of Manon as adored mother, innocently loved by a son she will reject; he wants nothing more than a happy nuclear family, and she refuses the comfort of triangular togetherness in favour of her right to make her own decisions for the two of them."[49] The problem with an oedipal model that places Manon in the role of mother lies in the very refusal that Segal points out. From the beginning, Manon refuses to be a wife. Despite her numerous sexual encounters, she never becomes a mother, and she flatly refuses any interaction with Des Grieux's father. For Manon, the labor of childbirth and rearing, traditionally attributed to the wife/mother, is replaced with a proliferation of the sexual act of reproduction itself. What Manon reproduces, however, is economic wealth rather than children. By accepting the masculine role of laborer (and breadwinner) and refusing to play the role of wife and mother, Manon renders impossible an oedipal formation via the maternal space of the woman. What she offers instead is an alternative gender economy, one that allows the woman to play a more active role in the domestic household as well as in the public sphere. Once Des Grieux accepts his role within the altered household, both characters are able to interrogate the type of gender roles that would grant a

48. As Lacan notes somewhat ironically in the sixth seminar, *père-version*, or a movement *vers le père*, is the perversion that takes place when the name-of-the-father becomes confused with the father himself. This is the result of mistaking the Imaginary for the Symbolic. See Jacques Lacan, *Desire and its interpretation: the seminar of Jacques Lacan, book VI*, ed. Jacques-Alain Miller, translated by Bruce Fink (Cambridge, 2019).
49. Segal, *The Unintended reader*, p.133.

public presence to men while forcing women to remain in the private sphere. Within this alternative gender economy, the hero remains subject to Manon's desires rather than his own.

Manon does not serve as a site of transfer for the *nom-du-père* as would a mother within a traditional oedipal construction; instead, she *interrupts* such a transferal. Standing outside of familial relationships, Manon radically alters the oedipal playing field, shifting the role of the son's romantic opponent from the father to other men (in this case M. de B., G. M., etc.), thus disempowering the father who does not possess the desired object. Castration *is* symbolically realized in this oedipal construction except that it is the father—not Des Grieux—who is symbolically castrated. Once the hero accepts her guidance unequivocally, Manon assumes the role of Des Grieux's superego, thus usurping paternal power from the father. The now impotent father would theoretically move aside, allowing Des Grieux to step in as the dominant male, except that in this novel Manon has castrated the father and so she alone possesses the masculine power in the relationship.[50] As Segal aptly points out, Manon does, after all, make the decisions. Her masculinization requires a counterpoint; Des Grieux, therefore, takes on a more feminine register. When the hero enters this relationship, he abandons his masculine origins rooted in the paternal home to take on the feminine characteristics lacking in Manon.

The scene in which Des Grieux rescues Manon from the Salpêtrière hospital offers a particularly striking example of this feminization. Analysis of the interactions between Des Grieux and Manon, and particularly the final sequence of the scene as the hero rescues Manon under cover of night, reveals that the hero takes on a particularly feminine persona:

> We returned to the hospital in the morning. I brought with me some linens, stockings, etc. for Manon, and over my body-coat, a waistcoat which concealed the bulk of everything in my pockets. We were in her room only for a moment. M. de T. gave her one of his shirts; I gave her my body-coat, the waistcoat being sufficient for me. There was nothing missing from her outfit, except the pantaloons, which I

50. Although we are still a long way from the types of female masculinity examined by Jack Halberstam in his groundbreaking *Female masculinity* (the androgyne, the tribade, or the butch lesbian, for instance), Manon does call into question the social markers of masculinity much like the masculine subjects Halberstam describes. See Halberstam, *Female masculinity* (Durham, NC, 1998).

had unfortunately forgotten. The lack of such a necessary piece of the outfit would have certainly amused us if the embarrassment it caused had been less serious. I was in despair that such a trifling error would get us caught. However, I made a decision which was to leave myself without pantaloons. *I gave mine to Manon.*

Nous retournâmes le matin à l'Hôpital. J'avais avec moi, pour Manon, du linge, des bas, etc., et par dessus mon juste-au-corps, un surtout qui ne laissait rien voir de trop enflé dans mes poches. Nous ne fûmes qu'un moment dans sa chambre. M. de T... lui laissa une de ses deux vestes; je lui donnai mon juste-au-corps, le surtout me suffisant pour sortir. Il ne se trouva rien de manque à son ajustement, excepté la culotte que j'avais malheureusement oubliée. L'oubli de cette pièce nécessaire nous eût sans doute apprêtés à rire si l'embarras où il nous mettait eût été moins sérieux. J'étais au désespoir qu'une bagatelle de cette nature fût capable de nous arrêter. Cependant je pris mon parti, qui fut de sortir moi-même sans culotte. *Je laissai la mienne à Manon.*[51]

By the end of this scene Manon is literally wearing the pants in the relationship. Rather than simply relying on brute force to rescue his damsel in distress as does Rosemont in the *Mémoires d'un homme de qualité* (who stabs a man in order to save his lover), Des Grieux plots and schemes, fretting about clothing and clever devices to facilitate Manon's escape. Since the moment of the lovers' first encounter, Manon has renounced traditional gender roles, refusing to marry, to become a mother, to enter the convent, and even to be a faithful lover.[52] In the absence of these feminine traits in the heroine, they are absorbed into the hero. The first hurdle to the completion of the oedipal cycle is the hero's own sexual ambiguity. Des Grieux's behavior and language not only designate him as feminine, but also go so far as to transform Manon into a part of himself, making Manon his masculine superego. From their first encounter, each sentence in which the hero pairs himself with her ("we talked," "we settled," "we would get married") is predicated upon an earlier proclamation of her

51. Prévost, *Manon Lescaut*, p.401 (emphasis added).
52. In this way, Manon serves as a counterexample to earlier traditional female characters. For example, if we look back to *La Princesse de Clèves*, the virtuous heroine chooses a life of solitude in the convent rather than indulging in carnal pleasures. In fact, we need look no further than the *Mémoires* and the character of Nadine, Renoncour's niece and Rosemont's lover, to see a perfect example of female virtuosity. Refusing to break up the father–son relationship, Nadine voluntarily goes to the convent to help quell Rosemont's desires.

desires ("she would be delighted," "she wanted to know") rather than
his own. Thus, the hero internalizes the influence of Manon almost
instantly. Her maturity and ingenuity guide his actions from the first
day he decides to flee the paternal home.

Because Des Grieux is feminized in this important intimate
relationship, his actions in other relationships are coded as feminine
as well. With his newfound sense of sexuality, even his homosocial
relationships are transformed. What appear to be masculine affective
bonds in fact reveal a different kind of attraction. Men offer the hero
money and protection while he plays the willing coquette, eliciting
favors from other men based not only on a gentlemanly sense of
honnêteté,[53] but also upon a sort of compassionate—at times sensual if
not sexual—attraction. In fact, during Renoncour's second encounter
with the hero in Calais, at the end of the latter's story and after his
return from America, he recognizes Des Grieux immediately, stating
that in spite of the chevalier's sad state, "his physiognomy was too
beautiful not to be easily recognized."[54] Segal argues that it is in his
financial transactions that Des Grieux assumes a feminine role:

> In receiving money from men—as he will, from now on, continue to
> do until Manon is dead—he similarly puts himself into the female
> position of one who, for love, is financially "protected." The discourse
> of comradeship, which is presented to overlay and transform the
> meaning of giving and receipt, is all the time subverted by his
> hypocritical and duplicitous "feminine" intention.[55]

It may have been the "noble air" that piqued Renoncour's interest in
the beginning, but after the time spent with Manon it is the hero's
beauty that serves as his most remarkable trait.

Des Grieux's feminine transformation becomes evident in his first
encounter with Tiberge after having met Manon and secured a hotel
room for his romantic tryst with her.[56] In the opening paragraphs of
the novel the hero describes Tiberge as the best and most virtuous

---

53. Translated as "honesty," *honnêteté* alludes to a much tighter and unspoken code
    between men of a certain quality.
54. Prévost, *Manon Lescaut*, p.367. "Il avait la physionomie trop belle pour n'être pas
    reconnu facilement."
55. Segal, *The Unintended reader*, p.150.
56. It is worth noting that Des Grieux uses a paternal connection (an old servant
    of his father's) to secure his first romantic tryst with Manon at the hotel. This
    exchange of paternal connections for sexual gratification reinforces Manon's
    role in the symbolic castration of the father.

of friends with whom he has always shared everything; in this scene, Tiberge waits at home for Des Grieux like a suspicious lover.

> I am sure, he said to me without any disguise, that you are planning some scheme that you wish to hide from me; I see it in your manner. I responded rather abruptly that I was not obligated to inform him about all of my plans. No, he replied, but you have always treated me as a friend, and this relationship implies a degree of confidence and openness. He pressed me so much and for so long to tell him my secret that, never having been reserved with him before, I confided in him completely the story of my passion. He listened with an air of disapproval which made me tremble.

> Je suis sûr, me dit-il sans déguisement, que vous méditez quelque dessein que vous me voulez cacher; je le vois à votre air. Je lui répondis assez brusquement que je n'étais pas obligé de lui rendre compte de tous mes desseins. Non, reprit-il, mais vous m'avez toujours traité en ami, et cette qualité suppose un peu de confiance et d'ouverture. Il me pressa si fort et si longtemps de lui découvrir mon secret, que n'ayant jamais eu de réserve avec lui, je lui fis l'entière confidence de ma passion. Il la reçut avec une apparence de mécontentement qui me fit frémir.[57]

Des Grieux's confession to Tiberge, which he thinks will bring them closer as brothers, is met with severity and the latter's apparent jealousy not of the hero's newfound passion, but of Manon's usurpation of power over his friend. Much like the brothers of *Totem and taboo*, these two men are divided—not united—by sexual desire.[58] In his passionate frenzy, Des Grieux has transgressed the bonds of heterosexual male friendship, assuming that his own sexual desire should be shared among friends. In the next sentence Tiberge chastises Des Grieux, making him promise to act in a wiser and more reasonable manner—in other words, to behave like a man. From this point until their reunion in America, this homosocial relationship verges on the romantic as Des Grieux coyly asks for favors, and Tiberge, like a disgruntled husband, begrudgingly gives in. E. Joe Johnson also notes the queer aspects in the chevalier's relationship with Tiberge,

---

57. Prévost, *Manon Lescaut*, p.369.
58. Freud writes, "sexual needs are not capable of uniting men in the same way as are the demands for self-preservation. Sexual satisfaction is essentially the private affair of each individual." *Totem and taboo*, p.86.

although, he places Tiberge in the feminine role.[59] This shift in gender roles among the two men does occur, but only later in the novel. Tiberge takes on a feminine role in the relationship in America, just after Manon's death, once the hero has returned to a comportment marked by masculine reflection and reason. In this situation, Tiberge's femininity counters Des Grieux's regained masculinity as the pair return to France after Manon's death. In his relationship with Tiberge, as well as in his other masculine relationships, the exchange of emotions for money and favors is directly correlated to Des Grieux's fluid understanding of gender roles.

While Tiberge chides him and implores him to act like a man, in M. de T. Des Grieux finds a friend who is willing to play along with his gender-bending behavior. In their first meeting, it is not money that Des Grieux desires, but Manon's freedom. Using his "natural" speech to excite M. de T.'s sympathetic nature, the hero actually places his heart in another man's hands: "the interest of my life and that of my heart are now in your hands."[60] Not only does his ruse work, but the two also become fast friends. At the end of this encounter Des Grieux informs the reader, "we embraced tenderly, and became friends, for no other reason than the goodness of our hearts and a simple disposition that leads a tender and generous man to love another man who resembles him," ending this tender discourse with "I am attached to you for life."[61] Unlike when he had first mentioned Manon to Tiberge, describing her to M. de T. does serve to bond the two men closer together, forming precisely the kind of homosocial relationship that Sedgwick describes as fundamental to Western literature. What makes this particular passage so revealing is its repetition three paragraphs later: "we embraced with an effusion of tenderness that an absence of three months makes so charming to two perfect lovers," but this time it is Manon who receives Des Grieux's affections while M. de T. stands watching in the corner of the room, the third point to this awkward love triangle.[62] At this moment Manon pronounces one of

59. See E. Joe Johnson, "Philosophical reflection, happiness, and male friendship in Prévost's *Manon Lescaut,*" *Studies in eighteenth-century culture* 31 (2002), p.169–90.
60. Prévost, *Manon Lescaut,* p.399. "L'intérêt de ma vie et celui de mon cœur sont maintenant entre vos mains."
61. Prévost, *Manon Lescaut,* p.400. "Nous nous embrassâmes avec tendresse, et nous devînmes amis, sans autre raison que la bonté de nos cœurs, et une simple disposition qui porte un homme tendre et généreux à aimer un autre homme qui lui ressemble [...] je vous suis attaché pour toute ma vie."
62. Prévost, *Manon Lescaut,* p.400. "Nous nous embrassâmes avec cette effusion de

the few lines directly attributed to her as she cries out, "Alas! What kind of place have you left me in!"[63] While her tender emotions are only hinted at by the hero who describes the embraces and intimate exchanges between himself and his beloved, her words betray a truer, masculine nature as she once again takes control of the situation, dictating actions for Des Grieux. The response to this statement does not come from the chevalier, who having now returned to his feminine character can only assent to following her commands. Instead, M. de T. replies, "as for this place [...] you must not call it the hospital; it is Versailles since a person who merits the reverence of every heart is held within it," imploring her to be more playful and imaginative—in other words he suggests that she act like a woman.[64] Not only does the language of this scene suggest a doubling of the romantic relationship as Des Grieux uses the same compassionate words with M. de T. and Manon, but it also reinforces the tension between Manon and M. de T. that relegates Des Grieux to the feminine role in their threesome. Thus, the emotional security of another man in this novel serves to undermine the hero's masculinity just as much as financial security; the hero can complete his subjective formation only once he understands how to be a man.

If Des Grieux is to learn how to be a man, he must first learn to self-identify with other men. Segal argues that his feminization reaches its apex in the Italian prince scene in which Manon spends the entire day tending to the chevalier's physical appearance and fixing his hair as if he were a girl. This period of playing dress-up ends with her showing off her lover to the Italian prince as a prized possession. At this point, Segal argues, "des Grieux reasserts himself, acquires the language of patriarchy, and the balance of power is fatally changed."[65] She reads the rest of the story as Manon's gradual acquisition of the traditional feminine role as she takes M. de T.'s advice and starts acting like a woman until her death. While we can see certain elements of Des Grieux's masculine assertion in his identification with the prince as a nobleman and in his desire to rectify the situation with

---

tendresse qu'une absence de trois mois fait trouver si charmante à deux parfaits amants."

63. Prévost, *Manon Lescaut*, p.400. "Hélas! dans quel lieu me laissez-vous!"

64. Prévost, *Manon Lescaut*, p.400. "Pour ce lieu [...] il ne faut plus l'appeler l'Hôpital; c'est Versailles, depuis qu'une personne qui mérite l'empire de tous les cœurs y est renfermée."

65. Segal, *The Unintended reader*, p.49.

gentlemanly *politesse*, he easily gives up and is once again incapable of taking control of the situation. In fact, in the very next scene Des Grieux's next rival, the young G. M., appears, an event which ends in the hero's return to excessive emotion and an inability to behave like a man with the prostitute Manon sends as a replacement lover.

This sequence of events does, however, end with a certain *prise de conscience* in Des Grieux of his masculine identity. When M. de T. offers to gather his friends together to kill the young G. M., the hero replies, "let's save our blood [...] for a last resort."[66] The "us" here represents not only Des Grieux and M. de T., but also the young G. M. and, by extension, all noble men. For the first time in the novel Des Grieux recognizes himself as a brother of men. In the next sentence, "I'm thinking of a much gentler approach, and which promises to be equally successful," the hero reacts with reason and reflection rather than excessive emotion.[67] Although the hero will continue to waver between the masculine and the feminine until his return from America, this self-identification with other men marks a turning point in the hero's perception of his gender. It is here that we see the beginning of his turn to the masculine realm.

The first step in Des Grieux's process of masculinization comes much later when he has left France (*la patrie*) for America. It is in the new land where he is spatially separated from paternal power that the hero finally realizes a sense of masculinity. We can see early versions of this realization in his ability to play the normative masculine gender role as he and Manon play house in Louisiana. In fact, in earlier scenes in which family roles have been assigned to him (by Manon and her brother), on the boat heading to America, the narrator finally invents a role for himself when he tells the captain that he and Manon are married. Moreover, when they finally arrive at their dirty cabin in New Orleans, Des Grieux becomes a caring husband, assuring Manon that she will make a good housewife: "you are an admirable alchemist [...] you transform everything into gold."[68] The pair live blissfully in America until the governor of the settlement learns that they are not lawfully married. According to the customs of the colony, he has the right to pair unmarried women with any man he chooses.

---

66. Prévost, *Manon Lescaut*, p.416. "Réservons notre sang [...] pour l'extrémité."
67. Prévost, *Manon Lescaut*, p.416. "Je médite une voie plus douce, et dont je n'espère pas moins de succès."
68. Prévost, *Manon Lescaut*, p.434. "Tu es une chimiste admirable [...] tu transformes tout en or."

Because of Manon's beauty, he decides that she should marry his own nephew, Synnelet, thus making a decision that ends the utopian pastoral life that Manon and Des Grieux had shared for a brief period. In a desperate attempt to keep Manon, the chevalier challenges his final rival to a duel. The ultimate reassertion of his male dominance comes with a final bloodshed. The hero disarms Synnelet with his first move, but in a display of noble benevolence he returns his opponent's sword, giving him another chance at a fair fight. Although Des Grieux is cut on his arm, he ultimately stabs Synnelet, spilling the latter's blood and believing he has killed him. However, the reader soon learns that the wound is not fatal. Instead of preserving the romantic relationship with Manon, this violent action serves to unite the two men. With each man having spilled the blood of the other, the two become united as blood brothers.

Realizing the sincerity of Des Grieux's romantic intentions, Synnelet endeavors to help his new friend obtain his desire (this time not just being with Manon, but the final possession of her as his wife), but he is too late. The hero's newfound brother arrives at the scene to find Des Grieux dying and Manon already dead. Synnelet then carries Des Grieux back to the town where he nurses him back to health, and in the meantime has Manon's body moved to a more respectable burial place. When the hero awakens, he finds that masculine bonds of friendship and brotherhood have replaced passionate bonds of desire. Des Grieux can finally retake his masculinity when he recognizes in Synnelet a brother, a *semblable*, a man. His masculinization necessarily corresponds to Manon's death. During his relationship with Manon, an oedipal formation was impossible because the hero was incapable of performing the masculine role. Once he sheds the woman who served as his masculine alter ego he returns to France as a man among men, even if the configuration of men has been altered due to the death of his father.

The story that kills

Upon reaching the scene of Manon's death in his narration to Renoncour, Des Grieux states, "Excuse me if I finish in just a few words a story that kills me."[69] Whereas the hero spends hour after hour (and page after page) recounting his promiscuous and immoral

69. Prévost, *Manon Lescaut*, p.438. "Pardonnez, si j'achève en peu de mots un récit qui me tue."

behavior during his time with Manon, her death marks the end of his confession to the *homme de qualité*, as well as the end of his period of rebellion. In the few paragraphs that follow Manon's death scene, we learn that Synnelet is so moved by the chevalier's love for Manon that he moves her body to a proper burial place; that on the brink of his own death Des Grieux is so moved by the death of Manon that he decides to return to France; that Tiberge is so moved by an earlier letter from Des Grieux (informing him of the latter's sad and imminent voyage to America with Manon) that the trusty friend makes the journey to America to assist the hero; that Des Grieux receives a letter from his brother upon arrival in France informing him that his own father has died; and, finally, that our hero runs into the *homme de qualité* once again where he is able to finish telling the story he began just before leaving for America—the story that kills him.

This constant movement of others around Des Grieux at the end of the story—emotionally (characters being compelled to action because of an excess of feeling), spatially (Manon's body being moved, Des Grieux and Tiberge moving from one country to another), and temporally (time accelerating in the story)—acts as a catalyzing force designed to propel the now emotionally fixed hero back into French society. While, as Sgard aptly notes, the calendar time that passes between Manon's death and Des Grieux's return to France amounts to nine months (the time needed to "give birth" to the story), it is important to remember that these nine months are recorded in just a few paragraphs.[70] These paragraphs thus serve as Manon's postmortem, uncovering the true reason for her death—the gestation of Des Grieux's story happens only in her ultimate absence. Ironically, in this gruesome birth/death story we find the possibility for an optimistic future, and that future is decidedly male. Much of Des Grieux's narration takes the tone of a confession of events; however, the last few paragraphs of *Manon* indicate a reflective turn in the hero's narration. With the death of Manon, his period of rebellion against the father comes to an end as he returns to a state of reason. Having now been purged of his frenetic and passionate behavior in the discursive space of his confession to Renoncour, the hero is finally able to return to his father's home.

At this point, the hero returns to France with Tiberge, the brother figure who has consistently allowed him passage back home without forcing it. Having shared his childhood with Tiberge, he is the only

---

70. See Jean Sgard, *L'Abbé Prévost: labyrinthes de la mémoire* (Paris, 1986), p.70.

friend who can accompany the hero back to his homeland even though he cannot complete the journey with Des Grieux all the way to the paternal household. Ultimately, the chevalier must shed both his romantic relationship (with Manon), which had rendered him feminine and incapable of inhabiting the masculine family, and the relationship with his sociable brother (Tiberge), who had replicated the older brother in function while holding even less power than the blood sibling. The hero's need for paternal rule leads him to leave the new world—a world of no fathers—to return to France, his *patrie*. Crossing the Atlantic with Tiberge by his side, neither child nor father, he is baptized a brother among men.

The hero returns to France just in time to learn of his father's death in a letter from his brother.

> I wrote to my family upon arrival. I learned of my father's death in a letter from my older brother, and I tremble with fear, rightfully so, to think that my escapades contributed to his death. The wind being favorable for Calais, I embarked right away with the intention of arriving a few miles away from this town, at the home of one of my relatives where my brother tells me he will be waiting for me.

> J'écrivis à ma famille en arrivant. J'ai appris, par la réponse de mon frère aîné, la triste nouvelle de la mort de mon père, à laquelle je tremble, avec trop de raison, que mes égarements n'aient contribué. Le vent étant favorable pour Calais, je me suis embarqué aussitôt, dans le dessein de me rendre, à quelques lieues de cette ville, chez un gentilhomme de mes parents, où mon frère m'écrit qu'il doit attendre mon arrivée.[71]

Arriving back in France, Des Grieux begins to feel, much like the son of Greuze's *Fils puni*, the guilt of a rebellious son whose actions contributed to his father's death. What separates him from the guilty brothers of *Totem and taboo* is that he does not share that guilt with his brother. The guiltless older brother is thus free to assume the role of father. Des Grieux may fear that he has killed off the father, but he has not eliminated fatherhood. Waiting at home for the prodigal son, the older brother now assumes the fatherly function. At this point brotherhood has transformed into a new type of fatherhood and, moreover, given the older brother's unique position somewhere

71. Prévost, *Manon Lescaut*, p.440.

between the paternal and the maternal, this fatherhood gives birth to a renewed form of motherhood as well. In America, the hero was able to act as the patriarch in his household with Manon. In their Louisiana home, Manon finally assumed a traditionally feminine role, performing domestic chores while Des Grieux worked outside of the home. Yet, for all the semblance of tradition, this picturesque scene of domestic bliss was fatally flawed. The hero, lacking a family name and paternal power, remained incapable of maintaining a patriarchal family. Their household was thus destined to inhabit a representational space nestled between fading models of patriarchy and modern models of domestic equality. Furthermore, the placement of their home so near the border separating the land of the colonizers from the "savage" nature of America highlights the extremity and unnaturalness of their union.[72] Although the idea of a complete equality among brothers will not acquire political expression for another sixty years, what we see in the transformation of fatherhood in *Manon* is one step in the development of a model of social identity based on liberty, equality, and fraternity.

As we have seen, lapses in time in *Manon* indicate to the reader important transformations in the hero. We can also detect moments of temporal slippage in *Grecque moderne*. Although the narrator remains largely within one timeframe—that of his time spent with Téophé—he occasionally hints to its position in the past through the use of linguistic markers. Most of these moments involve calling upon the reader to pay close attention to details or to decide on the heroine's fate, implying that he alone currently has the answers. One such moment occurs at the end of the first volume. "Today as I reflect on the past," he writes, "I perhaps have a clearer understanding of my feelings then, and it seems to me that what I secretly desired was for Téophé to feel for me some of the penchant I had for her, or at least that she let me see some evidence of it."[73] Although the entire story is

72. Des Grieux often describes New Orleans and its inhabitants as "savages" in an attempt to further distinguish himself as a respectable man worthy of Manon's love, saying of the land that it is "inhabited by ferocious beasts and savages just as barbaric" ("habité par des bêtes féroces, et par des sauvages aussi barbares qu'elles") (Prévost, *Manon Lescaut*, p.436).
73. Prévost, *Greek girl's story*, p.110; *Grecque moderne*, p.64. "Aujourd'hui qu'en réfléchissant sur le passé, je juge peut-être beaucoup mieux qu'alors quelles étaient mes dispositions, il me semble que ce que je désirais secrètement était que Téophé eut pris pour moi une partie de l'inclination que j'avais pour elle, ou du moins qu'elle m'en eut laissé voir quelques marques."

told in the past tense, with the exception of direct quotations, this is
the first temporal marker the narrator offers. We know that the story
has already passed, but now we hear his voice, the distanced voice of
an older man, reckoning with his past.

While the insertion of the voice in the present indicates two precise
temporal matrices within the novel, time in the narration remains
ambiguous. Although the narrator indicates his relatively youthful age
early in the story (he is at least young enough that his desire for women
is still acceptable), in the second volume of the novel he appears to age
at an increasingly rapid pace. It is shocking the rate at which he sheds
the virility of youth for the infirmity of old age. By the end of the novel
he can hardly leave his bed because of his diminished state. And yet,
it is the young Greek woman who dies first. Aside from a brief illness
earlier in the story, which the heroine caught because of her devotion
to the Ambassador, she appears a relatively healthy young woman.
She is only sixteen at the beginning of the story, and yet by the last
pages she is dead. In fact, much like the ending of *Manon*, time appears
to speed up and her death is recounted so quickly that the inattentive
reader might miss it altogether. In one brief sentence, halfway through
the final paragraph, we learn of her death: "I did not even learn of her
death until several months after the tragic event."[74]

The language the narrator choses to describe the events leading
to her death (*accident*) purposefully obfuscate his own role in it. The
"accident" to which he refers is, in fact, not an accident at all, but
a transgression against her by himself and a disgruntled servant. A
former governess who believes Téophé to have stolen her lover accuses
the heroine of carrying on an affair in the Ambassador's house. The
former governess tells her master that she has seen a young man
entering her former pupil's room at night and convinces the master
to storm in on his young ward to catch her in the act. Not finding
any man in the room, he continues to accuse Téophé of improper
behavior. The next day, having realized what happened, Téophé once
again asks the Ambassador to allow her to seek refuge in a convent.
His refusal is the final incident between the two prior to her death.
In fact, by refusing to let Téophé leave his house, he denies her the
subjectivity she so desperately craves. Imprisoned in the French
man's house, she remains nothing more than the object of his jealous
obsession. In the end, he becomes more brutish than the noblemen

74. Prévost, *Greek girl's story*, p.201; *Grecque moderne*, p.121. "Je n'ai même appris sa
    mort que plusieurs mois après ce funeste accident."

he met in Turkey as he slowly kills her spirit, leading to the eventual death of her body as well. Throughout the novel we watch as both the Ambassador's house and his mental capacities crumble. His story, like many of those in Prévost's novels, offers us a glimpse into the fragility of the (masculine) human spirit.

The fragility of the male spirit for Prévost hinges upon the availability (or not) of the woman. His desire to control her overwhelms him as he loses control of himself. We cannot think of this traumatic experience solely in individualistic terms. The unhinging of these men's spirits occurs when desire is confronted with social expectations. For Des Grieux, the expectation is that he fulfill his duties in the Order of Malta as should a second son, and for the Ambassador it is expected that he behave with a gentlemanly aplomb fit for a Frenchman abroad. Conversely, for Manon and Téophé, their histories as the sexual objects of men lead to expectations that they can be nothing more than a sexual object. What is so innovative in Prévost's novels is that we learn that, in the absence of a woman, a story about a woman will serve the same function. In fact, Srinivas Aravamuden has likened *Grecque moderne* to a much older oriental tale—the *Arabian nights*. Like Scheherazade, Téophé repays her debt to the Ambassador by telling him a story, except that rather than telling her story, which she does not know, the two protagonists uncover it together.[75] However, once her father is found (and rejects her), and once the Ambassador realizes that he cannot play the role of her lover, he has no more need for her story. Her untimely death is the price she pays for running out of things to say. They have already discovered it all and, as a now virtuous woman, she has little more to add. In this way, the end of the novel demonstrates an inability to reproduce. Since she will not sleep with him and she has no more stories to tell, her reproductive value is diminished, and she has no reason to exist. At this point her ghost is more valuable to the narrator than her presence.

For the women of these two novels, the stories we read are certainly stories that kill, but can the same be said for the men? Des Grieux and the Ambassador suffer in many ways throughout the stories, even being from time to time on the brink of death, and yet they live to tell the tale. Rather than a story that kills, what we read are *stories that must kill.* In order for the men to assert themselves as whole, they need to eliminate the source of heterosexual desire in favor of the more tolerable and productive homosociality. The death of the woman

75. Aravamudan, *Enlightenment orientalism*, p.167.

brings them back to reason and back to reasonable relations with men. While the brothers of *Totem and taboo* killed the father in order to be with the mother, these brothers must kill the object of desire itself. Only through the death of the woman can they form a regime of the brother.

The king is dead. Long live the brother!

Of modern mechanisms of governmental formation, MacCannell writes, "If in modernity (the time of self-governance, self-begetting, no fathers) formal arrangements—social, personal, aesthetic—are no longer laid out or programmed Oedipally, they must be rethought."[76] Although for Des Grieux an oedipal formation is impossible, for the older brother it is not. The knowledge of the older brother's eventual ascent to power signals the triumph of Oedipus in *Manon*. However, the plot's focus on the prodigal son for whom fatherhood is nothing more than an obstacle to his passionate desire suggests a different desire—a communal desire to rethink restrictive paternal bonds. By examining what can happen when a son is willing to unbind himself from patriarchal authority, Prévost explores the interstices of absolutism, and yet, by offering us a glimpse of the older brother, he reminds us that such authority does still exist. In *Manon*, rather than proposing an abandonment of Oedipus, the author allows for an exploration of its interruption and transformation.

To read *Manon* as the story of the prodigal son who moves laterally from one patriarchal regime to the next is to deny the richness of a story that rests in the breach *between* these two regimes. Calling into question traditional models of fatherhood requires a paradigmatic shift in thinking of the family as centering on a parents–children axis to one centered on a children–children axis, and it also requires an examination of how we arrive at the latter from the former. In other words, the family we find in Prévost's novels, while it still contains certain hierarchies, is laid out in a more lateral fashion. It is clear that an exploration of brotherhood and male homosociality is central to this novel. The chevalier Des Grieux is surrounded by brothers: Tiberge, Lescaut, M. de T., and Synnelet, each of whom fills a brotherly need for the hero throughout his time away from home.

In the hero's relationship with Tiberge we see most clearly the possibility of a fraternity that directly corresponds to eighteenth-century

76. MacCannell, *The Regime of the brother*, p.144.

notions of sociability (*sociabilité*). We have noted that Tiberge never enters the hero's childhood home, but he does enter Des Grieux's home in America. Just after their beach-side reunion, the hero declares, "I took him back to my place. I made him the master of all that I possessed."[77] Whereas Des Grieux's own brother becomes his master by blood, and his brother-in-law Lescaut usurps power by force, Des Grieux deems Tiberge a true brother, with whom he can share his life without any loss of power. In fact, it is not to Renoncour that the hero first confesses his story, but to Tiberge: "I told him everything that had happened to me since I left France."[78] Like the *homme de qualité*, Tiberge (also a man of the cloth) is equally qualified to take the hero's confession, but, unlike Renoncour, Tiberge does not prescribe it. Des Grieux confesses to Tiberge out of a sense of gentlemanly duty to share with a friend. Whereas the first discussion of Manon with Tiberge had driven the two men apart, recounting the story of his life with her which culminates in her death brings the pair closer together than ever before.

At this point, Des Grieux has confessed, he understands himself as the subject of his story and undertakes to atone for his sins. He could have begun his new life with his friend; he could have finally joined the clergy, as was his original, youthful desire, but instead he returns to the family. To end the novel with Tiberge, or with any of the other brother figures rather than his own brother, would be to transcend the oedipal structure of the narrative altogether. What we see in *Manon*, as well as in *Histoire d'une Grecque moderne*, is the emergence of a concept of brotherhood as one possible model for social governance.

In both novels we find intricate familial laboratories. In *Manon*, we read about a strange love story told as an interlude between two very different masculine regimes (the father and the older brother), in which the hero is incapable of escaping kinship bonds. As he moves throughout France and America, he tries out different familial structures, but in each of these experimental relationships (with Manon, Lescaut, Tiberge, the *homme de qualité*) his own role never diverges from brother, son, or lover. In *Histoire d'une Grecque moderne*, by contrast, kinship bonds are always only imaginarily maintained. The Ambassador inserts himself as a brother among men in Turkey,

---

77. Prévost, *Manon Lescaut*, p.440. "Je le conduisis chez moi. Je le rendis le maître de tout ce que je possédais."
78. Prévost, *Manon Lescaut*, p.440. "Je lui appris tout ce qui m'était arrivé depuis mon départ de France."

he imagines himself the lover of his slave, and he unwillingly plays the role of her father. Each of the novels betrays the anxiety the protagonists feel when kinship becomes obfuscated and masculinity can no longer be defined with and against a paternal figure. Although Des Grieux and the Ambassador exhibit anxiety in very different ways, they both demonstrate a confusion regarding the place of women in their masculine networks. Clearly, the woman's presence is crucial to their story, but it is not a story they can understand until she is gone. We will recall that MacCannell's regime of the brother must deny the sister, but Prévost's brotherly regime must also deny the mother and all other women. In these homosocial worlds all reproduction happens through men and men alone; although women are still necessary for reproduction, this form of reproduction requires their erasure. The death of the woman gives meaning to the life (in the form of memoirs) of the male narrators who share their stories with other men.

The woman's place in Prévost's fraternal regime is, therefore, extremely precarious. By killing off the women who give their names to the novels, the two male protagonists restore order to their otherwise topsy-turvy households. The death of the woman has meant the birth of a valuable commodity—a story. The exchange of women occurs on a narrative level that unites the brothers in a way that evens out social relationships. Although the Ambassador plays a paternal role throughout much of the novel, he ends it among family and friends. He is no longer in a position of power above others—he is a brother among equals. Similarly, Des Grieux does refuse paternal authority, but his refusal does not lead to a rejection of the family as such: It leads instead to an acceptance of a new type of authority, that of his brother. In *Manon Lescaut*, Oedipus is not destroyed—only interrupted; we thus see the potential for a future in which the stodgy old system of the father will eventually fall at the hands of the brothers. In such a future, "vive le roi!" will come to be replaced with "liberté, égalité, fraternité."

3. Wandering souls: the world of Crébillon fils

A singularity is indivisible from a plurality.

Une singularité est indissociable d'une pluralité.

Jean-Luc Nancy, *Etre singulier pluriel*

When we recall some of the *chefs d'œuvre* of libertine fiction in France, our mind likely turns to the works of the marquis de Sade or Choderlos de Laclos, two of the most famous libertine authors. The majority of libertine fiction that we continue to discuss today was published in the latter half of the eighteenth century and into the early years of the nineteenth. The stories these works tell are highly erotic, often quite violent, and generally convey some message of a materialist philosophy based on an immediate pleasure of the self. In most of Sade's novels, but especially in *Les Cent Vingt Journées de Sodome* (*The 120 days of Sodom*), what we read is a story of the id unleashed, the superego externalized and shut out from the space of pleasure altogether.[1] Given the novel's long descriptions of perverse desire and the intense pleasure the torturers feel at the pain of the victims, it is no wonder that many have argued that Sade, in many ways, anticipated Freud and psychoanalysis.[2] It seems he was every bit as interested in the extremities of

1. Donatien Alphonse, marquis de Sade, *Les Cent vingt journées de Sodome* (Paris, 1998).
2. When Sade's work began to be rereleased in France in the 1950s, it was embraced by Surrealists such as Breton and Dali, as well as existentialists such as Beauvoir and Sartre. These were among the first to see in Sade's work the explorations into the human psyche that would prefigure Freud. Since that time, this argument has been made numerous times. One famous objection to this hypothesis comes from Lacan, who argues that, rather than looking forward, Sade is actually looking to the past, completing the work of Kant by depicting empirically the "true reason" that Kant could describe only on a metaphysical

133

human nature as was the nineteenth-century psychoanalyst. However, one great distinction between Sade and Freud is that, for Sade, there is no distinction between the libido (the sex drive), Eros (the life drive), and Thanatos (the death drive). There is no *beyond* in Sade's pleasure principle—all pleasure is fair game.

The basis of the pleasure principle, for both Freud and Lacan, is simple: Human beings tend to avoid pain at all costs in order to seek out what is pleasurable—it is a natural animal instinct. More difficult to parse out and, consequently, more controversial, is first, the role the pleasure principle plays in the psyche of the individual, and second, what lies beyond its reach. In *Beyond the pleasure principle*, Freud introduces for the first time what he calls "Thanatos," or the death drive, which will forever change the study and practice of psychoanalysis. Realizing that humans are not governed by the search for pleasure and avoidance of pain alone, he argues that we have a natural, biological impulse to return to our original, precorporeal state. We came from dust, and our bodies are constantly moving closer to a return to dust. To combat this inevitable biological process, he argues, we have developed another drive, "Eros," the life drive, that compels us to stave off our untimely demise. It is the competition between these three forces—the libido, Eros, and Thanatos—that constitutes the human psychic experience.[3]

Lacan, however, does not believe that we are *always* trying to avoid death. In some cases, he argues, humans can find a certain perverse pleasure by straying just beyond the pleasure principle. This might explain why humans choose to bungee jump or skydive; we love the thrill of being within touching distance of death because it brings us back into our bodies and reminds us that we are alive. In other words, Lacan argues that we can find pleasure in the death drive—and this painful pleasure is what he calls *jouissance*. In addition to becoming an important concept for Lacan (especially in his seminar on anxiety), *jouissance* has become a key term in queer theory, particularly among those critics who argue for an anti-relational mode of politics such as Edelman or Bersani.[4] *Jouissance* is the pain experienced in the ultimate pursuit of pleasure. It is human nature, Lacan argues, to

---

      level. See Jacques Lacan, "Kant with Sade," translated by James B. Swenson Jr., *October* 51 (1989), p.55–75.

3.   See Sigmund Freud, *Beyond the pleasure principle*, translated by James Strachey (1920; New York, 1961).

4.   See Jacques Lacan, *Anxiety: the seminar of Jacques Lacan, book X*, ed. Jacques-Alain

try to transgress boundaries and, as such, we are always tempted to go beyond the pleasure principle. This is the very explicit goal of Sade's *Cent vingt journées*. The time devoted to preparing for the debauchery, the very precise dimensions of when the prostitutes will tell their stories; the detailed limits demarcating the various types of perversions, this is the clear link that Lacan draws between Kant and Sade; desire is linked not only to sexual pleasure, but also to the desire *of desire itself*. The very calculated schema of murderous torture for the pleasure of the four main characters demonstrates a desire to apply pure reason to that which has no reason; it is linked to the desire to control the drives, and those drives always remain imperceptible and, as such, uncontrollable.

In spite of its name, the "pleasure principle" is anything but pleasurable to experience for those who are the partial objects of desire (*objets petit a*). For Lacan, the expression of desire in language moves it from the unconscious into the conscious world, and thus constitutes the creation of desire. However, because the unconscious is not just unknown, it is *unknowable*, desire can never be attached to an object. The objects to which it attaches are only partial, reflecting the desiring individual's ego, and reminding the subject of what it cannot have. Put differently, desire is a lack that one tries, always unsuccessfully, to fill with an *objet petit a*. In this way, the objects of desire are doomed to remain objects—they are never considered in their subjectivity. This is why so many have described the function of desire as one that reinforces the hegemony of the master–slave narrative. The object of desire is emptied out of its humanity, rendered nothing more than a lack. This is the type of relationship that Horkheimer and Adorno assessed as being the hallmark of the Enlightenment and its most troubling legacy.

In fact, two decades before Lacan wrote "Kant with Sade," Horkheimer and Adorno had already made the connection between the two eighteenth-century philosophers. In a chapter on Enlightenment morality and Sade's *Juliette*, they write, "Reason is the organ of calculation, of planning; it is neutral with regard to ends; its element is coordination. More than a century before the emergence of sport, Sade demonstrated empirically what Kant grounded transcendentally: the affinity between knowledge and planning which has set its stamp of inescapable functionality on a bourgeois existence

---

Miller, translated by A. R. Price (Cambridge, 2016); Edelman's *No future*, and Bersani's *Homos*.

rationalized even in its breathing spaces."[5] The relation of knowledge to planning makes governing people a dangerous sport. It is a sport in which objects of desire are bent to the will of egomaniacal dictators.[6] Essentially, boiling everything down to reason removes all affective content, reducing humanity to no more than so many *objets petit a*. Like objects, they are evacuated of their own humanity and become mere receptacles for the other's desire. In the authors' opinion, one of the few philosophers to address this phenomenon in an honest manner was the marquis de Sade. While philosophers such as Kant appeal to some sort of higher Will that governs reasonable men, making them inherently good when living in society, Sade (and Nietzsche), they argue, demonstrate(s) that a higher "good" in the absence of religious mythology is nothing more than utopian optimism. Sade's Juliette, who teaches us to do away with all mythologies and pay homage to reason alone, finds that she is capable of providing logical arguments for torture, rape, and murder, among other crimes. Sade's *reductio ad absurdum* demonstrates the true power of reason—the good and the bad. "In Sade as in Mandeville," Horkheimer and Adorno write, "private vices are the anticipatory historiography of public virtues in the totalitarian era."[7] Once humans, like Juliette, use the world of reason and science for their own personal gain, there is no longer room for the common good so idealistically promised by the apostles of the Enlightenment.

According to Horkheimer and Adorno, the morality of the Enlightenment is a libertine one. Based as this morality is on pure reason (evacuated of affect), it sets the stage for an externalization of the master–slave dialectic as introduced by Georg W. F. Hegel in the *Phenomenology of the spirit*.[8] Hegel saw in Kant's pure reason a tyrant that exerts its force over all the other passions, thus creating a conflict within the subconscious mind. The totalitarian state becomes the master who tries to reason the other into subservience. That reason, however, serves only the will of a master ego and must be universal—it allows no room for difference or dissent. In the

5.   Horkheimer and Adorno, *Dialectic of Enlightenment*, p.69.
6.   The link between pure reason and tyrannical leadership was dramatized in an even more direct manner by Pier Paolo Pasolini in his film *Salò, or the 120 days of Sodom*. In the film, the director transposes Sade's novel onto the fascist regime in power in Salò, Italy.
7.   Horkheimer and Adorno, *Dialectic of Enlightenment*, p.92.
8.   Georg Wilhelm Friedrich Hegel, *Phenomenology of the spirit (The Phenomenology of the mind)* (1807; New York, 2009).

world of the libertine novels of authors such as Sade and Laclos, this universalism is relative to the desiring subject. In such a world, subjects are necessarily pitted against one another since no two unconscious desires could possibly be exactly the same at exactly the same time. This means that far from being a nurturing environment for both the body and the mind, kinship groups and other intimate communities would be nothing more than centers for the circulation of pain. Knowledge is produced within this group, but it is akin to Juliette's own libertine education—it is knowledge of the link between pain and power.

For this reason, libertine philosophy has long occupied a central place in critiques of the rise of fascist regimes in the West. In many libertine novels, encounters with others are presented in the most negative of lights, resulting in the pleasure of the subject alone. Yet it is important to note that critics who find in libertine fiction a key to the ills of modern, neoliberal societies often base their critiques, as do Horkheimer and Adorno, on works written in the latter half of the eighteenth century. The world in which Sade and Laclos were writing was one in which a discord was building in intensity until it finally reached a tipping point in 1789. True, Sade was already embroiled in his own personal scandals, but his writings, along with those of other libertine authors of the day, offered more than pornographic tales: they offered philosophical insight and equally sharp criticisms of politics and people. They spoke of Republicanism, reason, and revolution in ways that were specific to a France of the 1780s and 1790s. The libertinism of Sade and Laclos is, in many ways, the culmination of decades of libertine philosophy, but it is not where it began.

Much earlier in the century Claude Prosper Jolyot de Crébillon (Crébillon fils) was writing licentious novels and tales that would later be called some of the earliest examples of libertine fiction. In contrast to later libertine fiction, Crébillon focuses less on actions than on discourse. In lieu of long scenes of torture, we find long discussions about the nature of humans, sexuality, and society. Even in *La Nuit et le moment* (*The Night and the moment*), when Clitandre sneaks into bed with Cidalise, he does not immediately take advantage of her body. Instead, he regales her with stories of his sexual exploits. In these stories he lays bare his libertine debauchery, hoping to seduce the woman in bed with him by exciting her passions with tales of his previous sexual exploits. Crébillon's emphasis on talking and creating a language of libertinism make him, in many ways, a better precursor to Freud than

Sade. He too is fascinated by the perversions of humankind, but, more than anything, he wants to talk about it.[9]

Over the course of the century, libertine fiction moves away from discourse and toward actions, yet we can still see the traces of Crébillon's legacy in such authors as Denis Diderot and Vivant Denon. By focusing on the language of libertinism, these authors explore the potential of non-normative erotic systems in ways that allow a space to imagine utopian communities of desiring bodies. The discursive nature of this fiction necessitates a myriad of voices, which renders the practice of libertinism necessarily collective. In this chapter I will examine some of Crébillon's works, arguing that his early strand of libertinism is filled with a certain optimism for humanity that is difficult to find in later libertine fiction. In his novels, reason is not devoid of affect. Although reasoned discourse becomes the aphrodisiac par excellence in his works, there still exists the space for love, hope, and even hate. Instead of a *reductio ad absurdum* that leads to an affectless atomistic society, what emerges from his fiction is the possibility for a more ethical politics of encounter.[10] Like all of the authors studied in this book, Crébillon does quite a bit of world-building in his novels. He creates not only characters but also scenes and moods that draw the reader into the stories taking place. In order to better understand what a politics of encounter might resemble we must first take a closer look at Crébillon's world.

Le monde de Crébillon[11]

It may seem ironic that the man who in 1759 became a royal censor would be considered a progenitor of libertine fiction, but such is the

9. For an excellent study of the relation between seduction and language in Crébillon, see Geneviève Salvan, *Séduction et dialogue dans l'œuvre de Crébillon* (Paris, 2002).
10. The politics of encounter I propose is similar to Louis Althusser's notion of "aleatory materialism" in that something new emerges from the encounter between two or more bodies, but diverges from it in that I focus on the ethical possibilities of the encounters between bodies. For more on aleatory materialism, see L. Althusser, *Philosophy of the encounter: later writings 1978–1987*, ed. Oliver Corpet and François Matheron, translated by G. M. Goshgarian (New York, 2006).
11. Although this phrase translates as "Crébillon's world," I have chosen to leave it in French throughout this chapter to emphasize the ambiguity of the term *monde* as it is addressed in this section.

life of Crébillon fils. Son of the great tragedian Prosper Jolyot de Crébillon, he was born into a world of arts and literature. He was also born into a world of politics, as his father too was a royal censor. Although Crébillon lived a relatively modest life and experienced only a small amount of fame in his lifetime (in comparison to his father), he was an expert at his craft. In fact, many scholars have written on the impeccable quality of his prose, with Emeline Mossé even calling him "one of the greatest prose writers of his time next to Prévost, Marivaux, or Rousseau."[12] In his pieces he created complex worlds that involved dynamic characters, rich plots, and harsh critiques of French politics. As Carole Dornier argues, from his earliest publications, the author uses frames such as the oriental tales that were in vogue in France following the translation into French of the *Arabian nights* in order to veil critiques of the Catholic Church. For example, *Tanzaï and Néadarné*, she argues, "belongs to a wave of pamphlets and polemics that proliferated around the time of the *Unigenitus* bull affair."[13] Similarly, Dornier and many others have argued that *Le Sopha* is a *roman à clef*, describing the exorbitant behavior of Louis XV and his court. Crébillon fils knew perhaps better than any of his contemporaries how to take the world around him and transform it into a magical story that fascinates both in content and in language.

Yet, rather than merely reflecting upon the reality of eighteenth-century France, Crébillon's tales and novels open up new worlds and, with them, new possibilities. He may be alluding to the pope or the king, but in creating sultans, courtesans, and shahs, and by placing them in unfamiliar lands, he unlocks the potential for otherwise unimaginable outcomes. Certain rules of Western politics and sexuality no longer hold in these situations. As we saw in the first chapter with Montesquieu's *Lettres persanes*, interrogating political figures through the lens of the East brings a renewed focus on the

12. Emeline Mossé, *Le Langage de l'implicite dans l'œuvre de Crébillon fils* (Paris, 2009), p.7. Mossé points out that scholars often feel the need to make an argument for the importance of studying Crébillon since he had long been taken less seriously than authors such as Voltaire and Rousseau. She argues that this need not be the case since the author's work was well received in its time. Robert Darnton similarly points out Crébillon's popularity in the eighteenth century in *The Forbidden best-sellers of pre-revolutionary France*. Whatever the reasons may be, it has been only relatively recently that scholars have widely accepted the author's position among the greats of the century.

13. Carole Dornier, "Orient romanesque et satire de la religion: Claude Crébillon, *Tanzaï et Néadarné* et *Le Sopha*," *Eighteenth-century fiction* 11:3 (1999), p.445–58 (446).

ways in which politics are inseparable from marital, reproductive, and sexual practices. As Aravamudan argues, the use of the orientalist frames in these instances allows for more honest critiques of contemporary Western politics.[14]

Aravamudan likens the work of libertine authors such as Crébillon to that of visionaries. Specifically concerned with the ways in which orientalist aspects permeate several novels of the eighteenth century (especially the 1740s), Aravamudan argues that orientalism in these novels performs an important function that goes beyond promoting stereotypes or appropriating Eastern cultures. Orientalism is not a superfluous frame but an integral tool in denaturalizing politics, religion, and sexuality, as well as the relation of each one to the other. This denaturalizing effect is then doubled in libertine orientalist fiction. Of libertine fiction, Aravamudan writes that it "assumes that there can be surprising outcomes within normative expectations."[15] By creating a world in which the politics of sexuality, kinship, and desire can unfold in non-normative ways (as it does when the normal taboos on practices such as queerness, incest, and multiplications of partners are relaxed or absent), libertine fiction allows us to reassess some of the most pressing political problems outside of a patriarchal framework.

World-building may be an important task for any author, but, for Crébillon fils, the process is literalized and dramatized by frequent allusions to the ambiguous and amorphous nature of *le monde*. The first line of Crébillon's most famous novel, *Les Egarements du cœur et de l'esprit* (*The Wayward head and heart*),[16] indicates that, in this novel, the world the protagonist, Meilcour, inhabits will play a role just as important as that of the hero himself: "I made my entry *into society* [*le monde*] at the age of seventeen, with all the advantages that can make a man remarkable there."[17] Meilcour is displaced quickly from one

14. Aravamudan argues that, beyond understanding libertine fiction as pastiches of Eastern culture, we should also understand the revolutionary critiques of Western (in his study French and British) culture and politics. See Aravamudan, *Enlightenment orientalism*.
15. Aravamudan, *Enlightenment orientalism*, p.180.
16. Given the importance of cruising to my analysis, I would like to point out that a more literal translation of the title emphasizes the movement of the main character, *The Strayings of the heart and mind*.
17. Claude Prosper Jolyot de Crébillon, *The Wayward head and heart*, translated by Barbara Bray (Oxford, 1963), p.3; *Les Egarements du cœur et de l'esprit*, ed. René Etiemble (1736; Paris, 1977), p.47 (emphasis added). "J'entrai dans *le monde* à dix-sept ans, et avec tous les avantages qui peuvent y faire remarquer."

world (that of his mother and deceased father) to another in which his education will continue with a new cast of characters. The women and men who allow his entry into this other world circulate around the protagonist, constantly moving between locations familiar to the young Meilcour (such as the city of Paris or the childhood home), but that will be rendered unfamiliar in what follows. For decades, scholars have examined the key terms that constitute not only Crébillon fils's *œuvre*, but also his ethos of life, love, and possibly even happiness. These terms, such as "affix" (*fixer*), "gradation," and "taste" (*goût*), alert us to the importance of sexual and amorous desire in the construction of the Crébillonian self.[18] However, *le monde* is one term from this lexicon that has remained largely understudied and undertheorized.[19] It is a term that returns in multiple versions throughout the writer's career. Whether a veneration for being in the world, or the sadness that accompanies solitude, Crébillon's notion of the self was surprisingly forward-thinking: There is no self without an other, or, to be more precise, there is no self without an ensemble of others.

Mossé offers one of the few studies of the implications of *le monde* for Crébillon's *œuvre*.[20] She finds two distinct definitions of the term: It is simultaneously a social milieu and a "worldly knowledge" (*savoir-mondain*) to which one can gain entry only through an amorous initiation at the hands of an older master/mistress. As Mossé points out, each of Crébillon's works follows a similar pattern in which we encounter a young *ingénu* at precisely the moment of the character's entry into the world, and the story ends (often abruptly) once the initiation is complete. This is, in fact, a pattern that Laclos will later adopt in *Dangerous liaisons*. Mossé's important study demonstrates the inextricability of sexuality from *le monde*, yet, by focusing on the entry into the world, the discussion of what constitutes the social milieu is mostly limited to describing it as being aristocratic and courtly.

---

18. Some important studies of these terms come from René Etiemble (in the notes to his edition of *Les Egarements*), Jean Sgard, *Crébillon fils, le libertin moraliste* (Paris, 2002), and Mossé, *Le Langage de l'implicite*.
19. A few notable exceptions are Anne Giard, "Le 'monde' dans *Les Egarements*," *Stanford French review* 9:1 (1985), p.33–46; Colette Cazenobe, "Le monde de Crébillon ou une coupable innocence," in *Travaux de littérature: la culpabilité dans la littérature française* (Paris, 1995), p.193–208; and Mossé's *Langage de l'implicite*. While Peter Brooks does not study the term *monde* explicitly as a concept, he does offer an examination of "worldliness" in Crébillon in *The Novel of worldliness: Crébillon, Marivaux, Laclos, Stendhal* (Princeton, NJ, 1969).
20. Mossé, *Le Langage de l'implicite*.

By reorienting the discussion slightly, I hope to elaborate on the importance of the world itself, which plays a crucial role in the politics of encounter.

Take, for example, an excerpt from one of the author's later works, *Le Hasard du coin du feu, dialogue moral* (*Fortunes at the fireside*), in which the Duke, discussing past amorous relations with Célie, brings up the name of a former lover of hers, d'Alinteuil. After clarifying that her relationship with d'Alinteuil was not sexual, she asks the Duke why he would believe such a rumor. "I was not the only one to believe it," he responds, "and people in *le monde* were so persuaded by it that all those who had their sights on you—and it was not a small number—took them back."[21] The world in question here is, in fact, a very specific one consisting of aristocratic Parisians. Furthermore, this world is limited to those who would know, and discuss, the relationships of the dialogue's protagonist, Célie. Yet to imagine this world as a fixed entity that exists in relation to the main character alone would not be entirely accurate. The *monde* of which the Duke speaks is at once specific and vague. It is not situated geographically (as in *le monde in Paris* or *le monde at the marquise's place*), nor is it defined numerically. We know that within this world there was a more than "mediocre" amount of individuals interested in Célie, and we also know that this world comprised more people than that (given that there were presumably those *not* interested). The world invoked by the Duke in this conversation is sufficiently precise to make his point while remaining sufficiently vague to allow for interpretation. And yet, this entity *le monde* has defined Célie as something she is not—a woman who had an affair with d'Alinteuil. In this way, the world both constitutes and shapes individuals without regard for the individual in question. By contrast, the world into which the reader strays is that of the bedchamber of the protagonist, which consists of only two individuals—Célie and the Duke—and in which the words that define Célie are her own. The protagonist is thus doubled before the reader's eyes, and it becomes clear that who one *is* can be determined only in a particular place and time, in a particular world.

The idea of a multitude of worlds is implied by the term's common usage in early modern France. After initially defining *le monde* as

21. Crébillon, *La Nuit et le moment (suivi de) Le Hasard du coin du feu* (1763; Paris, 1998), p.183 (emphasis added). "Je n'ai pas été le seul qui l'aie cru; et l'on en fut même *dans le monde* si persuadé, que tous ceux qui avoient des prétentions sur vous—et le nombre n'en étoit pas médiocre—les retirèrent."

comprising the universe and everything in it, the 1694 edition of the *Dictionnaire de l'Académie française* provides the following secondary definition: "*Monde*, is also understood as the society of man in which one must live, or as a part of this society."[22] While notions of plurality and sexuality may rarely cross paths in the domestic fiction of the eighteenth century, we see this merger again and again in the work of Crébillon. Even the most solitary of sexual acts, masturbation, is transformed under his pen into a (be)coming together. In the author's first published work (the short story *Le Sylphe*), a young, desiring woman receives encouragement from the disembodied voice of a would-be male lover, who urges her to fulfill her desires immediately under the covers. The discussion of morals between the young woman and the voice that precedes the sexual act serves not only to entice the reader, but also to imply that, even when one is alone, the self is still a part of a larger world that informs it. Questions of embodiment and sexuality thus course vigorously through the works of Crébillon. So just what is this world? And who are its inhabitants? To answer these questions, I turn to two of the author's most famous novels: *Les Egarements* and *Le Sopha*.

Of all the author's tales and novels, these two remain the most studied today. *Les Egarements* follows the exploits of the young aristocrat Meilcour, as he leaves his mother's home and tries to make his way into the aristocratic society of Paris. *Le Sopha*, by contrast, is a tale that jumps between various degrees of exoticism, placing the Hindu narrator Amanzéi against a Persian backdrop, rewriting the *Arabian nights* story as a morally ambiguous and (softly) pornographic tale of reincarnation. In it, we read the stories of Amanzéi, who recounts a previous life in which he was forced to live out his days in a series of couches as punishment for earlier licentious behavior. In both novels the world is crucial, yet it is confusing; it shapes individuals and yet its own shape cannot be defined because it consists of many moving parts. In order to gain a better sense of those moving pieces, we must look at the moments when the form of the novel alerts us to the gaps between them.

The gaps between worlds are visible in *Les Egarements* from the very first lines of the novel when, as previously stated, Meilcour announces his entry into society ("J'entrai dans le monde"). At this point the

----

22. "Monde," in *Dictionnaire de l'Académie française* (Paris, [la Veuve de Jean Baptiste Coignard], 1694), vol.2. "*Monde*, Se prend aussi pour la société des hommes dans laquelle on a à vivre, ou pour une partie de cette société."

young Meilcour has no idea of the shape of the world that awaits him. The use of the past perfect, however, alerts the reader that the narrator recounting the story is none other than the older Meilcour, writing from a temporally distanced perspective. Even from the first lines of the novel, the protagonist is split between past and future and, thus, between two different worlds. The Meilcour of the first world (the younger) looks toward the world with optimism, hoping to take full advantage of all that life as a boy with means has led him to expect. The Meilcour of the other world makes judgments throughout the novel, relating details and opinions about himself and others that he could not possibly have known or sensed at the time. By writing his story, he is able to relive his youth with the knowledge of age; passion becomes tempered by reason.

Although reason plays a role in the judgment of others in this world, it does not eliminate the passions altogether. Before the hero's education, he begins to sense his feelings for Mme de Lursay:

> In spite of the care I took to conceal the feeling she inspired in me, she had understood me. My respect for her, which seemed to increase from day to day; the difficulty I had in addressing her, quite different now from the bashfulness of childhood; looks that were even more speaking than I supposed; my assiduous attempts to please her; my frequent visits, and perhaps most of all her own desire to attach me— all made her believe that I must secretly love her.

> Malgré mon attention à lui cacher ce qu'elle m'inspirait, elle m'avait pénétré: mon respect pour elle, et qui semblait s'accroître de jour en jour, mon embarras en lui parlant, embarras différent de celui qu'elle m'avait vu dans mon enfance, des regards même plus marqués que je ne le croyais, mon soin toujours pressant de lui plaire, mes fréquentes visites, et plus que tout, peut-être, l'envie qu'elle avait elle-même de m'engager, lui firent penser que je l'aimais en secret.[23]

What he is describing is, of course, the lust of a teenage boy, but it is a feeling new and foreign to him. It is unsurprising that he should choose a double for his mother to educate him in these feelings since his knowledge is based on the world he already knows, the one in which his mother took charge of his education. The narrator will use several adjectives, both flattering and hateful, to describe his teacher/ lover, and he remains open to the possibility of a fluctuation in affect.

23. Crébillon, *Wayward head*, p.7–8; *Les Egarements*, p.52–53.

Although the distanced perspective of the narrator allows him to pass judgment on those who constituted the world of his youth, he will forever remain unable to fix them in time because even within the context of his story his relation to those around him changes.

One of the key features of the relationship between Meilcour and Lursay, as well as each of the relationships featured in the novel, is an ability to play games—both literally and figuratively. We will recall the scene in the game room in which the language game playing out between the pair is amplified by the presence of others, as well as the game of cards being played. In order to embarrass Lursay in front of Meilcour, Versac brings to her dinner party Pranzi, her former lover. The dinner party is made more awkward by the presence of Meilcour's budding love interest, Mlle de Théville, as well as that of Mme de Senanges, who wishes to make Meilcour her own lover. In order to ease the tension placed on conversation alone, Pranzi suggests after dinner that they move the party to the game room. Within the game room desires become entangled in a web of relationality that renders each member simultaneously desiring subject and object of desire.[24] Within this game, language takes on a playful quality as well. When Senanges asks Meilcour to send her the lyrics to a crude song Versac sings during the game, Meilcour misunderstands the invitation. Believing that words are what she desires, he offers to send the lyrics over by way of one of his servants, not realizing that it is rather the messenger (Meilcour) that she wants. And when Meilcour finally makes a move to talk to Hortense, the conversation becomes confused when Lursay believes his playful messages to be meant for her. Meanwhile, Versac tries to veer Meilcour's romantic messages toward Senanges, and Mme de Théville misses the subtext of the language completely, mistaking her daughter's inexperience and reluctance to enter into the language game for a preference for solitude.

The expression of desire through playful language also has the result of tying language intimately to the sensations of the body. The connection is made all the more clear by Lursay's choice of game, *hombre* (Spanish for "man"). Lursay and Théville engage in this game as they literally, though unwittingly, battle to win the man. Unknowing of Meilcour's feelings for Théville, Lursay believes Senanges to be her

24. Two notable exceptions to this web of desire are Versac and Mme de Théville (Hortense's mother). These two characters stand at opposite poles in this game of desire, with Versac orchestrating in the manner of a sadistic hero, and Mme de Théville playing a neutral figure that keeps the game interesting.

true rival, and Théville has no desire for the man in question, "I find ombre wearisome."[25] Mlle de Théville's boredom with *hombre* becomes the subject of much discussion among the attendees of the party and ends with the introduction of the man who does love her, Meilcour, into her home. For one brief moment desire converges in this scene as everyone present wants to cure the young, virginal girl's boredom. In this world desire circulates, fixates, and dissipates within less than the time it takes to play a game of cards.

As Senanges tells Meilcour when he drops off the lyrics at her house the next evening, passions will do strange things to people, and these movements of the body emerge from deep within the unconscious. "I see women infatuated without in the least knowing why, and bringing into fashion little nobodies whom one can hardly bear to look at. One might almost think sometimes that we are living in the age of *Atoms*, might one not?"[26] Her reference to chaos and atoms indicates a split between interior and exterior, and between emotions and actions, that begins to suggest an emptying out of guilt or regret. If we are controlled by our uncontrollable atoms rather than our minds, we should not be held accountable for those actions. In this way, her discourse presages Sade's Juliette, who will offer a similar argument. In fact, we can find in Senanges's words a synecdoche of the story itself. Each of the characters in the book is like a single atom that moves freely among other atoms in the world, often circulating near and occasionally crossing paths with or bumping into one another. What distinguishes Crébillon's materialist philosophy from that of Sade is the optimism we find in these chance encounters. Encounters may cause pleasure or pain, but even in the painful encounters we are reminded of the hope of the next one.

Take for instance the last scene of the book in which Meilcour finally enters *le monde* in an encounter with Lursay. Along with Versac's moral treatise, this scene is one of the longest in the book. Once again, the scene of romantic language games full of deception and double entendres begins in the game room, only this time it is Meilcour who

25. Crébillon, *Wayward head*, p.104; *Les Egarements*, p.174. "C'est [...] que l'hombre m'ennuie." A more literal translation of the French would be "It's just that [...] ombre bores me."
26. Crébillon, *Wayward head*, p.127–28; *Les Egarements*, p.204. "Je vois les femmes s'entêter sans qu'elles sachent pourquoi, mettre à la mode de petits riens qui ne sont point faits seulement pour être regardés. Ne diriez-vous pas que c'est quelquefois le règne des *atomes*?"

is distracted by Lursay's other potential love interest. Bringing a young marquis back to her home from the country is the first move in Lursay's game, and it is quite a successful one. Although Meilcour's interest in her had been waning since meeting Mlle de Théville, he finds himself once again fascinated by Lursay. Once the occasional object of his desire appears to be no longer available, he is drawn back to her, although in the most selfish of ways. Of her actions he remarks, "these manoeuvres made me impatient at last: it was not that my heart was involved, but it seemed to me I was cast in a very disagreeable role."[27] The lovers' game that arises once the card games have finished is one of a long semantic seduction. Once Meilcour starts to leave, Lursay asks him to stay. When he feels she wants him to stay, he decides to leave. Once she decides to let him leave, he wants to stay. He behaves much like a child playing a game they do not quite understand but feel frustrated to be losing. His emotions continue to oscillate between attraction and repulsion throughout the conversation that follows until the two finally give in to their passions in what the narrator will call his "victory." Although he expresses some remorse afterwards (when he is reminded of Théville), mostly what he feels is ambivalence. We might expect his first sexual encounter to quell his active mind, but it has no such effect. The story does not end immediately after the act itself—the act that serves as his initiation into *le monde*; instead, it is followed by paragraphs in which the young Meilcour reasons with himself to give meaning to what has just happened. The book ends not with an erotic scene of wish fulfillment as we might expect, but with a discussion about it. In other words, the final scene of the book demonstrates the desire to match words to meaning in a system in which meaning has always already been in excess of speech.

One of the defining features of this world in which speech and meaning do not necessarily align is a desire to build a reputation. By using language, and manipulating the circulation of language within the world, characters are able to create an image of the self that remains separated from the self. Sometimes reputation-building is used for personal gain, other times it is used against another through the spreading of rumors, but in each case there is the possibility for a gap between self and reputation that allows one to exist as a fractured and complex being. In *Les Egarements*, when Lursay makes

27. Crébillon, *Wayward head*, p.178; *Les Egarements*, p.264. "Ce manège à la fin m'impatienta: ce n'était pas qu'il intéressât mon cœur, mais il me semblait que je jouais là un rôle désagréable."

clear that entering the world is distinct from being initiated into it, she demonstrates that *le monde* is not only a place, not only a group of people, it is also a transformative force that shapes individuals. In other words, the world itself becomes the collective superego of the individual. In fact, the disembodied yet ever-present nature of the superego is literalized in at least two of Crébillon's early works: *Le Sylphe* and *Le Sopha*. In the first, as previously mentioned, the disembodied voice encourages the main action of the story, pushing the plot forward and the young woman's excitement to its extreme. In the second, however, the voice is both narrator and character; the distinction between body and voice in this instance is a temporal one as the narrator recounts stories from his previous lives. Because he focuses on the time he spent relegated to a series of couches, he tells almost exclusively the stories of others (in these scenes he is a silent observer), offering these stories as vignettes designed to teach the true nature of human beings. In this way, he calls multiple worlds into being simultaneously, blending past, present, and future into one narrative.

The rapid movement of language and the misunderstandings that can happen are emblematic of Crébillon's world. In *Les Egarements*, these features are most evident in the constant mood swings of the narrator that remind us of his ever-changing sense of self and relation to society. In *Le Sopha*, these features of the world become most apparent in places in which diverging narratives overlap and collide. To demonstrate this phenomenon, I turn to the two chapters describing the relationship of Almaïde and Moclès. It is not so much the content of their story as its framing that is useful for my analysis here, but I shall give a brief account of these chapters for the sake of clarity. After having moved between a few couches and observed some immoral relations, Amanzéi decides to move to a new couch in the home of Almaïde, a woman in her forties who passes much of her time with a college professor of a certain age. Although both claim to be uninterested in sex, they both find themselves attracted to one another, even if unable to tell the other of their feelings. Instead, we see language games similar to those of the card-game scene in *Les Egarements*. After a certain amount of time passes, Almaïde tells the story of her rape. Although she tells the story of how she was violently pinned to a couch with her mouth covered so that she could not scream, this scene of sexual violence perversely serves to convey to her interlocutor her desire to engage in sexual relations with him. In this scene, therefore, we see how passions become confused by language and vice versa. To incite passion in another by describing a scene of violence demonstrates the absolute fluidity of language in Crébillon's world.[28]

The confusion of registers is duplicated in the narrative structure of the chapters. As Amanzéi tells the story, he is interrupted by the sultan: "Oh Good Lord!" he cries out, tired of the narrator's frequent expositions on the thoughts and morals of the characters of his story.[29] As soon as the sultan interrupts, he is also interrupted by the sultana, who contradicts the opinions of her husband. The pair is finally interrupted by Amanzéi, who returns to the story he had been telling. These frequent interruptions perform two important functions: First, they heighten the sensuality of the scene, repeating in action what is taking place discursively between the two lovers (a series of near misses that increases arousal); and second, they lay bare the divergent worlds of the novel. Amanzéi tells a story about a past world, and the present world comes crashing in.

Rather than smoothing over the edges, Crébillon consistently calls attention to the places where these worlds collide. As we have seen, in some stories, the blending of worlds results in characters such as Meilcour who are confused or hesitant. In others, such as *Le Sopha*, the seams become apparent through a series of interruptions (such as those described above). The author thus highlights the multiplicity and diversity of these worlds within the structure of his tales, dialogues, and novels. Distinct as these worlds may be, they each share two defining features: a proliferation of language through dialogue and storytelling and, correspondingly, a continuous deferral of sexual pleasure accompanied by an intensification of desire.

Because desire cannot be fixed, the characters cannot be fixed either. Even the flattest characters in these novels are allowed room to change or evolve. For example, Hortense de Théville, one character in *Les Egarements* who appears relatively flat, remains, in many ways, opaque to the reader, thus allowing for character growth. Take, for instance, the scene in which Meilcour and Lursay arrive at the home of Mme de Théville to find her daughter (in true romantic fashion) lost in a book. Eventually Meilcour starts a conversation with Hortense about the book she was reading. "It was," she tells him, "the story of an unhappy lover."[30] The conversation continues between the pair

---

28. As we have seen, this is a literary feature often exploited by Sade.
29. Crébillon, *Le Sopha* (1742; Paris, 1997), p.103. "Oh parbleu!"
30. Crébillon, *Wayward head*, p.117; *Les Egarements*, p.190. "C'était l'histoire d'un amant malheureux."

about love, passion, loss, and heartache. Although Meilcour is clearly expressing his own desires for Hortense, her desires remain unclear.

> Carried away by my passion, I should doubtless have unfolded the whole of it to Mademoiselle de Théville if Madame de Lursay, having just finished a letter that Madame de Théville had given her to read, had not come over to us. Deprived of the delight of telling Hortense how much I loved her, I had at least the consolation of thinking she must be able to guess it, and that the little I had been able to reveal to her of my feelings had not displeased her. We had both spoken with feeling, but I had seen no anger in her eyes, and though she had not said anything that I could positively turn to account, neither had there been any sign of the aversion I had hitherto suspected.

> Emporté par ma passion, j'allais sans doute la découvrir tout entière à Mademoiselle de Théville, si Madame de Lursay, qui venait de finir une lettre que Madame de Théville lui avait donnée à lire, ne se fût pas rapprochée de nous. Privé de la douceur de dire à Hortense combien je l'aimais, j'avais du moins celle de croire qu'elle l'avait pu deviner, et que le peu que je lui avais montré de mes sentiments ne lui avait pas déplu. Nous avions été tous deux émus en nous parlant, mais je n'avais pas trouvé de colère dans ses yeux, et quoiqu'elle ne m'eût répondu rien dont je pusse tirer avantage, je n'avais pas non plus lieu de penser qu'elle eût pour moi cette aversion dont jusque-là je l'avais soupçonnée.[31]

Meilcour, along with the reader, can only speculate as to Mlle de Théville's true desires. This sense of mystery, of not quite knowing of whom she speaks, saves her from being flattened into an object of desire alone because it also marks her as a subject with desires outside the scope of the narrator's knowledge. Like even the most seasoned of libertines, the young Théville has used the uncertainty of language to her advantage.

In these subtle ways, Crébillon adds a certain dynamism even to his minor characters. Reading Crébillon, we often feel that there is something *caché*, some little things that we do not, and cannot, know. But more than that, the fluidity of language, as well as the movement of desire through a complex web of characters, sets the stage for a *monde* that is plural, dynamic, and constantly changing and reinventing itself. Individuals, like desire, circulate throughout the

31. Crébillon, *Wayward head*, p.119; *Les Egarements*, p.193.

worlds, continuously changing and never fixating on one object for too long. While this may seem like precisely the kind of world we find in Sade, in which individuals are like atoms that do not feel and that bump into one another without caring or wondering why, in Crébillon this constant movement opens up the possibility for a different kind of relationality between individuals. The only way to navigate the sexual politics of this world is through the practice of cruising.

Cruising in Crébillon's world

In *Cruising utopia*, José Esteban Muñoz critiques the politics of many modern LGBTQ+ groups, arguing that the insistence on same-sex marriage as a political project—and thus on inclusion into the heteronormative institution of marriage—lacks the radical quality that has always been queer politics.[32] In making this critique Muñoz turns to the past, to 1971 to be precise, when a text called "What we want, what we believe" was published in the journal *Gay flames*. This text, Muñoz points out, demands not individual rights, but rather a radical rethinking of society, in which such exclusionary institutions as the family would be abolished in favor of a revolutionary socialist society. The absence of families signals a liberation of sexual relations that disrupts the link between sex and reproduction. Many would be tempted to dismiss the manifesto as merely utopian and therefore impractical, but Muñoz embraces the impulse of what he deems "a logic of futurity."[33] Rather than inclusion into the institutions that maintain and govern capitalist society, this document calls for revision, rethinking, reorganizing—refusing the status quo of patriarchal politics. It is within the framework of this argument that Muñoz writes the surprising phrase that would become a motto of sorts for a number of LGBTQ+ individuals who were also opposed to same-sex marriage for this very reason: "gay marriage is not natural—but then again, neither is marriage for any individual."[34]

---

32. *Cruising utopia* was published prior to 2015 when a ruling in the Obergefell vs. Hodges case in the United States deemed bans on same-sex marriage unconstitutional, thus allowing for same-sex marriage in all US states and territories.
33. Muñoz, *Cruising utopia*, p.20.
34. Muñoz, *Cruising utopia*, p.21. It is not my intention here to argue against the necessity of inclusion within the institution of marriage for all individuals within neoliberal societies that reserve certain rights (such as adoption, tax, and end-of-life rights among many others) for married couples only. Marriage is a necessity for many couples and for many different reasons. My intention is

Now I would like to evoke a turn back to earlier even than 1971—to a time and place when civil rights was a meaningless phrase that had yet to be invented.[35] During the 1730s and 1740s in France, marriage served a very different purpose. Marriage did govern society, although not through individual rights; instead, one's belonging to a particular clan determined the possibilities that would be opened to them throughout their lives. In other words, privileges, and not rights, governed this world. To be born into a noble family meant having the privilege of leisure and of being lazy; being born into a family of a lower station meant working hard and figuring out how to survive. In order to think about the construction of a political subject outside of the blood ties governing society, it is necessary, then, to eliminate or exteriorize marriage and families. As we shall see in what follows, Crébillon used many devices to think outside traditional familial networks.

Contrary to *Manon Lescaut* for example, the plot of which centered on the romantic escapades of a single heterosexual couple, the novels studied in this chapter demonstrate no such preference for monogamous heterosexuality. Instead, we find in them a proliferation of nodes in a web of relationality that questions both monogamy and heteronormativity. It is a desire for something other than romance that brings together this cast of unlikely characters; their desire has no particular object and remains ambiguous. Sometimes the symptoms of this desire are expressed as sexual, other times they are more familial, and still other times they are simply egotistical desires for recognition. Above all, these desires are enmeshed with, and impossible to disentangle from, one another. This is the desire of cruising.

Although the word "cruising" immediately calls up images of clandestine sex with strangers (usually among men) in parks, bathrooms, and other public spaces, this term, for Muñoz, also evokes the temporality of lived experience among others—a queer sociality. The use of the term "among" is key here. It involves not a time of others that would be separate from the self, but rather a

---

rather to invite serious reflection upon the exclusivity of "the family" as well as the organization of society as such.

35. Lynn Hunt points out that a practice did begin to emerge in the late eighteenth century that divided civil from political rights, especially in the case of women. Nevertheless, even at this late stage of the eighteenth century, the discourse of civil rights had not yet emerged. See L. Hunt, *Inventing human rights: a history* (New York, 2007).

time that is shared between the self and an Other (or others). This time takes shape only in the moment. Rather than being assessed in minutes, hours, and days, it is assessed affectively. It is a time that is felt internally (akin to the sensation of time passing faster when one is involved in pleasurable activities with friends, or the feeling of butterflies when one is nervous or excited), but it is also a time that recognizes the other as a feeling subject who is also experiencing time in similar—if not identical—ways. The utopian aspect of such forms of queer sociality lies both in their refusal of normative behavior in the present, and in their imagining of a potential form of socialization that allows being together to take shape in a myriad of ways that change and morph over time. It is this last point, in particular, that is important to the present analysis of cruising in the work of Crébillon. There are moments of outwardly queer desire, but even the moments of seemingly heteronormative desire call into question the forward motion through time implied by heterosexual marriage and its goals of reproduction.

Ironically, our discussion of the intimate communities borne of cruising begins with a language of kinship and reproduction. Given the many allusions to rebirths in Crébillon's novels, such a language seems the most fitting to describe the author's queer communities. *Les Egarements* opens with the narrator, an aging Meilcour, describing his entry into *le monde*:

> My father had left me a noble name, whose lustre he himself had increased, and from my mother I had expectations of considerable wealth. Left a widow when still of an age when there were no attachments she might not have formed; young, rich, and handsome, her devotion to me permitted her to contemplate no other pleasure than that of educating me, and of making up to me for all that I had lost in losing my father.

> Mon père m'avait laissé un grand nom, dont il avait lui-même augmenté l'éclat, et j'attendais de ma mère des biens considérables. Restée veuve dans un âge où il n'était pas d'engagements qu'elle ne pût former, belle, jeune et riche, sa tendresse pour moi ne lui fit envisager d'autre plaisir que celui de m'élever, et de me tenir lieu de tout ce que j'avais perdu en perdant mon père.[36]

36. Crébillon, *Wayward head*, p.3; *Les Egarements*, p.47.

From the very first pages of the novel, the oedipal triangle is disrupted through the loss of the father. Rather than writing out the father altogether, however, the narrator chooses to lead with this loss, indicating from the very beginning a lack that continues to be keenly felt throughout. As the narrator claims, rather than remarrying, and thus reinstating a heteronormative oedipal triangulation, his mother chooses instead to inhabit the roles of both mother and father. The original lack then manifests itself as a surplus of affection (*tendresse*) from the mother, which, as Meilcour points out in the next few paragraphs, renders him at least less smug (*fat*) than he might otherwise have been. Although the narrator speaks of all that his mother does for him (essentially fulfilling both parental roles), receiving such a feminine education does not serve him well. He enters the world unknowing of the conceitedness of others, ignorant of the games people play, and clueless as to the normal comportment of a young aristocratic guy in Paris.

In addition to defining the protagonist, the mention of the loss of the father within the first paragraph serves as an alibi. The hero could not have led a sage life, he suggests, because he did not have a male role model. A maternal education is all that he has known, and it is unsurprising, therefore, that he should seek out another kind of maternal education for his rebirth into another world. Leaving behind the world of his childhood in the maternal home, he re-enters the world from another (symbolic) womb—that of Lursay. Thus, the hero's journey begins and ends with his entry into a world. The pages between these two scenes take the reader through a whirlwind of constant movement. Meilcour follows his heart, his hormones, and his feet from one encounter to the next. His existence is tightly bound to those he encounters throughout the novel.

If, as I claim, the house of Mme de Lursay serves in this novel as a sort of symbolic womb, then we must take a closer look at Meilcour's "gestation" period to better understand the elements that inform his arrival. In the first few pages of the novel, the narrator's thoughts seem scattered. He invokes a desire for pleasure as his only guiding principle and wonders about the mysteries of love. Although he seeks pleasure, he does not understand how it works, knowing only that it should cure his boredom. Quickly, however, Meilcour links pleasure to love and, more specifically, to a love he does not have, or even know how to have: "I wanted to be in love, but there was no one I loved."[37] Love, in

37. Crébillon, *Wayward head*, p.4; *Les Egarements*, p.48. "Je voulais aimer, mais je n'aimais point."

this reflection, is coded through several distinct words: delight (*volupté*), passion, love (*amour*), and ecstasy (*félicité*) become fairly interchangeable to him. Each iteration of love (or something like it) ends in the same desire—to attach this emotion to an object (*un objet*).

Confused as he may be, Meilcour does offer some preliminary thoughts about what it means to love and be loved:

> That which both sexes then called love was a kind of commerce that they entered into often without inclination, where convenience was always preferred to sympathy, interest to pleasure, and vice to feeling. [...] For a man to please, it was not necessary for him to be in love; and in urgent cases he was even excused from being amiable. An affair would be decided at sight, *but would rarely survive the morrow*; yet even so swift a separation did not always preclude disgust.

> Ce qu'alors les deux sexes nommaient amour, était une sorte de commerce où l'on s'engageait, souvent même sans goût, où la commodité était toujours préférée à la sympathie, l'intérêt au plaisir, et le vice au sentiment. [...] Un homme, pour plaire, n'avait pas besoin d'être amoureux: dans des cas pressés, on le dispensait même d'être aimable. La première vue décidait une affaire, mais, en même temps, *il était rare que le lendemain la vit subsister*; encore, en se quittant avec cette promptitude, ne prévenait-on pas toujours le dégoût.[38]

Love, in Crébillon's world, is not about romance—it is about one-night stands. In other words, from the outset of the novel, the author introduces a culture of cruising. These encounters may not always be between strangers in the strictest sense of the word (they do involve an exchange of words prior to the act) but they are decided in an instant (pleasing words are of little use) and they are fleeting. This is an exchange that is repeated throughout the novel. The narrator's problem at this stage is simply finding a way into this vast network of bodies in spite of his shyness, indecisiveness, and inexperience. In need of an education, he turns to the incestuously maternal figure of Mme de Lursay.

"The Marquise de Lursay (for that was her name) saw me nearly every day, either at her own house or at my mother's, for they were close friends."[39] The first appearance of Lursay's name ties her directly to the protagonist's mother. As we will learn over the next several

---

38. Crébillon, *Wayward head*, p.5–6; *Les Egarements*, p.50 (emphasis added).
39. Crébillon, *Wayward head*, p.7; *Les Egarements*, p.52. "La Marquise de Lursay

pages, she is roughly the same age as Mme de Meilcour, and like his mother Lursay remains unmarried after the death of her husband. Although he describes her as beautiful and always well dressed, she is not coquettish and does not seek to please others. Lursay is like his mother in many respects, except one: She can teach him about sex and intimate relations. "She had applied herself to the study alike of her own sex and ours, and knew all the springs that *moved them both* [*les font agir*]."[40] One can imagine a relatively anodyne sense to this passage: As an aristocratic woman and hostess of many gatherings, Lursay is an astute observer of human behavior (which we see throughout the novel). "Knowing" both sexes in this case means simply that she knows men and women and what makes them tick.

Yet the last word of the sentence, along with the situation of this text within Crébillon's work more broadly, invites a second, more provocative reading. *Agir*—to take action, to make something happen (*faire agir*)—suggests a movement easily associated with the very physical and biological instance of the orgasm. Indeed, the next sentence returns to the central question of pleasure, explaining how the patient Lursay knows exactly how to wait for the perfect moment to seek out pleasure or, if necessary, revenge. She is, therefore, a master of desire, or, to put it differently, she is capable of walking the fine line between pleasure and pain that defines a well-adjusted individual. Her goal in this novel is not only to win Meilcour's affections, but also to impart to him a knowledge of desire and pleasure.[41]

In the second endeavor (that of managing his education), her progress is continuously interrupted by a number of interlocutors. Versac aims to take charge of Meilcour's education, but the education is also interrupted by his pupil's feelings for Mlle de Théville as well as his encounters with Mme de Senanges, Mme de Mongennes, and even Pranzi. Meilcour's knowledge of the world is diffuse—spread through a vast network of encounters. The most prominent of these educational encounters comes in the third part of the novel, during a conversation between Meilcour and Versac. Versac's much-studied

---

(c'était son nom) me voyait presque tous les jours, ou chez elle, ou chez ma mère avec qui elle était extrêmement liée."

40. Crébillon, *Wayward head*, p.9; *Les Egarements*, p.54 (emphasis added). "Elle avait étudié avec soin son sexe et le nôtre, et connaissait tous les ressorts qui *les font agir.*"

41. For a thorough discussion of Lursay's role as a mentor to Meilcour see Katherine Deimling, "The female mentor in Crébillon's *Les Egarements du cœur et de l'esprit*," *Eighteenth-century fiction* 16:1 (2003), p.13–31.

"moral treatise" continues for several pages, explaining the difference between the private self and public performances of the self.[42] We will recall that this is one of the disjunctions that defines the Crébillonian world. Versac's lesson reveals the meticulous, intelligent, and calculating man behind the facade of vapidity, lending credence to the kinds of critiques of libertine fiction as a cruel instantiation of the master–slave dialectic discussed earlier in this chapter. The libertine subject seeks out a desired object and takes pleasure in the object's pain and submission. We are not yet witness to the horrific scenes of malignant *jouissance* that we will find later in the century with Sade, but we do see the inklings of a pleasure to be had at the expense of the other.[43] If Versac's had been the dominant lesson—if his had been the story being told—then we might have been able to trace a more direct line between Crébillon's licentious tales and Sade's orgiastic scenes of terror. And yet, as we see throughout the novel, Meilcour resists a complete immersion into Versac's system largely through his utter indecisiveness. He remains unable to distinguish his own desires from the desires of those around him. As such, he cannot help but to care for others even when—or perhaps especially when—he wishes that he could remain distant and cold. In fact, the very structure of the novel attests to the failure of Versac's teachings. The older Meilcour narrates his own life, divulging his most intimate thoughts and moments; we know, therefore, that he is incapable of hiding his true self behind a mask of carefree frivolity.

Ultimately, however, neither Versac nor Lursay succeeds in completely taking charge of Meilcour's education. Although, as Katherine Deimling convincingly argues, Lursay does exert a large amount of power over Meilcour's life and actions, he does not always follow her advice, especially given that the novel closes as soon as the hero sleeps with her and re-emerges into the world.[44] The unfinished nature of the novel renders it impossible to say with any certainty the path the hero will take. We know from the preface only that he will eventually settle down and marry "an estimable woman," but we do not know the duration or extent of his wanderings (*égarements*) prior

42. For a more detailed study of the political, social, and moral implications of Versac's treatise see Colette Cazenobe, *Crébillon fils, ou la Politique dans le boudoir* (Paris, 1977), particularly ch.1 and 2.
43. In fact, Versac would later serve as a model for Laclos's calculating anti-hero Valmont, who abides strictly by this moral treatise.
44. See Deimling, "The female mentor."

to marriage. Meilcour's rebirth from the loins of Lursay might have rendered him an outwardly vapid yet inwardly reflexive libertine (as Versac or Pranzi); he may have become the sensitive part-time lover of his mother's double; or he may have run straight into the arms of the young Mlle de Théville who had captured his heart, becoming one of the romantic heroes that she so thoroughly enjoyed. Because we cannot know who he becomes, we must focus on what he is: a young man at the center of a web of relations.

Although heteronormative desire propels the narrative of this novel forward, the end product is not what we might expect as the result of heterosexual love. There is no marriage (except that of the narrator, which remains outside the primary narrative, appearing only in the preface), and there are no children. The resolution of this novel, if indeed it has one, is complete ambiguity. Meilcour leaves Lursay's house the next day excited yet remorseful, determined to return the following day but making no promise to do so. The novel, then, is less about the fulfillment of desire or wishes than about the very mundane ways in which queer families are formed. The protagonist's mother figure incestuously becomes his lover, his cousin may become his wife, and his best friends advise him to dress well, play dumb, and live for the moment. This cast of misfit characters comes together to form and inform the hero much in the ways that a family would, but with a twist: There is no maintaining society through the many rules of patriarchy, including marriage and the reproduction of children. In this society, there is only the perpetuation of desire to live life in the moment, allowing it to progress as it might without imposing upon it any restrictions. Meilcour may have lost his father and strayed away from his mother, but, in the brief time that passes in this novel, he has fashioned for himself a new family, and this is the family that constitutes his world.

Cruising takes a different form in *Le Sopha*, as the narrator's soul moves from one body to the next. Even prior to Amanzéi's punishment by Brahma (the very punishment that banishes him to the couches in the first place), he recalls his previous lives. Although it appears that he inhabited mostly male bodies, he implies that he has also experienced life as a woman.[45] Amanzéi is thus the ideal subject to explain sexual desire and pleasure, since he has experienced life in many different gradations of gender and animacy. The sultan may be the supreme

45. In fact, he blames his time spent as a woman for the bad behavior that led to his punishment.

leader of the land, but in this novel Amanzéi has an even greater power—a keen knowledge of sexual practices and human morality. He thus assumes the role of master in the slow dissemination of an *ars erotica* that will unfold over the course of the novel.

> A sofa was never a piece of furniture meant for the antechamber and I was placed in a small room in the home of the woman to whom I belonged that was separate from the rest of her palace, and where, she said, she often went just to meditate on her duties or devote herself to Brahma with fewer distractions.

> Un Sopha ne fut jamais un meuble d'antichambre et l'on me plaça chez la Dame à qui j'allais appartenir, dans un cabinet séparé du reste de son Palais, et où, disait-elle, elle n'allait souvent que pour méditer sur ses devoirs, et se livrer à Brama avec moins de distraction.[46]

The first sentence of chapter 2 plunges us into Amanzéi's observations from his peculiar vantage point embodied in a sofa. He first takes his listeners into the bedroom of Fatmé, a well-known and well-respected woman whom he had heard of in his previous life. By alerting the listener immediately to the placement of the sofa, the narrator sets the tone for the tales to come. Although it had already been clear that the purpose of his confinement was to learn about pure love, drawing attention to the seclusion of this room in particular reminds us that we are entering into scenes that are taking place behind closed doors. In Fatmé's story we see the danger of what can happen when the private is made public. Lasting only three chapters (which makes it a relatively short story within the novel), the story ends with Fatmé's murder at the hands of her husband when he finds her in bed with another man.

Fatmé's life is cut short in a horrific way but our witness, Amanzéi, is moved surprisingly little. He explains, "as terrifying as this spectacle was, I was not moved by it. They had both deserved death much too much to be able to complain about it and I was thrilled that such a terrible catastrophe taught all of Agra just what these two people, whom everyone had long regarded as models of virtue, had always been."[47] The narrator casts himself early as the arbiter of virtue, even though his punishment is the result of immoral behavior. Throughout

46. Crébillon, *Le Sopha*, p.43.
47. Crébillon, *Le Sopha*, p.55. "[Q]uelque affreux que fût ce spectacle, il ne me toucha pas. Ils avaient tous deux trop mérité la mort, pour qu'ils pussent être plaints, et je fus charmé qu'une aussi terrible catastrophe apprît à tout Agra, ce

the novel, Amanzéi will provide commentary to his audience, judging the choices of the lovers as he observes. However, a more salient function of Amanzéi's commentaries lies in the fact that they also point the reader and listener to the more erotic moments they have been waiting for. Similar to the language games in *Les Egarements*, language in this novel takes on an excess of meaning that produces a rupture between the speech act and its reception.

The split is heightened by the narrator's obliviousness, real or feigned, to the ways in which his own fate is tied to Fatmé's. Because his soul resides in her sofa, her death represents a rebirth of sorts for him. He may not be moved by her death emotionally, but her death will move him physically. Just after her death, his soul flies into the couch of a neighboring house where he finds an incredibly virtuous woman. From there he will move from couch to couch, each time based on the actions of the women and men to whom the sofas belong. Sometimes he gets bored and leaves; other times, as we shall see in the case of Zulica, he gets excited and decides to follow. In each instance, his existence is intimately tied to that of the individuals he follows.

The longest vignette in the narrative follows the exploits of Zulica and lasts nine chapters. Zulica's story is unique in that the narrator does not initially inhabit a sofa in her house, but rather he first encounters her in the house of a man. In chapter 10, bored with virtuous women, the narrator decides to move to a seedier part of town filled with love nests (*petites maisons*) designed specifically for clandestine romantic trysts. It is there that he begins to inhabit the couch of Mazulhim, the aristocratic man who will begin his seduction of Zulica in the next chapter. The Zulica chapters exploit more than any others the unhinged nature of the narrator's soul. Floating by chance into Mazulhim's bachelor pad, Amanzéi is struck by Zulica's vibrant spirit. Within the first few pages of her appearance, she becomes so enraged with Mazulhim that she breaks a porcelain vase in his house. The Zulica scenes also contain a lot of movement, with characters moving nearer to and farther from the couch. Amanzéi draws attention to the limits of his knowledge by pointing out the gaps occurring in the story when characters leave the room. Hearing that Zulica has other lovers and eager to learn more of her story, the narrator jumps first into her carriage, then into a sofa in her room, carried along by curiosity and fascination. After enjoying a tryst with Zulica and her primary lover,

qu'avaient été deux personnes qu'on y avait si longtemps regardées comme des modèles de vertu."

Zâdis, he decides to return with her to Mazulhim's *petite maison* where he will remain for a while.

Ultimately, Zulica's story is one of intense emotional violence. Zulica lies to Zâdis, telling him that she would never give herself to a man like Mazulhim and going so far as to taunt her lover for being jealous. Her immoral behavior is matched first by Mazulhim, who fails to show up for their second tryst, and then by Nassès, the man Mazulhim sends to tell Zulica he will not be coming. Both men, although Nassès more than Mazulhim, offer the same explanation used by so many men who take advantage of women—because of her behavior, she had it coming. In the end, Zulica, who is first presented as a libertine that Sade would have been proud of, is reduced to tears because of her mistreatment. The story that plays out in this, the longest episode of the novel, demonstrates the destructive nature of humans and feels anything but hopeful or utopian. If cruising in Crébillon's world results in so much pain and suffering, and if we participate in that pain through the voyeuristic framework of the novel itself, then where are we to find those utopian impulses to which I alluded earlier? To find utopian impulses, we must remember the overlapping nature of worlds, frames, and timelines and seek out those places when their boundaries meet and overlap with one another. Let us return now to Zulica's story, but this time read it through another frame.

While Zulica's story takes place in the main narrative, another story emerges from the frame of the novel. We will recall that the story we read is also being spoken aloud to an audience of the sultan and sultana. Their frequent interruptions into the narration break up the story's linear chronology. One of the sultan's most common complaints is his boredom and fatigue with all the little details he deems uninteresting. In one instance he even suggests that rearranging the stories (internally) might make them more interesting, to which Amanzéi responds, "if I were telling your majesty a story, it would be easy for me to arrange the pieces as you wish, but I am telling you what I saw, and I cannot attribute behavior to Mazulhim other than his own without altering the truth."[48] Crébillon borrows the technique of dialogistic story-framing so famously exploited by

48. Crébillon, *Le Sopha*, p.136. "Si je faisais un conte à votre Majesté, il me serait facile d'arranger les objets comme elle le voudrait, mais je raconte ce que j'ai vu, et je ne puis, sans altérer la vérité, donner à Mazulhim des procédés différents de ceux qu'il avait."

authors such as Marguerite de Navarre, but he alters it by inserting the commentaries of the interlocutors into the stories themselves. The interruptions become more and more frequent as the novel progresses, and the sultan becomes more and more impatient. The narrator may claim to remain true to his story, but his listeners' frequent commentaries provide a back and forth that alters the narrative as we read it. These interruptions signal a break in the erotic tales, allowing readers to participate in a little couch-surfing of their own. They cannot move from one piece of furniture to the next, but they move between narrative frames much in the way Amanzéi's soul travels from one room to another. The repetition of the plot within the frame itself allows the reader to see the gaps between worlds where there exists at least a potential for something different.

Lacking the more overtly orgiastic scenes of later libertine fiction, *Le Sopha* expresses that orgiastic energy in its language and narrative structure. Voices circulate, breaking into one another and rendering the different temporal registers difficult to disentangle. These frequent penetrations, particularly by the sultan, are littered with gasps and exclamation points ("Oh yes!" "Oh my god!" "Oh great!" "What?!"), providing the narrative equivalent of multiple orgasms. Furthermore, the sultan's interruptions are often seconded by the sultana, who asks follow-up questions, drawing the speech out of Amanzéi and thus prolonging the pleasure of the sexual speech acts. In contrast to libertine sexual encounters that render one individual a subject while the other is rendered object—thus establishing a structure in which one experiences pleasure as a result of another's pain—in Crébillon's narrative orgy everyone is allowed a voice; all are subjects and all feel pleasure together. Cruising in this world creates an astonishingly egalitarian form of human (and nonhuman) relationality.

Critics tend to interpret these frequent interruptions as a critique of the excesses of aristocratic leaders whose luxurious lifestyles have rendered them restless and incompetent. But I argue that this also presents another story of desire, one that has not only an exotic, but also a queer construction from the very beginning. We learn in the introduction that the sultan has been so spoiled with riches that he has nearly lost the ability to appreciate anything. Although he has a menagerie full of exotic and highly trained animals, as well as a harem full of beautiful wives, he is incapable of enjoying them:

> In spite of his pastimes and various pleasures, it was impossible for
> the sultan to avoid boredom. Even these famous tales, the perpetual

objects of his surprise and reverence and which it was forbidden on one's life to critique, would have become insipid to him if he had become accustomed to them. This boredom followed him all the way to the chamber of his wives, where he passed part of his life watching them embroider and make paper cutouts: arts for which he had a singular esteem, the invention of which he regarded as the masterpiece of the human spirit, and which he wished that all of his courtiers would practice.

Malgré de si grandes occupations, et des plaisirs aussi variés, il fut impossible au Sultan d'éviter l'ennui. Il n'y eut pas jusques à ces Contes fameux, objets perpétuels de son étonnement et de sa vénération, et dont il était défendu, sur peine de la vie, de faire la critique; qui à force de lui être connus, ne lui fussent devenus insipides. L'ennui enfin le suivait jusque dans l'appartement de ses femmes, où il passait une partie de sa vie à les voir broder, et faire des découpures: arts pour lesquels il avait une estime singulière, dont il regardait l'invention comme le chef d'œuvre de l'esprit humain, et auxquels il voulut enfin que tous ses Courtisans s'appliquassent.[49]

The sultan, bored with his female companions, seeks pleasure from the lips of another man. By reading the frame of the novel queerly, we see that queer desire is sublimated into the practices of telling, listening to, and building stories together.

In *Unlimited intimacy*, Tim Dean writes, "Often understood simply as the pursuit of new sex partners, cruising entails a remarkably hospitable disposition to strangers."[50] "Hospitable" in this sense is irreducible to affects such as happiness or excitement, and might just as well be linked to fear and nervous energy, but it does indicate an openness to whatever possibilities may come. This is the distinctive feature of Crébillon's brand of libertinism. Encounters that engender desire are every bit as important as they are to Laclos or Sade, but they come with no preconceived notions of how those encounters should go. One may find oneself with an older woman, a young man, a sultan, a slave, or even a couch, but the terms of the encounter are negotiated

---

49. Crébillon, *Le Sopha*, p.31. The "Contes fameux" to which the narrator refers are the *Arabian nights*, which had only recently been translated into French. This passage also announces the novel as a *roman à clef*, including an exaggerated portrait of life in the court of Louis XV.

50. Tim Dean, *Unlimited intimacy: reflections on the subculture of barebacking* (Chicago, IL, 2009), p.176.

between all participants. This type of cruising disrupts the master–slave dynamic by adding another (and often multiple others) who is capable of speaking, feeling, and being heard in return. Cruising in Crébillon's world is more optimistic than in Sade's, certainly, and it is also ethical.

A politics of encounter

In addition to illuminating the performative quality of Sade's fiction, in *Sade, Fourier, Loyola,* Roland Barthes also delineates a sort of community that forms between the moving pieces of the libertine author's novels. In fact, Barthes finds in Sade's fiction precisely the confusion and profusion of familial signifiers exploited by Sade in order to create his perverse communities. In the Sadian novel, he writes, there are two opposing definitions of family: The first is by its content (which consists of the affective bonds between individuals), and the second is by its form. The content of the family is mocked—in a system of atheistic materialism in which atoms merely cohabitate with one another, there is no room for affective bonds. The form of the family, by contrast, is shaped purely in linguistic terms and allows for a playful rearranging of pieces. As Barthes points out, because familial signifiers change in relation to certain practices (birth and marriage, for example), Sade is able to reorganize the pieces of this language to perform multiple sexual transgressions at once. The proliferation of simultaneous sexual offences is a defining feature of the material universe of Sade.

In fact, as Barthes points out, the very repetition of these transgressions makes them seem somehow insignificant. Indeed, reading Sade can give one the feeling of being stuck on a merry-go-round going a little too fast; the more one reads, the more one sees the familiar (if frightening and blurry) scenes that continue to pass by over and over again. Moreover, Barthes blames the Sadian novel's exclusion from the canon on these very repetitions:

> If the Sadian novel is excluded from our literature, it is because in it novelistic peregrination is never a quest for the Unique (temporal essence, truth, happiness), but a repetition of pleasure; Sadian errancy is *unseemly,* not because it is vicious and criminal, but because it is dull and somehow insignificant, withdrawn from transcendency, void of term: it does not reveal, does not transform, does not develop, does not educate, does not sublimate, does not accomplish, recuperates

nothing, save for the present itself, cut up, glittering, repeated; no patience, no experience; everything is carried immediately to the acme of knowledge, of power, of ejaculation; time does not arrange or derange it, it repeats, recalls, recommences, there is no scansion other than that which alternates the formation and the expenditure of sperm.[51]

In Sade, it is not only the shocking and terrifying acts that happen in the novels that scare off a number of readers. If this were the case, Navarre's *Heptameron*, with its gruesome and morbid scenes of murder and rape, might be stricken from the canon as well. Navarre's novel is recuperated from history, as it were, by the frame discussed in the previous section, in which interlocutors judge the actions of the story subsequently to telling it. By framing the action as wrong and/ or criminal, or even by debating the morality of the adventures, tales such as those told in *The Heptameron* are made palatable by taking on an edifying feature that serves as moral instruction for future generations.

Any notion of a future, aside from the assimilation of progeny into a system of perverse sexualities, is completely absent from Sade. In Sade we thus find an excellent illustration of Edelman's anti-reproductive futurism.[52] There is no living for tomorrow because who knows what it will bring (or if it will come at all); all action is bound to pleasure in the present, or, as Mme de Lorsange puts it in *Juliette*, "the past encourages me, the present electrifies me, I worry very little about the future."[53] In the Sadian universe, time ceases to move as it becomes lodged in the present moment with the subject making a particular effort to extract as much from the moment as possible. Futurity is also suspended in the world of Crébillon; however, the dilation of time happens at a slightly different pace and in a slightly different manner than in Sade. Understanding the role of the moment and of repetition in Crébillon will help us to understand the politics of encounter that emerges from his works.

In *Le Hasard du coin du feu*, Célie asks the Duke the meaning of "moment." He replies that it is "a certain disposition of the senses as

---

51. Roland Barthes, *Sade, Fourier, Loyola*, translated by Richard Miller (Berkeley, CA, 1989), p.150.
52. Edelman, *No future*.
53. Sade, *La Nouvelle Justine, ou les Malheurs de la vertu, suivie de l'Histoire de Juliette, sa sœur* (Brussels [en Hollande], n.n., 1797), p.343. "Le passé m'encourage, le présent m'électrise, je crains peu l'avenir."

unforeseen as it is involuntary."[54] In an edition of *Les Egarements* edited by Etiemble, the editor notes that the word *moment* in Crébillon's *œuvre* is almost never a banal measure of time but rather one of intense erotic emotion. Citing this passage from *Le Hasard* in a footnote, Etiemble further describes the *moment* as an *occasion*, a moment in time when the possibility for an erotic encounter will be ripe. In the passage the editor annotates, Crébillon does indeed seem to indicate the possibility of an erotic encounter as Meilcour expresses his compulsion to give himself over "at least for the moment" to Lursay.[55] Examining the Duke's response to Célie, however, offers another definition of the *moment*, one that seems intimately linked to the drives. His *moment* is not just the occasion for the encounter; it is also the physical manifestation of affect leading up to the encounter. The moment in Crébillon takes on the same presentism that we found in Sade, and indicates that the meeting of individuals in this world is something that happens at the level of the unconscious. If the drives govern erotic encounters, then choices in such matters are irrelevant. The drives wander uncontrollably, fixating on others and then breaking apart to take up the process of wandering anew and repeating this process over and over again.

The repetition of the drives is echoed in the structure of Crébillon's novels and dialogues, which often center on a series of sexual conquests.[56] *Le Sopha*, with its series of erotic tales told by a literal wandering soul demonstrates the importance of the repetition of the act. However, repetition takes on a narrative function as well in this novel. The scenes of romantic encounters may be repeated, but they each offer something different and new. It is easy to see in this structure a precursor to Sade. And yet, there is a transformative quality to the repetition of Crébillon's tales. The characters change throughout, and the narrator moves from couch to couch in search of new encounters. Like Sade's tales, these new encounters seek out various ways of describing the scenes of erotic pleasure and pain, but Crébillon diverges from Sade in his interest in the pedagogic function of the tales. Instead of the lessons in debauchery (particularly for young girls) that we read in Sade, the discussions framing Crébillon's

---

54. Crébillon, *Le Hasard*, p.169. "Une certaine disposition des sens aussi imprévue qu'elle est involontaire."
55. See Etiemble's note in *Les Egarements*, p.170. "Pour le moment du moins."
56. These conquests can either be described or, as in the case of *Le Hasard*, be recounted as a story.

tales provide a larger debate on morality and its place in (particularly aristocratic) society.

Because the erotic sensations of bodies are crucial to understanding Crébillon's sexual politics, let us return momentarily to our discussion of *jouissance*. In his earliest seminars, Lacan elaborates on *jouissance* through a discussion of the master–slave dialectic. As I mentioned previously, it is always a pleasure experienced for the Self at the expense of an Other. In later seminars, Lacan will expand upon this notion, linking *jouissance* to the unconscious, as a drive, in opposition to the conscious act of desire.[57] Desire, he argues, is what helps us to avoid the dangers of following our id and engaging in dangerous or criminal activity. Desire allows us to attach those incomprehensible sensations to an object, albeit erroneously, thus acting as a pressure valve for the drives. The problem with theories that center on *jouissance*, and the most common critique of such theories, is their inherently unethical nature.

Much as Barthes argued of Sade's literature, *jouissance* is not unethical because it is *bad*; it is unethical because it pertains only to the self. Once one enters into language (and thus the Symbolic Order), Lacan argues, they are forever separated from the Real, since all that exists around them becomes mediated by language. *Jouissance* is a remainder and a reminder of the real. It is an emotion emerging from the id that we can sense, but not truly understand. In other words, it is a deeply personal and unique drive incapable of being shared with another. It is the selfish nature of *jouissance* (selfish in the sense of pertaining to the self alone) that makes it unethical. However, scholars of queer studies such as Lee Edelman have made compelling arguments for reclaiming *jouissance* as an ethical practice. It remains an individualistic drive, but, in Edelman's work, it is transformed into a collective protest of queer individuals who do not belong to the future being maintained by the Symbolic Order. At the risk of being reductive, Edelman argues that, since the future is made for breeders and their children, those who do not participate in heteronormative reproductive practices should take a cue from Mme de Lorsange and not worry too much about the future.

In many ways the characters of Crébillon's novels engage in this type of anti-futural practice. For the most part, they inhabit the present,

---

57. Lacan touches upon the notion of *jouissance* in seminars 1–3, largely via discussions of Freud and Hegel. It is only in the seventh seminar that he will begin to explore the ethical implications of the concept, and these interrogations will continue to appear in later seminars.

they live in the moment (in all senses of that term), and they stretch pleasure to its limits, often veering into the realm of pain. And yet, one thing they cannot entirely escape is the future. Whether it is the near future (tomorrow) or the distant future (when the stories will be told and written), there is still a hope for, or at least a curiosity about, what lies beyond the moment of pleasure. Meilcour is constantly wondering what others will think of his actions, the sultan is constantly pressing Amanzéi to tell him what comes next, and even Zulica is devastated to learn that the future she envisioned first with Mazulhim and then with Nassès (both of which were to be thoroughly enjoyable but nonreproductive) has been an illusion. They do live in the moment, but they cannot cut themselves off from the future completely.

To think of a future means to think of the consequences for actions in relation to others in ways unseen in Sade. A collective action such as the practice described by Edelman still relies upon individualistic drives. What we find in Crébillon's fiction is the possibility for something a little more utopian. His practice is also collective, but it imagines the possibility of a collective—and shared— *jouissance*, opening up the space for an ethical politics of encounter. The introduction of another (or multiple others) into the scene of sexual pleasure causes Horkheimer and Adorno's vertical master–slave relation to fall on its side and expand, creating a horizontal network of relationality. This politics of encounter is based on the ethos of cruising discussed previously, and is produced from an encounter between beings (animate and inanimate, embodied and disembodied) in which pleasure is produced not from the pain of the Other, but from another pleasure. In these scenes sexual pleasure is multiplied as participants engage in similar goals. For example, in the masturbatory scene of *Le Sylphe* analyzed at the beginning of the chapter, the passions of the young girl are doubled by the disembodied voice that encourages her to bring herself to orgasm. One reading of this scene would understand the voice as that of the id externalized. The absence of the reasonable superego in the bedchamber allows the id to take its place. However, the externalized id appears in many forms throughout Crébillon's fiction in ways both corporeal and incorporeal, human and inhuman. This makes the id not an internal space of individual drives, but a separate subject in its own right, joining together with another subject and sharing the drive of *jouissance*. While remaining distinct subjects, they share that which normally cannot be shared—a drive.

The societies that emerge in Crébillon's fiction are built upon this foundation of collectivity. Each atom in the system defines the others along the way. There is no Meilcour, for instance, without Lursay, Versac, or Théville, just as there is no Amanzéi without the sutlan, the sultana, and all those who populate his previous lives. Put differently, these are societies that redefine what it means to be a subject amid other subjects, similar to what Jean-Luc Nancy describes in *Being singular plural*.[58] Nancy proposes a concept of community in which neither the self nor the other is primary. The one does not exist without the other. This community, then, moves from one based on individualized forms of subjectivity to a more communal model. His concept of being with (*être avec*) proposes a new ontology of human societies. A society based on *being with* resembles politically the act of cruising. *Being with* requires an openness and an abandonment to a society constantly in motion. In such a society, the individual comes to be defined by their relation to others. In Crébillon's fiction, a notion of *being with* combines with the pleasure of the sexual act multiplied, creating a society based on a *(be)coming with*. The moments of *jouissance* in Crébillon's world represent not only a coming together of bodies, but also a sharing of drives and desires in a way that brings to life a new form of being, precisely the kind that Nancy would call *being with*. Individuals become fused together, if only for a moment, thus producing a new, plural, individual. Although the reproduction of the family becomes fodder for perversity in libertine fiction, we can glimpse the production of another type of community, one in which coming together produces not pregnancy, but instead another form of life.

To demonstrate how bodies can become so fused as to share drives, we will first turn to the final episode of *Le Sopha*, that of Zéïnis and Phéléas. These are the two virginal lovers who will succumb to their desires for the very first time on the couch that is Amanzéi. When the narrator first enters Zéïnis's couch, he finds a young, beautiful, and virginal girl. As Zéïnis prepares to enjoy a little nap (*jouir des douceurs du sommeil*), the narrator becomes aroused as she moves toward him:

> A simple gauze tunic, almost completely open, was soon the only garment on Zéïnis; she threw herself nonchalantly on top of me. God! With what transport did I receive her! In consigning my soul to sofas, Brama had given it the liberty to go wherever it wanted; how happy I was to make use of that liberty in this instance. I carefully chose the

58. See Jean-Luc Nancy, *Being singular plural*, translated by Robert Richardson and Anne O'Byrne (Stanford, CA, 2000).

spot from which I could best observe Zéïnis's charms and I began to
contemplate them with the ardor of the most tender lover, and the
admiration that the most indifferent man could not deny!

Une simple tunique de gaze, et presque tout ouverte, fut bientôt le seul
habillement de Zéïnis; elle se jeta sur moi nonchalamment. Dieux!
avec quels transports je la reçus! Brama, en fixant mon Ame dans
des Sophas lui avait donné la liberté de s'y placer où elle le voudrait;
qu'avec plaisir en cet instant j'en fis usage! Je choisi avec soin l'endroit
d'où je pouvais le mieux observer les charmes de Zéïnis et je me mis à
les contempler avec l'ardeur de l'Amant le plus tendre, et l'admiration
que l'homme le plus indifférent n'aurait pu leur refuser![59]

From here the soul wanders from one part of the couch to the next,
interacting with the human on top of it. In fact, he ends up wandering
all the way up to a pillow, where he can be so close to her mouth
that he can almost touch her lips. Although he is stopped from going
inside her, he does not complain about it. Instead, he reflects upon the
inconvenience of the human body that he describes as a prison full of
bothersome organs that limit affective movement and inhibit the full
expression and sensation of pleasure and emotion.

The very last moments of the narrator's time as a couch are,
according to Brahma's plan, those of another couple's orgasm. "Finally,
a most piercing cry that she let out and the most vivid joy that I
saw burning in Phéléas's eyes alerted me to my misfortune and my
liberation; and my Soul full of love and pain, left, muttering, to receive
Brahma's orders and my new chains."[60] This moment that should be
shared only between the two lovers is shared, in a very intimate way,
with a third party who serves as a witness and a participant, the sofa.
The narrator talks once again of that inextricability of pleasure and
pain, so vital to Crébillon's fiction, and the words he uses might be
applied to the two lovers as well. The liberation (*délivrance*) is always
coupled with sadness in that first sexual encounter. One enters into
a new world, but there is always a bit of mourning that which has
been lost. The overlapping of individual desire is emphasized in the
last clause of the sentence. When Amanzéi talks of love (*son amour*)

59. Crébillon, *Le Sopha*, p.223.
60. Crébillon, *Le Sopha*, p.236–37. "Enfin, un cri plus perçant qu'elle poussa, une
    joie plus vive que je vis briller dans les yeux de Phéléas, m'annoncèrent mon
    malheur et ma délivrance; et mon Ame pleine de son amour, et de sa douleur,
    alla en murmurant, recevoir les ordres de Brama, et de nouvelle chaînes."

and pain (*sa douleur*), he is presumably referring to his soul (*mon Âme*), mentioned in the first half of the clause. However, at this point his own desire has become so entangled with that of Zéïnis that, given the possibility for multiple referents for the possessive articles *son* and *sa*, we might also assume that he speaks of her love (for her partner) and her pain (associated with the sexual act itself). In other words, his soul that has been exiled to a couch for so long has learned not only to feel for, but also to *feel with*. It is the communal nature of emotion and feeling that allows us to imagine a much more ethical form of *jouissance*.

As Zéïnis and Phéléas begin to become intimate, and just before they lose their virginity, Amanzéi realizes that the moment about to take place on top of him is the one that will return him to human form. He panics and tries to escape into another nearby sofa so as to keep his couch form, but is forced to remain in the couch until the two lovers reach orgasm (simultaneously), after which his soul is set free. In this scene, as in many others throughout the novel, we see that the narrator relishes the confusion between states of animacy. The inanimate form of the couch suits him well and allows him to implicate himself into a ménage à trois that disrupts the subject–object dialectic by introducing another into the pleasing act of sex. His soul may be residing in an inanimate object, but the narrator remains beholden to the three drives: the libido, the life drive, and the death drive. In this world, being means little if one is not coming with another.

Coming together is less literal in other Crébillonian novels and dialogues such as *Les Egarements* or *Le Hasard*, but, in these instances, narrative structure reminds us of his utopian project of creating a society in which drives can be shared. Characters are thrown together and engage in discussions of desire using the shared language of the drive. In *Les Egarements*, for instance, individuals are governed by drives (sublimated for some into desire) that bring them into contact and conversation with others meant to draw out the moment of *jouissance* for as long as possible.[61] Characters borrow language from one another to explain their own emotions, and bits of language spill into one another, creating an orgiastic effect of language that confuses desires, bodies, and relations.

Whereas desire in the oedipal structure circulates within the triangle, desire in this queer construction is quickly displaced outside

---

61. The term *jouissance* is chosen in this instance to indicate that the sexual act is not solely a pleasurable act.

of it, disrupting notions of continuity and wholeness. It is shortly after meeting the young Mlle de Théville that Meilcour's desire for Lursay begins to fade. Ironically, he uses Lursay's language to explain passion (and its lack) rather than his own:

> I should have liked to share with her [Lursay] that convenient relationship one establishes with a coquette, lively enough for the amusement of several days, and as easily broken as formed. But that was the last thing I could expect with Madame de Lursay. She had Platonic ideas, and continually repeated that the senses never counted for anything in the love of a person of breeding; that the disorders that the victims of the passion every day fell into were caused less by love than by the profligacy of their hearts; that love might be a weakness, but in a virtuous heart never a vice.

> J'aurais voulu d'elle [Lursay] enfin ce commerce commode qu'on lie avec une coquette, assez vif pour amuser quelques jours, et qui se rompt aussi facilement qu'il s'est formé. C'était ce que je ne croyais point attendre de Madame de Lursay, qui, platonicienne dans ces raisonnements, répétait sans cesse que les sens n'entraient jamais pour rien en amour, lorsqu'il s'emparait d'une personne bien née; que les désordres dans lesquels tombaient tous les jours ceux qui étaient atteints de cette passion, étaient moins causés par elle que par le dérèglement de leur cœur; qu'elle pouvait être une faiblesse, mais que dans une âme vertueuse elle ne devenait jamais un vice.[62]

In calling out Lursay as a *platonicienne* (one with platonic ideas), he has placed her in the world of the parents, the older generation, the démodé; and yet, he still wants to sleep with her even though he believes his desire to lie elsewhere. Olivier Delers has likened this kind of wandering desire to a "socialité en chaîne" in which the chain of sensual encounters represents an innovative form of social organization, utopian in its scope, that allows individuals to reinvent themselves in relation to others.[63] While a proliferation of sexual transgressions is one of the defining features of Sade's fiction, rebirth through reinvention is a defining feature of Crébillon's. For Crébillon, there is no desire to reproduce and maintain the status quo of kinship relations, but there is a future that lies outside of heteronormative

---

62. Crébillon, *Wayward head*, p.31; *Les Egarements*, p.82.
63. Olivier Delers, "La socialité en chaîne et en réseau dans *Les Egarements du cœur et de l'esprit* de Crébillon fils," *Dix-huitième siècle* 41 (2009), p.248-64.

reproduction; that future exists through a multiplication and proliferation of the self with and through others.

Although Meilcour has several desired objects, the sexual act is deferred until the very end of the novel, and then it occurs only with regret. Sleeping with Lursay, the surrogate mother, rather than signaling the moment of reproduction, signals a return to the womb. In essence, Meilcour reproduces himself. The last sentence of the novel highlights this ambiguous future: "thanks to the proprieties that Madame de Lursay observed so strictly, she dismissed me at last, and I quitted her, promising, in spite of my remorse, to see her early the next day, and *firmly resolved, moreover, to keep my word*."[64] We will never know whether or not Meilcour kept his promise, but we are left waiting for tomorrow. The protagonist's straying lifestyle and symbolic rebirth envision a utopian society, one in which power is neither fixed nor transferred. Parents are absent, and what remains is a cast of illegitimate children. In this utopia, the future is not defined by the succession of generations, but rather by drives, desire, and even whimsy. As such, it remains full of potential for that which is not-yet-here.

Reproduction of relations in the politics of encounter is based not on the future of a child, but on a present that is always communal. It is not always full of love, but it allows one to consider the other as One. Meilcour's wandering body, Amanzéi's wandering soul—the subjectivity of each of these protagonists is based on the interactions they have with others. With each new encounter, they learn something about themselves and about society. The interactions that Meilcour has with Lursay are vastly different from those he has with Théville or Versac, and yet he learns progressively through those long, sometimes erotic, discussions what it means to exist in a society with other people. The lesson becomes more starkly defined in *Le Sopha*, when the narrator can see but remains invisible; his form can be seen even if it is misunderstood, but it nevertheless takes part in the amorous liaisons of others as an unknown third party. From this he must only listen and learn. In his case, it is not only a being with, but it is also a coming with, and a becoming with, as he awaits his rebirth in human form.

64. Crébillon, *Wayward head*, p.202; *Les Egarements*, p.294–95 (emphasis added). "Grâce aux bienséances que Madame de Lursay observait sévèrement, elle me renvoya enfin, et je la quittai en lui promettant, malgré mes remords, de la voir le lendemain de bonne heure, *très déterminé, de plus, à lui tenir parole.*"

Wandering together

In the end, Meilcour understands the difference between desire and love. He understands that being need not be fixed, but can be a fractured and fragile thing, constantly changing. Amanzéi, by contrast, has lived a literally fractured existence for the vast majority of the novel. His soul moves throughout space and time. That he is returned to his human form at the end of the novel does not signal a return to a whole and individualistic state; it indicates only a formal change that continues to inform his journey. Both of these endings, then, introduce perspectival shifts. The world is constantly changing and with it the subject. The subject both understands and embraces the productive force of the world. Human reproduction is eschewed in favor of human coproduction. A body can be fixed in a moment and a place while its mind (*esprit*) wanders to another time and another place—longing for a future but without straying too far from the present. There is no predetermined path in the world of Crébillon: there are only winding paths, and the souls that encounter and produce one another along the way.

Straying, waywardness, cruising, and wandering—these are so many different words used to describe the crucial importance of Crébillon's political message. The author may have been a censor, regulating the circulation of literature in France, but in his own salacious literature he transforms language in such a way that rearticulates the primordial scene of desire as a communal and shared act. Through the use of allegory, Crébillon uses literature to engage in a form of protest. He critiques the excesses and the behaviors of Louis XV's court, French aristocratic society, and the Catholic Church. This is a political message that readers have understood for years and that even landed him in prison. And yet, we may still find another allegory in the larger body of his fiction. As those novels are disseminated, read, reread, and shared, his individualist form of protest becomes a shared event. Readers share not only in the *jouissance* of the virginal lovers that fill the pages of his literature, but also in the moment of political critique. In this way, much like the characters of Crébillon's fiction, the readers also participate in a *becoming with* in which the pleasure and pain that shape individuals are shared in the act of reading.

III

Narrative spinsters

4. Origin stories: maternal enlightenment in Marivaux

> I love you who are neither mother (forgive me, mother, I prefer a woman) nor sister. Neither daughter nor son. I love you—and where I love you, what do I care about the lineage of our fathers, or their desire for reproductions of men? Or their genealogical institutions? What need have I for husband or wife, for family, persona, role, function? Let's leave all those to men's reproductive laws.
>
> Je t'aime, toi qui n'es ni mère (pardon ma mère, je vous préfère une femme) ni sœur. Ni fille ou fils. Je t'aime—et que n'importe là où je t'aime les filiations de nos pères, et leurs désirs de semblants d'hommes. Et leurs institutions généalogiques—ni mari ni femme. Aucune famille. Aucun personnage, rôle ou fonction—leurs lois reproductrices.
>
> Luce Irigaray, "Quand nos lèvres se parlent"

In one of Pierre de Marivaux's later plays, *La Colonie* (*The Colony*) (1750), a group of individuals must reinvent society, creating a new government from the ground up after having been forced into exile on a remote island. The women of this island revolt after being excluded from political planning, insisting on establishing pure equality between the sexes. During one discussion between Arthénice, Mme Sorbin, and Sorbin's daughter, Lina, Arthénice declares that in addition to governmental representation for women, all sexist institutions, including marriage, should be abolished. When Lina complains that she wants to marry the man she loves, Arthénice responds: "And marriage, as it has been up until now, is no longer the same old servitude that we are abolishing, my dear, because we need to get to the point of it [*la servitude*] in order to fix it."[1] The women vow to abolish the misogynist practice of marriage, even if it means the end of the species, telling Arthénice and Mme Sorbin: "We will see the end of the world, the race of man will go extinct before we stop following your orders."[2] In fact, the women's insistence on rights in the present even at the expense of the future of humanity embraces a politics of anti-futurity similar to that of Edelman. These women understand this exile as a chance to start over and build a society upon a strong foundation of gender equality.[3]

One of the first challenges facing the women is finding a language to express their needs and concerns. Interactions between men and women in this play lead mainly to confusion and frustration. In the second scene of the one-act play, Sorbin and Arthénice encounter Timagène and M. Sorbin (Mme Sorbin's husband), their male counterparts who have been selected by the men of the island to draft the new laws. As Arthénice complains of the lack of laws, M. Sorbin responds, "There will be all of that in due course, they're waiting for us now to do just that."[4] The conversation that follows illustrates the frustrating exclusion of women not only from governance, but even from language:

Arthénice
Who, us? Who do you mean by us?

Mr. Sorbin
For heaven's sake, we mean us, it can't be others.

Arthénice
Hold on, these laws, who is going to make them? From whom will they come?

1. Pierre de Marivaux, *La Colonie*, in *Théâtre complet*, ed. Jacques Scherer (Paris, 1964), p.261–73 (265). "Et le mariage, tel qu'il a été jusqu'ici, n'est plus aussi qu'une pure servitude que nous abolissons, ma belle enfant, car il faut bien la mettre un peu au fait pour la consoler."
2. Marivaux, *La Colonie*, p.266. "On verra la fin du monde, la race des hommes s'éteindra avant que nous cessions d'obéir à vos ordres."
3. This is why scholars have described this play as an ultimate expression of Marivaux's feminism. See, for example, Susan Read Baker, "Sentimental feminism in Marivaux's *La Colonie*," in *To hold a mirror to nature: dramatic images and reflections*, ed. Karalisa Hartigan (Washington, DC, 1982), p.1–10; Aurora Wolfgang, *Gender and voice in the French novel 1730–1782* (Burlington, VT, 2004); Peter V. Conroy, "Marivaux's *The Colony*," *Signs* 9:2 (winter 1983), p.336–60.
4. Marivaux, *La Colonie*, p.264. "Il va y avoir de tout cela en diligence, on nous attend pour cet effet."

Mr. Sorbin, with disdain

From us.

Mrs. Sorbin

Men!

Mr. Sorbin

Obviously.

Arthénice

And these legislators, or rather, this position of legislator, from whom will it be chosen?

Mrs. Sorbin, with disdain

From men.

Mr. Sorbin

Oh! Obviously.

Arthénice

Who will it be?

Mrs. Sorbin

A man.

Mr. Sorbin

And who should it be then?

Arthénice

Qui, nous? Qui entendez-vous par nous?

Monsieur Sorbin

Eh pardi, nous entendons, nous, ce ne peut pas être d'autres.

Arthénice

Doucement, ces lois, qui est-ce qui va les faire, de qui viendront-elles?

Monsieur Sorbin, en dérision

De nous.

Madame Sorbin

Des hommes!

Monsieur Sorbin

Apparemment.

Arthénice

Ces maîtres, ou bien ce maître, de qui le tiendra-t-on?

Madame Sorbin, en dérision

Des hommes.

Monsieur Sorbin

Eh! Apparemment.

Arthénice

Qui sera-t-il?

Madame Sorbin

Un homme.

Monsieur Sorbin

Eh qui donc?[5]

Arthénice responds to M. Sorbin's last question with a sentence that will become a refrain of sorts for the rest of the long scene: "And always men and never women."[6] The confusion that occurs between the men and women over a seemingly simple word—"us" (*nous*)—demonstrates the vastly different ways in which language functions for men and women. The men take for granted that the "us" in question is all men. The women, who have long been excluded from this "us," envision this new island not only as a place to consider new forms of government that eliminate social and gender hierarchies, but also as a space to re-evaluate the very basis of gendered language. What the women propose is a government in which they are represented, but, in order to achieve this, they must first construct a common language. This play, therefore, imagines a link between language and laws similar to that of Lacanian psychoanalysis.

Since at least the seventeenth century, women have been ridiculed for engaging in forms of speech that do not adhere to masculine norms.[7] Such forms of ridicule reduce the political power of women who are viewed as less intelligent than their male counterparts. Women are criticized not only for what they say, but also for *how* they

---

5. Marivaux, *La Colonie*, p.264–65.
6. Marivaux, *La Colonie*, p.265. "Et toujours des hommes et jamais de femmes."
7. Although there are undoubtedly earlier examples, the mocking tone of Molière's *Précieuses ridicules* (1659) demonstrates how certain feminine forms of speech are held in contempt.

say it. In the twenty-first century, for instance, women are still passed over for jobs and promotions because of vocal traits such as upspeak and vocal fry, traits that are understood as innately "feminine," and, even when expressing the same views as men, they are often ignored or accused of being too "shrill." The problem facing women is not learning how to use language properly, but, as we see in Arthénice and Mme Sorbin's frustrations, engaging in the constant struggle to have their words signify properly in a language made for men.

Up to this point, I have largely discussed the formation of the masculine subject, relying on various interpretations of the oedipal crisis. As we turn to the formation of the feminine subject, however, we face an impasse. On the one hand, although critics and analysts diverge on the functioning and outcomes of the oedipal crisis in women, many agree that the psychic process is universal, and that it initiates subjects into symbolic language regardless of gender. On the other hand, certain critics (such as Julia Kristeva, Juliet Mitchell, and Luce Irigaray) have convincingly argued that language, along with its oedipal structure, is inherently masculine; female subjects thus remain trapped in an ultimately masculine symbolic. Irigaray laments, for example, that the lack of women's language means that we must understand ourselves as waste or excess.[8] In the 1960s and 1970s, many of these same French feminist philosophers began proposing alternatives to this masculine regime. Largely through the practice of *écriture féminine*, thinkers such as Kristeva, Irigaray, and Hélène Cixous proposed that women might find in writing practices certain forms of resistance to the masculine symbolic. Kristeva, for example, proposes the existence of a feminine, pre-oedipal semiotic language based on the drives.[9] These theories acknowledge that women exist, and must continue to exist, within the realm of the oedipal symbolic, but attempt to find feminine spaces within this masculine structure. Viewed in this light, women might find temporary respite from phallocentric language, but they will ultimately be trapped in its web.

But what if we could imagine a way out of this impasse? What if we could find a symbolic that didn't rely upon the violence or resistance of Oedipus but that also didn't relegate feminine language to the pre-oedipal and inarticulable? This symbolic would also be explained

8. Luce Irigaray, *This sex which is not one*, translated by Catherine Porter and Carolyn Burke (Ithaca, NY, 1985).
9. See Julia Kristeva, *Séméiôtiké: recherches pour une sémanalyse* (Paris, 1969); and *Revolution in poetic language*, translated by Margaret Waller (New York, 1984).

in terms of familial relations (given that family members are most often our earliest interlocutors), but, rather than designating the father as the ultimate arbiter of language (and thus power), in this symbolic, we would turn to the mother. Such a maternal symbolic is precisely what I hope to uncover in this chapter. The maternal symbolic emerges from the dyadic and contiguous relation between mothers and daughters. Whereas entry into the Symbolic Order, as it is theorized by Lacan, requires the successful resolution of the oedipal crisis ending in the father's interdiction of the child's desire for the mother (*le non-du-père*), entry into the maternal order is not predicated on crises. Instead, this order is based on complete acceptance and trust between women in a mutually beneficial relationship. Such relationships inspire women to continue bonding with other women—women who mother with no need for biological reproduction. As we shall see, this maternal language still contains the fractured meaning characteristic of oedipal language, but, rather than an individual subject who must navigate this fractured language alone, the subjectivity of the maternal order is shared and exists on a continuum of female desire.[10] Rather than an emergence of incestuous sexual desire, it is breastfeeding that serves as the paradigmatic event of the maternal order.

In his seminars on anxiety, Lacan situates the primary scene of anxiety in the maternal breast. The infant, who in utero had never experienced a lack (all of the child's needs were met instantly through the nourishment of the placenta), first experiences hunger (an incomprehensible feeling) only after birth. The first external fulfillment comes from the breast, and the infant thus experiences anxiety (unconsciously) in knowing that the sustaining breast might also be taken away. Although Lacan's formulation of desire has little to do with biology, he does provide this very biological process as the primal scene of anxiety.[11] Because of the physical and emotional connections of mother and child during breastfeeding, distinguishing subject from object becomes impossible; both mother and baby become simultaneously subject and object, and this subjective confusion, he argues,

---

10. The type of shared subjectivity that places women on a continuum of shared desires is the main reason why Eve Sedgwick argues that homosociality is a necessarily male phenomenon. While relations between men are predicated on an "obligatory heterosexuality," she argues that "women in our society who love women [...] are pursuing congruent and closely related activities." See Sedgwick, *Between men*, p.2–3.

11. Lacan discusses the maternal breast in several seminars dedicated to anxiety. See Lacan, *Anxiety*.

provokes anxiety. Furthermore, it is the overwhelming presence of the mother that provokes anxiety in the child and causes the fractured order of the symbolic to fall apart, or, to be more precise, to fuse together too tightly.

What Lacan expresses as a scene of anxiety for the infant is, at the same time, a scene of immense contentment. The child may fear the looming departure of the breast, but, in the moment, it receives nourishment and comfort. Furthermore, as analysts including Melanie Klein, Sigmund Freud, and Lacan himself have pointed out, breast-feeding provides an erotogenic function for the nursing mother. Therefore, what Lacan understands as a subjective problem (the mother and child become fused so tightly that boundaries between the two become difficult to define) can also be seen as a supreme example of the potential fluidity of women's bodies. There is, of course, a danger in expressing such a fluidity; first, there is the perceived diminution of women's bodies when they are often already viewed as less than one. Moreover, to focus on the act of breastfeeding would appear once again to reduce women to their biological (and maternal) functions. However, in this chapter I will show that the mechanics of breastfeeding, along with the process of weaning, can also provide useful conceptual tools in understanding the queer, utopian forms of feminine subjectivity that we find in the works of Pierre de Marivaux. In his depictions of desire among women, the eighteenth-century author proposes models of womanly collaboration and autonomy that place him alongside Olympe de Gouges, Françoise de Graffigny, and the marquis de Condorcet as one of the most progressive champions of women's rights of the century.

Given the absurdity of Marivaux's plays with their exceedingly happy outcomes, it may seem strange to take him seriously as a philosopher and, what's more, a political philosopher. Indeed, studies on his work have tended toward the structural and the hermeneutic, often favoring the aesthetic over the political. And yet, as Masano Yamashita points out, one need only look closely at those marginal, down-on-their-luck characters who make repeat appearances in his plays and novels to appreciate the serious political nature of his work.[12] And, while many have analyzed the importance of body and identity in Marivaux's works, few have extended that research outside of his

12. See Masano Yamashita, "The spectacle of poverty: Marivaux's beggars and chance in Enlightenment Paris," *L'Esprit créateur* 55:3 (2015), p.59–71.

texts to ask what his articulation of these categories might mean politically.[13]

Whereas Jean-Jacques Rousseau's sentimental heroine Julie dedicated her life to having and raising children (even dying in order to save her child), the protagonists of Marivaux's works are concerned more with the production of a self in relation to other women. In other words, motherhood in Marivaux's stories focuses less on the feminine duty of biological reproduction than on the nourishing and instructive bonds that form between women regardless of their familial connection. In his novels and plays, the scope and power of the mother–daughter relation is put to the test. Women unrelated by blood adopt the language of maternity and filiation (or rather, *fille-iation*), and biological mothers attempt to translate motherhood into friendship. The language of motherhood is confused but omnipresent. Given the author's attention to this primal relationship between women, it is crucial to examine how motherhood can articulate a subjectivity for women outside of patriarchal norms.

If, as I argue, Marivaux is more than a mere playwright, novelist, and journalist—he is also a keen observer of the human condition and an astute political theorist—what might we learn about the political construction of women's subjectivity by reading the works of a man writing over 300 years ago? To answer these questions, in this chapter I focus on three works in particular: *La Vie de Marianne, ou les Aventures de Mme la comtesse de *** (The Life of Marianne, or the Adventures of Madame the countess of ***)* (1731–1742), *L'Ecole des mères (School for mothers)* (1732), and *La Mère confidente (The Mother as confidant)* (1735). Although Marivaux explores the intricacies of kinship and class in almost all of his works, these three in particular highlight the ways in which the bond between mothers and daughters imitates, competes with, or replaces heterosexual romance, sublimating sexual desire into a desire of a different kind. *Marianne* might well be described as one orphan's search for the perfect mother, and the two plays center on the relationship between a mother and daughter. In one play, the mother is initially harsh and old-fashioned, and desires the perpetuation of wealth and tradition until she learns a lesson about compassion; in the other, we see a kind of premodern *Gilmore girls*, in which mothers

13. Some notable examples of studies on body and identity include Anne Deneys-Tunney's *Ecritures du corps: de Descartes à Laclos* (Paris, 1992); Aurora Wolfgang's *Gender and voice*; and Pierre Saint-Amand's "Les parures de Marianne," *Eighteenth-century fiction* 4:1 (1991), p.15–26.

and daughters can also be best friends who share everything with one another. Most importantly for our purposes in this chapter, each of these relationships is *different*. We may find the terms "mother" and "daughter," but these words have no fixed meaning. They may refer to the type of reproductive vessels and offspring discussed earlier, but they need not necessarily do so. They may be strained relationships or they may be close, they may be unbalanced or the pair may exist in complete harmony, but, in each relationship portrayed in these works, women are complex, dynamic, and desiring individuals who learn and grow as their stories progress.

Readers of Marivaux likely already know that one of the most frequent ways the author demonstrates growth in his fiction is by masking a character's origins from the very beginning only to unveil them at the end. In his plays and novels, the protagonists' histories are slowly revealed to readers over the course of scenes or volumes, each new encounter offering a glimpse of their stories. Origins thus play a crucial role in each of Marivaux's works, and yet they are most often ambiguous or purposefully made ambiguous. Women dress as men, peasants dress as nobles, and servants trade places with masters in scenes of carnivalesque subterfuge that unfailingly end in the happy restoration of order. In the plays examined in this chapter, however, the heroines' origins are surprisingly *not* ambiguous. In both plays, Angélique is a young aristocratic woman who knows both her place in society and her role within the network of relations.[14] Marianne's origins, however, are inherently ambiguous given her unusual beginnings. Because of the woman-centric constructions of kinship in each of these works, the oedipal circulations of desire traced in previous chapters here lose traction. What Marivaux demonstrates instead are the ways in which subjectivity for women emerges from encounters with the maternal body. By rehearsing maternity outside of patriarchal genealogical institutions (such as marriage), Marivaux queers the maternal relationship and shows what a feminine symbolic might look like, thus allowing us to imagine a world outside of patriarchy.

---

14. Angélique is the name of the protagonist in both *L'Ecole des mères* and *La Mère confidente*, and in each the mother retains the name Mme Argante. The use of names that signify character types across multiple plays is a characteristic that Marivaux borrows from the Italian *commedia dell'arte*.

Shared subjectivities

We know that the oedipal complex requires a triangulation of desire that unfailingly places the father in a position of power while evacuating the mother of subjectivity. In this construction, power (the power of language) is distributed unevenly and passes from fathers to sons. The final stage of the process, when the subject experiences castration anxiety, is a violent one based on fear (of losing a member), and the result is the creation of an individualized subject whose desires are regulated through (phallocentric) language. The subject understands the fractured nature of language, in which meaning is predicated upon a proliferation of signifiers. In psychoanalytic terms, the desire that has been turned away from the mother must constantly attach itself to other objects: these are the *objets petit a* that have been discussed more thoroughly in other chapters. In other words, entry into this Symbolic means a cutting of the cord—a complete turning away from the mother who had nurtured the child since before birth. The mother who seeks to draw her children nearer becomes, as Irigaray puts it, a "devouring monster," hated by the men who try to compensate for their inability to grow life by encompassing the entire extrauterine world with masculine language.[15]

Any language predicated upon such masculine power clearly places women, who must also use this language, at a disadvantage. This is why so many of the feminist critics mentioned so far discuss the dangers for women of phallocentric language. For example, one of the most important, if contested, points of Cixous's career is her engagement with the theory of *écriture féminine*. In her essay "The laugh of the Medusa," she writes, "a woman is never far from 'mother' (I mean outside her role functions: the 'mother' as nonname and as source of goods). There is always within her at least a little of that mother's milk. She writes in white ink."[16] Although this example would seem to definitively link *écriture féminine* and the biologically female by connecting the expression of language to the expression of breastmilk, Cixous argues that hers is *not* a biologically essentialist argument (in fact, she offers Jean Genet's writing as an exceptional example of *écriture féminine*), but rather one that offers an alternative to the masculine prison of symbolic language.

---

15. Luce Irigaray, *Le Corps-à-corps avec la mère* (Ottawa, 1981), p.22.
16. Hélène Cixous, "The laugh of the Medusa," translated by Keith Cohen and Paula Cohen, *Signs* 1:4 (summer 1976), p.875–94 (881).

Rather than focusing on practices of writing, Kristeva turns to a language that predates one's entry into the Symbolic—this is the language of the *chora*. It is a maternal and semiotic language based on the drives of the subject as yet unable to distinguish boundaries— particularly the boundary between the mother and the self. What results, in this stage of psycholinguistic development, is a semiotized body. Kristeva describes this body as "a place of permanent scission."[17] The semiotized body is constantly being pulled back and forth between a pre-oedipal and intuitive language of sound, emotion, and drives, and a phallocentric language where meaning is founded on the rules of a patriarchal society. Building on Plato's description of the *chora* as nurturing and maternal, Kristeva notes that all drives are mediated by the mother's body. Thus, she offers a place of power to the feminine and the maternal, inserting them into the hyper-masculinized treatment of psychosexual development as it is analyzed by Freud and Lacan. The *chora* is inherently feminine and not yet informed by masculine structures of, and strictures on, language. Included in these masculine structures within society is the patriarchal family.

Because of the ambiguous site of the subject in utero as well as in early infancy, it is no wonder that Kristeva situates the *chora* and semiotic language within the primal, prelinguistic phase of psychic development. However, this language never fully disappears—it coexists with the phallocentric (symbolic) language that accompanies a distancing from the abject figure of the mother.[18] There are many moments throughout our lives in which we return to this stage and, as Edith Frampton points out, these are not simply returns to the same place. "To become a mother," Frampton writes, "and thereby to re-enter the pre-Oedipal, Kristeva asserts, is also to have one's most basic drives and therefore one's identity undergo metamorphosis."[19] This means that the experience of semiotic language can be shared between mothers and children (the latter in an initial pre-oedipal stage, the former returning to that space) in ways that are mutually

17. Kristeva, *Revolution in poetic language*, p.27.
18. For a thorough examination of the relation between the *chora*, semiotic language, and abjection in Kristeva, see Deborah Caslav Covino, *Amending the abject body: aesthetic makeovers in medicine and culture* (New York, 2004), particularly ch.1, "Abjection."
19. Edith Frampton, "Fluid objects: Kleinian psychoanalytic theory and breast-feeding narratives," *Australian feminist studies* 19:45 (November 2004), p.357–68 (362).

transformative while remaining distinct experiences. In these moments, communication occurs through a language outside of representational meaning. Successful communication with another outside of the norms of symbolic language draws us into a collectivity that simultaneously brings the other more proximate while reaffirming one's own subjectivity. When desire circulates from one subject to another, altering each through the fluctuations of the other, to speak of a transfer of power (as we see in the oedipal crisis) is not entirely accurate. Rather than the selfish and narcissistic language of the father in which the power of language must be passed on, in this construction, the power of language is always shared.

Kristeva, Irigaray, and Cixous: Each of these French feminists believes that the woman's body is always already socialized by the masculine symbolic, and each draws on the maternal body as the site from which a non-phallocentric language—a feminine language—might emerge. Moreover, they argue that it is only within such a language that we might find a female subject, freed from the limitations of a symbolic that reduces her to her reproductive functions. As revolutionary as these approaches may be, the problem lies in their ultimate return to the masculine symbolic. *Ecriture féminine* and semiotic language provide forms of resistance for women but acknowledge the embeddedness of women within in a world structured by the phallic order. In fact, they have been largely criticized by other (mostly Anglophone) feminist critics for being overly utopian and impractical, especially given that they work from within the psychoanalytic frame.[20] The maternal order that I propose in this chapter is admittedly equally utopian (as are all of the literary experiments addressed in this book), but it builds upon these theories not only to imagine how we might think about temporary resistance to phallocentric language, but also to demonstrate how language might be articulated altogether differently. In order to do this, let us first return to that space which for Lacan is a scene of supreme anxiety, and for Cixous the very possibility for womanly artistic expression—the nursing mother.

---

20. Elaine Showalter's "gynocriticism," for instance, is a direct response to what she felt were the shortcomings of French feminism—namely their overinvestment in psychoanalysis which occluded discussions of women's lived experience. Judith Butler later critiqued these same notions for their gender essentialism. See Elaine Showalter, *A Literature of their own: British women novelists from Brontë to Lessing* (Princeton, NJ, 1977), and Butler, *Gender trouble*.

Generally speaking, the time of nursing a child corresponds roughly with its existence within that pre-oedipal stage while the process of weaning occurs when the child begins to realize that it is no longer one and the same as the mother. This biological process would then appear to mimic the psychic process as the child becomes more adept with the use of symbolic language. Although we tend to think about nursing as a unidirectional act in which a mother nourishes a child (the child being the receiver of the beneficial milk), it is actually a much more interactive affair. As the child latches on to the mother's breast, the child's saliva communicates its bodily needs through the breast to the mother, letting the maternal body know exactly which nutrients and antibodies the child needs at any given time. The physiological act, therefore, becomes literally an unspoken body language between mother and child. This language is amplified by the proximity of one to the other. The process of weaning, then, would appear to be the end of this shared body language—ending in an act of severance similar to that which we see in the oedipal crisis. Language becomes fractured as the physical bonds between mother and child become more and more distant.

And yet, as Cixous points out, women are already intimately familiar with detachment due to the initial separation of child from mother during childbirth. She writes, "bring the other to life. Women know how to live detachment; giving birth is neither losing nor increasing. It's adding to life an other."[21] In other words, the woman does not fear detachment in the same way that a man would because she is capable of practicing it in a way that allows her to experience detachment as another form of closeness. Life is not the life of the one or the other, it is life in general. In rehearsing detachment in this way, maternal language acknowledges fractures but also is not suspicious of them. This kind of language allows for a freeness unavailable to the masculine symbolic because it is built upon closeness and trust (rather than fear and paternal interdiction). It allows for the lines of flight assessed by Kristeva as being the hallmarks of the language of the *chora*, guided as that semiotic language is by the drives, but it also gives a *voice* to that language. Because this feminine language is based first and foremost upon the bond between mother and child (and also from the initial separation of mother from child), it is best assessed by examining works which feature mother–daughter relationships

21. Cixous, "The laugh of the Medusa," p.891.

that exclude the father.[22] Although Marivaux's novels and plays tend to abound with fathers, in the three works I examine in this chapter, fathers are notably absent. The relationships between these mothers and daughters provide a rare glimpse into the development of affective bonds between women, as well as of feminine subjectivity. To see how this maternal subjective process occurs, let us turn first to an example from *La Vie de Marianne.*

One of the most striking features of the eponymous Marianne is her ability to navigate seventeenth-century Parisian society with no discernable lineage. Although her orphan status renders her essentially a nobody in a society governed by the strict rules of alliance (in order to become *some*body she must somehow belong to a family), she manages to construct around her an intimate community, to define her role in it, and eventually to redefine the terms of kinship. I will discuss her origins more thoroughly in the next section of this chapter, but for now I would like to focus on the formation of her nurturing bond with Mme de Miran (her benefactor turned mother) as well as the weaning process she undertakes.

Because the narrator loses her parents before she can even speak, her true identity, including her name, is unknown. If she were believed to be noble, then the choice of her assumed name would seem a supreme act of irony. In a study of the cultural functions of La Marianne (the symbol of the French Republic), Maurice Agulhon explains that the name "Marianne" is a combination of the two most common names in the French Catholic tradition, "Marie" and "Anne."[23] This invented name, so plain in its origins, becomes a sort of placeholder standing in for the true identity during the narrator's quest for a proper name. Early in the novel, this common name signifies all of the shame the narrator feels at her lack of origins. While each of the other characters is known by last name alone (Mme Dutour, Mlle de La Fare, Mlle Varthon, etc.) and thus by descriptors of their kinship bonds, Marianne has only a first name that communicates in the language of the fathers her absolute lack of connections. Her shame is quite clear in an early passage from the novel when Valville asks for her name in order to send a note to her family. Troubled by the

22. Although one need not be a woman to mother, in Marivaux's *œuvre* the act of mothering remains the work of female characters. For that reason, I will focus on mother–daughter pairs at the exclusion of mother–son pairs.

23. See Maurice Agulhon, *Marianne into battle: Republican imagery and symbolism in France, 1789–1880*, translated by Janet Lloyd (London, 1981).

question, Marianne bursts into tears rather than divulge her secret. She also demonstrates her shame in much subtler ways. For example, when Marianne writes a note to Mme Dutour stating that the latter should recount Marianne's story to the young nun (*tourière*) who will report back to Mme de Miran, she signs the note "Marianne." In this instance, writing to a non-noble woman allows her the freedom to use her chosen name. However, just after this scene, Marianne writes a note to Valville in which she once again forgoes any signature, preferring not to divulge any evidence of her exclusion from noble, patriarchal society.

As the story progresses, the name that has caused so much shame gradually shifts to a source of pride for the narrator. Her feelings toward the name begin to change once she becomes close to Miran. Having a mother figure who repeats her name next to the words "my daughter" (*ma fille*) brings to this nominal signifier a comforting feeling that it previously lacked. When a young boarder at the convent becomes jealous of the attention Marianne receives, she refers to the narrator by her first name "Marianne," transforming the name into an insult. "You have a beautiful dress there, *Marianne*," she declares, "and everything that goes with it; it's expensive at least, and the woman who takes care of you must be very generous."[24] When one of the sisters comes to Marianne's aid to admonish the other woman for calling the heroine by her name rather than using the proper address of *Mademoiselle*, the protagonist stops her, taking a newly found pride in a name that otherwise means nothing. She writes, "I have nothing, God took everything from me, and I must believe that I am beneath everyone; but I would much rather be how I am, than to have all the things that Mademoiselle has that I do not."[25]

At this point, Marianne has found the mother who nurtures and supports her. Miran provides her with love, affection, financial security, and the all-important touch and proximity of a mother. Eventually, both women will repeat that initial detachment—the one both have practiced before—as Marianne returns to the convent and Miran to her home. Yet, unlike Marianne's previous maternal detachment (after the

---

24. Marivaux, *La Vie de Marianne* (Paris, 1978), p.222 (emphasis added). "Vous avez là une belle robe, *Marianne*, et tout y répond; cela est cher au moins, et il faut que la dame qui a soin de vous soit très généreuse."
25. Marivaux, *La Vie de Marianne*, p.223. "Je n'ai rien, Dieu m'a tout ôté, et je dois croire que je suis au-dessous de tout le monde; mais j'aime encore mieux être comme je suis, que d'avoir tout ce que Mademoiselle a de plus que moi."

death of her mother), this separation is comfortable, and it is one that allows each woman to acknowledge their proximity to one another in ways made more meaningful by the detachment. As Marianne begins slowly to wean herself from Miran, she begins to experiment with the emotional yet symbolic language that the maternal bond has taught her. We see how this process arrives at its completion by returning to the seemingly plain name the narrator has chosen for herself. While the transfer of the father's name requires both sexes (the father as possessor of the name and the mother as the conduit of transfer), this construction requires no masculine intervention. Miran is a widower, and her son does not share her name. Miran is thus able to share her name with the protagonist, and we see the result in the name the older narrator has chosen to represent herself in the novel. "Marianne," the name the narrator invents for herself in the first letter, is not only a plain name, a common name, but, as Saint-Amand points out, it also contains the name of her mother anagrammatically.[26] M-I-R-A-N is rearranged and expanded as it becomes M-A-R-I-A-N-N-E. In choosing this name, Marianne leaves no doubt about her origins. If Marianne's life consists, as she affirms it does, of the pages she writes, then the very title of the story indicates Marianne's true mother, and thus the collective nature of her subjective formation.[27]

The egalitarian nature of the maternal symbolic is perhaps even more clear in *La Mère confidente*. Early in the play, we learn of the very tight bond between Mme Argante and Angélique. In act 1, scene 2, the daughter discusses her love interest (Dorante) with Lisette, her lady's maid. As the daughter worries about her mother's response to the choice of romantic partner, she laments, "this mother who idolizes me, who has shown only love for me, who always wants only what I want."[28] Lisette attempts to point out the flaw in Angélique's assessment of her mother, stating that maybe Angélique wants only the things that her mother loves without truly having a will of her own. In other words, the maid suggests that the mother's desires have occluded those of the daughter throughout the latter's life. Angélique

26. Saint-Amand, "Les parures de Marianne," p.23.
27. Moreover, the distinction of Miran's name from that of her son serves to mask the semi-incestuous relationship that transpires between Marianne and Valville once they share a mother.
28. Marivaux, *La Mère confidente*, in *Théâtre complet*, ed. J. Scherer, p.414–31 (416). "Cette mère qui m'idolâtre, qui ne m'a jamais fait sentir que son amour, qui ne veut jamais que ce que je veux."

responds with a question that suggests that the proximity of desires might be more inextricable than Lisette understands: "but if she has done so well that what she likes is pleasing to me as well, isn't it the same as if I always got what I wanted?"[29] At this point in the play, desires between mother and daughter are fused together. Rather than exemplifying a maternal symbolic, this scene highlights instead the anxiety of the maternal breast proposed by Lacan. Angélique does not yet understand herself as a subject separate from her mother, and she appears to fear the event that might provoke a separation—an inappropriate romantic choice.

Yet the scene that unfolds when the mother does learn of the extent of Angélique's desire for Dorante is not the separation that we might expect. Even though Dorante is poor, and even though he has made the indiscretion of suggesting that Angélique run away with him, Argante proposes a scheme which would allow her to match her own desires to those of her daughter. In an attempt to hide Dorante's error (the error of proposing a forced split between mother and daughter), and at the suggestion of Lisette, Angélique lies to her mother for the first time. After she has told her mother she has ended the relationship with Dorante, the mother's praise is enough to bring her to tears as she admits the lie, sadly telling her mother, "I have lied to you."[30] The moment of separation the daughter had feared due to this breach of trust, however, never comes. After a brief instance of incredulity ("You?" the mother asks), Argante reaffirms the closeness of the two, "no, you have not lied to me because you just admitted it."[31] Angélique expects that the separation she introduces between language and meaning by lying will also result in a severing (or at least a distancing) of the relationship between mother and daughter, but, rather than scolding Angélique for the lie, Argante lets her daughter know that fractured language can bring the pair closer together. In fact, it is just after these lines that Argante devises a plan to meet Dorante and learn more about his character. Once she is assured that the daughter's romantic desires are well placed, she admits that her own desire (that her daughter be happy) will also be satisfied by this match, rendering the match mutually pleasing. The play may end with the awareness

29. Marivaux, *La Mère*, p.416. "Mais si elle fait si bien que ce qui lui plaît me plaise aussi, n'est-ce pas comme si je faisais toujours mes volontés?"
30. Marivaux, *La Mère*, p.426. "Je vous trompe."
31. Marivaux, *La Mère*, p.426. "Toi? non, tu ne me trompes point puisque tu me l'avoues."

of a happy marriage to come, but it does not end with that marriage; instead, the final scenes communicate an abundance of expressions of tenderness between mother and daughter who realize that, although their desires are distinct, they are mutually beneficial.

As we have seen from these examples, entry into the maternal symbolic requires both a preliminary closeness between mother and daughter, and a moment when that proximity will be put to the test. The test may come in the form of inappropriate romantic choices, physical separation, or a seemingly unavoidable gulf between the desires of mother and daughter. This process of weaning does produce a fracture, but, rather than severing one subject from another, it ultimately brings them back together differently. We might think of it, as Melanie Klein suggests, not as a *weaning from* but as a *weaning to* a new kind of relationship.[32] In this more communal subjectivity, where women negotiate desire to ensure the well-being of other women, daughters might find a little white ink of their own. This is how the maternal symbolic begins. Let us now explore further how maternal language functions in Marivaux's literature.

Abject origins

An initial reading of Marivaux's unfinished novel, *La Vie de Marianne*, reveals a very familiar, sentimental tale. The protagonist, Marianne, falls in love with a man (Valville), the relationship is rendered difficult first by the fact that he is noble while she is not, and second because the man's uncle, M. de Climal (who is also the heroine's initial benefactor), also desires Marianne. Still, the young lovers vow to be together until Valville breaks her heart by falling for another woman, and Marianne enters a convent to live out her days alone. The story of young love and heartbreak is, as the saying goes, a tale as old as time. However, to read this novel another way, the love story occupies only a small and relatively peripheral part of the plot. In fact, the story we actually read in this voluminous novel is a story of one woman's search for, and discovery of, a mother. The proliferation of maternal figures in the

---

32. In an essay on weaning, Klein reminds us that in Old English the word was used in the sense of weaning both *from* and *to*. "Applying these two senses of the word," she writes, "we may say that when real adaptation to frustration has taken place, the individual is weaned not only from his mother's breasts, but towards substitutes." See Melanie Klein, *Love, guilt and reparation and other works, 1921–1945* (London, 1988), p.304.

novel suggests a moving beyond the pervasiveness of what Shelley Park calls "monomaternalism," or the necessity within patriarchal societies to limit mothering functions to one woman per child.[33] Marianne assesses her desire for each successive mother figure she meets, looking for a perfect match. That the maternal and romantic love stories overlap with one another throughout the novel produces a transposition of female–female desire onto that of heteronormative romance and renders this a fairly queer love story.

A queer love story invites a queer language with which to transmit it, and who better to provide such a language than Pierre de Marivaux, an author famous for his innovative use of prose. The author was so well known for his unique style of expression, in fact, that his contemporaries tried to imitate it, and his critics gave it its own name— Marivaudage.[34] Although the term was originally intended as an insult, already by the nineteenth century literary critics such as Jean Fleury began to consider the aesthetic value of the author's language.[35] With its meandering sentences, ornate language, and fusing together of philosophical and mundane registers, Marivaudage displays many of the traits that are central to the symbolic language of the maternal as articulated in this chapter. Let us now examine how the frame of *Marianne* works in tandem with its content to turn masculine symbolic language on its head.

The story of Marianne's life begins:

While I was crying under the body of the dead woman who was the youngest of the women, five or six officers who were patrolling nearby

33. Park calls for a queering of motherhood that allows for the multiplication of mothers in a child's life. See Shelley Park, *Mothering queerly, queering motherhood* (New York, 2013).
34. One of these imitations was Marie-Jeanne Riccoboni's *Suites* to *La Vie de Marianne*. After making a bet with the author and some friends that she could imitate his style so well that readers would be unable to distinguish her writing from his, she produced two more volumes of the novel and did, indeed, trick many readers. For more on this subject, see Gérard Genette, *Palimpsests: literature in the second degree*, translated by Channa Newman and Claude Doubinsky (Lincoln, NE, 1997), especially ch.29 (p.165–70).
35. Horace Walpole is often accredited with coining the term "Marivaudage." In a letter to Thomas Gray dated November 19, 1765, he wrote that "*marivauder* and *marivaudage* are established terms for being prolix and tiresome." See Horace Walpole, *The Letters of Horace Walpole*, vol.4, ed. Peter Cunningham (Edinburgh, 1908), p.436. For Fleury's writing on Marivaux, see *Marivaux et le marivaudage* (Paris, 1881).

came upon the scene, and seeing some persons lying dead near the coach and hearing the cries of a child within, stopped at this terrible spectacle, either because of that curiosity one feels when seeing such a horror, or to check out the crying baby and offer their assistance [...] They removed the woman and pulled me, covered in blood, from underneath her.

Pendant que je criais sous le corps de cette femme morte qui était la plus jeune, cinq ou six officiers qui courraient la poste passèrent, et voyant quelques personnes étendues mortes auprès du carrosse qui ne bougeait, entendant un enfant qui criait dedans; s'arrêtèrent à ce terrible spectacle, ou par la curiosité qu'on a souvent pour des choses qui ont une certaine horreur, ou pour voir ce que c'était que cet enfant qui criait, et pour lui donner du secours [...] Ils repoussèrent cette dame, et toute sanglante me retirèrent de dessous elle.[36]

This passage, a scene of death, resembles a birth scene in its chaotic nature. The crying baby is found wedged between two women—one young and dressed nobly, and another older and dressed as a servant. Covered in the blood of the younger woman whose body pins hers to the ground, this child is delivered into her new world both literally (as she arrives in Bordeaux from a foreign land) and figuratively (as she must begin life without any parents) when she is pulled from underneath the young woman's body. The child is promptly wrapped in a coat and carried to the nearest village where she is adopted by a vicar and his sister who take care of her until their own deaths almost fourteen years later. For all intents and purposes, this is the day of Marianne's birth.

This scene is striking in its abject portrayal of birth. In fact, one could not ask for a better example to dramatize Kristeva's notion of abjection in literary form. It is a scene that repulses us but that excites our curiosity. It is familiar in its allusions to birth but unfamiliar and terrifying in its allusions to death. In this scene, the binaries that constitute humanity and selfhood collapse into one another and what we sense is that there is a boundary—this bloody boundary— separating one subject in the process of becoming (Marianne) from another in the process of expiring (the young woman). Furthermore, this scene fuses together the two most prominent examples of abjection that Kristeva offers in *Powers of horror*: the maternal body and the

36. Marivaux, *La Vie de Marianne*, p.52.

cadaver.[37] The abject misunderstands or obfuscates the normal rules of subjectivity, eschewing the wholeness of the psychically normative self so famously prescribed by Lacan. There is no One, no Big Other, no sign. This scene portrays a series of signifying processes, but a series that muddies the subjectivity of the self.

Further complicating the subjectivity of the self are the circumstances surrounding the telling of the story. The language the narrator uses to describe that primal scene is, in fact, merely the reproduction of a story told to her later in life. The insertion of phrases tacked on anachronistically, as details seemingly forgotten, suggests an almost mechanical retelling of the story. Indeed, within the novel she retells her story at least three times. Ironically, the story she knows so little about, that she tries to skip over to get to the more interesting portions of her life, is exactly the story that elicits the most sympathy and that thus serves as her most prized possession. Saint-Amand notes that the protagonist's incessant retelling of the story adds to the mystery of her persona each time, to the point that Marianne becomes an enigma. "The name Marianne," he writes, "is stated as if it had no referent, or rather, it is refused the status of proper name."[38] However, in this vacant reproduction, Marianne brands herself, trading her mysterious name in order to receive everything she needs for subsistence.

That Marianne can take possession of a story about her own origins—a story that should be a part of her—highlights the fractured nature of the narrator. In the last chapter, we saw how Crébillon's anti-hero Versac details the task of the (male) libertine as working very hard to feign ease and indifference. The same traits in *Marianne* might be defined as what Aurora Wolfgang calls "coquettish language." Wolfgang claims that, for Marivaux, "the figure of the coquette is the very paragon of the writer," and the essential task of the coquette is to work very hard to appear as if every jest, every word, every movement is completely effortless.[39] In Marivaux's novels, such coquettish behavior blends together seamlessly feminine *naïveté* and masculine chicanery to produce the language games so essential to his works. The work involved in presenting a coquettish simplicity through speech is doubly intensified first when Marivaux, a man, writes in the female voice, and

37. Julia Kristeva, *Powers of horror: an essay on abjection*, translated by Leon Roudiez (New York, 1982).
38. Saint-Amand, "Les parures de Marianne," p.16.
39. Wolfgang, *Gender and voice*, p.69.

second, when Marianne, now an older noblewoman, takes up the pen to write the stories of her youth.

The narrator begins the very first letter (which is actually the continuation of a previous conversation) with an admission: "It's true that [my] story is strange but I will ruin it by writing it down because how am I supposed to figure out a style?"[40] This sentence is quickly followed by a passage in which she describes how the charms of young, feminine beauty can mask the idiocy of dull and/ or frivolous conversation. This example serves as a synecdoche of the novel itself. We see how the layers of narration peel apart, like Russian dolls: The young Marianne's words are less important than the manner in which she deploys them; more interesting than the story that the older Marianne recounts is the way she communicates it to the reader; and, finally, Marivaux's own masculine voice remains hidden behind the feminine voice he creates, and, if this separation were not complicated enough, we find the additional mediating editorial figure who alerts us that the words we are about to read are found letters that had been tucked away for years. In each case, coquettish language, that is, language hard at work to mask the work of language, replicates the coquettish behavior of the protagonist. Because she is keenly aware of the impact of her speech upon her interlocutors, she is able to manipulate language to turn it in her favor.

Similarly, Marivaux's use of contrasting registers creates a confusion within the novel that replicates the confusion regarding the protagonist's origins. Although the narrator claims to be ashamed of her philosophical asides, writing, for example, "let's return to the story; I am so ashamed of the argument I just made," this will not stop her from repeating this behavior: "you'll see that I will get a taste for it; because, as they say, it's the first one that counts."[41] The narrator continues throughout the novel to interrupt the narrative with personal reflection, all while offering apologies about this matter that does not belong. For a woman who repeatedly tells her reader that she *does not* and *cannot* have a "style," she spills much ink explaining that she will continue to write in this style that is not one. This strong

---

40. Marivaux, *La Vie de Marianne*, p.50. "Il est vrai que [mon] histoire en est particulière, mais je la gâterai, si je l'écris; car où voulez-vous que je prenne un style?"
41. Marivaux, *La Vie de Marianne*, p.60. "Reprenons vite mon récit; je suis toute honteuse du raisonnement que je viens de faire"; "Vous verrez que j'y prendrai goût; car dans tout il n'y a, dit-on, que le premier qui coute."

will in writing that narrator-Marianne exhibits is the same strong will we see in the young Marianne who convinces those around her of her noble origins, even in the absence of any proof. To put it differently, Marianne has no need to "figure out a style" because the style is continuous with her own mannerisms and is, thus, something that precedes the act of writing itself.

If we know that the writer-narrator-character adeptly manipulates her story in order to fulfill her needs, then we must look carefully at the story she tells. As we already know, the story with which the narrator begins (and to which she often returns) is that of the day she was found at the scene of a carriage robbery gone wrong. This is the event that begins the protagonist's unconscious search for a mother. After the death of her first adoptive mother (the vicar's sister) in Paris, Marianne is placed first in Mme Dutour's atelier, where she assesses the maternal potential of this woman who houses and cares for her, and who gives her advice. When she eventually describes Dutour as "a sort of parent, even a sort of fatherland," she acknowledges the familial connection between the two, but relegates Dutour to a more distant role.[42] Moreover, by using the term "fatherland" (*une patrie*)—in French a feminine noun to express a paternal homeland—she emphasizes Dutour's gender neutrality, which, in Marianne's world, makes her ill-suited to be a mother. Once she leaves Dutour's atelier, she meets a second mother figure, Mme de Miran (who, we will discover, is also Valville's mother and Climal's sister). Ironically, the traits of the carriage scene are repeated, if in a perverse way, on the day she meets Miran, the woman who will become the mother Marianne so desperately desires.

After an embarrassing encounter with a priest and M. de Climal (Marianne's first benefactor in Paris), a despondent Marianne realizes her inability to grasp the complexities of symbolic language. Having previously mistaken Climal's sexual desire for general kindness, and then having been unable to communicate the gravity of her situation to the priest, Marianne temporarily gives up on language. She best summarizes the failure of language as she bids farewell to the priest: "I bid him farewell, incapable of pronouncing a single word."[43] She has no money, no family, and she is alone in Paris as she steps out

---

42. Marivaux, *La Vie de Marianne*, p.166. "Une espèce de parente, et même une espèce de patrie."
43. Marivaux, *La Vie de Marianne*, p.155. "Je le saluai sans pouvoir prononcer un seul mot."

of the church and into the desolate streets of the city. Almost as if by providence, her attention is drawn to a convent, and she enters it "half out of a religious sentiment that came to me in the moment, and half out of a desire to go sit and cry in peace."[44] As she enters the church this time, she realizes that she is completely alone.

> There, I let myself wallow in my affliction and I didn't hide my whimpering or my cries. I say my whimpering because I was complaining, I formed words and I raised my voice, saying, "Why was I placed in this world, pitiful as I am? What am I doing on this earth? My God, you put me here, help me." And other such things.

> Là, je m'abandonnai à mon affliction, et je ne gênai ni mes gémissements ni mes sanglots; je dis mes gémissements, parce que je me plaignais, parce que je prononçais des mots, et que je disais: Pourquoi suis-je venue au monde, malheureuse que je suis? Que fais-je sur la terre? Mon Dieu, vous m'y avez mise, secourez-moi. Et autres choses semblables.[45]

In this scene, the language of the body corresponds exactly to the words she pronounces, the whimpering (*gémissements*) and the cries (*sanglots*) highlighting her existential crisis. This time it is not her nude head or her beautiful clothes that excite the reader, but rather her tears—the very same language that had attracted the officers that saved her so many years prior. In this instance the heroine is secluded in a feminine space in which the actions and emotions communicated through her speech are replicated in the movements of her body. Much like the scene of her initial discovery, this time her cries bring exactly the kind of help she needs, but, rather than a handful of men, in this scene it is a woman who comes to her rescue.

After crying alone in the chapel for half an hour, Marianne is greeted by a young nun who informs her that the church is closing. Sensitive to Marianne's state, the young woman leads the crying girl to the chamber of the head nun where Marianne also encounters Miran, who had seen her crying in the chapel earlier. The scene that follows performs two very important functions: First, it mirrors the preceding scene (with Climal and the priest) but replaces all male figures with women; and second, it serves as a sublimation for Marianne's initial,

---

44. Marivaux, *La Vie de Marianne*, p.155. "Moitié par un sentiment de religion qui me vint en ce moment, moitié dans la pensée d'aller soupirer à mon aise."
45. Marivaux, *La Vie de Marianne*, p.155.

traumatic origin story. Once again, the heroine finds herself between the bodies of two maternal women, but this time she will gain, rather than lose, a mother.

Prior to this scene, Marianne is most often depicted as separate from all that surrounds her. In a previous church scene (just before she meets Valville), she separates herself from the crowd and observes those around her from the distant perspective of an onlooker. Although, as Wolfgang points out, this distance allows her to manipulate the gaze by displaying her own body in a manner of her choosing, it also keeps her at a distance from the language of the crowd that she still does not fully understand.[46] The boundary between her body and that of those around her is clear and reinforces her exclusion. In the convent, however, human contact becomes a welcome and calming act. As she begins to excuse herself from the nun's chambers upon seeing the two women in discussion, it is Mme de Miran who gently touches her hand, pulling her back into the room, urging her to explain her situation. And when she throws herself at the nun's feet in a sign of humility, the nun gently touches her arm, pulling her back up. Once her body comes into contact with another woman's body, her language becomes freer and she begins to recount her story from her origins in the carriage to the present moment. In this space, her body is recognizable. The touch of other women serves as a turning point in the protagonist's understanding both of language and of the self.

Anne Deneys-Tunney cites these moments of touching as examples of the absence of a body in the novel. Assessing the confusion between body and discourse, she argues that Marianne exists merely as a series of metonymic relations, in which clothing and instants of contact with other bodies discursively erase the body of the protagonist. In *Marianne*, Deneys-Tunney claims, the body can be seen only in glimpses, when it is unaware of the gaze upon it.[47] However, we might also understand these moments of encounter not as instances of erasure, but instead as moments that highlight the porous boundary of Marianne's body. Although at times the protagonist relishes the display of her body's boundaries (for instance when she shows off her neck or her wrist in a church full of onlookers in order to excite them), the touch of the two women draws her into a larger body—a kinship of women. Almost immediately after their introduction, Miran and Marianne adopt the language of mother and daughter, and Marianne

46. See Wolfgang, *Gender and voice*, p.80.
47. See Deneys-Tunney, *Ecritures du corps*, particularly ch.1.

begins to understand that she belongs to and with someone. Although the mothers that Marianne adopts throughout her narrative never carry her within their bodies, the language she uses to describe their relationships fuses the women together, blurring the boundary between self and other, and between unconscious desire and language, as much as any pregnant body otherwise could.

In fact, after this encounter, which occurs near the end of part 3 of the novel, part 4 begins with a meditation on the bonds between people who are close with one another. In discussing the trouble with putting into words the description of people she knows so well, the older Marianne writes, "They are sentimental objects so complicated and of such a delicate construction that they become scrambled as soon as my memory becomes involved; I no longer know how to gather the pieces together in order to explain them: it is as if they are *in me* but do not *belong to me*."[48] At the time Marianne writes the letters, it is unclear whether or not Miran and the others with whom she interacts are alive or dead, but the idea that they live in her expresses a form of communal being that is paramount to the maternal symbolic. In this particular instance, the people she wishes to describe, and who will occupy the next two volumes of the story, are Miran and Mme Dorsin. Although Dorsin is featured only briefly at the end of part 4 and the beginning of part 5, she plays a crucial role in the protagonist's familial desires.

Dorsin is presented as simultaneously more and less feminine than Marianne or Miran. From Marianne's portraits of Dorsin, we learn that this woman possesses all the most envious bodily traits a woman could want, and in addition has the straightforward and well-reasoned thoughts of a man. Here is one of the first descriptions we read about her: "Madame Dorsin was much younger than my benefactor [Miran]. There is scarcely a physiognomy like hers, and never has a woman's face so merited the use of the term physiognomy to define and express all that one thinks of as good."[49] Marianne will spend

---

48. Marivaux, *La Vie de Marianne*, p.170 (emphasis added). "Ce sont des objets de sentiment si compliqués et d'une netteté si délicate qu'ils se brouillent dès que ma réflexion s'en mêle; je ne sais plus par où les prendre pour les exprimer: de sorte qu'ils sont *en moi*, et non pas *à moi*."
49. Marivaux, *La Vie de Marianne*, p.206. "Mme Dorsin était beaucoup plus jeune que ma bienfaitrice [Miran]. Il n'y a guère de physionomie comme la sienne, et jamais aucun visage de femme n'a tant mérité que le sien qu'on se servît de ce terme de physionomie pour le définir et pour exprimer tout ce qu'on en pensait en bien."

the next several paragraphs praising in minute detail Dorsin's beauty in a manner that wavers between a tone of respect and one of desire. "Let's personify beauty," she writes, "and let's suppose that she gets tired of being so incredibly beautiful [...] that she tempers her beauty without losing any of the charm, and that she dresses herself in grace; it is Madame Dorsin that she hopes to resemble."[50] After finishing the fourth letter with a description of the physical beauty of Dorsin, the fifth letter opens with a description of her character. The desire becomes more and more apparent as the protagonist describes this woman as having a "male spirit" (*esprit mâle*) and even hinting that she would make a great mistress. As we see from Marianne's descriptions, Dorsin's gender-queer nature serves her well as the organizer of a salon, allowing her to draw on her sensitive as well as her reasonable side.[51]

Aside from offering Dorsin as the embodiment of a utopian existence that would allow all individuals to exercise sensitivity and reason regardless of gender, the detailed descriptions of Miran's friend, which often compare and contrast the two women, place Marianne once again at the center of a triad of women. Even from the description of Dorsin above, we hear echoes of that first traumatic scene. We will recall that Marianne began that story by telling us that one of the women was much younger than the other, and that the younger of the women was much better dressed than the older. Similarly, Marianne focuses on the discrepancies in age and appearance between Miran and Dorsin. The description of this scene from the distanced perspective of the aging narrator who reflects on her life as a young woman cannot help but mirror that initial carriage scene in content if not in form. The orphan finds herself once again torn between two bodies, two different models of maternity, and, just as she had in her retelling of the carriage scene, she draws parallels and points out dissimilarities between herself and each of the

---

50. Marivaux, *La Vie de Marianne*, p.206. "Personnifions la beauté et supposons qu'elle s'ennuie d'être si sérieusement belle [...] qu'elle tempère sa beauté sans la perdre, et qu'elle se déguise en grâce; c'est à Mme Dorsin à qui elle voudra ressembler."

51. Jean-Marc Kehrès notes that Dorsin's gender queerness serves as the embodiment for the ideals of her salon in which opposing thoughts are brought together in civil dialogue, preferring reason to appearance. He points to the meritocratic nature of the salon, highlighting the politics at play in her description as being social. See Kehrès, "Travestissement discursif et discours utopique: Marivaux et les digressions de Marianne," *French forum* 33:3 (2008), p.17–34.

women. Marianne appears once again to be at a crossroads in terms
of defining herself, only this time the trauma of the previous scene is
sublimated into a new vision of a utopian family consisting solely of
women. In this way, Dorsin's gender queerness might be understood
less as a political demonstration of the ability to bring opposites
together in harmony than as an opening up of what it means to be a
woman and a mother. By highlighting the young woman's masculine
qualities, she imagines the possibility of a father-like figure to provide
a counterpart to her mother, Miran.

The repetition of the traumatic birth scene, along with the
masculinization of Dorsin, might seem to indicate little more than a
reconfiguration of the oedipal triangle. Marianne's desire has shifted
from maternal Miran to the more masculine figure of Dorsin, in a
manner that mimics the oedipal displacement of desire, if in a slightly
queerer manner. However, to read the triad as such would be to
ignore both Marianne's return to Miran, and her own act of autore-
production as she shares her narrative voice with her fellow sister in
the convent, Mlle Tervire. Dorsin does not restrict Marianne's desire,
as would an oedipal father: The three women share in a mutual
desire for the rest of the novel. The recurring caresses of Miran are
amplified by Dorsin; as Marianne points out after a dinner between
the three, "As usual, Madame Dorsin heaped caresses on me."[52] And
when Valville's extended family attempts to interrupt the young
lovers' union by sending Marianne away, rather than fighting to keep
Valville, she declares her love for his mother:

> I cannot think of it [Miran's love], I cannot even look at her without
> crying out of love and gratitude, without telling her from the bottom
> of my heart that my life is hers, without wishing that I had a thousand
> lives so that I could give them all to her if she needed them to save her
> own [...] yes, Madame, I am nothing but a stranger, an unfortunate
> orphan that God, who is the Master, left to all the misery imaginable:
> but if someone came and told me I was the daughter of a queen, that I
> was inheriting an entire kingdom, I would not want any of it if I could
> only have it by leaving you.

> Je ne saurais y songer [à l'amour de Miran], je ne saurais la regarder
> elle-même sans pleurer d'amour et de reconnaissance, sans lui dire

52. Marivaux, *La Vie de Marianne*, p.226. "Mme Dorsin, suivant sa coutume,
m'accabla de caresses."

dans mon cœur que ma vie est à elle, sans souhaiter d'avoir mille vies pour les lui donner toutes, si elle en avait besoin pour sauver la sienne [...] Oui, madame, je ne suis qu'une étrangère, qu'une malheureuse orpheline, que Dieu, qui est le maître, a abandonnée à toutes les misères imaginables: mais quand on viendrait m'apprendre que je suis la fille d'une reine, quand j'aurais un royaume pour héritage, je ne voudrais rien de tout cela, si je ne pouvais l'avoir qu'en me séparant de vous.[53]

In this scene of subjective confusion (in which family members piece together the story of Marianne), Marianne very clearly weaves her own subjectivity together with that of Miran. At the end of her diatribe, she explains that she could not live if Miran were to die. And, although the protagonist will suffer many more times throughout the novel (at the hands of men and women alike), by discursively linking her body with Miran's, she has recreated the umbilical cord that sustains her. With Miran's protection, she not only graciously navigates pain and heartache, but she effectively learns what it means to bond with another woman (as we see in the ninth volume when her story gives birth to that of Mlle Tervire).

In the novel, the existence of this family of women, as fleeting as it may be, signals a distinct change in the protagonist, one that allows her to grow as an individual subject. Dorsin fades into the background of the story almost as quickly as she enters it, mentioned only in passing after the description of her party. And yet, after the brief moment of bliss that Marianne spends at her salon, the protagonist seems to grasp more completely what it means to exist independently of others, all while creating a family of her own. At this point, she is no longer constituted through a series of body parts, but rather through the intimate connections she forms with other women. The capacity to build an all-female family facilitates the protagonist's entry into a new, maternal symbolic through which she will understand the collective nature of subjectivity.

A school of the mothers

La Vie de Marianne demonstrates the difficulties of articulating feminine subjectivity from a place of relative obscurity. Because Marianne is an orphan, she is able to seek out and construct intimate bonds without

53. Marivaux, *La Vie de Marianne*, p.302.

preconceived notions about what those bonds should resemble. The kinds of family romances we have seen in previous chapters fail to signify in a world without parents. The analysis of this novel, therefore, provides us with a unique opportunity to see the construction of queer forms of kinship in the process of unfolding. But what happens when women already have mothers? Given that motherhood tends to be defined within the masculine and heteronormative context of marriage, is it even possible to find forms of subversion within this familial relationship? To answer these questions, I will turn to two of Marivaux's plays written around the same time as *Marianne*, which demonstrate how even mothers and daughters related by blood can create relationships that signify outside of a patriarchal context.

In *Marianne*, maternal desire is transposed upon heterosexual romantic desire, thus heightening the intimacy of the mother–daughter bond. In the two plays, we see the reverse—romantic desires introduce a break in the intimacy of the mother–daughter relationship. In *L'Ecole des mères*, Angélique has been betrothed by her mother, Mme Argante, to the exceedingly older Damis, even though the young woman is actually in love with Damis's son, Eraste. In *La Mère confidente*, Argante finds a suitor she believes to be a perfect match for her daughter, a wealthy man named Ergaste. Ergaste is young and handsome, but as a philosopher he is described as boring and excessively shy. Angélique has fallen in love instead with Dorante, Ergaste's nephew. In this play Argante's maternal influence is much subtler than in *L'Ecole des mères* and lies in the powers of persuasion resulting from the intimate bond she shares with her daughter. There are many plays about marrying off daughters in the eighteenth century. What makes these two plays so unique is the absence of fathers, and the reliance upon mothers to perform a pivotal role in the exchange of women. As we will see, they often perform this role clumsily. In the domestic homes of these aristocratic women, we are far from such gruesome scenes as that of Marianne's abject birth, but we do continue to see in these plays a confusion of the boundaries separating out female desires, as well as those separating one woman from another. Like Marianne and Miran, Angélique and Argante also learn the important role that boundaries play (in their abilities both to bring together and to divide) in the construction of a female subject.

After a series of inane and unlikely events, *L'Ecole des mères* ends happily with Angélique's marriage to the young Eraste on the night she was supposed to marry his father, Damis. The father decides to continue with the *divertissement* he had planned for his own wedding, singing the song for his son's marriage rather than his own. The first verse of his song sums up the lesson to be learned from the play:

> You, who toward your little daughters
> Speak forever harshly *(encore)*,
> Of the error you are in mothers,
> The god of love laughs and will laugh eternally *(encore)*.
> Your opinions are prudent, your maxims are smart;
> But in spite of your care, in spite of your tenacity,
> You cannot close off completely
> All of the paths to a young heart;
> That there will never a vanquisher of it be.

> Vous, qui sans cesse à vos fillettes
> Tenez de sévères discours *(bis)*,
> Mamans, de l'erreur où vous êtes
> Le dieu d'amour se rit et se rira toujours *(bis)*.
> Vos avis sont prudents, vos maximes sont sages;
> Mais malgré tant de soins, malgré tant de rigueur,
> Vous ne pouvez d'un jeune cœur
> Si bien fermer tous les passages,
> Qu'il n'en reste toujours quelqu'un pour le vainqueur.[54]

Centuries before Rebecca Solnit introduced the concept of "mansplaining," we find in Damis's song a perfect example.[55] He is not explaining just *anything* to the women around him; he is explaining how they should do their job. According to these verses, the strict mothers may be wise but they are in error as well; hiding their daughters away and saving them for a marriage of the mother's own choosing leads to silly girls who are willing to give away their heart to the first young man who offers them love. The song continues with a simple message as the refrain, telling mothers of their daughters: "You must send her off to school" (*Il faut l'envoyer à l'école*). The song's message of the need to educate young women in order to save them from the pain and heartache of love is made incredibly strange by the fact that it is sung by the old and inappropriately matched man originally destined for one such young woman. Having benefited from what he

54. Pierre de Marivaux, *L'Ecole des mères*, in *Théâtre complet*, ed. J. Scherer, p.347–56 (356).
55. Rebecca Solnit introduces the term in *Men explain things to me* (Chicago, IL, 2014).

felt was a miseducation on the part of mothers, he now endeavors to school both Argante and the woman who would have been his new bride.

Once he renounces his claim to Angélique, the narrative of the play unfolds as a fairly typical dramatization of precisely the exchange of women that undergirds patriarchal systems of alliance. The young girl's fate is decided by all those around her and she appears as an accessory to her own love story, but with one major exception—the father is absent. Ironically, the paternal figure in this scene is not Angélique's father but the man she was supposed to marry, and his words of wisdom appear only in the last pages of the final scene. Marriage and fatherhood become entangled in this world of no fathers in ways that we are meant to understand as dangerous. The insertion of Damis's paternal voice at the conclusion of the play appears to indicate that only the restoration of heteronormative desire and kinship formations (in which Damis assumes a paternal role and creates a more fitting union between a young man and woman) can bring about true happiness.

The play may end on a happy note of heteronormative bliss, but this cannot negate the action of the entire play preceding it. Damis calls for an education of women so that they may avoid unfavorable matches, an education for which they must be sent away. And yet, the daughters of these two plays end up with precisely the matches they desired all along in spite of their maternal education. In both plays, the girls' education has taken place within the maternal household and has created a strong bond between mother and daughter. The fusion of the two lives is so great that it leads to misunderstandings in the sharing of desire. In one telling comment early in scene 4 of *L'Ecole des mères*, Argante makes one such error when she mistakes her daughter's sadness (because of the mother's poor marital choice) for a sorrow at the mere thought of leaving her mother. Upon learning that her daughter has been distraught since the announcement of the wedding, Argante feels proud: "it's a sign that she has a good heart; she's getting married, she's leaving me, she loves me, and our separation is painful for her."[56] Maternal love thus subsumes the daughter, transforming the latter into an object of motherly affection.

In *La Mère confidente*, maternal confusion is amplified due to the intense nature of the mother–daughter relationship. As in *L'Ecole des*

---

56. Marivaux, *L'Ecole*, p.349. "C'est une marque qu'elle a le cœur bon; elle va se marier, elle me quitte, elle m'aime, et notre séparation lui est douloureuse."

mères, the reason for the father's absence is unclear (although given that neither play mentions the father in any way we may confidently assume they are dead), but this time rather than seeking out an older paternal figure, Argante, because of the intimate bond she shares with her daughter, aims to create a good match based on mutual desire between lovers. Unfortunately, the mother of this play also mistakes her own desires for those of her daughter, creating a match based on a profound ignorance of the daughter as a subject with separate passions and drives. In this play, then, we see a perversion of female desire. Rather than serving as a superego to the daughter as does the father in masculine (and oedipal) constructions of the subject, Argante ties herself so tightly to her daughter as to render the two of them a single desiring subject. Her repeated requests that the daughter call her "friend" or "confidant" rather than "mother" serve the function of collapsing the barrier between mother and daughter. Like the mother of *L'Ecole des mères*, this mother has her daughter's best interests at heart, and, like that same mother, she must learn to accept her daughter as a separate entity from herself.

These two examples in which mothers are unable or unwilling to understand their daughters as autonomous subjects, guarding them tightly in a kind of womb that extends beyond the body to envelop the maternal household, demonstrate precisely the dangers that Damis feared of such an education. Incapable of imagining filial desire, the mother takes no measures, in Damis's opinion, to provide the most important instruction to her—an education on passion and love. By "sending her off to school," the old man introduces a separation of women, one that he believes would allow for girls to be educated free from the maternal love that blinds the mother-teachers. Forming proper female subjects, he suggests, requires separating women from their mothers. Not to do so would lead to frivolous and naive women who are no good for French society.

Damis's suggestion that women be separated from their mothers is not unusual. Prior to the eighteenth century, affluent children were most often sent off first to a wet nurse, and then to a tutor. As the family household and its importance in society begin to change and become more private over the course of the century, female seclusion takes a new form. As feminist critics such as Adrienne Rich and Nancy Chodorow have long argued, the creation of the family home as a separate domestic space removed from society, the very kind of space that was beginning to take shape in the eighteenth century, served the function of keeping women apart.[57] Once a woman marries and enters the husband's household, she relinquishes her own world and remains trapped in the patriarchal home. As she is removed from contact with women, the only other females who inhabit that space will eventually be her daughters, who will withdraw from the home as well once they marry and enter another patriarchal space of their own. The fact that separation of women is so common in early modern France makes the closeness between Argante and Angélique all the more remarkable. If we read these two plays a little queerly, we can find traits of a feminine symbolic, even in plays that end in marriages that maintain and reproduce patriarchal society. Prior to the fulfillment of heterosexual desire, these daughters first complete a subjective formation in the complete absence of men.

The French title of the first play (*L'Ecole des mères*) can be translated in two ways: The first is the most common English translation, *School for mothers*. This suggests that what follows will be a tale of mothers learning how to be better parents to their children. A secondary translation, however, might be *School of the mothers*. In this school the mothers are instructors, teaching their daughters all they need to know. What Damis presents in his *divertissement* is the need for a school *for* mothers. What we discover in the play that precedes his pronouncement and what we find in *La Mère confidente* is a school *of the* mother. Now let us take a look and see just what the daughters learn, and what we might learn from these maternal schools.

The length and formal structure of the two plays are varied and the names of the masculine characters change, but there are many similarities in the narrative structure of both plays. In each, a

57. Jürgen Habermas argues that the increasing separation of the family home from public society goes hand in hand with the rise of the free-market economy. The family (or intimate sphere) in this new cultural and political landscape serves as an agent of society, as well as a hope for emancipation from society. He notes that, although the family is held together by human closeness, it is also maintained through patriarchal authority. It is the patriarchal authority of this increasingly closed-off space that is so detrimental to women and that is critiqued by Rich and Chodorow. Habermas discusses the relationship between the public, private, and intimate spheres in chapter 2 of *The Structural transformation of the public sphere: an inquiry into a category of bourgeois society*, translated by Thomas Burger and Frederick Lawrence (1962; Cambridge, MA, 1991). For feminist critiques of the isolation of families that takes place during this transformation, see Adrienne Rich, *Of woman born: motherhood as experience and institution* (New York, 1995); and Nancy Chodorow, *The Reproduction of mothering: psychoanalysis and the sociology of gender* (Oakland, CA, 1999).

daughter (Angélique) who loves a young man (who loves her in return) is promised by a mother (Argante) to another man with whom she is inappropriately matched; both daughters plot with servants and lovers to convince their mothers by reason or ruse that they should be married to the man of their choice; and both daughters eventually succeed in changing their mothers' minds. The striking similarities between the two plays make their differences stand out all the more clearly. For instance, the mother of *L'Ecole des mères* is severe and seeks to impose her authority over her child, as would a father. She does ask Angélique's opinion of the man she has chosen as a husband; nevertheless, she expects only agreement. "Don't you think that you are so lucky to be marrying a man like Monsieur Damis, whose fortune, whose wise and reasonable character assure you a quiet and peaceful life, one that corresponds to the beliefs and morals I've always taught you?" she asks Angélique. When the daughter responds, "you order me to, then?" Argante replies frankly, "yes, of course."[58] The discord between the mother's desire on the one hand to make her daughter happy and, on the other, to impose her choice by forcing the daughter's sense of filial duty has the effect of fracturing Angélique's identity. Whereas Marianne felt happy and whole in the world of the mothers, Angélique struggles with the conflicting desires of amorous passion and of familial duty. She is afraid to speak her mind because to do so would be to betray one or another of those desires.

The responses she offers her mother are therefore short, often broken up by her mother's continued questions and insistences, and, much like Damis's song, they also contain a refrain: "but" (*mais*). "What, are you not happy with your lot?" Argante asks, to which the daughter responds:

Angélique

But...

Mrs. Argante

What! But! I would like for you to respond to me reasonably; I expect your gratitude and not your "buts"...

---

58. Marivaux, *L'Ecole*, p.350. "Ne trouvez-vous pas qu'il est heureux pour vous d'épouser un homme comme Monsieur Damis, dont la fortune, dont le caractère sûr et plein de raison vous assurent une vie douce et paisible, telle qui convient à vos mœurs et aux sentiments que je vous ai toujours inspirés"; "Vous me l'ordonnez donc?"; "Oui, sans doute."

Angélique (with reverence)
I will speak of it no more, Mother.

Mrs. Argante
I release you from the obligation of respect; tell me what you think.

Angélique
What I think?

Mrs. Argante
Yes: how do you feel about the marriage in question?

Angélique
But…

Mrs. Argante
Always with the buts.

Angélique
Mais…

Madame Argante
Quoi! mais! je veux qu'on me réponde raisonnablement; je m'attends à votre reconnaissance, et non pas à des mais…

Angélique (saluant)
Je n'en dirais plus ma mère.

Madame Argante
Je vous dispense des révérences; dites-moi ce que vous pensez.

Angélique
Ce que je pense?

Madame Argante
Oui: comment regardez-vous le mariage en question?

Angélique
Mais…

Madame Argante
Toujours des mais.[59]

59. Marivaux, *L'Ecole*, p.350 (emphasis added). "Voyons, n'êtes-vous pas satisfaite de votre sort?"

As the mother becomes increasingly upset and impatient, Angélique's response remains the same. This small word, only one syllable, communicates what the daughter cannot say, that she is unhappy with her mother's choice. Because her own desires do not match those of her mother, communication between the two becomes difficult. This word becomes the interruption that dispels the illusion of wholeness between mother and daughter. As the mother laments the repetition of the nonanswer, she pushes her daughter closer and closer to the response the latter had hoped to avoid. "This marriage is not pleasing to you?" Argante asks Angélique who finally responds in the negative, "no."[60] The daughter's "no" performs a similar function to that uttered by the oedipal father—it alters the circulation of desire. The myth of a unifying desire between daughter and mother is dispelled, and the daughter's "no" alerts the mother to the boundary separating the two. Maternal and romantic desire, in this instance, do not tend toward the same objects.

Similarly, the first scene between mother and daughter in *La Mère confidente* (scene 8) alerts the pair to their diverging desires. This gentler Argante also asks her daughter's opinion on the choice of Ergaste for a husband, but she does not wish to impose her choice by authority. Instead, the mother of this play sets out to change her daughter's mind through gentle language and reasoned discourse. The spectator is first alerted to this course of action in the mother's subtle pronominal switch. The scene begins in a very formal register: "I was asking about you [*vous*] to Lubin, my dear."[61] The two exchange some pleasantries, using the formal "vous" to address one another up until the moment when Argante learns that Angélique is not pleased with the choice of Ergaste. The mother first attempts both to remind the daughter of their close relationship ("You [*vous*] know well how we are together") and to give her daughter the final power to make a decision. When she realizes that her daughter is still unhappy, she slips mid-scene into a more intimate and less formal register:

Mrs. Argante
Do you [*tu*] believe that I love you?

Angélique
Not a day passes in which I do not receive proof of it.

60. Marivaux, *L'Ecole*, p.350. "Ce mariage ne vous plaît donc pas?"
61. Marivaux, *La Mère*, p.419. "Je vous demandais à Lubin, ma fille."

Mrs. Argante

And you [*toi*], my dear, do you love me as much?

Angélique

I flatter myself to think that you [*vous*] do not doubt it.

Mrs. Argante

No, but to reassure me, you [*tu*] must do me a favor.

Angélique

A favor, mother! There's an ill-suited word, command me and I will obey you [*vous*].

Mrs. Argante

Oh! If you [*tu*] are going to take on that tone, then you don't love me as much as I thought. I have no orders to give you [*vous*], my dear, I am your friend and you are mine, and if you treat me differently, I have nothing left to say to you.

Madame Argante

Es-tu bien persuadée que je t'aime?

Angélique

Il n'y a point de jour qui ne m'en donne des preuves.

Madame Argante

Et toi, ma fille, m'aimes-tu autant?

Angélique

Je me flatte que vous n'en doutez pas, assurément.

Madame Argante

Non, mais pour m'en rendre encore plus sûre, il faut que tu m'accordes une grâce.

Angélique

Une grâce, ma mère! Voilà un mot qui ne me convient point, ordonnez, et je vous obéirai.

Madame Argante

Oh! si tu le prends sur ce ton-là, tu ne m'aimes pas tant que je croyais. Je n'ai point d'ordre à vous donner, ma fille, je suis votre amie, et vous êtes la mienne, et si vous me traitez autrement, je n'ai plus rien à vous dire.[62]

We will note that Argante first switches to the pronoun *tu*, reinforcing the love for her daughter. She is to be understood no longer as a mother, but rather as a friend. Friends do not give orders to one another, and there is no inherent hierarchy that exists between them. This intimate code-switching, coupled with a language that asks for favors rather than giving orders, has the effect of evacuating the discussion of the power otherwise invested in it. Ultimately the mother does have the power to dictate orders to her daughter, but she chooses to efface this fact in order to render her daughter more open to suggestion.

And yet, the formal *vous* that is reintroduced in the last line of the passage alerts the spectator to the presence of the lie. The persistence of maternal power cannot be erased by simply wishing it away. In each of the scenes between mother and daughter, pronouns and registers become confused and, while the Angélique of *La Mère confidente* may appear surer of herself than she did in *L'Ecole des mères*, the ambiguous parental relationship leads to confusion in other areas. She is not afraid to speak her mind to her mother-confidant, and yet her mother's friendly advice often leads her to question her own desire. If she does love her mother so much, and if the mother loves her and wants only what will make her happy, should she not want the same things as her mother? This is the question that haunts Angélique throughout the play as we see in her consistently confusing conversations with her lover, Dorante. Each discussion with Dorante reignites her desire for him, and each conversation with her mother calls that desire into question. The solution to this problem is to introduce a break into the mother–daughter relationship, but it is not, as Damis would have it, through the introduction of a father. In true Marivaudian style, the break in this play comes in the form of familial transvestism.

In order to intervene in the scene of daughterly desire without affecting its outcome, Argante decides once again to leave her maternal role, this time distancing the familial connection to that of aunt. As an aunt, she can enter the romantic scene of the two lovers in order to better understand her daughter's desires without imposing the authority that her parental position would otherwise signal. In fact, her discourse in this scene draws on the distinction between signs and signifiers in a manner that heightens the sensitivity of both of the

<hr>

62. Marivaux, *La Mère*, p.419. "Vous savez bien comme nous vivons ensemble."

young lovers. When Dorante reasons that running off with Angélique would be justified because they would live in the sanctity of marriage, Argante counters that pronouncing the words of husband and wife does not, in fact, make them true. "Her husband," she replies, "is it sufficient to call yourself that for it to be so?"[63] Her own position in this scene as a false aunt adds credence to her words. Things are not always what they appear—it is actions and emotions that bring about truth. The truth of her words provokes a crisis in the young lovers, who renounce their plans to run away. Once their actions demonstrate the truth of their desires (they just want to love one another), Argante tears away her own mask, revealing her true relation to Angélique and granting her blessing for the marriage. At this point, maternal and filial desire are once again matched, but through a process of negotiation that grants both a position of subjectivity. While Argante acknowledges the fractured nature of language, she uses the gaps between meaning to her advantage. She does not prohibit desire; she merely helps to alter its course. Put differently, rather than a castrating "no," this mother performs an act of weaning by incrementally shifting the very meaning of desire for mother and daughter until both can be satisfied simultaneously.

Much as we saw in *La Vie de Marianne*, maternal language in this play emerges through a process of drawing desires nearer to one another rather than the kind of splitting off that defines the oedipal crisis. Instead of emphasizing the separation of mother–daughter desires, language works in *La Mère confidente* to bring them closer and closer together, without wholly collapsing one into the other. The desires of both parties remain the same as they had been at the beginning of the play; the mother desires the daughter's happiness and the daughter desires a romantic love that will strengthen, rather than sever, maternal relations. Although the language with which Angélique communicates her feelings remains relatively static throughout the play (she, for instance, never hesitates between pronouns for her mother), the language of her emotions vacillates between personal and filial desire. In the end, the back and forth of language between mother and daughter that shifts between a language of reason and one of emotion, and that changes in register and levels of intensity, provides the space of negotiation that evens out desire and leaves the boundary between the two bodies intact, but permeable. As Angélique tells Dorante, love and trust have replaced fear and duty in the parental relation:

63. Marivaux, *La Mère*, p.430. "Son époux, suffit-il d'en prendre le nom pour l'être?"

"I told her about it [our relationship]; her kindness, her tenderness compelled me to; she has been my confidant, my friend, she only ever kept the right to counsel me; she relied on my tenderness for her to guide my conduct, and she left me the mistress of everything [...] she promised me that I would be free."[64] The freedom to examine her own desires has provided the space necessary to become a subject that, like Marianne, feels once again whole in the world of the mothers.

And what of our other Angélique? How does she fare in this subjective formation? In scene 18 of L'Ecole, Angélique complains to her lover, Eraste, about the education her mother has given her. If only her mother had done what Damis will later suggest and sent her out into the world, then perhaps she would not have been so foolish as to tell this man she loved him; instead, she reasons, "maybe I would love you without telling you; I would make you languish to find out."[65] In other words, had she been raised in society, she would have known better how to play the game of love. The conversation turns to masculine reason when Eraste responds that he, at least, has a reasonable father and, therefore, he will be reasonable enough for both of them. Throughout the play, masculine reason competes with feminine passions, and each character offers differing models of how to manage passionate emotions within the institutions such as marriage that govern society.

Even the mother of this play displays an inner conflict regarding the place of masculine and feminine systems of symbolic logic. A firm believer that a wife gives herself over completely to her husband, she teaches her daughter that once married she need not have any friends because her husband will be the only friend she needs. She states further that the wife need not seek out advice from others (including a mother) because her husband's desires will dictate her own. When Angélique asks what will become of the love she has for her friends, her mother responds:

Mrs. Argante
You must no longer have any [friends] other than those of Mr. Damis,

64. Marivaux, La Mère, p.431. "[J]e l'avais instruite [de notre relation], ses bontés, ses tendresses m'y avaient obligée, elle a été ma confidente, mon amie, elle n'a jamais gardé que le droit de me conseiller; elle ne s'est reposée de ma conduite que sur ma tendresse pour elle, et m'a laissée la maîtresse de tout [...] elle avait promis que je serais libre."
65. Marivaux, L'Ecole, p.355. "Je vous aimerais peut-être sans vous le dire; je vous ferais languir pour le savoir."

to whose wishes you must always conform, my dear; that's our place in marriage.

Angélique
His wishes! And what will become of mine?

Mrs. Argante
I know that this can be a little mortifying, but you must give in, my dear; it's a kind of law that's imposed on us, and that, in the end, honors us, because when two people live together, it is always the most reasonable one who is charged with being the most docile, and this docility will be easy for you since you never had any will with me; you know only obedience.

Madame Argante
Vous n'en devez point avoir d'autres que ceux de Monsieur Damis, aux volontés de qui vous vous conformerez toujours ma fille; nous sommes sur ce pied-là dans le mariage.

Angélique
Ses volontés! Et que deviendront les miennes?

Madame Argante
Je sais que cet article-là a quelque chose d'un peu mortifiant, mais il faut s'y rendre, ma fille; c'est une espèce de loi qu'on nous a imposée, et qui dans le fond nous fait honneur; car entre deux personnes qui vivent ensemble, c'est toujours la plus raisonnable qu'on charge d'être la plus docile, et cette docilité-là vous sera facile; car vous n'avez jamais eu de volonté avec moi, vous ne connaissez que l'obéissance.[66]

Angélique's lesson from this conversation is this: In order to fulfill your natural role as wife, you must be obedient and docile. The mother's words suggest that entering into marriage requires leaving behind personal desire and will. However, the language Argante uses in the rest of the scene betrays her harsh reasoning. As a woman in a patriarchal society, her duty is to marry, reproduce, and then assure the transmission of the same duties to her female children. Argante explains this duty to the daughter whom she has promised to a man old enough to be the latter's grandfather, and yet she also explains that she understands the violence such practices perpetuate toward women. It is at this point that Argante demonstrates a confusion of

66. Marivaux, *L'Ecole*, p.350.

parental and marital bonds. Rather than trying to understand her daughter's desires (as had the other Argante), this mother tries to assuage Angélique's fear of marriage by posing it as a move from one form of subordination to another ("you never had any will with me"). It is the daughter who points out the error in this argument: "Yes, but my husband will not be my mother."[67] After this "but," Angélique demonstrates the same understanding of symbolic language that Argante displayed in the other play. When asked by her maid if she will marry Damis, she replies, "I assure you I will not; it's enough that he's marrying me."[68] She will continue to manipulate language masterfully in a private conversation with Damis, refusing to play along with her mother's desire (she will not tell Damis she wants to marry him), but also refusing to outwardly disobey her mother (she will not openly state that she does *not* want to marry him). Although she has received a maternal education, her keen understanding of desire and duty allows her to grasp symbolic language innately.

Although Angélique's use of language does not immediately provoke a change in the mother, it does set off a series of events that will bring the pair closer together, all while allowing for the fulfillment of romantic desire. In true Marivaudian style, the final event will rely upon mistaken identity. Angélique, Argante, Damis, and Eraste all find themselves together in a dark room where the two young lovers remain oblivious to the presence of Argante and Damis. Words of love are passed inadvertently between father and son, and then between confused lovers, before finally the room is illuminated, and everything comes into focus. It is only after this scene of bodily confusion that both Angélique and Argante emerge as distinct subjects who become closer than they had ever been before. In this womb-like space of the dark room, the boundaries separating bodies become obfuscated, and individuals are linked by a language of pure desire. Each subject will emerge from this room with a better understanding of the desire of the other. Furthermore, the reason, which Argante is constantly accused of lacking, resurfaces in Angélique, who then opens the space for her mother to be reasonable as well. Although the mother–daughter relationship in this play is quite different from the relationship we find in *La Mère confidente*, the endings demonstrate the same outcomes. Mothers and daughters are brought together by complementary—though distinct—desires. We will not witness

67. Marivaux, *L'Ecole*, p.350. "Oui, mais mon mari ne sera pas ma mère."
68. Marivaux, *L'Ecole*, p.350. "Je t'assure que non; c'est assez bien qu'il m'épouse."

the same lengthy negotiation of maternal and filial desire that we witnessed in the previous play, but we do see how feminine language is capable of bringing together reason and emotion, and ultimately of satisfying multiple desires.

In both "schools" of the mothers, maternal education is questioned and interrogated, pitted against the masculine traditions with which they collide. Secluded from society and thus from interaction with men, the two Angéliques have received educations in intimacy and duty that are far superior to those they would have otherwise received. Had they been raised in conventional societies, their outcomes may have resembled more those we saw in the last chapter; education in the last chapter came from cruising, but here it comes from staying in one place—a place full of women.

La Vie de Marianne opened with a scene of abjection par excellence. Angélique's subjective birth may not be as obviously abject as Marianne's, but the confusion of feminine desires does call into question the boundaries separating one subject from the next. What we see instead is what Cixous calls a "defamilialization" of the subject.[69] This type of subject is not borne of a mother and a father because, much as declaring oneself husband or wife does not make it so, having a child does not transform one into a mother or father. This subject also refuses to fetishize the oedipal triad. Ultimately, a reaffirmation of boundaries separating one subject from another produces a new type of family. The daughter need not leave the world of the mothers to enter the world of the husband. The mother, offering a "yes" instead of a "no," provides the daughter with something new: the opportunity to fuse together maternal and romantic desire into a harmonious union. The women of this symbolic have learned not only what language is, but also how to fuse it with the drives in order to communicate beyond language. The maternal symbolic thus proposes an alternative type of enlightenment—one that favors a coming together, rather than a dividing out, of knowledge.

Maternal enlightenment

The examples from this chapter demonstrate that, well before the first performance of *La Colonie*, Marivaux was already imagining how to

69. Cixous, "The laugh of the Medusa," p.890. According to Cixous, this subject would be free from the familial signifiers that define the subject in phallocentric language.

construct a language within which women could revolt against sexist, patriarchal regimes. The mothers and daughters of these plays work together to fuse the emotions of the drives, or semiotic language, with representational language that does not return to the ultimate phallic signifier. And yet, these are not the plays that we most remember when thinking of Marivaux. The novel certainly holds an important place within the canon of eighteenth-century French literature, but the plays that are most often staged are those that focus more on the resolution of heterosexual romantic love, such as *Le Jeu de l'amour et du hasard* (*The Game of love and chance*) or *Le Triomphe de l'amour* (*The Triumph of love*). These plays provide spectators with the humor based on mistaken identity and double entendres that we have grown to love and expect from the playwright.

There is one venue in which the author's work on female desire has experienced somewhat of a renaissance in France—film. In recent years screenwriters such as Abdel Kechiche have incorporated the author and playwright's works into their films.[70] In particular, Kechiche's 2013 *La Vie d'Adèle* seizes upon the female desire of Marivaux's works, and amplifies it through a reading of Julie Maroh's *Le Bleu est une couleur chaude* (*Blue is the warmest color*) (which provides the title of the movie's English translation), a graphic novel about a young woman's awakening to her lesbian sexuality. Throughout the movie, several references are made to *La Vie de Marianne*, and the movie even opens with a shot of the book cover itself as Adèle reads it for her high school class. While adaptations such as this one highlight, on the one hand, precisely the themes discussed in this chapter (that women transcend the role of object to become desiring subjects, for instance), on the other hand, they also demonstrate the dangers of reading this novel through a completely masculine framework. By offering female sexuality as seen through the male gaze, Kechiche flattens out the complexity of women that is so important to Marivaux's work. The director evacuates the possibility for caring love, and with it all of the utopian qualities of Marivaux's work, and replaces it with narcissistic passion. One scene in particular, in which the director plays a young man at a party explaining the female orgasm to a group of mostly

70. Louisa Shea argues that it is the playful nature of Marivaux's works that makes him so appealing as a modern-day hero of the disaffected youth, and thus equally appealing to filmmakers such as Kechiche. See Louisa Shea, "Exit Voltaire, enter Marivaux: Abdellatif Kechiche on the legacy of the Enlightenment," *The French review* 85:6 (2012), p.1136–48.

lesbians, highlights the problematic nature of the gaze.[71] In this scene, the male actor/director assumes the role of Damis, trying to send these women off to school to learn how to live a feminine life in a man's world.

The women of Kechiche's films may be sexually liberated in ways that the women of Marivaux's novels and plays are not, but they are still subjected to the rules of masculine society. These are not the lessons that one should learn from Marivaux's works. The mothers and daughters of these novels and plays are strong and, aside from possibly Argante (*L'Ecole*), not desirous or in need of a man to explain their worth. These women do not die for their children, as did Rousseau's Julie, they *live* for them. They pass on education and they also pass on love. Marivaux does not need to kill off women or subject them to the violences of masculine societies to prove their worth. Instead, he proves their worth by demonstrating that they are complex, desiring subjects who yearn for both passion and caring intimate relationships with other women. What is produced in each of these works is a new means of expression. Rather than centering on the traditional heterosexual marriage plot, these stories focus on relations between women. As the Angélique of *L'Ecole des mères* moves from the monosyllabic "but" to a complete expression of emotions and desires; as the Angélique of *La Mère confidente* learns to articulate her own desire to her mother (even if that mother is disguised as her aunt); and as Marianne accepts her name and passes her voice on to another woman, female expression, to put it bluntly, finds its voice.

In each of the works examined here, fathers are absent, and lovers play only secondary roles. What is revolutionary about Marivaux's articulation of feminine subjectivity is that it all takes place outside patriarchal institutions such as fatherhood and marriage. While sharing one's maternal voice may seem like precisely the kind of reproduction of motherhood that Chodorow critiques, it is actually a production of a different kind. As Kristeva points out, each encounter with the *chora* (for mother and for child) is not a return but an event that produces something completely new. In the end, when marriage does occur, it is outside of the frame of the stories, and couples are certainly not having children. Instead, we see the amplification of women's voices in a feminine symbolic that requires no Other, simply

---

71. In fact, in interviews after the movie's release, the actors starring in the film had these same criticisms of the director, who, they felt, completely misunderstood female sexuality.

others with which to share language and love. We tend to think of the Enlightenment as the birth of the individual (male) pursuit of contentment through knowledge. We learn the opposite in Marivaux; the happiness that accompanies knowledge is a feminine construction and is found in collective being.

5. Knotty relations: Graffigny's regime of the sister

> We are taught that women are "natural"
> enemies, that solidarity will never exist between
> us because we cannot, should not, and do not
> bond with one another. We have learned these
> lessons well. We must unlearn them if we are to
> build a sustained feminist movement. We must
> learn to live and work in solidarity. We must
> learn the true value and meaning of Sisterhood.
>
> bell hooks, "Sisterhood: political solidarity
> between women"

> Documentation is a feminist project; a life
> project.
>
> Sara Ahmed, *Living a feminist life*

If there is one person who ties together each of the authors studied
in this book, as well as many of the most elite French authors and
philosophers of the early eighteenth century, that person is Françoise
de Graffigny.[1] Thanks to Graffigny's abundant correspondence (which
comprises sixteen volumes), we have records of meetings, exchanges,
dinners, and letters between the country's most prominent authors. For
instance, Graffigny had a brief but intense friendship with Crébillon
fils, whom she referred to alternately as "le Génie Jonquille," "le
Grand Drôle," and, most often, "le Petit."[2] The letters passed between

---

1. Portions of this chapter have previously been printed in *French forum*. See Tracy
    Rutler, "Liberté, égalité, sororité: the regime of the sister in Graffigny's *Lettres
    d'une Péruvienne*," *French forum* 39:2–3 (2014), p.1–15.
2. "Le Génie Jonquille" refers to Crébillon's oriental tale *L'Ecumoire*, in which
    the sovereign of the Ile Jonquille (or Ile des plaisirs) is a cynical libertine who

the two authors highlight a mood that is easily felt in the novels of both; there is an ease and a capacity to play with language in their back-and-forth banter that demonstrate the importance both authors place on exploring the link between language, bodies, and a certain desire to have a good time. However, one of Graffigny's strongest critiques of Crébillon (a critique that eventually led to the end of their friendship) was that the latter focused too intensely on worldly pleasures (often at the expense of his writing), so much so that he became lazy. In fact, in letters to her longtime friend François-Antoine Devaux written toward the end of her friendship with Crébillon, she becomes ever more annoyed with the author's laziness. In a letter to Devaux written early in the morning of March 2, 1745, she writes that "le Petit" told her at one of their weekly gatherings that he was finally going to get back to work. "I maintained that he wouldn't," she replies, "and I think I'll win since he is such a lazy man who lets everyone eat up his time."[3] Although she discusses Crébillon's work in later letters, this is the last time she writes about their encounters. For Graffigny, fun between friends was a stimulating experience, but one that ultimately should lead to the development and production of literature for the enjoyment of the public.[4]

Nowhere in her *œuvre* is this devotion to writing and experimenting with writing depicted more clearly than in her extremely successful novel, *Lettres d'une Péruvienne* (*Letters from a Peruvian woman*). In the novel, a Peruvian princess is kidnapped by Spaniards on the day she is to marry her betrothed, Aza. In his absence, she finds solace, and eventually takes pleasure, in the only activity that can tie her

---

    has incredible powers of persuasion which he uses to convince his victims to succumb to him. Among this group of authors, it was common to refer to each other by the names of the characters in their works and, in this case, Graffigny seems to use the nickname to paint a less than flattering portrait of her friend.

3.   Graffigny to Devaux, in *Correspondance*, vol.6, p.227. "Je lui soutins que non et je crois que je gagnerai, car c'est un vray paresseux et qui se laisse manger son tems par tout le monde."

4.   In fact, Graffigny often complains about the laziness of her intellectual companions at the Société du bout du banc, a salon hosted by Jeanne Quinault and attended by the most prominent authors of the day. In one letter written in September 1744, Graffigny also complains at length about Marivaux's laziness. Within this company, laziness, as a way of life and a practice of writing, was embraced by some and disdained by others. For a detailed assessment of the link between laziness and literary production, see Jacqueline Hellegouarc'h, "Ces messieurs du Bout-du-banc: *L'Eloge de la paresse et du paresseux* est-il de Marivaux?," *Revue d'histoire littéraire de la France* 102 (2002/2003), p.455–59.

to him—writing. This novel has been called by some a sentimental novel, by others an exotic tale, by still others a novel of education, and it is all of those things. It is also a novel that focuses perhaps more than any other on the process of learning about the world through writing. Robin Howells has argued that *Lettres d'une Péruvienne* is, at least in part, a work of autobiography, and he focuses largely on the treatment of marriage and relationships between women and men.[5] However, I believe that an even more telling autobiographical trait in this novel is the author's treatment of the process of writing. Much like her protagonist, Zilia, Graffigny also insists on writing each and every day. And, in addition to the copious amounts of letters the author wrote to friends, family, and lovers in which she documented her life in great detail, she also continued to work on the *Lettres* long past its first publication date. The first edition, published in 1747, was a resounding success, with people passing around counterfeited copies within the first weeks of its publication. Readers loved the novel, although they desired a happier ending in which Zilia would be married either to her Peruvian prince or to her French doctor. Five years later, in 1752, Graffigny published a second edition. If readers were hoping to finally have the romantic ending they desired, they were sadly let down. Not only does the Zilia of the second version still refuse to marry, but she also amplifies the tone of her aversion to the patriarchal institution of marriage, harshly critiquing the French system of education for girls and expressing outrage over the hypocritical treatment of women in France. In other words, the pleasure of learning through writing that Zilia expresses throughout the novel reinforces her displeasure with French customs that systematically disenfranchise women.

The changes that appear in the 1752 edition did not emerge from a void of five years. In addition to revising the manuscript, between 1747 and 1752 the author wrote three plays: *Ziman et Zénise* (*Ziman and Zénise*) (1747), *Phaza* (1747), and *Cénie* (1750), each of which offers us a glimpse into Graffigny's revisionary process. Although *Cénie* was among the most successful plays of its time, after its last public performance it was largely forgotten.[6] *Ziman et Zénise* and *Phaza*, however, were only ever

---

5. Robin Howells, "Mme de Graffigny's story," *The Modern language review* 99:1 (2004), p.36–44.
6. There are many theories about the play's disappearance from the canon, including unfounded speculations that Graffigny plagiarized the story from Pierre-Claude Nivelle de La Chaussée's *La Gouvernante* (even though La Chaussée denies the accusation of plagiarism against Graffigny while admitting

performed privately (the former in 1748 for the Viennese emperor's children and the latter in 1753 on the private stage of the comte de Clermont in Berny), and were published posthumously in 1770, twelve years after Graffigny's death. As a result, these three plays remain largely understudied today, in spite of their whimsical stories and surprisingly forward-thinking ideas, which include lessons in gender queerness, critiques of girls' education, and exemplary instances of female autonomy. Reading these plays as the interlude between editions of the *Lettres*, we can actually trace the author's process of writing. Although the plays feature different characters and even fantastical scenarios (in the case of *Ziman* and *Phaza*), they each, along with *Lettres d'une Péruvienne*, work through the same problematic: What does it mean to be a woman in a society that depends so heavily upon the exchange of women? And furthermore, what can women do to resist? Rather than providing an answer to these questions, Graffigny offers several possibilities and in the process demonstrates the richness and diversity that women may experience once freed from the shackles of masculine domination.

Like so many women writers, Graffigny has often been accused over the centuries of plagiarizing the work of men. In addition to being dismissive and condescending, such claims deny the depths to which the author plumbs human nature, orienting her works, as she does, around intimacy in its many forms. Indeed, close analysis of her literature reveals a rethinking of society more radical than many have given her credit for up until now. As with many of the utopian experiments studied in previous chapters, we see that restructuring the family is often at odds with maintaining social norms. Graffigny understood firsthand this dilemma (given her often unusual living situations), and this is perhaps why she is not content to think only about how we might change the structures of kinship.[7] Her fiction goes

---

a similarity between their works). For a thorough discussion of the play's elusive history see Diane Dufrin Kelley, "The morality of plagiarism: Voltaire, Diderot, and the legacy of Graffigny's *Cénie,*" *New perspectives on the eighteenth century* 7:1 (2010), p.48–62.

7.   Financial hardship, combined with Graffigny's refusal to remarry following her divorce, left her with a relatively nomadic lifestyle. Her brief stay with Voltaire and Emilie Du Châtelet at Cirey is well known (in part because of the trio's ultimate falling out), but she also lived in apartments and took odd jobs which required her to move and find creative ways to continue her affairs. The best biography of her life remains English Showalter's *Françoise de Graffigny: her life and works, SVEC* 2004:11. For an intriguing take on her sexuality and aging, see Joan

beyond a restructuring of the family to think about a restructuring of society as a whole. She does ponder how we might create families that provide a safer and more positive space for women, but beyond that she imagines how we might rebuild our economic and educational systems in ways that do not privilege men. In her fiction, we see that only a society organized around such concepts can be capable of supporting such a feminocentric family. By featuring brave and smart women, gender nonconforming characters, and strong relationships between women, Graffigny shows what it could mean to become a woman in a world *made for women*.

In this chapter we will examine not only what a world made for women might look like, but also the types of relationships that constitute this world. Graffigny uses several techniques to subtract her female protagonists from male-dominated spaces, including placing characters in a magical land or a foreign milieu, writing characters who question familial connections, or, much like Marivaux, orphaning a character early in the story. These devices allow the protagonists to create worlds that are drastically different from the domestic spaces they might otherwise have known. That the heroines encounter difficulty when their worlds collide with traditionally masculine ones is to be expected. However, Graffigny's characters do not simply revert to old ways. Instead, the strength of her female characters, which comes through a process of imagining, questioning, writing, and revising women's experiences, enables them to alter how they exist in the world, and how they relate to others. The new relations they form may be difficult to define and name, but they depend upon a sisterhood of strong, autonomous women.

Building a sisterhood of women is no easy task. As critics such as Foucault and Habermas have taught us, the transformation of the bourgeois family was carried out in the eighteenth century largely by means of cultural, religious, and medical practices, as well as by restructuring space itself. As I pointed out in the last chapter, architectural shifts made the family home into an ever more intimate—and isolated—sphere. Doctors augmented the mother's supervisory role with regard to the children, resulting in her being further detached from public society, as her presence was constantly required at home. Such structural and cultural changes led to new practices which ensured the reproduction of both motherhood and

Hinde Stewart, *The Enlightenment of age: women, letters, and growing old in 18th-century France, SVEC* 2010:09.

women's dependency upon men. Graffigny herself notes the dangers of practices of female exclusion in many of her texts, lamenting that women are locked up in convents until the moment they become locked up in the familial home with their husbands. While the convent in *La Vie de Marianne* provided a unique space for the development of the female subject, the revolutionary potential of such spaces is, in Graffigny's view, diminished; they serve only the function of strengthening patriarchal practices that disenfranchise women. Graffigny knew then what bell hooks would remind us of over 200 years later: In order to build a community of women united in solidarity, we must first do a bit of unlearning. In order to parse out Graffigny's process of building a better world for women, I will trace the author's revisionary process both across time and from one work to another, spotting the moments when she embraces what others saw as flaws in her stories. Rather than revising her narratives to suit the desires of others, the author uses the revisionary process to strengthen her own visions and to introduce alternative models of knowledge production.

Writing, revising, and rehearsing

Like most young, aristocratic women in eighteenth-century France, the woman born Françoise d'Issembourg Du Buisson d'Happoncourt was married at a young age to an older man chosen by her parents. This was a disastrous marriage; her husband abused her, spent all of her money, and eventually left her virtually penniless. She made several unsuccessful appeals to her father to extract her from this marriage. In fact, one of the earliest pieces of her writing that remains is a letter addressed to her father, desperately imploring him to save her from this brutish husband:

> My Dear Father,
> I am obliged, because of the dire circumstances I find myself in, to beg you not to abandon me and to send Mr. Rarecour to fetch me as soon as possible because I am in grave danger and am all broken from the blows. I throw myself in your graces and beg you to act quickly. I must say that it is people other than me who summon you because everyone knows about it. With respect, I am your humble and obedient servant,
> F. D'Haponcour de Grafigny

Mon cher pere,

Je suis obligés dans l'extremité ou je me trouvee de vous suplier de ne
me point abandoner et de m'envoier au plus vite chercher par Mr de
Rarecour car je suis en grand danger et suis toutes brisé de coups. Je
me jete a votre misericorde et vous prie que ce soit bien vite. Il faut
dire que c'est d'autre que moy qui vous l'on mandé, car tout le monde
le sait. Je suis avec bien du respect,

Vostre tres humble et tres obeisante servante,

F. D'Haponcour de Grafigny[8]

One cannot help but notice the impassioned tone of a scared young
woman who, like many women before and after her, cried out for
someone to hear her, believe her, and save her from a terrible situation.
Also striking, however, is the formality with which she addresses her
father, even when discussing something so delicate and personal as
spousal abuse. It is clear that writing to her father was a last resort.
She did not want to write to him, she was *obligated* to do so because
of the dire circumstances. Even at this relatively young age, Graffigny
believed in the power of written expression.

There was only one problem: Her father, evidently, did not. Try as
she might, Graffigny could not convince her father to help. Help would
have to come through other means. And so, the author continued to
write, keep records, and talk to those she thought might be able to assist
her. In the end, she was able to obtain a divorce after eleven years of
marriage and three children (all of whom died in early childhood), but
it would not be thanks to the help of her parents; it would be due to
the juridical demonstration of her husband's mental instability. On the
one hand, we might be tempted to see in this example a shortcoming
of the written word. Letters to her father were sent to no avail; even
though she sent the first letter to him in 1716, she was unable to obtain
a divorce until seven years later in 1723. On the other hand, we could
see this as the success of another kind of writing. When personal letters
failed to work, Graffigny turned to a different kind of writing—one
that kept track of the facts and documented a pattern of neglect and
abuse. What we ultimately learn from this story is that Graffigny was
not one to give up and resign herself to an undeserved fate. When one
method failed to work, she sought out others, continually writing and
revising her plans. Her divorce in 1723 demonstrates the power of
persistence, and her successful career as a writer that followed stands

8.   Graffigny, *Correspondance*, vol.1, p.1.

as a testament to the power of female resiliency. Adapting and making revisions were therefore as crucial to her legacy as were writing and relentlessly documenting her life and relationships with others. These are themes that recur again and again in her fiction.

Although *Lettres d'une Péruvienne* was internationally celebrated as one of the greatest novels of its time, it was not without its criticisms as well. For example, shortly after the publication of the first edition, Graffigny sent a letter to her friend the economist and then up-and-coming statesman Anne Robert Jacques Turgot, asking for his opinion of the novel. His response echoes what much of the public was saying, and he sums it up with three major suggestions: First, he proposes that the author make Zilia more French—"you seemed to make a main point of showing Zilia as French after having shown her to us as Peruvian."[9] Making this change would help to efface Zilia's otherness, allowing her, in his opinion, to stand in more easily as a symbol of feminine virtue for France. Next, he advises her to lessen the kinship bond between Zilia and Aza from brother and sister to distant relatives. This familial alteration would make the pair's love affair more palatable for a European audience. Finally, he urges her to conclude the novel with Zilia's marriage to Aza, proposing that a marriage between the two would augment the moral utility of the text, teaching readers not just about marriage, but more precisely about what he calls "good marriage," wherein individuals enter happily and willingly into the eternal union.[10]

Graffigny does indeed make some revisions to the novel in the second edition, but, instead of following Turgot's advice, the Zilia of the second version extols the virtues of friendship over marriage and continues to spend her days translating her letters in a home of her own, living on the margins of both French and Peruvian society. Rather than crossing an imaginary dichotomous line separating Peruvian from French, Incan traditions from European customs,

9. Portions of Turgot's letters to Graffigny can be found in *Œuvres de Turgot et documents le concernant*, ed. F. Alcon (Paris, 1913–1923), p.43. "[V]ous m'avez paru goûter la principale qui est de montrer *Zélia* [*sic*] française après nous l'avoir fait voir péruvienne."

10. For a more detailed study of the relationship between Graffigny and Turgot see Gilbert Mercier, *Madame Péruvienne: Françoise de Graffigny, une femme sensible au siècle des Lumières* (Paris, 2008); and Showalter, *Françoise de Graffigny: her life and works*. For a detailed account of the reader reception of the work see David Smith, "The popularity of Mme de Graffigny's *Lettres d'une Péruvienne*: the bibliographical evidence," *Eighteenth-century fiction* 3:1 (1990), p.1–20.

woman from wife and mother, Zilia doggedly toes that line as she remains firmly between worlds, between languages, and between cultures.

Undoubtedly, one of the most unique aspects of *Lettres d'une Péruvienne* is the protagonist's use of the Peruvian *quipos* to construct the first seventeen letters.[11] As the author writes in the historical introduction (added for the second edition), "Their *quapas*, or *quipus*, replaced for them the art of writing"; in other words, she understands the *quipos* as akin to written language although she distinguishes it from the French art of writing by likening it to a ritualistic practice of the guardians of the word (*Quipocamaios*) in the sentences that follow.[12] In Peru, *quipos* were, above all, a language of trade, a way of keeping track of business. In Graffigny's hands, however, the *quipos* come alive. They are no longer the expression of a rudimentary language of exchange; they become a method of exchanging the most complex and intricate thoughts and emotions one can express. In fact, they are even capable of communicating asides or parentheticals, thoughts that might better be left out. In the first letter, for example, Zilia writes:

> From that terrible moment (*which should have been torn from the chain of time and resubmerged in the eternal store of ideas*), that moment of horror when those impious savages stole me away from the worship of the Sun, from myself, and from your love, I have experienced nothing save the effects of unhappiness without being able to discover their cause, held as I am in strict captivity, denied all communication with our citizens, and not knowing the language of these ferocious men whose bonds I bear.

> Depuis le moment terrible (*qui aurait dû être arraché de la chaîne du temps, et replongé dans les idées éternelles*) depuis le moment d'horreur où ces sauvages impies m'ont enlevée au culte du Soleil, à moi-même, à ton amour; retenue dans une étroite captivité, privée de toute communication avec nos citoyens, ignorant la langue de ces hommes féroces

11. *Quipos*, or more commonly spelled *quipu*, is an Incan method of tying knots from various colored threads used to keep records and communicate information.
12. Françoise de Graffigny, *Letters of a Peruvian woman*, translated by David Kornacker (New York, 1993), p.13; *Lettres d'une Péruvienne*, ed. Joan DeJean and Nancy K. Miller (New York, 1993), p.13. "Les *quipos* leur tenaient lieu de notre art d'écrire."

dont je porte les fers, je n'éprouve que les effets du malheur, sans
pouvoir en découvrir la cause.[13]

The impious savages to whom Zilia refers are her Spanish captors, and
the citizens are her fellow Incans. Throwing the reader into the story
in media res, the narrator gives the impression of frenzy, confusion, and
panic, precisely the feelings of a woman being kidnapped and dragged
by unknown captors to an unknown location. Such feelings are
reinforced by the language of the narrator who laments the "terrible
moment," the "ferocious men," and the "effects of unhappiness." The
use of the present tense in the first-person singular "I have experienced"
(*je n'éprouve*), combined with the effusive display of adjectives, enhances
the impression that the reader is receiving a firsthand account of a
specific moment as yet unmediated by time.[14] Yet the words in between
the parentheses betray the instantaneity of the rest of the letter. The
use of the past conditional in the parenthetical clause, coupled with
its visual segregation from the rest of the sentence, indicates that the
notion of ripping apart time (communicated within the parentheses) is
grafted onto the event of the main clause at some point after the initial
event, thus representing another temporal matrix—the distanced
perspective of the letter's author. The moment of crisis has passed and
should, in the narrator's opinion, not simply be erased, but ripped
completely from the fabric of time, leaving the frayed edges of the
moment to be patched together through the work of narration and
translation.

It is Zilia's task, we soon learn, to weave this story together
into a coherent narrative consisting of several disparate pieces. In
describing and transcribing this moment of rupture, the narrator
draws a distinction between what Mikhail Bakhtin has called epic
time (of events which have already happened or will inevitably
happen) and historical time (which can be altered and manipulated).[15]
Thomas Kavanagh describes the notion of an alterable historical

13. Graffigny, *Letters*, p.17–18; *Lettres*, p.17–18 (emphasis added).
14. While technically a present tense, the use of the present perfect ("I have
    experienced") in English does not convey the same urgency of the original
    French, which, for my purposes, might be more accurately translated into the
    present continuous, "I am experiencing."
15. In drawing on these terms from Bakhtin, I also intend to stress that Zilia's
    understanding of time is simultaneously individual and collective in nature.
    Although the *quipos*, as described in the introduction, serve as an archive of
    Peruvian history and knowledge, the task of the narrator is to disentangle the

time in *Lettres d'une Péruvienne* as an "aesthetics of the moment," where unpredictable events produce ruptures in the fabric of time.[16] Zilia's deep understanding of diverse temporalities and her ability to manipulate the French language so adeptly show us that the author of these love letters is not simply a sensitive woman, painfully and dutifully writing to a geographically distant lover, nor a *primitive*, naively describing a culture of which she is not a part, but that she is also a philosopher and historian, whose collection of letters serves as much as collective annals of Incan and French history and culture as it does an individual story about a desire for love. Knowing that the epic past cannot be changed, she suggests that the narrative of the past is at least capable of being manipulated. First, through the act of untying and retying the knots of the *quipos*, and second, by translating her story from Peruvian to French, Zilia alters the narrative of her own past. In this way her story—the woman's story—and particularly the sister's story that is undervalued under both patriarchy and the regime of the brother (as we saw in chapter 2) can be written into a masculine history.

Although rewriting masculine history in this particular fashion ultimately falls to the capable hands of Zilia, Graffigny offered help to her Peruvian princess in the form of several other strong female characters. Discussions of gender, education, love, friendship, and marriage among the characters of the three plays written and/ or performed between the first and second editions of *Lettres d'une Péruvienne* demonstrate just how Graffigny experiments with different ways of addressing how women can alter both histories and episte-mologies. While readers may be familiar with her successful play *Cénie*, few will likely have seen or read *Ziman et Zénise* or *Phaza*.[17] To facilitate

---

individual's story in order to construct a new temporal matrix. M. Bakhtin discusses these notions in *The Dialogic imagination: four essays* (Austin, TX, 1982).

16. See Thomas M. Kavanagh's "Reading the moment and the moment of reading in Graffigny's *Lettres d'une Péruvienne*," *Modern language quarterly* 55:2 (1994), p.125–47. While Kavanagh's notion of "the moment" in the *Lettres* is helpful in understanding Graffigny's ability to rewrite historical time, it too easily denies the possibility of female agency in the novel. Because such a notion is experience-driven, it tends to fall into the type of reading that Nancy K. Miller criticizes when she writes of the constricting female plot (the female protagonist is led from place to place—or event to event—by a male guide) in many novels that deal with female writing. See N. K. Miller's *Subject to change: reading feminist writing* (New York, 1988).

17. Although English Showalter unearthed these two posthumously published plays in the 1960s and briefly discusses *Phaza* in his later works, very few scholars

our discussion of the relationship between *Lettres d'une Péruvienne* and these three plays, I will provide brief summaries of each.

Ziman et Zénise

Written in 1747 and performed for the children of the imperial court of Vienna in 1749, this play features the two titular characters alongside another young boy and girl, Mirflot and Philette. Although the play's bill (published posthumously in 1775) lists Ziman and Zénise as a young prince and princess while listing the other two as peasants (*païsan*), the plot is based on the premise that neither pair knows which is which. The children have each been taken from their parents at a very young age by a good fairy who raises them together and provides them with the same education (although this education is gendered—the boys are taught separately from the girls). As they grow, the children endure a series of trials in order to demonstrate their virtues. Only once they reach the age of fourteen does the fairy reveal the true nature of her pupils' social rank when Mirflot's father arrives from the farm to reclaim his son. Demonstrating benevolence fit for a prince, Ziman offers to keep Mirflot by his side as a marquis, allowing him to take Philette for his wife and bring his father to the court with him as well.

In the last scene of the play, each of the characters (with the exception of the fairy) is surprised to discover their rank. The spectator, however, most certainly is not. The emphasis on Mirflot's physical strength versus Ziman's sensitivity, coupled with Philette's desire for power versus Zénise's tender concern for others, draws on long-held stereotypes of nobility and baseness. Furthermore, Ziman and Zénise express such concern about each other to the fairy that it is clear early within the play that these two share a natural attraction to one another and therefore will ultimately be paired. Conversely,

---

have since considered them. To my knowledge, only four other scholarly works discussing these plays exist: Heidi Bostic's "The difference she makes: staging gender identity in Graffigny's *Phaza*," *Tulsa studies in women's literature* (2010), p.291–309; Charlotte Simonin's "Phaza, la 'fille-garçon' de Mme de Graffigny," in *Le Mâle en France, 1715–1830: représentations de la masculinité*, ed. Katherine Astbury and Marie-Emmanuelle Plagnol-Diéval (New York, 2004), p.51–62; Mariangela Miotti's "Il mito dell' 'enfant de nature' e il teatro di Mme de Graffigny," *Studi di letteratura francese* 16 (1990), p.126–37; and, most recently, Theresa Varney Kennedy's *Women's deliberation: the heroine in early modern French women's theater (1650–1750)* (New York, 2018).

Mirflot and Philette appear to desire whichever partner will afford them the power of nobility. In the end, it would not have mattered much if the viewer had known the children's rank in advance—this play may be fun and informative, but it is not subtle.

In lieu of surprise, this play offers its viewers an instructional tale of human kindness and decency. Even though Ziman and Zénise take up the positions of prince and princess, they implore the fairy to provide a proper station to the two who have become their brother and sister. They insist that the education that Mirflot and Philette have received would make it impossible for them to return to life on a farm. Education has a truly transformative quality. It can change peasants into nobility, and it can even render great leaders compassionate. One of the biggest lessons this play teaches is that, in order to change the world, one must first provide children with a proper education. However, the fairy of this play adheres to practices which separate boys and girls, offering different kinds of education to each. In her next play, *Phaza*, Graffigny will try a different approach.

Phaza[18]

Rather than being unaware of social status, this play centers on an ignorance of gender. Phaza (to whom Graffigny often refers in letters as her "fille en garçon," or girl-boy) is kidnapped from her parents as a baby and taken to a magical land where she is raised by a fairy, La Singulière, as a boy. Until the last scene of the play, Phaza believes himself to be, and presents as, a boy. It is only with the arrival of another fairy, Clémentine, along with her son and niece, that his beliefs begin to be shaken. Clémentine's son Azor, we come to find, has been to the magical land before and has fallen in love with Phaza, sensing immediately the latter's "true" identity. Unfortunately, he learns that he cannot share this information with Phaza without causing the latter's death. Only when Phaza kneels before a true love will the

18. According to Graffigny's letters, she wrote *Phaza* in 1747. However, the play was not performed until 1753 and published only posthumously in 1775 along with *Ziman et Zénise*. Since we have no documentation of the scripts for either in their earliest forms, these two plays present an interesting case for the argument of revision. Because the versions we have are definitive, we can only speculate as to the originals, especially given the author's proclivity toward revising. These plays then stand out as a particularly fertile test-ground for revising the themes she addresses in *Lettres d'une Péruvienne* since she only shared pieces of the play with intimate friends.

spell be broken. Phaza reciprocates Azor's love but not understanding romantic love he recognizes it as friendship. Because of their devotion to one another they both vow never to marry a woman, a plan which becomes more difficult when Zamie, Clémentine's niece, is promised first to Phaza and then to Azor. Through an elaborate series of ruses involving a masquerade ball and a scene of transvestism in which Phaza dresses up as a girl, Graffigny's *fille-garçon* finally kneels before his love (Azor), offering up his name and land and thus breaking the spell. Phaza now learns of her sex, assumes a female identity, and becomes engaged to Azor in a scene of heteronormative bliss.

Although much of the plot revolves around the love (or more accurately betrothal) triangle that forms between Phaza, Azor, and Zamie, the play ultimately offers an important meditation on the legitimacy of gender essentialism and the fate of women in patriarchal societies. The longest scenes are those in which characters discuss candidly the disastrous effects that marriage has on women, the disadvantage we put women at by teaching them to be modest and timid, and even the problems with raising men to be strong and independent. In short, the most important conversations that take place in this play focus on problems that have now become discourses with important cultural and political implications: gender equality, domestic abuse, and toxic masculinity. One of the devices that allowed Graffigny to conduct such radical experiments was the use of the fairy play genre: Because she placed her characters in a magical land, the rules normally governing polite society did not necessarily have to apply. In the last play she wrote before publishing the second edition of the *Lettres*, the author brings these discussions back down to earth.

Cénie

There are no fairies in this play—just a girl, her governess, and a handful of men who make up her family. In many ways, this play follows the structure of Marivaux's plays; there are various scenes of misrecognition, familial origins are called into question, and, although Cénie has found a supreme confidant in her governess, Orphise, she is ultimately betrayed by another servant. When the play opens, Mélisse, Cénie's mother, has died, but not before confiding a terrible secret to her nephew, Méricourt: She is not Cénie's mother and nor is Dorimond her father. Seeing in this confession an opportunity to receive his uncle's inheritance (which would otherwise go to Cénie), Méricourt tries to force his cousin to marry him, threatening to reveal

the secret if she refuses. The virtuous young woman, who happens to
be in love with Méricourt's brother Clerval, is devastated but refuses
to marry him, and instead tells Dorimond the truth. At that time,
Méricourt produces a second letter from Mélisse, which indicates that
the child's mother, who believed her daughter to be dead, is none
other than Cénie's governess, Orphise. In an abrupt reversal of the
family romance, Cénie learns that the confidant who had long been
dear to her is actually her mother. The two women plan to move to a
convent when Clerval's friend, who has just returned from the Indies
(*les Indes*), reveals himself to be Orphise's long-lost husband and Cénie's
father, Dorsainville. Familial order is restored, and the two families
are fused together when Dorsainville gives his permission for Clerval
to marry Cénie.

This play both most closely mirrors and most sharply diverges
from *Lettres d'une Péruvienne*. Set once again in the domestic sphere of
a bourgeois household, it repeats the story of love, loss, betrayal, and
reunion. In this play, however, the betrayal is at the hands of a foe
rather than a lover. In contrast to Déterville, Méricourt is harsh to
Cénie and tries to force her hand in marriage. Instead of declaring his
love for her, he declares his love for her inheritance. And Dorsainville
(Cénie's long-lost father), is, as Robin Howells points out, essentially
"Aza rectified"; whereas Aza returns only to let Zilia know that he
is engaged to someone else, Dorsainville has remained faithful to
Orphise the entire fifteen years since he last saw her.[19] Thus, while
the other two plays performed experiments in genres and themes, this
play experiments with different outcomes for what is more or less the
same story.

These three plays, although drastically different from one another,
each return to questions of equality between individuals of different
genders, races, and social stations. In reading them one after the
other, we can see how the plays help the author to revise the *Lettres*
in preparation for the second edition. To illustrate this revisionary
process, I will now turn to discussions of the unfair treatment of
women, demonstrating how its depiction evolves across the works.

In both editions of the *Lettres*, Zilia spends a lot of time explaining
to Aza the mistreatment of women in France. She blames the abuses
largely on the disjunction between an education that teaches women
to focus on their outward appearance (or what she refers to as a "false"
appearance) and then punishes them for being vain and frivolous.

19. Howells, "Mme de Graffigny's story."

In fact, although Zilia's harsh words might paint her as disdainful of most French women, they in fact betray a certain sympathy for them and a sadness for their condition. In the 1747 version, she often focuses on the victimization of these women, writing in letter 31 for instance: "insolence and effrontery are the first sentiments that we teach men; timidity, gentleness, and patience are the sole virtues we cultivate in women. How could they [women] not become victims of [masculine] impunity?"[20] In the letters immediately preceding this one, Zilia had lamented the bad behavior of men. At Céline's wedding, she complains of bold men interrupting her thoughts and even claims that Déterville is not exempt from such behavior. This is the first letter in which we see such clarity on the issue from the heroine. She has finally realized that it is not only the way boys are raised that causes them to behave so terribly, it is also because girls are raised to allow it. In this letter, therefore, we see the first seeds of a larger discussion on girls' education that will appear more fully in the second edition.

In *Ziman et Zénise*, education takes on a central role, and stereotypes of masculinity and nobility are called into question. As early as the first scene, we encounter long-held beliefs about what it means to be a man. In one test to prove their worth, both boys, Ziman and Mirflot, must fight a lion. Although both succeed in vanquishing the beast, Mirflot does so with much more gusto. When Zénise points out this fact to the fairy, the latter's response opens up a much larger discussion on masculinity and nobility. "And because he [Mirflot] is strong, I presume you have concluded that he is of a lower status?" she asks.[21] Zénise is flustered, and instead responds by focusing on the noble qualities she sees in Ziman: courage, gentleness, kindness, and a good heart. The scenes that follow continue to simultaneously reinforce and question such norms. Although the actions of Ziman and Zénise are clearly meant to indicate their moral superiority—and therefore their nobility—whereas the actions of Philette and Mirflot demonstrate their baseness, in the end, the equal education they all

20. Françoise de Graffigny, *Lettres d'une Péruvienne* (Paris, A Peine, 1747), p.280–81. "L'impudence & l'effronterie sont les premiers sentimens que l'on inspire aux hommes, la timidité, la douceur & la patience sont les seules vertus que l'on cultive dans les femmes: comment ne seroient-elles pas les victimes de l'impunité?"

21. Françoise de Graffigny, *Ziman et Zénise*, in *Œuvres posthumes de Madame de Graffigny* (Amsterdam [Paris?], n.n., 1775), p.1–44 (2). "Et parce qu'il [Mirflot] a de la force, je gage que vous en concluez qu'il est de basse naissance?"

receive renders such stark hierarchical divisions irrelevant. Education, in this play, has functioned to re-evaluate the structures that divide societies.

Phaza's focus on education is narrower. In this play, education is also transformative, but here it attempts to correct for an education that teaches women to be victims. If girls are taught to be submissive, it asks, why not reverse this by changing their gender and providing them with an education normally reserved for boys, one that teaches them to be assertive and bold? While this might seem to simply reproduce masculine domination by creating more brutish men, there is one key difference: The fairy's boys, or at least Phaza, are keenly aware of the power they hold in relationships with women. Graffigny's *fille-garçon* introduces us to gender queerness as a way of thinking about how access to knowledge is gendered. When Zamie tells Phaza that they share an interest in thwarting the marriage that neither of them desires, the latter responds by telling her, in earnest, that they do not.[22] He reprises the vocabulary of victimization to explain the unequal balance of power in relationships to Zamie:

> A man marries, he takes a wife, or he doesn't, it's basically the same thing. Held less accountable by the bonds of marriage than simply by his word, he remains free, independent, and the master of his desires. But you, *victims* of our desires, when you take a husband you give up all rights to your liberty, your person, and even your heart.

> Qu'un homme se marie, qu'il ait une femme, ou qu'il n'en ait pas, c'est à peu près la même chose. Moins engagé par les liens de l'himen que par une simple parole d'honneur, il reste libre, indépendant, maître absolu de ses volontés. Mais vous, *victimes* de nos prérogatives, en prenant un époux, vous renoncez à vos droits sur votre liberté, sur votre personne, & même sur votre cœur.[23]

22. The reasons for Zamie's dislike of Phaza are also indebted to a common trope of eighteenth-century fiction—the pair who know instinctually that they should not be together. This often occurs between siblings who are unaware of their kinship (as in Diderot's *Le Fils naturel*), or between people of different social stations (as in Marivaux's *Les Jeux de l'amour et du hasard*). In this case, we can assume that Graffigny is also hinting at Zamie's aversion to Phaza because he is a woman and the former knows, at least subconsciously, that the two cannot be paired.

23. Françoise de Graffigny, *Phaza*, in *Œuvres posthumes*, p.45–107 (72) (emphasis added).

In this scene we see first what happens when men become aware of their privilege, and second, what happens when they share that knowledge with others. At first Zamie is shocked—"I don't believe any of that," she tells Phaza. Although Phaza points out that all men feel this way about marriage, Zamie refuses to believe him based on what she understands as fundamental differences between Phaza and Azor, the only two men we encounter in the play. As the scenes continue, Zamie begins to notice similarities between the two and, little by little, she begins to believe that what Phaza says might be true. In discussions with Phaza and Azor, she frequently points out the ways she is being mistreated, citing the "unkind things" that have been said to her along with the harsh conduct she receives from others.[24] *Phaza* creates a space for enacting gender equality by demonstrating the unbreakable link between women's education and their treatment in society.

By the time Graffigny publishes the second edition of *Lettres d'une Péruvienne* in 1752, she has had several years to reflect on just how she wants to address this victimization in a more direct manner. She makes some revisions throughout, and adds two new letters. In the second of these letters she explains more thoroughly the mistreatment of women. She critiques the practice of marrying young girls to inappropriate men, and blames men for all the ills of society. Most importantly though, she shifts the conversation away from victimization and toward a possible response:

> how could these women not be revolted by the injustice of laws that tolerate men's impunity, which is pushed to the same extreme as their authority? [...] In the end, dearest Aza, it seems that in France the bonds of marriage are reciprocal only at the moment the wedding is celebrated, and that thereafter only wives must be subject to them.

> comment ne seraient-elles [les femmes] pas révoltées contre l'injustice des lois qui tolèrent l'impunité des hommes, poussée au même excès que leur autorité? [...] Enfin, mon cher Aza, il semble qu'en France les liens du mariage ne soient réciproques qu'au moment de la célébration, et que dans la suite les femmes seules y doivent être assujetties.[25]

In this passage we can almost imagine the voice of Zamie all grown up and outraged by what she had been forced to believe and accept for so

---

24. Graffigny, *Phaza*, p.73 and 88. "Je ne crois rien de tout cela"; "choses désobligeantes."
25. Graffigny, *Letters*, p.148–49; *Lettres*, p.143–44.

long. Zilia calls for women to stop accepting their position as victim—
she tells them that this is not normal. What she calls for finally, with
the help of her sisters, is a revolution. These women are revolted and
revolting. In her fiction, Graffigny offers possible solutions to some of
the problems women face, thinking about how we might rebuild our
economic and educational systems in ways that no longer privilege
men. However, revolting against centuries of masculine oppression
will mean first doing a bit of unlearning. Unlearning means extracting
oneself from masculine epistemologies and refusing to accept the
supposed "natural" order of things. Only then, she proposes, can we
create something entirely new.

In defense of ignorance

The 1747 edition of *Lettres d'une Péruvienne* begins with the following
exclamation of fear, sadness, and shock from Zilia:

> Aza! my dear Aza! Like a morning mist, the cries of your tender Zilia
> rise up and dissipate before reaching you. In vain do I call to you for
> help, in vain do I wait for your love to come and break the bonds
> of my enslavement. But alas, perhaps those misfortunes of which I
> remain unaware are the most dreadful! Perhaps your woes surpass
> mine!

> Aza! mon cher Aza! les cris de ta tendre Zilia, tels qu'une vapeur du
> matin, s'exhalent & sont dissipés avant d'arriver jusqu'à toi; en vain
> je t'appelle à mon secours; en vain j'attens que ton amour vienne
> briser les chaînes de mon esclavage: hélas! peut-être les malheurs que
> j'ignore sont-ils les plus affreux! peut-être tes maux surpassent-ils les
> miens![26]

From the earliest pages, Zilia begins to realize there is much she does
not know. She does not know, for example, where she is or who has
taken her, she does not know the language of her captors, she does
not know where Aza is, and she has absolutely no idea what is in store
for either of them. At this point, the reader, just like Zilia, is also in
the dark. Readers may believe this to be the beginning of a damsel-
in-distress story (which in many ways it is), but they do not know of
her background. They do not know that this is a princess, and an

---

26. Graffigny, *Lettres* (1747), p.1–2.

educated one. The beginning of the story places both the protagonist and the reader in a place of shared ignorance.

Like many of the early letters of the novel, this one remains relatively untouched in the 1752 edition. Thus, from the first paragraph, the reader of the second edition might expect to read the same book they had read five years earlier. In fact, up until letter 28, the changes are very minor. A different word choice here, a spelling change there, but nothing that would alert the reader to anything drastically different. Even the major changes, which come largely with the addition of two letters (29 and 34), could be argued to change very little the overall narrative of the book. So why add them at all? Why spend so much time revising, rewriting, adding, and cutting, only to reproduce the very same narrative?

There are many possible answers to these questions. First, as any writer knows, a work written is never truly a work finished. Submission of a manuscript will never satisfy that deeply felt itch that there are still parts that could have been done differently—better even. This is certainly true in the case of Graffigny (it is a fact we can ascertain from her letters), but it does not provide us with a complete answer. Beyond wishing to improve the writing, *this* story in particular is one the author cannot let go of. The story of a woman out of place, a woman in love, a woman scorned, a woman determined, and a woman who remains single even when pressured to marry is one that Graffigny knows well and tells in each of her works in one way or another. It is not the story of ignorance per se, but it is a story which requires an act of willful ignorance. In other words, in order to think about a different way of existing in a world in which one feels out of place, it is first necessary to forget the proper or traditional ways of inhabiting that world and proceed accordingly. Ironic as it may seem given the author's attention to education for girls in each of her works, ignorance provides one very crucial path to empowering women.

It should come as no surprise that philosophers since Antiquity have been fascinated with ignorance and its role in the production of knowledge, self, systems, even communities. The entirety of the Socratic method is based on a presupposition of ignorance. The philosophical embracing of ignorance might be said to experience a shift in Europe during the period of the Enlightenment, particularly with the utterance of two words: *Sapere aude!* (Dare to know!). Ignorance was beginning to seem juvenile in an era in which we had the means to know things in ways we never had before. Science and technology were evolving at such a rapid pace that ignorance meant one of two things: Either one was choosing to remain ignorant in a willful act of defiance, or one did not have the means (materially, emotionally, intellectually) to learn. Necessarily and involuntarily stuck in this second category, according to Kant at least, were women and children.

Although Kant's "What is Enlightenment?" would not be published until well after Graffigny's death, it is fair to say that the intellectual climate had been shifting toward an embrace of amassing knowledge since at least the publication of Descartes's *Meditations on first philosophy*. Descartes's assertion that the purest knowledge comes from the absence of doubt suggests that ignorance is a state that one is meant to shed (and forget)—and the sooner the better. In a climate in which knowledge is prized above all, and women are actively excluded from the realm of knowledge production, what is a female writer-philosopher to do?[27] In the case of Graffigny, she made a move that will feel familiar to many modern-day feminists and activists—she reclaimed ignorance, making it a central theme in much of her *œuvre*. By shedding light on women's ignorance, she raised awareness of the inadequacies of female education, forcing readers to reckon with the situatedness (materially, geographically, culturally) of knowledge.

Let me be clear, ignorance does not equate to stupidity or a lack of knowledge. Ignorance can also be a refusal to accept the status quo, and can even forge a new path to different forms of knowledge. In a provocative essay on female sexual pleasure, Nancy Tuana proposes that, in order for any epistemology to be complete, it must include a study of ignorance, as well as knowledge. "Ignorance," she writes, "far from being a simple, innocent lack of knowledge—is a complex phenomenon that like knowledge, is interrelated with power."[28] The power of ignorance lies in rebuffing the dominant episteme, thus destabilizing truths believed to be self-evident. In fact, Eve Kosofsky Sedgwick describes the Enlightenment will to knowledge as a "violence of epistemological enforcement."[29] Focusing

27. It is important to point out that, while some philosophers and politicians were proposing that women were incapable of producing knowledge and therefore must be excluded from politics, studies have shown various ways women were actively shaping the intellectual and political spheres. See, for example, Goodman, *The Republic of Letters*; Carla Hesse, *The Other Enlightenment: how French women became modern* (Princeton, NJ, 2001); and Roberts, *Sentimental savants*.

28. Nancy Tuana, "Coming to understand: orgasm and the epistemology of ignorance," *Hypatia* 19:1 (2004), p.194–232 (226).

29. Eve Kosofsky Sedgwick, "Privilege of unknowing," *Genders* 1 (1988), p.102–24 (120).

on another fictional convent of eighteenth-century literature (that of Diderot's *La Religieuse*), Sedgwick demonstrates how ignorance, especially when it concerns sexuality, can serve not only as an excuse for perpetrating sexual violence (we can think of the many abusers who claim ignorance of a victim's unwillingness to participate in sexual acts), but also as a means to empower victims. She describes, for instance, how Suzanne's insistence on ignorance of sexual knowledge allows her to participate in a lesbian relationship without feeling the shame or guilt of that encounter. While Sedgwick's assessment of ignorance in the novel ultimately paints a relatively negative picture of its role in economic and patriarchal systems, her insistence on "deglobalizing and pluralizing" the idea of ignorance allows us to see how ignorance might be thought of as more than the reification of a rejection of knowledge.[30]

A refusal to accept the status quo of knowledge or even to propose an alternative can be a very powerful move. Take, for instance, the case of Philette in *Ziman et Zénise*. Although all four children know that one boy and one girl will be revealed as the true prince and princess once they turn fourteen, for most of the play they all remain oblivious to their true social status. In this literary experiment ignorance plays an important role in the redistribution of power. If the children must simultaneously imagine themselves as noble *and* common, they must also alter how they treat their mates since they do not know if they will be leading or serving them in the coming years. Philette, who eventually learns that she is not a princess, understands the power of this lack of knowledge, and embraces the opportunity to declare herself the princess many times over throughout the play. Her only remaining line after the revelation of her common birth are full of the sadness that accompanies the newly acquired knowledge that she is just a peasant. In this instance, ignorance had allowed Philette to imagine a world in which she was more than simply a peasant. Ignorance, for her, was indeed bliss, but it was also power.

Conversely, ignorance is often a key component to the continued foothold of systems of oppression such as sexism and racism. One cannot fight the power without knowledge of its existence. Sara Ahmed points out a friction that occurs when one becomes aware of oppression, describing it as stopping in the middle of a large crowd that is moving in one direction.[31] When we become aware, we stop

---

30. Segwick, "Privilege of unknowing," p.116.
31. Sara Ahmed, *Living a feminist life* (Charleston, NC, 2017).

moving—interrupting the flow of traffic and causing problems for those who want to continue on their way. When we become aware, that is, we disrupt the natural (if superficially imposed) flow of power, and seize a little power of a different sort for ourselves.

To demonstrate how ignorance can become entangled in systems of power and oppression, let us return to the scene from *Phaza* in which Phaza describes marriage to Zamie. We will recall the frankness with which the protagonist describes the different ways men and women experience marriage, noting that women lose themselves completely within its bonds (symbolized by women taking the husband's name). Men, he points out, remain free to do as they wish. In this scene, ignorance functions very differently for Zamie and Phaza. For the former, ignorance of the condition of women in marriage has been something imposed upon her in order to keep the exchange of women running smoothly. She is so deeply entrenched in this system that she cannot even believe what she is hearing. Phaza uses this as an opportunity to point out that her ignorance is the natural outcome of the terrible education given to girls.

It is ironic that Phaza should cite his own education as a source of liberation, since his knowledge relies very heavily on an ignorance of a quite different nature. Although his ignorance is also imposed upon him (by the fairy who has raised him as a boy), in this case it allows him to learn about the world in ways inaccessible to girls like Zamie. Zamie is taught to desire marriage; it is, after all, what everyone wants for her— why should she not want it herself? What she is never taught is what comes after. Her education consists of learning tasks to render her a good and desirable wife. Put simply, her education consists in learning how to best be enslaved in marriage. Being raised as a boy, Phaza has never had to think about marriage except when confronted with it directly. He is taught to read, to think, to hunt—in short, to live a fulfilling life. His happiness is not coupled with an event or another person; it is found in day-to-day activities. Education has been the central focus of his upbringing, but equally important to his knowledge is ignorance. In this case, ignorance isn't just a simple, innocent lack, nor is it a state to be passed through on the way to some better knowledge; instead, ignorance is an important tool for thinking outside the gendered box.

Elsewhere in Graffigny's work, willful acts of ignorance open up the space to think more broadly about the meaning of knowledge itself. One such example can be found in the *Lettres*. As Zilia learns more about French society, she relays this information to Aza through letters, and the more she learns about it, the more she laments the state of education for women in France. Over the last few decades, many scholars have offered up Zilia as a paragon of Enlightenment knowledge production.[32] Even as early as the eighteenth century the chevalier de Jaucourt cited the fictional princess in five articles in Diderot and D'Alembert's famous encyclopedia. Many scholars have argued that his crediting of Zilia, the fictional heroine, rather than Graffigny, the novel's author, with the knowledge produced in the *Lettres* can be understood as a move to present his own thoughts as more natural, given that Zilia is a noble savage. Yet I believe that the encyclopedist's citation of the Peruvian woman goes beyond the use of a narrative device; his citation of the fictional woman can also be read as a displacement of women's knowledge. To acknowledge a female author would be to admit the possibility for an enlightened *female* subject. By citing Zilia, Jaucourt performs a double displacement. First, he places the potential for an enlightened woman outside of Europe, in the exotic woman; and second, as if Peru were not distant enough from France's border, he relegates the potential for female knowledge—and therefore female power—to the realm of fiction. In other words, even though he is praising a woman for her philosophical acumen, he reinforces notions of the intellectual inferiority of women.

To return to *Lettres d'une Péruvienne*, while someone in Zilia's situation might be tempted to turn toward the education received by boys to figure out what is lacking for girls, Zilia makes no such move. After discussing the way girls are treated inhumanely by their parents and tutors, she tells Aza that she has no idea of the education for boys. She makes it clear that she is not interested in learning about boys' education, stating that she had "not informed [her]self in that regard."[33] Rather than turning to French notions of what a true education should look like, Zilia reflects back on her own education in the Temple of the Virgins where she was raised. In the temple she was tutored by the wise older women, but she received an education from some of the male Peruvian educators as well. She insists on both the masculine and the feminine qualities of her education, with the end result being an education in both reason and sentiment.

In the historical introduction to the novel that Graffigny wrote for

32. See Jean-Paul Schneider, "*Les Lettres d'une Péruvienne*: roman ouvert ou roman fermé," in *Vierge du soleil/fille des Lumières* (Strasbourg, 1989), p.7–48; Miller, *Subject to change*; and Heidi Bostic, *The Fiction of Enlightenment: women of reason in the French eighteenth century* (Newark, NJ, 2010).
33. Graffigny, *Letters*, p.143; *Lettres*, p.138. "Je ne m'en suis pas informée."

the second edition, she explains that in Incan lore the prince is the sun and the princess is the moon—the sun and the moon being brother and sister just like Zilia and Aza. While the term "Enlightenment" is often associated with solar illumination, Zilia's enlightenment is associated with the moon. Zilia, therefore, proposes a radically different Enlightenment, one based on the general principles of Enlightenment ideology (daring to know, waking up from a self-imposed immaturity) while running counter to it by creating a place for women. Women's immaturity or dependency is not self-imposed, but rather imposed by men. As daughter, wife, and mother, a woman's primary duty is to obey the male head of the family, and, as we see from much domestic literature of the day, her role with regard to knowledge acquisition is to inspire the desire to learn in her male offspring. In order to create a space where a woman can become an active member of the family—a space where she can act in her own best interest—she must enjoy a relative independence from male dominance. She must occupy the role of the sister.

Zilia's refusal to marry at the end of the novel solidifies her place as a sister. She continues to live near her French family (Déterville and Céline), but she lives alone in her own house. She has no children and so her reproductive labor is devoted to writing, translating, and revising. She willfully refuses both male and female systems of education in France, and in so doing proposes something radically new. By revising and translating her experience to share with others, she proposes that others might do well to also ignore the systems that restrict access to knowledge, and instead to create new paths, as well as new types of knowledge.

Given that raising awareness about injustice has become such a crucial practice in our political era—especially with regard to race and gender—it may seem counterintuitive to propose an argument in favor of ignorance as a feminist praxis. And yet, if there is one thing we see again and again in Graffigny's fiction, it is that where there is ignorance, there is hope. Awareness may be an endpoint, but focusing on the origins of doubt, uncertainty, and insecurity allows us to see that being aware means different things for different people in different situations. If knowledge is historically and materially situated, then we must acknowledge that a universal understanding of the "truth" of the world is impossible. Or, as Sara Ahmed puts it, "reality is usually just someone else's tired explanation."[34] Tired of those worn-out

34. Ahmed, *Living a feminist life*, p.29.

explanations, Graffigny offers us something unusual—a chance to
enter into another world and think through a different explanation,
one that might make sense to a woman in a woman's world.

Building a woman's world, in Zilia's words

In the last chapter, we saw how a maternal symbolic offers an
alternative to phallocentric language. Graffigny demonstrates another
alternative language, this time focused on the act of translation. In
both form and content, *Lettres d'une Péruvienne* provides an innovative
view of how language can be a transformative force in a woman's
world. There are several factors that distinguish Graffigny's novel
from other epistolary novels of the day like those of Richardson,
Montesquieu, or Rousseau (for instance, the woman's voice is written
by a woman and there is only one letter-writer), but perhaps the most
intriguing distinction is the unique delivery of the first seventeen letters
in *quipos*.[35] Although the anthropological studies upon which Graffigny
bases her knowledge of Peruvian culture suggest that *quipos* serve as a
mnemonic device that aids in the retelling of collective history, what
is particularly interesting about the exchange of the *quipos* as imagined
by Graffigny is that, once the reader receives the letter, they must
untie and then retie the knots in such a way as to insert themself into
the display of events. In this way, the knotted letter intertwines various
individuals' separate events and emotions into a collective story.[36]
With the *quipos*, Zilia weaves together various moments, people, and
places from her past and present to record her story and to leave it as
a legacy for future generations.

The colorful cords knotted together thus serve as a physical
extension of her nostalgia or, in her own words, her "malady" as she

35. For a discussion of the impact of *Lettres d'une Péruvienne* on writing and Enlightenment book culture see Lorraine Piroux, "The encyclopedist and the Peruvian
princess: the poetics of illegibility in French Enlightenment book culture,"
PMLA 121:1 (2006), p.107–23; and François Rosset, "Les nœuds du langage
dans *Les Lettres d'une Péruvienne*," *Revue d'histoire littéraire de la France* 96:6 (1996),
p.1106–27.
36. Although Graffigny's novel would suggest that *quipos* is a form of writing, it is
interesting to note that both Graffigny and Jaucourt (in his article "Quipos" for
the *Encyclopédie*) refer to *quipos* as a system of communication used by the Incans
in the absence of writing (see Graffigny's historical introduction). In this way the
author of the work negates the work of the hand as well as the work in hand,
making the story legible only once it has been translated into French.

yearns for a connection to her homeland. Zilia describes her symptoms in the fourth letter as "the violence of the pain that devours me," and shortly thereafter the French doctor on the boat diagnoses her writing-induced illness.[37] However, when he separates Zilia from writing her condition worsens. The heroine understands that the ability to write means access to knowledge, and that knowledge will provide her with the means to return to Aza, Peru, and most importantly a state of freedom.

Throughout the first seventeen letters, Zilia reflects on the pain of remembering as she gives existence to her thoughts through writing.[38] In her reflections, she offers an elegant discourse on the evolution of language and its relation to expression. As Diane Fourny points out, the heroine's account of the development of language in the sixteenth and seventeenth letters (the last two written in *quipos*) closely resembles Rousseau's arguments in the *Essay on the origin of languages* (published three decades later), in which language moves from the gestural to the intuitive, and finally to the symbolic.[39] Zilia begins in the seventeenth letter with an assessment of sounds. She explains that sound must be the most natural form of communication because its meaning is universal.[40] Language, by contrast, is a contrivance of man that is culturally

---

37. Graffigny, *Letters*, p.34; *Lettres*, p.33. "La violence du mal qui me dévore."

38. In this type of lamenting, what Svetlana Boym calls "reflective nostalgia," the desiring subject is obsessed with the *algia*, or the pain of longing itself, rather than with the dislocated object. Boym contrasts this form of nostalgia with what she calls "restorative nostalgia," in which the subject focuses on the *nostos* or the home (the desired object), often inventing a past moment that never existed. The latter, Boym explains, can be pernicious because the longing subject idolizes a fictive past and becomes detached from the present. See S. Boym's *The Future of nostalgia* (New York, 2001).

39. See Diane Fourny, "Language and reality in Françoise de Graffigny's *Lettres d'une Péruvienne*," *Eighteenth-century fiction* 4:3 (1992), p.221–38.

40. Zilia also draws a connection between sound and sentiment, stating, "If it is true that piercing sounds better express the need for help in a state of violent fear or of acute pain than do words understood in one part of the world that have no meaning in the other; it is no less certain that tender moans instill a much more effective compassion in our hearts than do words whose strange arrangement often has the opposite effect" ("S'il est vrai que les sons aigus expriment mieux le besoin de secours dans une crainte violente ou dans une douleur vive, que des paroles entendues dans une partie du monde, et qui n'ont aucune signification dans l'autre, il n'est pas moins certain que de tendres gémissements frappent nos cœurs d'une compassion bien plus efficace que des mots dont l'arrangement bizarre fait souvent un effet contraire"). Graffigny, *Letters*, p.77–78; *Lettres*, p.75–76.

constructed. The heroine's lack of knowledge of the Spanish language, coupled with the fear she feels in the presence of her captors, leads her to convey this language in her letters as nothing more than a series of shrill sounds and barbarous gestures. Her native Incan, conversely, expertly communicates emotions, based as it is on the truths of the heart and soul. True to the conventions of the primitive trope, this "savage" language seems to correspond to Rousseau's theories of the first languages, which he describes as brought about by passion rather than need.

Rousseau's conception of language departs from Graffigny's when language reaches the symbolic. Zilia is resistant to learning French because of the misleading quality she sees in this language: "In general, I suspect this nation of not being at all as it appears; affectation seems to me to be its dominant trait."[41] Whereas in the *Lettres* Graffigny posits "truth" as antithetic to the French language, Rousseau understands all language as constantly in the process of assimilation, whereby affectation is merely the result of truth's catching up to passion, creating both figurative and literal meaning; "let us conclude that visible signs render imitation more precise, but that our interest is better piqued by sounds."[42] While Rousseau holds a logocentric view of French in which the written word serves as a supplement to spoken language and as a record of the truth produced in the presence of the utterance—the written word becoming what Jacques Derrida would call a signifier of a signifier—Graffigny's heroine has difficulty conceiving of the distinction between written and spoken language, going so far as to believe that learning to speak French will allow her to understand Déterville's soul ("Would the comprehension of languages also be that of the soul?").[43] To sever either written or spoken language from thought would produce a rupture in the production of truth that would be, for the Zilia of the first half of the novel, unethical.

Zilia begins to grasp more completely the notion of excitation by sound as she learns French. During the time when she remains incapable of understanding the French language Déterville endeavors

---

41. Graffigny, *Letters*, p.75; *Lettres*, p.73. "En général, je soupçonne cette nation de n'être point telle qu'elle paraît; l'affectation me paraît son caractère dominant."

42. Jean-Jacques Rousseau, *Essai sur l'origine des langues, où il est parlé de la mélodie et de l'imitation musicale* (1781; Paris, 1993), p.91. "[C]oncluons que les signes visibles rendent l'imitation plus exacte, mais que l'intérêt s'excite mieux par les sons."

43. Graffigny, *Letters*, p.50; *Lettres*, p.49. "L'intelligence des langues serait-elle celle de l'âme?"

to excite her emotion and lead her to his own desires of passionate love through a repetition of romantic language: "As soon as I have repeated, 'yes, I love you,' or 'I promise to be yours,' joy spreads over his face."[44] However, for the protagonist, these remain empty signifiers that mean nothing to her. Passionate love (*eros*) is comprehensible to her only as being attached to Aza, and does not translate when it comes from the mouth of another man. Only later, as she realizes the necessity of learning French (once she runs out of cords), does she begin to understand the complexity of emotion that exists in spoken language. After going to the opera for the first time she explains that the ability to understand sounds must be universal, "for I had no more difficulty experiencing the emotion of the various passions being depicted than I would have had they been expressed in our language, and this seems quite natural to me."[45] In her unique linguistic system, sounds correspond to feeling—written signs (*quipos*) correspond to truths. For Zilia, Incan is an intuitive language that conveys emotions by fusing together sign and signifier, offering immutable meaning.[46]

In the written Peruvian language, Zilia feels secure because each knot corresponds to an event and an emotion that she understands on a deeply personal level. Even collective history becomes an individual experience between her fingers. Writing is what makes the heroine feel whole because it is the extension of her thoughts, and, as such, it is a part of her. When she first falls into the hands of the French and her cords are taken away from her, she feels as if her soul is being ripped out and as though she will die. Moreover, although she speaks and writes in her native language, throughout the first seventeen letters Zilia is repeatedly infantilized due to her inability to communicate with those around her. Like a child she is innocent and pure, awkwardly repeating new words and phrases that bring a smile to the faces of those around her. Until the eighteenth letter she remains locked in a *chora*-like, pre-oedipal space within the French-speaking world. At this point, writing becomes like a pharmakon—a poison that is killing her but that is also a cure for her nostalgia.

---

44. Graffigny, *Letters*, p.49; *Lettres*, p.48. "Dès que j'ai répété après lui, *oui, je vous aime*, ou bien *je vous promets d'être à vous*, la joie se répand sur son visage."
45. Graffigny, *Letters*, p.75; *Lettres*, p.75. "Car il ne m'a pas été plus difficile de m'affecter des différentes passions que l'on a représentées que si elles eussent été exprimées dans notre langue, et cela me paraît bien naturel."
46. The immutable meaning corresponds to a belief in the truth communicated through language. In fact, a footnote to the third letter informs the reader that it is inconceivable that an Incan could lie.

Put differently, it is an activity that draws her away from the present moment, but that also grounds her more firmly within herself.[47] In this symbolic no-man's-land, Zilia has not yet accepted the rules of a phallocentric society. Within the womb-like haven of this suspended moment the heroine makes a transformative return to the *chora* and is able to formulate a female subjectivity that can be iterated positively rather than from a position of lack.

As she begins to panic at the thought of running out of cords, which would render her incapable of writing, the heroine learns that the French also possess a system that can "give a kind of existence to thoughts."[48] Consequently, her fears of losing her sole means of communication seem to lessen. In fact, as her cords run out, the violence of the illness she describes in the first letters begins to dissipate. At first, she panics in the sixteenth letter as she sees the end of her cords, afraid to write because it will bring the end not only of her favorite activity (writing), but also of her love affair. Once the cords finally do run out in the seventeenth letter, Zilia laments, "these knots, which seemed to me to be a line of communication linking my heart to yours, are already nothing more than the sad objects of my regret."[49] Once she ties the last knot, she understands that she must learn a new language. This decision leads to an experience that will alter her very being.

Because these cords have served as the physical extension of her nostalgia, a sickness or disease, the cure must lie in removing them from the body. This nostalgectomy that occurs at the end of the seventeenth letter leaves Zilia linguistically comatose. Without language she has no means of expression, and therefore her thoughts are left to float in the void between languages. The Aza her memory has created will become once and for all hypostatized in the past, unable to be revived in the present. Consequently, she resists the desire to learn French, and, although she is constantly surrounded by

47. Both the written and the spoken language in Peruvian are directly linked to thoughts and therefore the "truth" of the soul. This fact highlights the Derridean observation, which seeks to collapse oppositions. This is perhaps where Graffigny most fruitfully departs from Rousseau in her conception of the origins of language, as she posits ideas that will later become central to the deconstructionist movement.

48. Graffigny, *Letters*, p.74; *Lettres*, p.72. "Donner une sorte d'existence aux pensées."

49. Graffigny, *Letters*, p.79; *Lettres*, p.77. "Ces nœuds, qui me semblaient être une chaîne de communication de mon cœur au tien, ne sont déjà plus que les tristes objets de mes regrets."

her new French family (Déterville and Céline), it is not until she runs out of cords that she finally *must* learn to speak, read, and of course write in French. Only a linguistic reintegration can bring her out of her coma.

If, as Fourny writes, the times when Zilia is between letters are a sort of non-moment, or a space where time does not exist and Zilia's universe fades away, then the break between letters 17 and 18 is tremendously important. Once she loses the ability to communicate, she can no longer exist in the present. While the first line of the eighteenth letter reinforces the idea of a death between languages ("How much time has been erased from my life [my dearest Aza!]"), it is quickly followed by declarations of life, in which she embraces a completely new universe full of infinite symbolic possibility.[50] In fact, Zilia remarks that, during the time she could not write, she lived only in the future, stating: "I lived only in the future, for the present no longer seemed worthy of being counted."[51] The cords of the *quipos* allow her simultaneously to experience the present moment while still serving as an umbilical cord tying her to the past (Aza and Peru), but once that cord is cut she is forced into an abyss of darkness, surviving on the yearning for a future moment when she will once again be able to express herself in writing, and therefore exist materially (in the form of letters).

Within the non-moment, time ceases to exist, yet, when she is thrust back into the present (in the eighteenth letter), time speeds up exponentially. Whereas time in her native language is arranged spatially (life is communicated through insular, communal events), French introduces a sense of temporal progression and a necessity to demarcate time. Just after she learns French, Déterville leaves Zilia for the first time, and she learns that he will be gone for six months. Because words describing units of time mean nothing to Zilia, she translates them into the only language capable of transgressing linguistic boundaries, the language of emotions; "when he left, I was still ignorant of the use of his language. From the sharp pain he manifested in taking leave of his sister and me, however, I understood that we were losing him for a long time."[52] The emotion-filled departure of her friend provides

50. Graffigny, *Letters*, p.79; *Lettres*, p.78. "Combien de temps effacé de ma vie, mon cher Aza!"
51. Graffigny, *Letters*, p.80; *Lettres*, p.78. "[J]e ne vivais que dans l'avenir, le présent ne me paraissait plus digne d'être compté."
52. Graffigny, *Letters*, p.82; *Lettres*, p.80. "J'ignorais encore l'usage de sa langue;

her with a second desired moment of reunion and, therefore, another limit to time. Rather than reflecting on the past, she must yearn for the future and the possibilities that lie therein. It is thus during the moments outside of language, when Zilia is forced to live in the present, that her illness is cured.

In the sixteenth letter, before learning French, Zilia compares the words of this language to women's makeup, in the way they cover up the truth of thoughts to make them pretty. Moreover, once she has learned to write in French, she complains of the difficulty in directly and honestly conveying thoughts in the language, stating, "it takes me an endless amount of time to form a very few lines. It often happens that after having written a great deal, I myself cannot figure out what I believed myself to be expressing."[53] Although she finds the symbolic French language false, a language in which the proliferation of signifiers confuses meaning, the Zilia of the second half of the novel begins to grasp the utility of affectation in language. By writing letters in French, she can actually revive Aza. In the earnest Peruvian language, he was forced to remain in the past, but in the creative French language he can be reconstructed in the present.

As soon as she is finally reunited with the Aza of flesh and blood, when her desire has finally been fulfilled, Zilia learns of his infidelity. While the heroine has dedicated her existence to resisting integration into French society by holding onto the Peruvian language and refusing to learn French, Aza has converted to Christianity and found a Spanish wife. Once Zilia learns of Aza's treachery, the past that she had created for herself is proven to be a lie. Although the intuitive Peruvian language does not allow for lies, the more symbolic French is predicated upon an art of minor falsehoods and double entendres. Her world is shattered not only because of Aza's betrayal, but also because language has become obfuscated. She realizes that she has been lied to for the first time, and she understands that her own recollections of the past have been faulty. It is at this moment, when language fails because she cannot reconcile truth with language, that Zilia becomes a victim of the infidelity of both her lover and language. For the first time she longs to forget the past, dedicating the present to imagining

---

cependant, à la vive douleur qu'il fit paraître en se séparant de sa sœur et moi, je compris que nous le perdions pour longtemps."

53. Graffigny, *Letters*, p.81–82; *Lettres*, p.79. "Il me faut un temps infini pour former très peu de lignes. Il arrive souvent qu'après avoir beaucoup écrit, je ne puis deviner moi-même ce que j'ai cru exprimer."

the future. Ironically, the future she imagines is the same as the one she had imagined in the past. Unlike historic time, Zilia's internal time is mutable, allowing her to revive the faithful Aza she had previously imagined, bringing this memory back to life in the present moment and fusing experience and expectation. Forgetting the tragic event that separates her imagined past from the present, Zilia decides instead to imagine a future that can never exist.

Zilia's turn from reflection on a past moment to imagination of the future signals a shift in her own understanding of nostalgia. Her emotions are now mediated by language (from Peruvian to French) and by time (the year that has passed since she last saw Aza), and, although her heart is broken, her violent illness is cured. Because of the slowness of writing in French, her feelings become temporally mediated and necessarily more reflective. With her new language she can reflect on a lost time while imagining a time that will never come, a new utopian future to which I will now turn.

In a letter written to Déterville just after Zilia's disastrous reunion with Aza she laments: "No longer is it the loss of my freedom, my rank, or my homeland that I regret, no longer the anxieties of an innocent tenderness that wring tears from me; rather, it is good faith betrayed and love scorned that rend my soul."[54] As a final act of tearing Zilia's soul apart, Aza returns her letters. Not only has Zilia lost the cords that were once attached to her person, the cords she used to create her story, but now the cords that tied her to Aza have also been severed once and for all. This event marks the painful progression of Zilia's internal time, yet she also realizes that she now holds Aza's very existence in her hands. By restoring her cords to her, the Aza of flesh and blood has given her the tools to recreate historical time. The heroine's postscript desire to rewrite the past is predicated upon her willingness to tear all of the terrible moments from her past out of the fabric of time, throwing them back into the realm of what she calls "eternal ideas." From this realm, she can choose moments, weave together experiences, and reorganize time in whatever manner she sees fit. By reducing history to a series of spatially disjointed concepts rather than a teleological series of events, the narrator of the *Lettres*

---

54. Graffigny, *Letters*, p.164; *Lettres*, p.159. "Ce n'est plus la perte de ma liberté, de mon rang, de ma patrie que je regrette; ce ne sont plus les inquiétudes d'une tendresse innocente qui m'arrachent des pleurs; c'est la bonne foi violée, c'est l'amour méprisé, qui déchirent mon âme."

combines the spatial element of her original written language (*quipos*) with the logocentrism of her learned language (French).

Such a mode of describing a reorganization of time is, in fact, in line with Zilia's initial mode of writing. When inserting parenthetical comments into her story as she translates the knots from *quipos* to French, the heroine must unravel the fabric of her story in order to insert (anachronistically) the French language. Zilia decides simply to erase the moment of betrayal itself. Instead of destroying Aza, forgetting him completely and ripping the memory of him from the fabric of her own timeline, Zilia participates in a bit of *hauntology*, bringing him back to life on her own terms because, as she puts it, her heart will be his "until death." Rather than a specter of patriarchy, here we see a specter of brotherhood and love. In this queer relationship, nothing but a ghost can fulfill all of Zilia's desires.

Although Zilia laments Aza's infidelity, his sudden removal from her life toward the end of the novel does not result in a near-death experience or a suicide attempt as it had in the past because this time the cords that tied her identity so tightly to his have been severed and returned to her. Within the ruptures in space and time she has created her own identity, independent of Aza. In fact, the last letters of the novel are no longer addressed to him. Instead, she writes to Déterville, and even responds to letters from him.[55] Because her heart will forever belong to Aza, she refuses to marry Déterville. She cannot share her heart with him, but she can share a much more important organ— her brain. She has become an active subject, capable of exchanging thoughts and ideas with men as an equal.

The final letter, addressed to Déterville, concretizes the heroine's decision to lead a solitary life in her country home. Zilia has now resolved to live out her days reflecting on a past, lost moment, imagining the possibility of a future that cannot exist. The decision to sit at home pining over a missed opportunity would seem a tragic ending for the heroine, reminiscent of the sad but dutiful princesse de Clèves, knitting by the fire until her untimely death. However, rather than signaling an end, this letter signals a return to the beginning. From the beginning the absent hero's name suggested a circular story.

55. Although the reader never sees the letters to which she is responding, Zilia does address questions and issues brought up by Déterville in his letters. There is, however, one piece of writing inserted into the novel that is not her own, that is the brief note Déterville writes explaining how he came upon the Peruvian treasures that are transformed into gold to buy Zilia's house.

From A to Z and back to A, this is finally the point at which Zilia—whose name begins only at the end with Z—can break free from the strong hold of her memory of Aza and begin to live in the reality of her own constructed world, which is no less real to her than the world broken by Aza's betrayal. At this moment, she can finally weave her past into the present as she translates the seventeen letters from *quipos* into French, inscribing her memories in the indelible ink that produces the French language.

Through the work of translation, the heroine embraces the symbolic possibilities of French, but in a controlled environment. She has seen the deceit that comes with a language based on symbolism rather than emotion, but, instead of rejecting that language, she decides to use it to her advantage, inventing a world in which she alone controls the language, a world in which Aza will return in the form she has created, and in which the violence of her nostalgia has dissipated. Her individual illness cured, she can finally begin a treatment for the malady plaguing not only herself, but all the women surrounding her. Guided by feminine reason and a knowledge that blends French and Peruvian languages and customs, Zilia lays the foundation for a new female identity as she writes her legacy. By inventing a space where girls' education is taken seriously and where women have the potential to be equal to men, Graffigny's novel offers a utopian sense of hope for a world welcoming of all citizens, regardless of sex or gender. This is not yet Gayle Rubin's androgynous utopia, but it does force us to reckon with the treatment of women in a society built around patriarchal practices.[56]

The heroine's moments of reflection, the end that signals a new beginning in a woman's retreating to her country home to rewrite her past, serve as an incredibly powerful metaphor for feminine desire in eighteenth-century France. If Zilia can translate her Peruvian story into French, weaving together past moments in a way that creates a new present, so too can woman positively insert herself into a phallo-centric history. By constantly writing and revising, Graffigny—like Zilia—translates her experience into her own letters, leaving behind a material legacy in which she enters into philosophical discourse and begins to assess the ills of an unequal society. Much like her protag-onists, Graffigny offers alternative paths to enlightenment. In the

56. The final lines of Rubin's "Traffic in women" call for a revolution that would produce an androgynous society in which gender will no longer be a reason for withholding power from large portions of the population.

end, Zilia's nostalgic desire for the familiar (Aza and Peru) translates into something completely new and different. Rather than offering a repeat of the beginning, the end of this novel signals a return to a beginning that has been altered. Zilia has mastered speech, has become integrated into French society without giving up her Peruvian identity, and has disentangled all of the knots that made her foreign. In the end she is neither French nor Peruvian, she is Woman—existing independent of a man and possessing a desire to learn. She combines the truth of Peruvian language with the affective ornament of French to produce a new, more powerful truth. By taking fragments of her Peruvian and French identities and weaving them together, Zilia breaks free from nationalistic stereotypes to become a cosmopolitan, enlightened citizen—collapsing distinctive spaces and synthesizing competing notions of identity.

The traditional teleological narrative for an eighteenth-century woman, like the narrative of Zilia's trajectory (told with the first three French words she learns), can be summed up in three nouns: daughter, wife, mother. Because Zilia's independence is predicated upon her refusal of Déterville's hand in favor of Aza's memory, she must create a new family that interrupts (and disrupts) the cycle of life that women have been forced to accept. Such a family does not involve the production of children, but instead offers an exchange of ideas. Zilia is not an individual who exists only within and as an extension of the intimate sphere of the family; rather, her individuality serves as the basis for her own notion of kinship structures. The family bonds that emerge, and that we see repeated in Graffigny's other works, rely upon the strength and the vulnerability of an intimacy detached from passion—one that enacts the solidarity of sisterhood.

Sisterhood, or something like it

Zilia's willful ignorance (of language, of time) contrasts starkly with Cénie's obliviousness to the identity of her parents, Phaza's confusion surrounding gender, or Zénise's and Philette's lack of knowledge regarding their respective ranks. And yet, we see traces of each of these characters in each of the others. They are all young but they are wise; at times they appear naive but they are bold; they know what they want, and, when their plans unexpectedly go awry, they adapt. Their stories are very different, as are the challenges they face, but there is a commonality in their resiliency. In other words, if we think of these novels and plays not as a constellation of solitary works about individual women, but rather as a more cohesive *œuvre*, we see that, in offering individual worlds made for women, Graffigny has offered us a whole world of potential for women. In the second chapter, I discussed how relations between men are transformed in the absence of a father, or, to be more accurate, of a symbolic patriarch. The "regime of the brother," as MacCannell calls it, offers a world of brothers with imaginary—rather than symbolic—power whose fragile sense of worth (and therefore power) rests upon the utter exclusion of women from the political sphere. To conclude this chapter, I would like to examine how Graffigny's fiction might allow us to theorize a regime of the sister.

It may seem anachronistic to think of sisterhood as a uniting concept among unrelated women when considering eighteenth-century fiction. It is a term that, for many, evokes images from the 1960s of women taking to the streets, marching arm in arm, and burning bras in protest of the patriarchy. For others, this term might bring to mind a much more sober image of groups of women in robes who have devoted their lives to prayer and worship. And yet, as early as at least the seventeenth century (and likely even earlier), the term "sister" had uses outside of familial and religious contexts. Although the first definitions in the 1694 edition of the Académie française's dictionary describe women related by blood or religion, the third signals its use for groups of women united for nonreligious reasons, as in the Sisters of Charity. We might also recall the frequent usage of the term *sœurs de lait* (milk sisters, or those nursed by the same wet nurse), which indicates women not necessarily bonded by blood but sharing an intimate bond (through a nursing woman) nonetheless. In short, sisterhood has been uniting women—related by blood or not—for centuries.

To think of sisterhood, therefore, is to think of a form of intimate community whose *raison d'être* does not necessarily lie in maintaining the traditions of any masculine regime. Put differently, to think sisterhood does not mean thinking about family. As I noted in the previous chapter, the language of kinship, particularly with regard to designators for women, has to stretch and morph to imagine what the role of women outside of the intimate sphere of the family household might look like. While masculine regimes prescribe roles that relegate women to a reproductive function and exclude them from the public and political sphere, feminine regimes hold no such limitations, and do not appear beholden to gender exclusion. As I demonstrated in my discussion of *Phaza* (and to a certain extent *Lettres d'une Péruvienne*), Graffigny's conception of gender allows for a fluidity that breaks down binary notions of what "men" and "women" should look like and do. What I am calling the regime of the sister, then, does not require the exclusion of men; conversely, it calls for a transformation of gender roles for all.

How might anything resembling a "regime" not require exclusionary tactics for the maintenance of power? How might it be open and adaptive? Simply put, while the brother seeks out a symbolic power that he does not and cannot have because he is not the progenitor of the familial dynamic, the sister has no such pretentions to symbolic power. Having been marginalized from the beginning, the female child sees her journey as one from a man (the father) to another man (the husband). Within this triangulation of power, she may *represent* power (in the form of reproductive possibilities), but she never holds it. That the family should include a wife or a mother matters little once her primary functions have been fulfilled. As we see in each of the works studied in this chapter, what power each of the female characters has garnered has emerged from a space of symbolic exclusion. These protagonists are often subject to real exclusions that take a geographic form (taking place in distant lands), but such real exclusions are also inextricable from the social, sexual, and linguistic positionality of the protagonists. Even when sharing a language (in each case the shared language is French), the meanings and emotions communicated through language are often misunderstood, misconstrued, or ignored because of the gendered and social position of the speaker. Being out of sync with the symbolic order (because of that order's inherent masculinity), these women must figure out alternative pathways to power by experimenting with the relationality of people to and by language.

To understand the unique position of these characters to language and knowledge, let us turn briefly to a discussion of *parrhesia*. As Foucault points out, *parrhesia* runs counter to Cartesian notions of doubt and certainty, by implying that the *parrhesiastes* (the one who uses *parrhesia*) speaks the truth inherently and without recourse to rhetorical flourishes.[57] To speak frankly is to take a risk and to offer critique of what one understands as flawed. Although ancient notions of *parrhesia* reserve such verbal activity for men (and beyond that for relatively powerful men), the elements of such speech activities can be found in each of our protagonists. Does Zilia not take a risk in critiquing French customs in her letters to Aza, especially when she

57. Michel Foucault, *Fearless speech*, ed. Joseph Pearson (Los Angeles, CA, 2001).

requires a mediating figure to deliver the letters—one who might read what she has to say? Does Cénie not take a risk in declaring to Méricourt that she would rather be cast away from her home for the truth than to live with him in a lie? And does not Phaza risk hurting Zamie by opening up her eyes to the truth about marriage? Each of these examples demonstrates not only a risk, but also the perceived notion within the speaker that what they speak is the truth, so much so that they feel a moral obligation to share the knowledge in spite of such risks.

Although few have analyzed the convergences between the dialogic process of speech and power inherent to *parrhesia* and the psychoanalytic process of subjectivation, the constant negotiation that mediates each is crucial to the construction of a regime of the sister.[58] We understand that the process of subjectivation involves a negotiation between the framework of the ego ideal (which is shaped by culturally appropriate norms) and the unconscious drives of the id. This is a process that is continually repeated throughout the life of the subject. *Parrhesia*, by contrast, involves a process of negotiation between the *parrhesiastes* and the listener. As Nancy Luxon argues, both speaker and listener place themselves into a vulnerable position in the encounter—the speaker because they critique what is accepted as a norm, the listener because they must trust in the good will of the speaker.[59] Bringing these two concepts together, therefore, allows us to account for a process of power through knowledge, first of all, that is both inter- and intrasubjective; secondly, that is constantly adapting to new contexts; and finally, that accounts for a type of power through knowledge that is not attained (as from a master) but that is created collaboratively and shared.

Collaborative creation is precisely what we see across the works of fiction studied in this chapter. These characters are not speaking to a void—they speak to each other and they speak to others. Their voices echo and alter one another across texts, and, in the process, they speak out to others by virtue of their being shared. That so many "suites" to *Lettres d'une Péruvienne* appeared within weeks of its publication (mostly penned by anonymous authors) attests to the power of the novel, and the enormous success of *Cénie* in its day stands as a tribute to the

58. A few notable exceptions are Luxon, *Crisis of authority*, and Gentile, *Feminine law*.
59. Because "ground zero" for each of these processes relies upon a male subject, to begin from the position of female is to place oneself in an increased state of vulnerability.

importance spectators placed on fully developed voices of women on stage. Furthermore, these strong voices do not require the exclusion of men. Déterville, Dorimond, and Clerval, among others, support the women they love without prescribing their behavior. The regime of the sister, as theorized through the works of Graffigny, relies upon the participation of individuals of all genders. The citizens of the author's world are united in a struggle to end gender inequality by actually talking about what women experience and what they want, and then fighting to achieve those goals. In feminist terms, this is also the goal of a sisterhood based on what bell hooks calls solidarity. Arguing against previous notions of sisterhood among mostly white feminists who favored support as the dominant method of caring for one another, hooks proposes that solidarity is the only feminist praxis capable of uniting women of diverse racial and economic backgrounds. Support, she argues, can be given and taken away; solidarity requires "sustained, ongoing commitment."[60] Several scholars have analyzed these forms of sustained and ongoing commitment in Graffigny's fiction through discussions of *amitié*, or friendship.[61] In each of the novels and plays discussed in this chapter, friendship does indeed play a central role. In Graffigny's fiction, any intimate society inclusive of women must be organized around a strong network of friendships. However, I believe that what the author envisions with this word is much larger in scope.

  Friendship has a long and varied history from Antiquity up through the eighteenth century. At its simplest, friendship indicates a mutual affection between two people. The prevailing understanding of friendship in Europe throughout much of the sixteenth to eighteenth centuries is based on the neoplatonic model most famously articulated by Michel de Montaigne in the sixteenth century. This model is repeated in the dictionaries of the time, which most often describe friendship as existing between two people of relatively equal condition. Claude Yvon and Denis Diderot depict a more precarious yet more democratic vision of friendship in the article they authored for the *Encyclopédie*. The need for people to be of the same condition is

60. bell hooks, "Sisterhood: political solidarity between women," in *Feminist theory from margin to center* (Cambridge, MA, 1984), p.43–66 (64).
61. See, for example, Laura Burch, "La nouvelle République des lettres: Graffigny et l'amitié philosophique," *SVEC* 2004:12, p.319–27; and Heidi Bostic, "Friendship, *fainéantise*, and fraternal correction in Graffigny's letters to Devaux 1752–53," *Eighteenth-century fiction* 26:3 (2014), p.355–74.

less important in their view than habit, charity, and pleasure, but, once these conditions are no longer met, friendship can disappear. Notions of friendship may vary, but they each describe very personal relationships between two people, and these relationships have very few effects for those outside of the friendship.

In Graffigny's work, friendship takes on a much more political dimension. It can exist between people of different races, genders, and social stations, and thus acts as a democratizing force. It is so important, in fact, that one of the letters the author added for the second edition of the *Lettres* focuses almost exclusively on the virtues of male–female friendship. In that instance, friendship is more than a supportive and nurturing relationship: It is a replacement for marriage. Friendship, therefore, is a concept that would allow women to remove themselves from the marriage market altogether, thus bringing to a halt the exchange of women necessary to maintain patriarchal society. Friendship then is not only personal, but also political. Although the author might not have used the word "sisterhood," it is that kind of ongoing commitment to the proper treatment of women that is being expressed in the term "friendship." "Friendship" is thus a key term in Graffigny's sentimental vocabulary, but at the center of that friendship is what hooks would call solidarity, or what is expressed in Graffigny's own words as *confiance.*[62]

To understand the importance of *confiance*, let us look at a scene from *Cénie*. After Cénie has confided in Orphise her belief that a marriage based on love rather than obligation will be a better and stronger marriage, Orphise expresses her disagreement: "Alas!" the governess cries,

> your error is only natural. Only experience can uncover for us the pains that are inseparable from a deep love. But this happiness, the image of which seduces you, depends too much on the life of sentiments, even on the happiness of the loved object, to be durable. Tenderness doubles our natural sensitivity: it doubles the pain, and the repetition of these details overwhelms us. The true misfortunes are those of the heart.

62. Howells suggests that in Graffigny's work *confiance* is relatively synonymous with solidarity. While the two words share mutual characteristics and concerns, they are, in fact, distinct. Like solidarity, *confiance* also requires a consistent commitment over time, but, unlike solidarity, it can be formed in an instant and based on gut feelings. See Howells's "Mme de Graffigny's story," as well as his *Regressive fictions: Graffigny, Rousseau, Bernardin* (London, 2007).

votre erreur est bien naturelle. L'expérience peut seule nous découvrir les peines inséparables d'un attachement trop tendre. Mais cette félicité, dont l'image vous séduit, dépend trop de la vie des sentimens, du bonheur même de l'objet aimé, pour qu'elle soit durable. La tendresse double notre sensibilité naturelle: elle multiplie les peines de détail dont la répétition nous accable. Les véritables malheurs sont ceux du cœur.[63]

These seemingly wise words from Orphise reveal wounds much deeper than she lets on. In beginning her advice by referring to experience, she implies to her young mistress that this pain is one she is intimately familiar with. Ironically, in proposing a colder, more distant relationship with men in marriage, she opens herself up to a closer relationship with her ward. Cénie senses this drawing out and seizes the opportunity to connect with Orphise more intimately, asking her to explain the terrible things that happened to her to make her believe in such a cold version of marriage. Realizing that she has crossed a boundary and wishing to restore the teacher–pupil order, Orphise draws back, apologizing for her abundance of emotion and attempting to refocus the conversation on Cénie's problem. Rather than restoring order, however, these words hurt the pupil, who responds, "you [*vous*] don't believe that I merit your *confiance*: however, my heart would be worthy."[64] In this scene we see how relationships between women become easily confused. The pair exist at this point in the play in a teacher–student relationship that replicates the mother–daughter relationship, and yet the notion of *confiance* introduces a more egalitarian element than had previously existed.

Confiance is thus a word that indicates intimacy in Graffigny's work, but it is used in very specific ways. Intimacy can occur between mothers and children, husbands and wives, lovers, or friends, but the word *confiance* is reserved exclusively for the closest friendships. Zilia, for instance, talks of an instant feeling of *confiance* with Céline and later, when she finally has her own country home, she talks of spending the day with Céline and Déterville "savoring the delights of confidence [*confiance*] and friendship."[65] Much like *parrhesia*, *confiance* involves

---

63. Françoise de Graffigny, *Cénie, pièce en cinq actes* (Paris, Cailleau, 1750), p.33.
64. Graffigny, *Cénie*, p.33 (emphasis added). "Vous croyez que je ne mérite pas encore votre *confiance*: cependant mon cœur en seroit digne."
65. Graffigny, *Letters*, p.159; *Lettres*, p.153. "Dans les délices de la confiance et de l'amitié."

taking a risk. Opening oneself up to a friendship also means relying on the other's goodwill. Whereas blood relations are predetermined, and marriages are often arranged, friendships are the single relationship one enters into of one's own accord. This relationship does not require the submission of one to another (as in marriage), nor does it involve a sense of duty (as in the parent–child relation). Instead, *confiance* means trusting that the other shares your goals even when your needs and desires diverge from their own.

As we have seen, the fight for gender equality was an important project for Graffigny, and one that she addressed in each of her works in one way or another. When there was a lack of female voices, she amplified them, creating more and more as she revised her works. Gender equality was even on the lips of her male characters, whose friendship with strong women helped them to understand the struggle in ways previously inaccessible to them. Building a community of women and men united in the struggle to end gender inequality through experimentation and revision was a necessary step not only for the characters of Graffigny's fiction, but also for the author herself. Women may never have had a place in a symbolic order that understood them only as daughters, wives, and mothers. By opening up the space for a sister, one who disrupted the Symbolic Order by refusing to reproduce (children, patriarchy, tradition), by understanding and presenting herself as naturally equal to men, and by refusing to accept that authority came only at the exclusion of a portion of society, Graffigny theorized a potential counterpart to the regime of the brother. Although her world may have remained a distant utopia for centuries to come, she opened up the possibility for a regime of the sister.

A new legacy

Earlier in the chapter I discussed possible reasons why most of Graffigny's work, aside from *Lettres d'une Péruvienne*, remains largely forgotten today. These theories ranged from a lack of performances to accusations of plagiarism. But maybe there is another reason we remember, read, and study the *Lettres* above all others. Perhaps *Lettres d'une Péruvienne*, when it was revived first by Showalter in the 1960s, then again by feminist scholars in the 1980s, provided us with the legacy of Graffigny that we desperately needed. This was the story of a woman who stood up to the men around her and remained faithful to her own image of herself. Zilia was a woman who continued to write, even when doctors and friends told her that she should not. She was a woman who told us just what was wrong with patriarchal society and gave us a model to follow for thriving in its margins.

In 2021, however, times are different. As if by happenstance, the relatively recent success of the #metoo and the #timesup movements coincided with the publication of the final volume of Graffigny's correspondences in 2018. This happy coincidence allows us to see simultaneously the proximity and the chasm between the struggles of women in the eighteenth century and those of women today. On the one hand, the author, like many women today, struggled to be a self-sufficient woman in a field dominated by men. On the other hand, the voices supporting her the most in those letters (aside from her friend Devaux) are those she creates in her fiction. As Dena Goodman teaches us, becoming a woman in the age of Enlightenment meant writing, but writing could take many forms. For Graffigny, this meant a constant devotion both to her personal correspondence and to her fiction. And as Joan Hinde Stewart points out, Graffigny's writing in particular allowed us to see not just a snapshot of the author, but rather a detailed account of her life—a real life—as she aged through her letters. As she aged, as her financial and social situation changed, so did her struggles. She was never one-note, and her writing reflected that diversity.[66]

Maybe then it is time to re-evaluate Graffigny's legacy. As all the brilliant Graffigny scholars before me have pointed out, not only was Françoise de Graffigny an excellent writer of prose, but she was also an astute philosopher, a woman who faced adversity and survived, a devoted (if sometimes creative) historian, a faithful friend (but one who held her friends to the highest standards), and a woman who inspired writers for generations to come. But, as these relatively forgotten stories tell us, she was also a woman whose theories of gender and class were well ahead of her time. Sure, she had the inspiration of authors such as Isaac de Benserade, Christine de Pizan, and Marie-Jeanne L'Héritier, among others—authors before her who were also interrogating notions of class, gender, and sexuality in exciting ways—but, by weaving these questions into fantastical theater and domestic fiction alike, she bridges the gap between the exotic and the domestic, the queer and the banal, even between fact and fiction. The fictional tapestry she weaves throughout her works shows us that her legacy can

66. See D. Goodman, *Becoming a woman in the age of letters* (Ithaca, NY, 2009); and Stewart, *The Enlightenment of age*.

hardly be neatly relegated to being among the first critically acclaimed female writers in France. No, her legacy is just a little knottier than all that.

Conclusion: queering the Enlightenment, today

In many ways, the utopian experiments examined in this book were failures. If we are to learn anything from Foucault's ironic discussion of sexual liberation in the first volume of *History of sexuality*, it is that, from the premodern to the modern period, we (Westerners) have become more, not less, uptight about sex. The desire to categorize, name, and normalize evacuates the queer from queer theory. The authors examined in this book proposed radical forms of human relationality that focused on the intimacy of community rather than the blood bonds of kinship. The new families created in their pages allowed readers to journey into an alternate universe (that still looked strikingly familiar) in which love and sexuality were unhinged from the business of marriage and reproduction. This coterie of literary political philosophers embraced what they sensed as an era of change, and displayed many of the possibilities open to a society in the mood for something new. Still, by the end of the 1740s, we began to see the rise of a very heteronormative strand of domesticity in the works of Rousseau or in the popularity of translations of Richardson, for example. These ideas, embraced by so many leaders of the new Republic, immortalized the new model of the bourgeois family built upon hierarchies of gender and sexuality that continue to haunt us today. Unmarried women continue to be perceived as oddities (and spinsters) by many, and, although same-sex couples have won certain legal rights in many countries, there is an increasing pressure on these families to fit into a mold of normativity (what Lisa Duggan calls "homonormativity") that encourages biological reproduction and product consumption.[1]

1. See L. Duggan's "The new homonormativity: the sexual politics of neoliberalism," in *Materializing democracy: toward a revitalized cultural politics*, ed. Russ Castronovo and Dana D. Nelson (Durham, NC, 2002), p.175–94.

As I hope to have demonstrated, however, failure should not be understood in a purely negative light. These stories may not have changed minds overnight, but they were beloved stories that were read, shared, and even continued anonymously through what has now become the genre we call "fan fiction." These were the stories circulating through France in the first half of the eighteenth century, working their way into a body of common cultural knowledge. Over the years they have only gained in stature, becoming a wealth of cultural capital. If any of this were in doubt, one need only to browse through the reading lists for the *baccalauréat*, in which these authors appear year after year.

As we have seen, the novels and plays studied in this book repeatedly attempt to represent the emergence of alternative kinship structures. These structures are characterized by forms of relation that exceed and undermine both patriarchy and heteronormativity. The difficulty with the articulation of such alternatives is that the terms deployed to describe kinship have become sedimented—so burdened by the passage of history—that they constitute monuments of almost sublime proportions. Psychoanalysis and structuralism both have gone so far as to say that the structures of kinship are foundational to the very use of language. So how then are we to even imagine names for what lies beyond *the family*? Rather than simply giving us those names and telling us what some new family would look like, the works examined in this book insistently repeat the very failure to imagine such a thing. But perhaps the problem lies in our desire to encapsulate the future of relations with the names of the present, for we might ask with these novels and plays if failure—the failure of the family, the failure of representation, the failure of marriage—might not gain its own substance, and if, by reading these works a little queerly, we might find that this substance could be the beginning of a social structure whose existence lies just beyond the threshold of the text.

Bibliography

Agulhon, Maurice, *Marianne into battle: Republican imagery and symbolism in France, 1789–1880*, translated by Janet Lloyd (London, 1981).

Ahmed, Sara, *Living a feminist life* (Charleston, NC, 2017).

Althusser, Louis, *Philosophy of the encounter: later writings 1978–1987*, ed. Oliver Corpet and François Matheron, translated by G. M. Goshgarian (New York, 2006).

Altmon, Janet Gurkin, "Strategic timing: women's questions, domestic servitude, and the dating game in Montesquieu," *Eighteenth-century fiction* 13:2–3 (2001), p.325–48.

Aravamudan, Srinivas, *Enlightenment orientalism: resisting the rise of the novel* (Chicago, IL, 2011).

–, *Tropicopolitans: colonialism and agency, 1688–1804* (Durham, NC, 1999).

Ariès, Philippe, *Centuries of childhood: a social history of family life*, translated by Robert Baldick (New York, 1960).

Aristodemou, Maria, "To be or not to be a (dead) father," *Journal of international dispute settlement* 9:1 (2018), p.103–22.

Armstrong, Nancy, *Desire and domestic fiction: a political history of the novel* (Oxford, 1990).

Baker, Susan Read, "Sentimental feminism in Marivaux's *La Colonie*," in *To hold a mirror to nature: dramatic images and reflections*, ed. Karalisa Hartigan (Washington, DC, 1982), p.1–10.

Bakhtin, Mikhail, *The Dialogic imagination: four essays* (Austin, TX, 1982).

Balzac, Honoré de, *Le Père Goriot* (Paris, 1971).

–, *Père Goriot*, translated by A. J. Krailsheimer (Oxford, 1991).

Barthes, Roland, *Sade, Fourier, Loyola*, translated by Richard Miller (Berkeley, CA, 1989).

Beauvoir, Simone de, *The Second sex*, translated by Constance Borde and Sheila Malovany-Chevallier (New York, 2011).

Berlant, Lauren, *Cruel optimism* (Durham, NC, 2011).

Bersani, Leo, *Homos* (Cambridge, MA, 1996).

Bilis, Hélène, "Corneille's *Œdipe* and the politics of seventeenth-century royal succession," *MLN* 125:4 (2010), p.873–94.

–, "Poétique tragique et pensée politique: la mise en scène de la souveraineté dans l'*Œdipe* de Voltaire," *Symposium* 64:4 (2010), p.258–74.

Boe, Ana de Freitas, and Abby Coykendall (ed.), *Heteronormativity in eighteenth-century literature and culture* (New York, 2014).

Bostic, Heidi, "The difference she makes: staging gender identity in Graffigny's *Phaza*," *Tulsa studies in women's literature* (2010), p.291–309.

–, *The Fiction of Enlightenment: women of reason in the French eighteenth century* (Newark, NJ, 2010).

–, "Friendship, *fainéantise*, and fraternal correction in Graffigny's letters to Devaux 1752–53," *Eighteenth-century fiction* 26:3 (2014), p.355–74.

Boym, Svetlana, *The Future of nostalgia* (New York, 2001).

Braun, Theodore E. D., "Montesquieu, *Lettres persanes*, and chaos," in *Disrupted patterns: on chaos and order in the Enlightenment*, ed. Theodore E. D. Braun and John Aloysius McCarthy (Amsterdam, 2000), p.79–90.

Brooks, Peter, *The Novel of worldliness: Crébillon, Marivaux, Laclos, Stendhal* (Princeton, NJ, 1969).

Burch, Laura, "La nouvelle République des lettres: Graffigny et l'amitié philosophique," *SVEC* 2004:12, p.319–27.

Butler, Judith, *Antigone's claim: kinship between life and death* (New York, 2000).

–, *Gender trouble: feminism and the subversion of identity* (New York, 1990).

Caplan, Jay, *In the king's wake: post-absolutist culture in France* (Chicago, IL, 1999).

Caron, Jean-Claude, "La fraternité face à la question sociale dans la France des années 1830," in *Fraternité: regards croisés*, ed. Frédéric Brahami and Odile Roynette (Besançon, 2009), p.135–57.

Cassirer, Ernst, *The Philosophy of the Enlightenment*, translated by Fritz C. A. Koelln and James P. Pettegrove (1932; Princeton, NJ, 2009).

Cazenobe, Colette, *Crébillon fils, ou la Politique dans le boudoir* (Paris, 1977).

–, "Le monde de Crébillon ou une coupable innocence," in *Travaux de littérature: la culpabilité dans la littérature française* (Paris, 1995), p.193–208.

Chambers, Samuel A., and Michael O'Rourke (ed.), *Borderlands* 8:2 (2009), special issue: *Jacques Rancière on the shores of queer theory*.

Chodorow, Nancy, *The Reproduction of mothering: psychoanalysis and the sociology of gender* (Oakland, CA, 1999).

Cixous, Hélène, "The laugh of the Medusa," translated by Keith Cohen and Paula Cohen, *Signs* 1:4 (summer 1976), p.875–94.

Conroy, Peter V., "Marivaux's *The Colony*," *Signs* 9:2 (winter 1983), p.336–60.

Cook, Elizabeth, *Epistolary bodies: gender and genre in the eighteenth-century Republic of Letters* (Stanford, CA, 1996).

Corp, Edward (ed.), *A Court in exile: the Stuarts in France, 1680–1718* (Cambridge, 2009).

Covino, Deborah Caslav, *Amending the abject body: aesthetic makeovers in medicine and culture* (New York, 2004).

Crébillon, Claude Prosper Jolyot de, *Les Egarements du cœur et de l'esprit*, ed. René Etiemble (1736; Paris, 1977).

–, *La Nuit et le moment (suivi de) Le Hasard du coin du feu* (1763; Paris, 1998).

–, *Le Sopha* (1742; Paris, 1997).

–, *The Wayward head and heart*, translated by Barbara Bray (Oxford, 1963).

Cusset, Catherine, "Loi du père et symbolique de l'espace dans *Manon Lescaut*," *Eighteenth-century fiction* 5:2 (1993), p.93–103.

Darnton, Robert, *The Forbidden best-sellers of pre-revolutionary France* (New York, 1996).

Daumas, Maurice, *Le Syndrome Des Grieux: la relation père/fils au XVIIIᵉ siècle* (Paris, 1990).

David, Marcel, *Fraternité et Révolution française* (Paris, 1987).

Davidson, Ian, *Voltaire, a life* (New York, 2010).

Davis, Oliver, *Jacques Rancière* (Malden, MA, 2010).

Dean, Tim, *Unlimited intimacy: reflections on the subculture of barebacking* (Chicago, IL, 2009).

Degauque, Isabelle, *Les Tragédies de Voltaire au miroir de leurs parodies dramatiques: d'Œdipe (1718) à Tancrède (1760)* (Paris, 2007).

Deimling, Katherine, "The female mentor in Crébillon's *Les Egarements du cœur et de l'esprit*," *Eighteenth-century fiction* 16:1 (2003), p.13–31.

DeJean, Joan, *Tender geographies: women and the origins of the novel in France* (New York, 1991).

Delers, Olivier, "La socialité en chaîne et en réseau dans *Les Egarements du cœur et de l'esprit* de Crébillon fils," *Dix-huitième siècle* 41 (2009), p.248–64.

Delon, Michel, "Un monde d'eunuques," *Europe* 574 (1977), p.79–88.

–, *Le Savoir-vivre libertin* (Paris, 2004).

Démoris, René, *Le Silence de Manon* (Paris, 1995).

Deneys-Tunney, Anne, *Ecritures du corps: de Descartes à Laclos* (Paris, 1992).

Deranty, Jean-Philippe (ed.), *Jacques Rancière: key concepts* (New York, 2010).

Dictionnaire de l'Académie française (Paris, [la Veuve de Jean Baptiste Coignard], 1694).

Diderot, Denis, *Diderot on art: the salon of 1765 and notes on painting*, translated by John Goodman (New Haven, CT, 1995).

–, *Œuvres complètes*, vol.14: *Salon de 1765: essais sur la peinture*, ed. Else Marie Bukdahl, Annette Lorenceau, and Gita May (Paris, 1975).

Dornier, Carole, "Orient romanesque et satire de la religion: Claude Crébillon, *Tanzaï et Néadarné* et *Le Sopha*," *Eighteenth-century fiction* 11:3 (1999), p.445–58.

Douthwaite, Julia, "Embattled eros: the cultural politics of Prévost's *Grecque moderne*," *L'Esprit créateur* 32:3 (1992), p.87–97.

Dufrin Kelley, Diane, "The morality of plagiarism: Voltaire, Diderot, and the legacy of Graffigny's *Cénie*," *New perspectives on the eighteenth century* 7:1 (2010), p.48–62.

Duggan, Lisa, "The new homonormativity: the sexual politics of neoliberalism," in *Materializing democracy: toward a revitalized cultural politics*, ed. Russ Castronovo and Dana D. Nelson (Durham, NC, 2002), p.175–94.

Edelman, Lee, *Homographesis: essays in gay literary and cultural theory* (New York, 1994).

–, *No future: queer theory and the death drive* (Durham, NC, 2004).

Edmiston, William F., *Sade: queer theorist*, *SVEC* 2013:03.

Feder, Helena, *Ecocriticism and the idea of culture: biology and the bildungsroman* (Burlington, VT, 2014).

Felski, Rita, *The Limits of critique* (Chicago, IL, 2015).

Festa, Lynn, *Sentimental figures in eighteenth-century Britain and France* (Baltimore, MD, 2006).

Finch, Alison, "The French bildungsroman," in *A History of the bildungsroman*, ed. Sarah Graham (Cambridge, 2019), p.33–56.

Fleury, Jean, *Marivaux et le marivaudage* (Paris, 1881).

Foucault, Michel, *Fearless speech*, ed. Joseph Pearson (Los Angeles, CA, 2001).

–, *The History of sexuality: an introduction*, vol.1, translated by Robert Hurley (New York, 1991).

–, "Qu'est-ce que les Lumières?," in *Dits et écrits*, vol.4 (Paris, 1984), p.562–78.

Fourny, Diane, "Language and reality in Françoise de Graffigny's *Lettres d'une Péruvienne*," *Eighteenth-century fiction* 4:3 (1992), p.221–38.

Frampton, Edith, "Fluid objects: Kleinian psychoanalytic theory and breastfeeding narratives," *Australian feminist studies* 19:45 (November 2004), p.357–68.

Fraser, Nancy, *Unruly practices: power, discourse, and gender in contemporary social theory* (Minneapolis, MN, 1989).

Frautschi, R. L., "The would-be invisible chain in *Les Lettres persanes*," *The French review* 40:5 (1967), p.604–12.

Freccero, Carla, *Queer/early/modern* (Durham, NC, 2006).

Freud, Sigmund, *Beyond the pleasure principle*, translated by James Strachey (1920; New York, 1961).

–, *Collected papers*, vol.5, ed. and translated by James Strachey (New York, 1959).

–, *The Interpretation of dreams*, translated by James Strachey (1899; New York, 1955).

–, *Totem and taboo: resemblances between the psychic lives of savages and neurotics*, translated by James Strachey (1913; London, 1950).

Garraway, Doris, *The Libertine colony: creolization in the early French Caribbean* (Durham, NC, 2005).

Gauthier, Florence, *Triomphe et mort du droit en Révolution 1789–1795–1802* (Paris, 1992).

Gay, Peter, *The Enlightenment*, vol.1: *The Rise of modern paganism* (New York, 1966).

–, *The Enlightenment*, vol.2: *The Science of freedom* (New York, 1969).

Genette, Gérard, *Palimpsests: literature in the second degree*, translated by Channa Newman and Claude Doubinsky (Lincoln, NE, 1997).

Gentile, Jill, *Feminine law: Freud, free speech, and the voice of desire* (New York, 2016).

Giard, Anne, "Le 'monde' dans *Les Egarements*," *Stanford French review* 9:1 (1985), p.33–46.

Gilroy, James, "Prévost's Théophé: a liberated heroine in search of herself," *The French review* 60:3 (1987), p.311–18.

Goldzink, Jean, "La métaphysique du mal," *Revue Europe* 72 (1994), p.63–78.

Goodman, Dena, *Becoming a woman in the age of letters* (Ithaca, NY, 2009).

–, *The Republic of Letters: a cultural history of the French Enlightenment* (Ithaca, NY, 1994).

Gossman, Lionel, "Male and female in two short novels by Prévost," *The Modern language review* 77:1 (1982), p.29–37.

Graffigny, Françoise de, *Cénie, pièce en cinq actes* (Paris, Cailleau, 1750).

–, *Correspondance de Mme de Graffigny*, ed. J. A. Dainard *et al.* (Oxford, 1985–2018).

–, *Letters of a Peruvian woman*, translated by David Kornacker (New York, 1993).

–, *Lettres d'une Péruvienne* (Paris, A Peine, 1747).

–, *Lettres d'une Péruvienne*, ed. Joan DeJean and Nancy K. Miller (New York, 1993).

–, *Œuvres posthumes de Madame de Graffigny* (Amsterdam [Paris?], n.n., 1775).

Grosz, Elizabeth, *Volatile bodies: toward a corporeal feminism* (Bloomington, IN, 1994).

Habermas, Jürgen, *The Structural transformation of the public sphere: an inquiry into a category of bourgeois society*, translated by Thomas Burger and Frederick Lawrence (1962; Cambridge, MA, 1991).

Halberstam, Jack, *Female masculinity* (Durham, NC, 1998).

–, *The Queer art of failure* (Durham, NC, 2011).

Hartsock, Nancy, "Foucault on power: a theory for women?," in *Feminism/postmodernism*, ed. Linda Nicholson (New York, 1990), p.157–75.

Hegel, Georg Wilhelm Friedrich, *Phenomenology of the spirit (The Phenomenology of the mind)* (1807; New York, 2009).

Hellegouarc'h, Jacqueline, "Ces messieurs du Bout-du-banc: *L'Eloge de la paresse et du paresseux* est-il de Marivaux?," *Revue d'histoire littéraire de la France* 102 (2002/2003), p.455–59.

Henry, Patrick, "Raisonner in *Candide*," *Romanic review* 80:3 (1989), p.363–70.

Hesse, Carla, *The Other Enlightenment: how French women became modern* (Princeton, NJ, 2001).

Hirvonen, Ari, "Voltaire's garden," *Pólemos* 8:2 (2014), p.223–34.

hooks, bell, "Sisterhood: political solidarity between women," in *Feminist theory from margin to center* (Cambridge, MA, 1984), p.43–66.

Horkheimer, Max, and Theodor Adorno, *Dialectic of Enlightenment*, ed. Gunzelin Schmid Noerr, translated by Edmund Jephcott (Stanford, CA, 2002).

Howells, Robin, "*Candide* and *La Nouvelle Héloïse*," *Journal for eighteenth-century studies* 29:1 (2006), p.33–46.

–, "Mme de Graffigny's story," *The Modern language review* 99:1 (2004), p.36–44.

–, *Regressive fictions: Graffigny, Rousseau, Bernardin* (London, 2007).

Hunt, Lynn, *The Family romance of the French Revolution* (Oakland, CA, 1992).

–, *Inventing human rights: a history* (New York, 2007).

Irigaray, Luce, *Le Corps-à-corps avec la mère* (Ottawa, 1981).

–, *Speculum of the other woman*, translated by Gillian Gill (Ithaca, NY, 1985).

–, *This sex which is not one*, translated by Catherine Porter and Carolyn Burke (Ithaca, NY, 1985).

Israel, Jonathan, *Radical Enlightenment* (Oxford, 2001).

Johnson, E. Joe, "Philosophical reflection, happiness, and male friendship in Prévost's *Manon Lescaut*," *Studies in eighteenth-century culture* 31 (2002), p.169–90.

Jones, Matthew J., "'Enough of being basely tearful': 'glitter and be gay' and the camp politics of queer resistance," *Journal of the Society for American music* 10:4 (2016), p.422–45.

Kant, Immanuel, *Political writings*, ed. H. S. Reiss, translated by H. B. Nisbet, 2nd ed. (Cambridge, 1970).

Kantorowicz, Ernst, *The King's two bodies: a study in medieval political theology* (Princeton, NJ, 2016).

Kavanagh, Thomas M., "Reading the moment and the moment of reading in Graffigny's *Lettres d'une Péruvienne*," *Modern language quarterly* 55:2 (1994), p.125–47.

Kehrès, Jean-Marc, "Travestissement discursif et discours utopique: Marivaux et les digressions de Marianne," *French forum* 33:3 (2008), p.17–34.

Kennedy, Theresa Varney, *Women's deliberation: the heroine in early modern French women's theater (1650–1750)* (New York, 2018).

Klein, Melanie, *Love, guilt and reparation and other works, 1921–1945* (London, 1988).

Kra, Pauline, "Montesquieu and women," in *French women and the Enlightenment*, ed. Samia Spencer (Bloomington, IN, 1984), p.272–84.

Kristeva, Julia, *Powers of horror: an essay on abjection*, translated by Leon Roudiez (New York, 1982).

–, *Revolution in poetic language*, translated by Margaret Waller (New York, 1984).

–, *Séméiôtiké: recherches pour une sémanalyse* (Paris, 1969).

Lacan, Jacques, *Anxiety: the seminar of Jacques Lacan, book X*, ed. Jacques-Alain Miller, translated by A. R. Price (Cambridge, 2016).

–, *Desire and its interpretation: the seminar of Jacques Lacan, book VI*, ed. Jacques-Alain Miller, translated by Bruce Fink (Cambridge, 2019).

–, "Kant with Sade," translated by James B. Swenson Jr., *October* 51 (1989), p.55–75.

–, *The Seminar of Jacques Lacan VII: the ethics of psychoanalysis 1959–60*, ed. Jacques-Alain Miller, translated by Dennis Porter (New York, 1992).

–, *The Seminar of Jacques Lacan XX: on feminine sexuality, the limits of love and knowledge 1972–73*, ed. Jacques-Alain Miller, translated by Bruce Fink (New York, 1998).

Landes, Joan B., *Visualizing the nation: gender, representation and revolution in eighteenth-century France* (Ithaca, NY, 2001).

–, *Women and the public sphere in the age of the French Revolution* (Ithaca, NY, 1988).

Lanser, Susan, *The Sexuality of history: modernity and the sapphic, 1565–1830* (Chicago, IL, 2014).

Lévi-Strauss, Claude, *The Elementary structures of kinship*, translated by James H. Bell, John R. von Sturmer, and Rodney Needham (Boston, MA, 1969).

Loraux, Nicole, *Tragic ways of killing a woman*, translated by Anthony Forster (Cambridge, MA, 1987).

Love, Heather, "Truth and consequences: on paranoid reading and reparative reading," *Criticism* 52:2 (spring 2010), p.235–41.

Lukács, Georg, *Theory of the novel: a historico-philosophical essay on the forms of great epic literature* (Cambridge, MA, 1971).

Luxon, Nancy, *Crisis of authority: politics, trust, and truth-telling in Freud and Foucault* (Cambridge, 2013).

MacCannell, Juliet Flower, *The Regime of the brother: after the patriarchy* (New York, 1991).

Margon, Joseph, "The death of Antigone," *California studies in classical Antiquity* 3 (1997), p.177–83.

Marivaux, Pierre de, *La Colonie*, in *Théâtre complet*, ed. Jacques Scherer (Paris, 1964), p.261–73.

–, *L'Ecole des mères*, in *Théâtre complet*, ed. Jacques Scherer (Paris, 1964), p.347–56.

–, *La Fausse suivante, L'Ecole des mères, La Mère confidente*, ed. Jean Goldzink (Paris, 1992).

–, *La Mère confidente*, in *Théâtre complet*, ed. Jacques Scherer (Paris, 1964), p.414–31.

–, *Théâtre complet*, vol.1, ed. Henri Coulet and Michel Gilot (Paris, 1994).

–, *La Vie de Marianne* (Paris, 1978).

Martin, Christophe, "L'institution du sérail: quelques réflexions sur le livre XVI de *L'Esprit des lois*," *Revue Montesquieu* 5 (2001), p.41–57.

McAlpin, Mary, "Between men for all eternity: feminocentrism in Montesquieu's *Lettres persanes*," *Eighteenth-century life* 24:1 (2000), p.45–61.

–, "The rape of Roxane and the end of the world in Montesquieu's *Lettres persanes*," *Romanic review* 107:1–4 (2016), p.55–74.

–, "Utopia in the seraglio: feminist hermeneutics and Montesquieu's *Lettres persanes*," in *Gender and utopia in the eighteenth century: essays in English and French utopian writing*, ed. Nicole Pohl and Brenda Tooley (New York, 2007), p.87–106.

Mélanchon, Jean-Luc, "Addresse à l'Assemblée nationale: compte rendu intégral de l'Assemblée nationale XVe *législature*, seconde session extraordinaire de 2018–2019, première séance du mercredi 25 septembre 2019," http://www.assemblee-nationale.fr/15/cri/2018-2019-extra2/20192011.asp (last accessed February 22, 2021).

Mercier, Gilbert, *Madame Péruvienne: Françoise de Graffigny, une femme sensible au siècle des Lumières* (Paris, 2008).

Miller, Nancy K., *Subject to change: reading feminist writing* (New York, 1988).

Miotti, Mariangela, "Il mito dell' 'enfant de nature' e il teatro di Mme de Graffigny," *Studi di letteratura francese* 16 (1990), p.126–37.

Mitchell, Juliet, *Psychoanalysis and feminism: a radical reassessment of Freudian psychoanalysis* (New York, 2000).

Montesquieu, Charles de Secondat, baron de, *Lettres persanes*, ed. Jean Starobinski (1721; Paris, 2003).

–, *Persian letters*, translated by C. J. Betts (New York, 2004).

–, *The Spirit of the laws*, ed. Anne M. Cohler, Basia C. Miller, and Harold S. Stone (1748; New York, 2002).

Mordrelle, Hélène, "De l'*Œdipe Roi* de Sophocle à l'*Œdipe* de Voltaire: l'histoire et les enjeux d'une réécriture," *Bulletin de l'Association Guillaume Budé* 1 (2010), p.210–32.

Moretti, Franco, *The Way of the world: the bildungsroman in European culture* (New York, 2000).

Mossé, Emeline, *Le Langage de l'implicite dans l'œuvre de Crébillon fils* (Paris, 2009).

Muñoz, José Esteban, *Cruising utopia: the then and there of queer futurity* (New York, 2009).

Nancy, Jean-Luc, *Being singular plural*, translated by Robert Richardson and Anne O'Byrne (Stanford, CA, 2000).

Nesbitt, Nick, *Universal emancipation: the Haitian Revolution and the radical Enlightenment* (Richmond, VA, 2008).

Ozouf, Mona, "Fraternité," in *Dictionnaire critique de la Révolution française*, ed. Mona Ozouf and François Furet (Paris, 1988).

–, "Liberté, égalité, fraternité," in *Les Lieux de mémoire*, vol.3, ed. Pierre Nora (Paris, 1992), p.583–629.

Palmer, Jennifer, *Intimate bonds: family and slavery in the French Atlantic* (Philadelphia, PA, 2016).

Park, Shelley, *Mothering queerly, queering motherhood* (New York, 2013).

Piroux, Lorraine, "The encyclopedist and the Peruvian princess: the poetics of illegibility in French Enlightenment book culture," *PMLA* 121:1 (2006), p.107–23.

Pomeau, René, "Candide entre Marx et Freud," *SVEC* 89 (1972), p.1305–23.

Power, Nina, "Non-reproductive futurism: Rancière's rational equality against Edelman's body apolitic," *Borderlands* 8:2 (2009), special issue: *Jacques Rancière on the shores of queer theory*, ed. Samuel A. Chambers and Michael O'Rourke, unpaginated.

Prévost, Antoine, abbé, *The Greek girl's story*, translated by Alan J. Singerman (University Park, PA, 2014).

–, *Histoire d'une Grecque moderne*, in *Œuvres de Prévost*, vol.4, ed. Allan Holland (Grenoble, 1978), p.11–121.

–, *Mémoires et aventures d'un homme de qualité qui s'est retiré du monde: histoire du chevalier Des Grieux et de Manon Lescaut*, in *Œuvres de Prévost*, vol.1, ed. Pierre Berthiaume and Jean Sgard (Grenoble, 1978).

Pucci, Suzanne Rodin, "Letters from the harem: veiled figures of writing in Montesquieu's *Lettres persanes*," in *Writing the female voice: essays on epistolary literature*, ed. Elizabeth Goldsmith (Boston, MA, 1989), p.114–34.

Rancière, Jacques, *Aux bords du politique* (Paris, 1998).

–, *Disagreement*, translated by Julie Rose (Minneapolis, MN, 1999).

–, "L'héritage difficile de Michel Foucault," in *Chroniques des temps consensuels* (Paris, 2005), p.183–89.

–, *The Ignorant schoolmaster*, translated by Kristin Ross (Stanford, CA, 1991).

–, *The Philosopher and his poor*, translated by John Drury, Corinne Oster, and Andrew Parker (Durham, NC, 2004).

–, *Proletarian nights*, translated by John Drury (London, 2012).

Respaut, Michèle, "Des Grieux's duplicity: Manon Lescaut and the tragedy of repetition," *Symposium* 88:1 (1984), p.70–80.

Rich, Adrienne, *Of woman born: motherhood as experience and institution* (New York, 1995).

Robert, Marthe, *Origins of the novel*, translated by Sacha Rabinovitch (Brighton, 1980).

Roberts, Meghan K., *Sentimental savants: philosophical families in Enlightenment France* (Chicago, IL, 2016).

Rogers, Katherine M., "Subversion of the patriarchy in *Les Lettres persanes*," *Philological quarterly* 65:1 (1986), p.61–78.

Rosset, François, "Les nœuds du langage dans les *Lettres d'une Péruvienne*," *Revue d'histoire littéraire de la France* 96:6 (1996), p.1106–27.

Rousseau, Jean-Jacques, *Essai sur l'origine des langues, où il est parlé de la mélodie et de l'imitation musicale* (1781; Paris, 1993).

Rubin, Gayle, "The traffic in women: notes on the 'political economy' of sex," in *Toward an anthropology of women*, ed. Rayna Reiter (New York, 1975), p.157–210.

Runyon, Randolph, *The Art of the Persian letters: unlocking Montesquieu's "secret chain"* (Newark, DE, 2005).

Russo, Elena, "Libidinal economy and gender trouble in Marivaux's *La Fausse suivante*," *MLN* 115:4 (2000), p.690–713.

Ruti, Mari, *The Ethics of opting out: queer theory's defiant subjects* (New York, 2017).

Rutler, Tracy, "Liberté, égalité, sororité: the regime of the sister in Graffigny's *Lettres d'une Péruvienne*," *French forum* 39:2–3 (2014), p.1–15.

Sade, Donatien Alphonse, marquis de, *Les Cent vingt journées de Sodome* (Paris, 1998).

–, *La Nouvelle Justine, ou les Malheurs de la vertu, suivie de l'Histoire de Juliette, sa sœur* (Brussels [en Hollande], n.n., 1797).

Saint-Amand, Pierre, "Les parures de Marianne," *Eighteenth-century fiction* 4:1 (1991), p.15–26.

Salvan, Geneviève, *Séduction et dialogue dans l'œuvre de Crébillon* (Paris, 2002).

Santner, Eric, *The Royal remains: the people's two bodies and the endgames of sovereignty* (Chicago, IL, 2012).

Schneider, Jean-Paul, "*Les Lettres d'une Péruvienne*: roman ouvert ou roman fermé," in *Vierge du soleil/ fille des Lumières* (Strasbourg, 1989), p.7–48.

Sedgwick, Eve Kosofsky, *Between men: English literature and male homosocial desire* (New York, 2016).

–, *Epistemology of the closet* (Berkeley, CA, 2008).

–, "Paranoid reading and reparative reading, or, you're so paranoid, you probably think this essay is about you," in *Touching feeling: affect, pedagogy, performativity* (Durham, NC, 2003), p.123–51

–, "Privilege of unknowing," *Genders* 1 (1988), p.102–24.

Segal, Naomi, *The Unintended reader: feminism and Manon Lescaut* (New York, 1986).

Sgard, Jean, *L'Abbé Prévost: labyrinthes de la mémoire* (Paris, 1986).

–, *Crébillon fils, le libertin moraliste* (Paris, 2002).

–, *Prévost romancier*, 2nd ed. (Paris, 1989).

Shackleton, Robert, "The Moslem chronology of the *Lettres persanes*," *French studies* 1 (1954), p.17–27.

Shea, Louisa, "Exit Voltaire, enter Marivaux: Abdellatif Kechiche on the legacy of the Enlightenment," *The French review* 85:6 (2012), p.1136–48.

Sherman, Carol L., *The Family crucible in eighteenth-century literature* (Burlington, VT, 2005).

Showalter, Elaine, *A Literature of their own: British women novelists from Brontë to Lessing* (Princeton, NJ, 1977).

Showalter, English, *Françoise de Graffigny: her life and works, SVEC* 2004:11.

Simonin, Charlotte, "Phaza, la 'fille-garçon' de Mme de Graffigny," in *Le Mâle en France, 1715–1830: représentations de la masculinité*, ed. Katherine Astbury and Marie-Emmanuelle Plagnol-Diéval (New York, 2004), p.51–62.

Singerman, Allan J., "The abbé Prévost's 'Grecque moderne': a witness for the defense," *The French review* 46:5 (1973), p.938–45.

Smart, Annie, *Citoyennes: women and the ideal of citizenship in eighteenth-century France* (Newark, NJ, 2011).

Smith, David, "The popularity of Mme de Graffigny's *Lettres d'une Péruvienne*: the bibliographical evidence," *Eighteenth-century fiction* 3:1 (1990), p.1–20.

Snediker, Michael D., *Queer optimism: lyric personhood and other felicitous persuasions* (Minneapolis, MN, 2008).

Solnit, Rebecca, *Men explain things to me* (Chicago, IL, 2014).

Stewart, Joan Hinde, *The Enlightenment of age: women, letters, and growing old in 18th-century France*, SVEC 2010:09.

Stewart, Philip, "Holding the mirror up to fiction: generic parody in *Candide*," *French studies* 4 (1979), p.411–19.

Summerfield, Giovanna, and Lisa Downward, *New perspectives on the European bildungsroman* (London, 2010).

Tuana, Nancy, "Coming to understand: orgasm and the epistemology of ignorance," *Hypatia* 19:1 (2004), p.194–232.

Turgot, Anne Robert Jacques, *Œuvres de Turgot et documents le concernant*, ed. F. Alcon (Paris, 1913–1923).

Voltaire, François Marie Arouet de, *Artémire*, ed. David Jory and John Renwick, in *Œuvres complètes de Voltaire*, vol.1A (Oxford, 2001), p.409–61.

–, *Candide, ou l'Optimisme*, ed. Michelle Béguin and Jean Goldzink (Paris, 1998).

–, *Correspondence and related documents*, ed. Th. Besterman, in *Œuvres complètes de Voltaire*, vol.85–135 (Oxford, 1968–1977).

–, "Lettres écrites par l'auteur qui contiennent la critique de l'Œdipe de Sophocle, de celui de Corneille, et du sien," ed. David Jory and John Renwick, in *Œuvres complètes de Voltaire*, vol.1A (Oxford, 2001), p.323–81.

–, *Œdipe*, ed. David Jory and John Renwick, in *Œuvres complètes de Voltaire*, vol.1A (Oxford, 2001), p.15–284.

Walpole, Horace, *The Letters of Horace Walpole*, vol.4, ed. Peter Cunningham (Edinburgh, 1908).

Watt, Ian, *The Rise of the novel* (Oakland, CA, 1974).

Wittig, Monique, *The Straight mind and other essays* (Boston, MA, 1992).

Wolfgang, Aurora, *Gender and voice in the French novel 1730–1782* (Burlington, VT, 2004).

Wynn, Thomas, "Collaboration and authorship in eighteenth-century French theater," *Romanic review* 103:3–4 (2012), p.465–81.

Yamashita, Masano, "The spectacle of poverty: Marivaux's beggars and chance in Enlightenment Paris," *L'Esprit créateur* 55:3 (2015), p.59–71.

Zanger, Abby E., *Scenes from the marriage of Louis XIV: nuptial fictions and the making of absolutist power* (Stanford, CA, 1997).

Index